STEAMBOATS
AND THE RISE OF THE COTTON KINGDOM

ROBERT
GUDMESTAD

STEAMBOATS
AND THE RISE OF THE COTTON KINGDOM

LOUISIANA STATE UNIVERSITY PRESS
BATON ROUGE

Published by Louisiana State University Press
Copyright © 2011 by Louisiana State University Press
All rights reserved
Manufactured in the United States of America
First printing

DESIGNER: Michelle A. Neustrom
TYPEFACE: Adobe Minion Pro
PRINTER: McNaughton & Gunn, Inc.
BINDER: Acme Bookbinding

LIBRARY OF CONGRESS CATALOGING-IN-PUBLICATION DATA

Gudmestad, Robert H., 1964–
  Steamboats and the rise of the cotton kingdom / Robert Gudmestad.
    p. cm.
  Includes bibliographical references and index.
  ISBN 978-0-8071-3839-7 (cloth : alk. paper) — ISBN 978-0-8071-3840-3 (mobi) — ISBN
978-0-8071-3841-0 (pdf) — ISBN 978-0-8071-3842-7 (epub) 1. Inland water transportation
—Southern States—History—19th century. 2. Steamboats—Southern States—History—19th
century. 3. River steamers—Southern States—History—19th century. 4. Cotton trade—
Southern States—History—19th century. 5. Southern States—Commerce—History—19th
century. 6. Indians of North America—Relocation—Southern States—History—19th
century. I. Title.
  HE631.S6G84 2011
  386'.244—dc22

                                                                    2011006962

All maps by Mary Lee Eggart.

Portions reprinted from *Technology, Innovation, and Southern Industrialization: From the
Antebellum Era to the Computer Age*, edited by Susanna Delfino and Michele Gillespie, by
permission of the University of Missouri Press. Copyright © 2008 by the Curators of the
University of Missouri.

For the memory of my parents

CONTENTS

Illustrations follow page 96

MAPS AND TABLES

MAPS

TABLES

ACKNOWLEDGMENTS

This book began several years ago when I was preparing to teach a class on Jacksonian America at Southwest Baptist University. I was writing a lecture on the transportation revolution and needed good material on steamboats. The best I could find was Louis Hunter's *Steamboats on the Western Rivers: An Economic and Technological History.* A treasure of a book that will probably not be surpassed, Hunter's volume dates back to Harry Truman's presidency. The book is also more generally about the West and, being an historian of the South, I was frustrated that there was not more about slavery, plantations, and southern culture. That lecture, which I have since lost, sparked this book and sent me in unexpected directions in my quest to understand the influence of riverboats on the Southwest.

I saw much of the South while researching this book, and the M. Michael Awad travel grant from Southwest Baptist University and a fellowship to use the Herman T. Pott Inland Waterways Library at the St. Louis Mercantile Library provided much needed financial assistance. The staff at the various libraries and archives I visited were courteous and helpful, and I gratefully thank them for their assistance. Special thanks go to individuals at the Oneida County Historical Society and the University of Houston, who copied materials and mailed them to me. What I could not physically access I requested from interlibrary loan. Donna Young at Southwest Baptist University deserves special mention for her indefatigable labors, but the interlibrary loan staffs at the University of Memphis and Colorado State University also merit much credit. Without exception, they fulfilled my requests in an efficient and timely manner. Diane Mallstrom at the Public Library of Cincinnati and Hamilton County provided some crucial, last-minute assistance with illustrations, while Mary Lee Eggart created the excellent maps that grace this book. As always,

Rand Dotson at LSU Press was a helpful and patient editor, while Derik Shelor was a perceptive and indefatigable copy editor.

While thinking about and writing the manuscript, I benefited from the advice and direction of patient colleagues and friends. Those who read parts of the manuscript and provided useful suggestions include Charlie Royster, Paul Paskoff, Mike Allen, Ed Skeen, Tom Buchanan, John Larson, Michele Gillespie, Chris Leahy, Aaron Marrs, Mark Fiege, Jared Orsi, Prakash Kumar, and my colleagues at Colorado State. Ari Kelman deserves a special thanks because, despite the fact that he probably could not pick me out of a line-up, he graciously consented to my email request to read a chapter. His compelling insights greatly improved my efforts. Similarly, my predecessor in Fort Collins, Frank Towers, provided excellent comments that were not only voluble, but valuable. Josh Rothman read the entire manuscript and profoundly shaped the final product with his trenchant insights.

While I have heavily relied on my friends and colleagues for their good ideas, I am even more indebted to my family. Because of my career, they have endured moves from Baton Rouge, to Bolivar, Missouri, to Memphis, and now to Fort Collins, Colorado. They have done so with good cheer, even though my son, Sam, observed that he has lived in four states and seven different houses. Sometime between the preparation for that class on steamboats and the composition of these acknowledgments, Sadie joined our family and has proved to be an expert at pestering her brother. My wife, Beth, has provided the love, stability, and encouragement that are the essential glue for a project such as this; she has shaped the final product more than she knows. My parents were enthusiastic champions of my academic career, and it was my hope that they could have seen this book. It is my deep regret that they did not live to see and hold a more precious creation: their granddaughter. It is to their memory that this book is dedicated.

STEAMBOATS
AND THE RISE OF THE COTTON KINGDOM

THE *NEW ORLEANS*

A raucous crowd gathered at the Pittsburgh waterfront on October 20, 1811, to see the *New Orleans*. In many ways the boat was typical of other craft built for the Mississippi and Ohio River system. Its white pine came from local forests, where lumberjacks hacked down trees and floated the logs to Pittsburgh. Workers in a huge new saw pit at the foot of Boyd's Hill sliced the trunks into planks, and local shipwrights fit the boards together into what looked like a keelboat. The rounded hull cradled two cabins. The forward, or gentlemen's, cabin had small berths lining the outside walls and a long dining table in the room's open center. A smaller ladies' cabin with four berths in the boat's aft took less time to complete, but the boat was still behind schedule. Workers quickly constructed a bowsprit, lined the portholes, raised two sailing masts, and painted the hull sky blue. A sudden rise in the river almost carried the *New Orleans* into the Monongahela and further delayed construction. After workmen hauled the boat back to the shipyard, they added a long box-like superstructure on the main deck. It could shelter cargo and hold up to eighty deck passengers. There was no pilothouse on the superstructure, just the steering wheel perched amidships. The final product was massive. At 148 feet by 32 feet and 371 tons burden, the *New Orleans* was double the size of most keelboats and could carry more than twice their cargo. Not only was it the largest boat built in Pittsburgh, but its $38,000 price tag made it the most expensive. When the boat shoved off into the Monongahela River, men tossed their caps in the air and women waved handkerchiefs. The *New Orleans* went upstream a short distance, slowly arced around, and then disappeared down the Ohio River.[1]

The inelegant *New Orleans* drew a large throng on that chilly Pennsylvania Sunday not because of its huge size or cost but because it was unlike anything seen on the western waters. The boat had two paddle wheels, a steam engine sandwiched in the hold between the men's and ladies' cabins, and a smoke-stack rising from the superstructure. Each of the ten-foot paddle wheels had six iron paddles and could be raised or lowered to compensate for the boat's displacement, but typically reached three feet underwater. The low-pressure engine that turned the wheels weighed about 100 tons and had one copper boiler connected to a thirty-four-inch cylinder. It was forged in New York, dis-assembled, hauled in wagons to Pittsburgh, and then reassembled. The steady cadence of the piston's firing enabled the engine to reach 18 rpm and propel the boat downstream at the robust speed of ten miles per hour.[2]

Nicholas Roosevelt, great grand-uncle of Theodore Roosevelt, supervised construction of the *New Orleans*. He had moved to Pittsburgh at the behest of his two business partners, Robert Livingston and Robert Fulton. The fabu-lously wealthy Livingston, who styled himself as an inventor, had helped ne-gotiate the Louisiana Purchase, while Fulton was known for building the first commercially successful steamboat. Roosevelt brought his wife, Lydia, with him to Pittsburgh and she insisted on being a passenger for the maiden voyage despite being eight months pregnant. Andrew Jack, the pilot, guided the craft while an unnamed captain gave the actual orders directing the boat's opera-tions. An engineer and his six firemen kept the fire stoked in the small boiler room. A cook, a waiter, and two female servants rounded out the thirteen-person crew. The Roosevelts' huge Newfoundland dog went along for good measure.[3]

Once the *New Orleans* left Pittsburgh it made good time, thrashing its way to Cincinnati in two days and to Louisville in two more. Along the way, it alarmed keelboatmen, farmers, and townfolk as it roared past. Few people had heard of the boat and fewer still expected it. According to an account writ-ten fifty years after the fact, the boat's rhythmic puffing so scared a Kentucky farmer that he rode from farm to farm yelling, "The British are coming!" This Revere-like sentinel was on guard because tensions between the United States and England had been rising for several years. (The two countries went to war less than a year after the *New Orleans*'s historic voyage.) His edgy neighbors supposedly rushed to the riverbank to repel a British invasion only to see "the monster of the waters" pass. The boat blazed into Louisville at night and, ac-cording to another legend, started a panic. When the engineer released steam from the boiler, the ear-splitting whistle supposedly roused some of the town's residents from their sleep. Confused and scared, they fled to the woods lest a comet fall from the sky and obliterate them. Accurate or not, these stories convey the sense of novelty and wonder isolated westerners experienced upon seeing and hearing the *New Orleans*.[4]

At Louisville the *New Orleans* faced its first significant test. Water was only trickling over the Falls of the Ohio, the greatest natural impediment on the Ohio River. The Falls was a series of dangerous rapids created by limestone ridges. When the water was high, according to a later steamboat passenger, it "boils and splashes about in a most violent manner, and in one place resembles exactly the surf of the sea." Although frightening to behold, the high water was usually not dangerous. Low water was another story, and even intrepid boatmen waited for a rise in the river because the menacing rocks were known to smash a dozen boats a year. Roosevelt chose prudence over recklessness and waited. He took the opportunity to invite city leaders aboard the *New Orleans* for dinner. When the boat suddenly lurched, many guests feared that it was drifting toward the Falls and certain destruction. Roosevelt watched them rush to the deck and prepare to dive into the river. Much to the guests' surprise the boat was chugging away from the Falls, and Roosevelt used his ruse to open the company's stock book for subscriptions. There were no takers. Skeptical investors were waiting for the *New Orleans* to make it unscathed over the Falls. Roosevelt refused to sit in Louisville, so he steered the boat back to Cincinnati, where he gave rides for a dollar.[5]

Even while Roosevelt was entertaining the multitude, he was keeping a close eye on the river level. When the Ohio began to rise in late November, the *New Orleans* returned to Louisville. Local experts reported that the water running over the Falls exceeded the boat's draft by five inches. Convinced that this was his best opportunity, Roosevelt hired a local pilot and gave the order for the boat to shoot the rapids on December 8. The key to a successful journey over the Falls was speed, since a fast boat could steer over the rapids and avoid getting caught in the swirling waters. Engineer Baker and his men tossed extra wood onto the fire and the engine reached its maximum power. The *New Orleans* roared into the rapids, spray striking the men as they clutched the rails. Pilot Jack and the local pilot communicated with one another by hand signals, since the din of the engine and rapids drowned out all shouting. The boat lurched and pitched, but made it over the Falls without incident. Roosevelt halted the craft at Shippingport to inspect her, but there was no significant damage. The crew loaded supplies, Lydia and her new son boarded the boat, and the *New Orleans* resumed its voyage.

The steamer traveled three days to present-day Owensboro, Kentucky, where it stopped at dusk on December 15 to load coal. About two o'clock the next morning a powerful earthquake shook the region, churning waters into fourteen-foot waves that roused the crew from their sleep. It was the first of three magnitude 8 earthquakes and hundreds of aftershocks that shook the region for three months. Known collectively as the New Madrid earthquakes, they were the most powerful quakes to strike the United States. Tremors were felt as far away as Quebec, and the final upheaval in February of 1812 caused the Mississippi River to run backward for a time and created Reelfoot Lake in Tennessee. The crew had little choice but to continue the trip, but hushed voices betrayed their nervousness. Constant aftershocks roiled the waters, brown waves washed away huge chunks of land, trees choked the river, and a nasty sulfur smell hung in the air. Loud gunshot-like cracks signaled explosions of water that spouted mud, sticks, and debris thirty feet into the air. Worse yet, the powerful quake had obliterated the traditional landmarks and changed the topography along the river as huge chunks of shore slid into the river. Jack directed the boat as best he could through this new and confusing reality. Since the riverbanks were constantly caving in, Roosevelt decided to moor the *New Orleans* to islands at dusk. Even this strategy failed. One night Roosevelt awoke to the bumping of wood against the hull. He thought an unusually large number of trees were grinding against the boat but was startled to discover that the island had disappeared during an earthquake, leaving the boat floating downstream.[6]

Despite a few more exciting events, including a fire on board and a race with Native Americans rowing a canoe, the *New Orleans* made it to Natchez on December 30. "[T]housands were assembled on the bluff and at the foot of it" to watch the boat arrive. No doubt they heard the boat before they saw it. The *New Orleans* took on supplies and its first freight—fittingly, Samuel Davis's cotton bales. It was also in Natchez that the ship's captain successfully proposed to Lydia Roosevelt's maid. The last leg of the journey was uneventful. With all the excitement of the voyage, it was almost anticlimactic when the *New Orleans* arrived in the city for which it was named on January 10, 1812. Bobbing in the wharf within site of the French Quarter, the riverboat was soon host to the territorial governor and a throng of prominent citizens.[7]

The *New Orleans* entered the American bloodstream at a propitious moment. The Louisiana Purchase had recently doubled the country's size and Americans were eagerly moving over the Appalachian Mountains. The states and territories of the West were home to about 1 million of the nation's 7 million residents and Louisiana was not yet a state. Five decades later, nearly half of the country's residents lived in states that bordered the Mississippi River and its tributaries. The interior South—those slave states west of the Appalachian Mountains—figured prominently in these changes. Its population shot from 806,000 to nearly 7 million people, or, put another way, went from 11 percent of the nation's population to 22 percent. When the *New Orleans* completed its first voyage, over 17,000 people lived in New Orleans. Fifty years later, 168,675 people dwelled there. Memphis, a city that did not exist in 1812 and owed its existence to riverboats, was the country's thirty-eighth largest city in 1860. The river towns of St. Louis, Louisville, and Mobile ranked in the top thirty for national population, and five of the South's seven largest cities in 1860 were on the western waters. Steamboats played an important part in building these small towns into bustling trading centers.[8]

Reciting population statistics is only part of the story and, more importantly, does not demonstrate that riverboats brought about the changes. But a rise in steamboat activity accompanied this population surge. A decade after the first riverboat touched the New Orleans levee, over seventy steamers prowled the western waters. By the time Abraham Lincoln took up residence in the White House, the number surpassed eight hundred. The majority of these boats, particularly before 1830, listed a southern town as their home port. In five decades riverboats brought significant change to southern economics, demographics, agricultural practices, social expectations, commercial relations, and the environment.[9]

This book is about those changes. Soon after the War of 1812, southwestern entrepreneurs built new and improved steamboats that not only put the interior South on the cutting edge of technological sophistication, they reduced the region's isolation. Employment on riverboats brought upward mobility to ambitious whites and geographic mobility to free blacks and slaves. White southerners migrated across the region in steamers, bringing thousands of enslaved Americans with them. And as plantations and farms consumed geographic space, they pushed Native Americans out of the way. Steamboats became central to the Indian Removal process, not only creating conditions for it but also serving as the means of moving Native Americans to Oklahoma. A string of riverboat explosions, many of them linked to racing, triggered the first federal regulation of a transportation industry and forced residents of the interior South to reexamine the goodness of steamboats. Riverboats, though, were too important to the region's political economy to be abandoned, and the residents of the Southwest lobbied the federal government to alter the shape of the western waters. In doing so, they revealed an identity that was not only southern but western. While steamboats extracted a significant toll on the environment, they changed the course of the southern economy. Riverboats became an essential component of the Southwest's cotton trade and helped create an international age of cotton. But as southerners grew frustrated with the limitations of steamboats and railroads siphoned off the river trade, steamboat traffic started to decline. Even as residents of the interior South stopped looking to the federal government to promote economic development, they shed their commonality with the Midwest. Steamboats helped make, and then undo, the Cotton Kingdom.

The centrality of steamboats for the social and economic development of the interior South—also called the Southwest in this study—is widely assumed but not well studied. Even though steamers carried more southern freight than railroads between 1820 and 1860, the iron horse occupies a much more prominent place in the historiography of the antebellum South. The recent works of Ari Kelman, Tom Buchanan, Paul Paskoff, and Carl A. Brasseaux and Keith P. Fontenot have begun to address this imbalance, but the present study seeks to clarify the role of riverboats in bringing social, environmental, economic, and political change to the interior South.[10]

Riverboats exerted profound influences on other parts of the country, but a comprehensive history of steamboating in the United States is beyond the scope of this narrative. Certainly steamers changed life and labor on the Hudson River and the streams that jutted into the Atlantic coastline. Steamboats, moreover, penetrated the Far West and connected Montana with the rest of the country. More obviously, riverboats chugged the waters of the Midwest. While those stories are important, they are only briefly recounted in this book. It is my intention to focus on a particular region (the Southwest) in order to see how steamboats transformed it in the years prior to the Civil War. Riverboats brought the various regions—South, West, and Midwest—into contact with one another, and there will be times that such interactions unfold in this narrative. But, for the most part, the regions along the great rivers of the interior South remain the setting for the story that follows.

It is not too much to say that steamboats were like the New Madrid earthquake that caused the Mississippi River to run backward. The unnatural seemed natural. Moving upstream—conquering the mighty currents of the western rivers—greatly facilitated the rise of the Cotton Kingdom in the Southwest. Steamboats did not completely reshape the region, just as the New Madrid earthquake did not obliterate all it touched, but their influence, as a veteran riverman noted, was obvious even to the "most dull and stupid."[11]

ONE

SOUTHERN STEAMBOAT ENTREPRENEURS

ost people heard the *General Jackson* before they saw it chugging up the Cumberland River. The engine's rhythmic puffing—and the booms of the cannon mounted on the boat's bow—echoed across Tennessee's rolling hills. Curious farmers hurried to the water's edge to catch a glimpse of the unusual-looking craft. When the *General Jackson* hove into view in Nashville, the thousand or so spectators at the waterfront cheered. It was March 11, 1819, and the first steamboat had arrived in Tennessee's capital city. At first a novelty, the steamer's repeat visit three weeks later prompted perceptive observers to imagine possibilities that were unthinkable a year earlier. In only three weeks the boat had traveled to New Orleans and back, this at a time when keelboats took more than three months to make the same trip. Regular steamboat traffic with that great southern city could elevate Nashville from a sleepy backwater to a bustling emporium. As the local newspaper pointed out, "what a promise of realizing wealth is confirmed by the two late trips of this fine vessel."[1]

James Winchester was one of the people who understood that steamboats stood at the intersection of risk, opportunity, and power in the burgeoning Southwest. Winchester had moved from Maryland to Tennessee in search of riches but nearly sullied his reputation beyond repair during the War of 1812. He had wrangled his way into command of the Kentucky militia, then promptly became the laughingstock of his troops. Pranksters tricked him into sitting on a porcupine skin during a nighttime latrine visit and later ran part of his uniform up a flagpole. Worse still, he was captured and his army was destroyed at the Battle of River Raisin. After his humiliation, Winchester had returned to Tennessee and dabbled in all types of speculative gambles: mercantile houses, flatboats, plantations, and land sales. One of his most successful ventures became the city of Memphis, which he helped found with

Andrew Jackson and John Overton. But when steamboats appeared, the ambitious Winchester jumped at the chance to own the new technology. He was sixty-seven when he organized the Cumberland Steamboat Company, a concern that diffused risk and made it possible for savvy businessmen to secure a reliable means of transportation for their products. The company made the $1,000 down payment for its flagship vessel, the *Cumberland,* a 246-ton boat built in Pittsburgh.[2]

The Cumberland Steamboat Company used its boat to haul cotton and tobacco downriver to New Orleans, and a wide variety of hard-to-get items upriver on the return trips. Coffee and sugar, precious and expensive commodities, were in high demand, but the company's steamers also carried wine, brandy, china, candles, cigars, raisins, and iron. The firm even shipped an "Elegant Hair Sofa," a dozen "Fancy flag Bottom Chairs," and a "Turkey carpet" from New Orleans to Nashville in 1822. Winchester's various businesses became so dependent on riverboats that any delays, repairs, or accidents took huge bites out of his potential profits. When the *Cumberland* had to be fixed, he impatiently demanded to know when the repairs would be finished. The foreman explained that work had slowed when one laborer cut off his toe and nearly severed the whole leg. Worse yet, he added, "our grogg has been stopped for ten days and we cannot get a seam tight without it."[3]

Winchester was just one of many southerners who were willing to risk their money on an unproven technology. In 1816 five prominent Nashville citizens pledged to line the banks of the Cumberland with "powerful and useful engines." Within eight years more than a dozen steamboats traveled regularly between Nashville and New Orleans despite the Cumberland River's tendency to be a barrier rather than a thoroughfare. Ice, low water, and natural obstacles like the Harpeth Shoals near Gallatin eliminated river traffic for much of the year. Steamboats often stopped short of the capital city and offloaded their goods to keelboats for the final few miles of the journey. Despite these irregularities and difficult conditions, steamboat traffic thrived in Nashville. Local entrepreneurs like William Carroll, Thomas Yeatman, and James and Robert Woods invested their money in steamers. This high degree of local ownership was something that quickly became typical for southern river towns. These merchant entrepreneurs, perhaps more so than their fellow residents, understood that steamboat ownership allowed them to exert greater control over their businesses and exact greater earnings. As one riverboat investor put it, "The profits are great indeed."[4]

9

The scene in Nashville was repeated across the southern interior. Collectively, the actions of early steamboat entrepreneurs produced startling transformations in boat design as they learned to accommodate their craft to environmental conditions. These new boats took shape at the same time that riverboat ownership shifted. The first riverboats on the western waters were the products of eastern money and ingenuity. Their owners hoped to penetrate the markets of the South by creating monopolies that would control the flow of steamers on America's major rivers. The monopolies could not last and only served to attract competitors, who scrambled to build and operate steamboats along the western waters. Southerners were at the center of this rush, as merchants, lawyers, planters, and men on the make like James Winchester revealed a strong southern entrepreneurial spirit in their haste to adopt the latest technology. Steamboats not only were integral to a new communications network, but they became one of the South's most important businesses and put the interior South on the leading edge of technological sophistication in early nineteenth-century America.

"LITERALLY SKIN'D LIKE A RABBIT"

Early nineteenth-century transportation in the southern interior was fraught with all types of difficulty. Roads were rough paths that might have rocks, holes, fallen trees, or other obstacles. The deplorable conditions—one Englishman lamented that "no one can imagine what a bad road is until he has travelled in the Western States of America"—made movement of goods and people difficult at best and impossible at worst. Passengers traveling by stage could expect numerous delays, perils, and discomfort on even the most routine trips. Mosquitoes, dust, heat, rain, mud, smelly passengers, and boredom were commonplace on stages. Teamsters urging their mules forward found their situation even worse. Freight moved at a snail's pace and many towns were inaccessible during bad weather.[5]

Given the dismal state of American roads, rivers were natural avenues for moving goods, animals, and people. The vast water network that crisscrossed the interior South became the roadmap for early white settlement of the region, and by 1800 most settlers lived within a day's journey of the major rivers. Flatboats handled most downstream travel, which constituted 90 percent of Mississippi River traffic in 1810. They were large (sixty feet long and fifteen feet wide) floating boxes made of rough logs nailed together. Flatboats often traveled in groups of four or five and were sometimes tied together. These disposable "wooden prisons" made their appearance on the western waters around the time of the American Revolution and had many aliases: Kentucky boats, Natchez boats, broadhorns, and arks. Their chief virtue was their cheap price, as it cost around $45 to build a broadhorn in 1810. The first broadhorns held no more than thirty tons of cargo, while their more advanced descendants could transport five times that amount. They came equipped with four huge sweeps—long poles with boards attached—at the front and an even larger stern sweep. The heavy oars took considerable strength and skill to manage, but even then navigation was no easy task. Eddies, strong currents, sandbars, and snags threatened flatboats, a situation that was only magnified when they took on large amounts of cargo. Davy Crockett learned that flatboats' bulkiness often left them at the mercy of nature. Crockett and some business partners loaded 30,000 staves on two flatboats but quickly learned they were in over their heads. The flatboats careened out of control on the Mississippi River and started to get sucked underwater. Crockett barely escaped through a small hole in the boat's side, admitting he was "literally skin'd like a rabbit" when he showed up naked on the Memphis levee. Landing flatboats required expertise, patience, and sometimes luck. Usually two crewmen rowed a skiff to shore, pulling a long rope behind them. They quickly tied the line to a tree and the boat then swung around when the rope snapped taut. If the line broke, the crew tried again further downstream. Not surprisingly, flatboat losses were high. When William Noble of Cincinnati, for instance, sent cargo on six flatboats in 1820, only three of them made it as far as the Mississippi River. These difficult craft were also inefficient; once a broadhorn reached its destination, the crew broke it apart, sold the wood, and normally walked back home.[6]

Going upriver was even worse. The strong currents of the Mississippi River made upstream travel a slow, painful process that reduced commercial activity to almost nothing. Keelboats and their larger cousins, barges, became common around 1780 and handled all upriver traffic. They resembled sailing ships and were meant to cut through the water. Keelboats were typically sixty feet by eight feet and carried from 40 to 100 tons of freight. They came equipped with oars and sails, but such methods of propulsion were unreliable and hardly used. Instead, sinewy, profane, and callused crews overcame the river's current by poling the craft forward. Upon command, each crew member faced the stern and planted a long pole in the riverbed. Bracing his shoulder against the pole's end, he trudged along a cleated running board. In essence, he was walking in place but pushing the boat upstream with his legs. Another command signaled crew members to lift their poles and quickly return to the bow, only to begin the process again. This was exhausting work, particularly in the hot and humid climes of the lower Mississippi. When poling failed, as it often did, crews resorted to cordelling, where a sailor dog-paddled to shore with a thick, heavy rope called a cordelle. Other members followed and then pulled the ship upriver by trudging along the shore. Should the bank prove unsteady, crews turned to warping, where they fastened the cordelle to a tree and then hauled it in, thus propelling the boat forward in a tedious tug-of-war contest. If the shore was heavily wooded, the crews might try bushwacking. They stood on the boat's edge, grabbed trees, and pulled the craft forward. A keelboat might travel thirty miles on a good day, but most crews managed no more than half that. The 1,350 mile journey from New Orleans to Louisville became a tedious odyssey that typically took three to four months. These grueling conditions limited upstream freight on the Mississippi River to not more than 6,500 tons a year. Steamboat tonnage provides a measure of comparison to show how the expense and difficulty of keelboat travel kept the supply of goods from outside the region at low levels. In 1820 western river steamboats had a total carrying capacity of 13,890 tons. In two weeks they carried twice as much freight as went upriver in all of 1811.[7]

A WEDDING CAKE WITHOUT THE COMPLICATIONS

Steamboats changed everything because they overcame the Mississippi River's most obvious environmental barrier: the strong current. The first boats to prove their worth were unusual looking craft, since they were essentially keelboats with steam engines grafted onto them. Most boats had freight and passenger accommodations beneath the main deck, and sheer hulls, sails, and bowsprits were common; the square sail of the *Vesuvius,* for instance, supplemented the engine's meager power. The *General Pike,* built in Cincinnati in 1818, anticipated later designs with a boxy structure that ran the boat's length and housed staterooms and the main cabin. Probably the strangest looking craft was the *Western Engineer.* Built for the Yellowstone Expedition that traveled up the Missouri River, it featured a serpent's head at its bow that blew smoke.[8]

In 1816 Henry Shreve's *Washington* moved steamboat design in important new directions by placing the boilers on the main deck and tipping them so they were horizontal. This radical new design eliminated some heavy gearing while simultaneously increasing horsepower. The rhythmic cadence of these high-pressure engines was deafening. One traveler likened it to the "hard breathing of some huge mastodon labouring under the asthma." Engines also shook the boats, especially when working at high capacity. The vibration could be so intense that common activities like eating, writing, or reading became chores. Bazil Kiger later complained that the *Sultana* shook so much that "I can't easily write" and abruptly ended his letter. These large, powerful engines naturally increased steamboat speed. Early boats struggled along at three to eight miles per hour, but by the 1830s steamers averaged about ten miles per hour upstream and fifteen or more with the current.[9]

Further modifications reveal how southerners learned to adapt steamboats to the particular geography of the West. Not only were river levels unpredictable, but obstacles such as shoals, sandbars, and snags were menacing. By 1820 the deep displacement of keelboats gave way to shallow-draft steamers modeled more like flatboats. Boats with less draft could operate longer into the dry season and were more likely to avoid underwater threats, crucial factors that ensured their economic viability. The gradual curve, or rake, of the bow allowed steamers to ease themselves onto muddy riverbanks so the crew could hop out and secure the boat to a mooring post or tree. One of western steamboats' great features was the ability to stop just about anywhere along the shore, not just in the river towns.[10]

Boat builders tinkered with structural designs in other ways. Most steamboats built between 1820 and 1850 had paddle wheels on both sides of the boat, usually about two-thirds of the way to the stern. In the late 1840s stern-wheels made a comeback and became the favored design because they were ideal for shallower water and were protected from floating debris. Hulls became flat and long. Most of the early steamers were less than 120 feet in length, but after 1830 they consistently stretched more than 200 feet and drew about eight feet of water. A few behemoths were as long as a football field, and the famous *Eclipse* set the record at 350 feet. The width of steamboats, though, remained remarkably constant in the half century after the *New Orleans* steamed out of Pittsburgh. Ninety percent of western boats were no broader than the thirty-two-foot-wide *New Orleans,* which was huge for its time. The 1853 *Crystal Palace,* for instance, was one foot wider than the *New Orleans* but twice as long and carried 170 tons more cargo. Thin boats were fast boats, and the elongated design satisfied the public's desire for speed.[11]

Hundreds of smaller shallow-draft steamers, "perfectly adapted to the depth of the waters on which they operate," complemented the giant riverboats of the Mississippi. They prowled rivers like the Tennessee, Arkansas, Tombigbee, Apalachicola, and Sabine. At 100 to 200 tons, they drew perhaps two feet of water and extended the reach of steamboats far away from the main rivers. One boat on the Kentucky River, for instance, drew an amazing eleven inches without cargo and operated far into the dry season. While it is not true that boats were so light that when "the river is low and the sandbars come out for air, the first mate can tap a keg of beer and run the boat four miles on the suds," it was not unusual for captains of low-water boats to send crew members ahead with lanterns to walk the river and pick out the deepest channel. Boats dispatched yawls to take soundings, and cub pilots like Samuel Clemens competed for the opportunity to go out sounding.[12]

The cargo capacity of steamers became steadily larger, thanks in large part to a huge main deck. Most of the space was actually on the guards, which were the portions of the deck that stretched beyond the hull and normally did not touch the water. Guards might be as wide as thirty feet per side and protected the hull from scraping and grinding against objects. Hog chains were the key to this leap forward in design. They ran from the forward hull, up and over the hurricane deck, and back down to the stern and were tightened with turnbuckles to prevent the boats from "hogging," or sagging, at the extremities. Large guards were the primary reason for an increase in riverboat tonnage. Downstream cargo capacity for steamboats on the Mississippi River rose from an average of 110 tons before 1820 to 630 tons in the decade of the 1850s. More freight meant higher profits. Steamboats, in short, became an attractive investment option because they were adapted to the environment, held more freight, and penetrated further along shallow rivers.[13]

Early steamboats had one deck, but that changed in the mid-1820s. The main deck contained the engine, the freight room, and was home to deck passengers and most of the cargo. The second level was the boiler deck, since it was built on the roof of the boiler room. It became the domain of cabin passengers, and conditions on it were noticeably different from those on the main deck. The hurricane deck was the roof for the cabins and was the location of the ship's signal bell and occasionally became the repository of small cargo. It was so named for its ever-present breeze. Up until the early 1840s this was the highest deck, but the need for more cargo capacity led to the creation of the texas. The texas received its name, as the story goes, because it was annexed to the steamer, just like the Lonestar State was added to the United States in 1845. It was shorter and narrower than the boiler deck, being at most one-third the length of the vessel, and was home for the crew. The pilothouse, resting on the highest deck of the steamboat, might be forty feet or more above the main deck and had a commanding view of the river. Most were aft of the chimneys, had windows on all four sides, and contained the huge wheel, a bench, and a stove. On either side of the pilothouse were the chimneys, or stacks, which got progressively taller during the 1820s and 1830s. Not only did the tall stacks add to the majestic appearance of steamboats, but they served a practical purpose. High chimneys gave embers more of a chance to burn out before floating into the air and possibly setting the boat on fire. Additionally, builders added fluting, a wire mesh at the stop of the stacks, to break the embers into smaller pieces. Also called Indian feathers, the fluting became ornamental and gave rise to the expression high falutin'. Riverboats also had distinctive symbols between the stacks as a way to differentiate them from other crafts. The whole appearance, as Mark Twain supposedly remarked, was like a wedding cake without the complications.[14]

"BY THE FORCE OF STEAM OR FIRE"

The New Orleans was merely a primitive version of its eventual huge descendants when it "fumigate[d]" from New Orleans to Natchez and back in fifteen days. Helped by the monopoly that the Ohio Steam-Boat Navigation Company secured for the waters of Louisiana, the boat hauled so many passengers and so much freight that it was rumored to have cleared $20,000 its first year. On the basis of this success, Robert Fulton and Robert Livingston launched two more boats, the Vesuvius in 1814 and the Aetna in 1815, and appeared to be fulfilling their promise of dominating the western trade by introducing a fleet of steamboats that would operate between the major cities of the West. Already southerners were learning that steam power was the key to overcoming the restrictive conditions of nature because, compared to human or animal muscle, it was "portable, cheap, and efficient."[15]

Before the Ohio Steam-Boat Navigation Company could secure its grip on western commerce, rivals appeared. Daniel French started the onslaught by chartering the Monongahela and Ohio Steamboat Company and building the Enterprise. French selected Shreve, a seasoned keelboatman who was crucial for the development of riverboats and navigation on the western waters, as captain of the *Enterprise* and sent him to Louisiana. Shreve guided the little boat to New Orleans and did everything possible to thumb his nose at the monopoly. He steamed the boat up the Red River, to Natchez, and to the mouth of the Mississippi River before returning to New Orleans in May 1815. Only when Shreve announced that the *Enterprise* would leave for Brownsville did the Ohio Steam-Boat Navigation Company take action. As Shreve was making final preparations to depart, a deputy arrested him for violating the Fulton-Livingston monopoly. Shreve had anticipated the gambit and had hired Abner Duncan, one of the city's best attorneys. Duncan quickly bailed out Shreve, who steamed upriver the same day.[16]

The presence of a legitimate competitor caused many Louisiana residents to question the wisdom of granting a monopoly to the Ohio Steam-Boat Navigation Company. The source of the criticism is unclear, but the *New Orleans Louisiana Courier* steadfastly defended the company. It argued that the "privileges" granted Fulton and Livingston "contain nothing which may be considered 'odious.'" Governor William C. Claiborne, who had lobbied for the monopoly, concurred. In a private letter to Livingston, Claiborne pledged himself to the "prevention of intrusion on your rights." For the time being, the Fulton-Livingston monopoly was safe.[17]

The monopoly, though, was dependent on public support for enforcement and involved more than just Louisiana. Livingston used his influence to protect his New York monopoly, but lacked the power to stifle dissent in the West. Along the Ohio River, newspapers and state legislatures argued that the company prevented economic growth rather than promoted it. The business had not been able to keep enough boats consistently in the water to satisfy demand and the confrontations with Shreve smacked of arrogance. It was in Louisiana, however, that the monopoly mattered most, and events were swiftly moving to end the privilege. The state legislature twice debated the wisdom of its grant to Fulton, but Jasper Lynch, the company's local representative, pressured key legislators to uphold the monopoly. The House committee released its report in January 1817 by noting how the company's steamboats reduced freight costs and would soon create "an extensive commerce with the interior of the country."[18]

Even though the legislature was still in his pocket, Lynch was fighting a rearguard action. Rival steamboats chugged into New Orleans like so many pesky flies, and their steady presence showed not only the impracticality of enforcing the monopoly but also the enthusiasm of southerners in adopting the new technology. Although Lynch succeeded in forcing the *Dispatch* to leave its cargo of sugar on the levee, the *Pike* docked on October 2, 1816. Shreve's *Washington* arrived in the Crescent City five days later. The latter boat presented the greatest threat because of Shreve's persistence. In a desperate move that betrayed weakness, Lynch offered Shreve one-half interest in the monopoly. When Shreve rebuffed the offer, Lynch tersely wrote, "I have failed in making the arrangement I had expected with Captain Schrieve." Lynch prepared to sue his rival for violation of the monopoly, but Shreve once more fled Louisiana.[19]

When Shreve returned to New Orleans on March 12, 1817, Lynch was ready. He filed suit against the Quaker, charging that Shreve had twice "impelled and driven [a boat] thro the water [of Louisiana] by the force of steam or fire." Duncan anticipated the suit and executed a brilliant counter-strategy. He advised Shreve to await arrest aboard the *Washington*. Most people associated with the levee were sympathetic to Shreve and hated Livingston, whose family had tried to build a private batture, or boat enclosure. When the city marshal hauled Shreve away, a large crowd protested and threatened to storm the jail. Duncan correctly assumed the sight of Shreve in chains would play upon public perceptions of Livingston as a privileged outsider. Shreve spent one night in jail and left New Orleans before learning that the judge dismissed the case on April 21, 1817, for lack of jurisdiction. The Fulton-Livingston monopoly was dead.[20]

The monopoly's demise anticipated the more famous *Gibbons v. Ogden* Supreme Court case of 1824, where the heirs of Fulton and Livingston had also fought to retain their monopoly in New York. A number of competitors emerged, including Aaron Ogden, who bought a license from Livingston to operate a ferry. Thomas Gibbons deliberately violated the monopoly, so Ogden sued. Once the case made it to the Supreme Court, Chief Justice John Marshall overturned the New York law that granted the monopoly and asserted the federal government's power to regulate interstate commerce. The issue was already a dead letter in Louisiana thanks to Shreve and Duncan.[21]

A tangled skein of troubles ultimately brought down the Ohio Steam-Boat Navigation Company. The petulant Fulton quarreled with nearly all of his employees and pushed an ambitious construction program that saddled the company with too much debt. Snags, sandbars, and fires also took their toll. The Fulton-Livingston monopoly predated most of the significant design changes to steamboats—perhaps even stifling innovation—and relied on boats that were not reliable enough nor technically advanced enough to guarantee consistent profits. Worse yet, the monopoly was unenforceable in a place where it did not enjoy public support.

"SPLITTING OPEN THE RIVER"

The death of the Fulton-Livingston monopoly coincided with the spread of steamboats across the country. Starting about 1820, revolutions in communications and transportation reoriented the arc of trade within the United States. Riverboats became a common sight on the upper Ohio River between Louisville and Pittsburgh and also worked the upper Mississippi River. By 1835 the western waters had more steam tonnage than the Atlantic coast and almost as much as the whole British Empire. Steamboats also roiled the tidal rivers of the East coast and the Great Lakes, traveled up the Missouri as far as Montana, and paddled up the short rivers of the slave states along the Atlantic Ocean. But environmental conditions limited the operation of riverboats everywhere except the interior South. The shipping season in the North and the Far West was significantly shorter than in the lower Mississippi River valley, and the rivers in Virginia, North Carolina, South Carolina, and Georgia were not long enough to warrant much traffic. Compared to the western waters, steamboat traffic there was negligible. The Cape Fear River, for instance, was one of the busiest streams, and its traffic peaked at a mere fifteen boats in 1850.[22]

The interior South was on the vanguard of radical change, especially as information moved across watery networks with unprecedented speed. The logbooks of the Natchez landings show just how quickly fact and fiction filtered through the region. Steamboats from all points of the compass (Pittsburgh, Cincinnati, Louisville, St. Louis, Nashville, Memphis, Vicksburg, Yalobusha [Mississippi], Florence [Alabama], Alexandria [Louisiana], Point Chicot [Arkansas], Mobile, Natchitoches, New Orleans) passed through Natchez, and their captains recorded their activities in the city's logbooks. The ledgers were a combination of brag book, gossip sheet, political column, environmental study, and commercial diary where captains explained why they ventured to Natchez, boasted about their boats' capabilities, and mentioned information that might affect navigation. Military events dotted the ledgers. On June 22, 1836, the *Tuskina* stopped in Natchez with three hundred volunteers headed to Texas, men who probably were filled with patriotic fervor after hearing news of the Alamo. When the Panic of 1837 struck, a captain who had just come from Louisville scrawled, "Reports all Cincinnati & Louisville banks

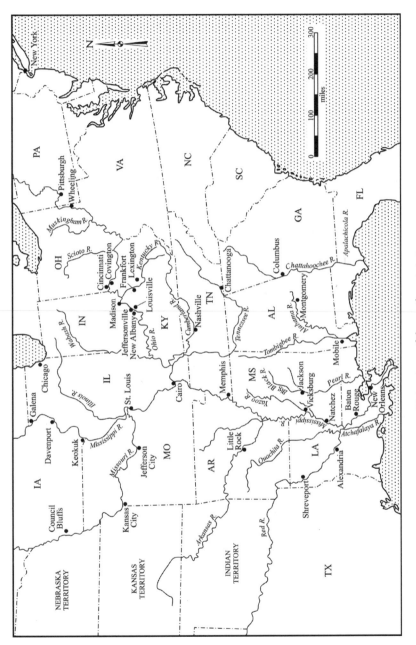

Major rivers of the southern interior

stopped!," to which another visitor added, "God Dam." Political news was also prominent, in one case the likely victory of William Henry Harrison and John Tyler, when the captain of the *Monongahela* wrote, "Reports 17,000 votes majority in Pennsylvania for T[ippecanoe] & T[yler], to[o]." Water levels and the spread of yellow fever were other frequent notations on the logbooks.[23]

The point is that riverboats created information networks that transmitted the important and the trivial in hours or days rather than weeks or months. River towns like Natchez, Vicksburg, and Memphis were situated at the center of this web, and information flowed in and out of these central points with amazing (at least for the era) rapidity. The *Diana* went from New Orleans to Natchez in only 26 hours and 45 minutes, its captain boasted, because it was "splitting open the River." It is no surprise that the most common entries in the Natchez logbooks dealt with a boat's speed or its abilities. "She Runs like the Devil coming out of Hell," crowed the *Pittsburgh's* captain in a typical entry. Boats from Natchez to St. Louis took only three days, and made it to Louisville in four. Information and ideas converged in these central river towns and then spread out on steamboats.[24]

Once riverboats received government contracts to carry mail, their function as bearers of information was formalized. The first boats carried letters as a favor to their customers, but Shreve's 1819 *Post Boy* was the first steamboat with a formal mail contract, in this case between Louisville and New Orleans. The postal system enlarged dramatically during the 1820s and 1830s, thanks in part to steamboats and stagecoaches. Once riverboats became established as postal carriers, southerners tracked their arrivals and departures with precision and tailored their activities and writing schedules around the boats. Like most Americans, they came to assume that postal access was a basic necessity of life. When southerners were not included in the riverine postal system, they complained to the federal government. Residents of northwestern Louisiana petitioned to have steamboat mail service on the Red River, arguing that horseback mail was too slow and unreliable. Since there was an "abundance of boats engaged in the Red river trade," they hoped to improve upon the two- to three-month overland trip from Fort Adams, Mississippi. Letters carried on steamboats could be powerful tools that enabled producers of cash crops to receive current information on prices and markets. One cotton factor sent word by riverboat for his client to ship his cotton immediately so he could "take advantage of present good prices." The ability of steamers to move information privileged residents along the main rivers at the expense of people along the smaller tributaries or those away from the riverside. As people, letters, and stories transferred to subsequently smaller boats, the information moved more slowly and had the potential to become garbled, lost, or outdated.[25]

When letters proved to slow and southerners found it necessary to handle their own business affairs, steamers gave them the opportunity. The fast trip and low cost meant that commerce could be conducted face to face and not at a distance. William Kenner repeatedly asked his client to steam from Natchez to New Orleans so they could speak directly about some bills. "Can't you take a trip down in a good Steamboat before the Season is too far advanced?" he wondered. By 1827, the *Western Monthly Review* reported with exaggeration that most merchants, planters, and farmers in the South had traveled to New Orleans on a steamboat. To a significant degree, the people of the Mississippi River valley became more time conscious as they waited on steamers to bring vital information. And those who ran out of patience, or needed that extra measure of control, found steamers a welcome tool.[26]

Steamboats also fostered the ability to access other cultures and sensibilities in an unexpected way: floating circuses. Several circus groups, including Spaulding and Rogers, Dan Rice, Chapman's Floating Theatre, and Stickney's Mammoth Pavilion and Great Western Gymnastic Arena Company, traveled along the rivers of the southern interior. The first circus groups used steamboats as a means of transportation, but by the 1840s they built showboats that they towed behind riverboats. The most elaborate showboat was Spaulding and Rogers' Floating Circus Palace, a "vast Floating Amphitheatre" that was twice the size of the St. Charles Theater in New Orleans. Although accounts vary, it had at least 1,100 cane-bottomed arm chairs, cushioned settees that could accommodate 500 people, and benches for another 1,200 people on the second deck. Huge mirrors on both sides of the arena made the space seem even larger. Brussels carpeting, massive paintings, and ornamental chandeliers with gas lights made the theater as much of an attraction as the amusements within it. The two hundred-foot-long showboat also had stables, a green room, dressing rooms, living quarters, and a business office. The riverine circuses mapped out itineraries that included only the larger towns. Advance men went ahead to place advertisements in newspapers and plaster towns with posters. The calliope, a standard feature by the 1850s, banged out tunes that could be heard miles away. When the showboat arrived in town, a huge parade of performers, the brass band, and animals marched through the streets. Circus Day became its own spectacle, as curious residents abandoned their work to catch a glimpse of the exotic.[27]

Circuses became quite popular in the Southwest because they featured amusements and spectacles that most people had never seen before. Menageries of animals (elephants, camels, lions, and orangutans, for instance), skilled equestrian riders, clowns, bugle players, and singers from Europe were a few of the acts that southerners clamored to see. Circuses sometimes shocked traditional sensibilities, as in the case of Chapman's Floating Theatre, which stopped in Memphis in 1836. The painting that featured a young maiden's bare foot and calf was too risqué for public consumption, so workers quickly painted over the unfortunate girl. Most circuses, though, featured safe entertainment that was supposed to enlighten and edify the backwoods rubes who were fortunate enough to gain admission. One Natchez newspaper, for instance, was grateful that one recent circus did not feature "low and vulgar jokes" but instead presented "acts of a high and classic order." Such paeans to the redemptive value of circuses should not be taken at face value, but it is clear that residents of the southern interior recognized the ability of floating circuses to reduce their provincialism. Circuses were one of the few forms of professional entertainment that rural southerners could see, and their continued presence along the rivers testifies to the desire of southerners to experience life outside their small worlds.[28]

Riverboats bearing ideas, information, letters, newspapers, journals, visitors, and migrants were a crucial component in reducing the Southwest's insularity. Although the region was rural, it was not isolated. The leading intellectual and political leaders were modernizing cosmopolitans who made decisions in a national and global context. Natchez merchants, for instance, explored the possibility bankrolling steamboats that provided direct service between Natchez and New York or Philadelphia. The plan, which proved unworkable because of technological difficulties, was intended to bypass "excessive handling charges" in New Orleans and prompted Memphis merchants to consider a similar scheme. The *Western Monthly Review* captured this sense of steamboats effacing differences of time and space when it noted that steamboats carried all manner of goods and ideas to "Atlantic" citizens who were also known as "backwoodsmen." By the late 1820s, steamboats enabled southerners to expand their expectations about which ideas and products they could consume.[29]

"A STEAM BOAT BY G——D"

Southerners did not have to understand how steamboats created new communications networks to be in awe of them. Like other Americans, residents of the southern interior fell under the spell of the "technological sublime." A traveler to Natchez in 1819 struggled to capture his thoughts the first time he boarded a riverboat. "I wish I could convey an adequate description of this craft," he wrote after carefully studying the unnamed boat. The traveler correctly predicted that steam navigation would come to dominate life along the Mississippi River and its tributaries. Even more flabbergasted was a riverman who arrived in Maysville, Kentucky, in a broadhorn and saw his first riverboat. The thundering paddle wheels and the roar of the steam pipe frightened observers and created "not a little excitement and admiration." At that time, a steamboat was "almost as great a wonder as a Flying angel would Be at present."[30]

Ambitious southerners scrambled to put boats in the water. Riverboat production, ownership, and operation rapidly spread along the waters of the Southwest. Up until 1817—the last year of the Fulton-Livingston monopoly—only fifteen steamers designated a town in the southern interior as their home port. That number doubled in 1818, and 190 new boats took to the water during the 1820s. Heavy demand coupled with the short life span of steamboats meant that between 1820 and 1860 workers turned out over two thousand boats for the southern interior, or about one boat per week. Particularly during the two decades after the War of 1812, the massive production of riverboats and their innovative designs put the interior South on the cutting edge of technological advance in America. Steamboats came of age at the tail end of a surge of American industrialization between 1780 and 1820 and before the rapid advance of the railroad in the late 1830s. Between these technological bursts, steamboats were the premier machine in America. See table 1 for specific information on the number of southern steamboats.[31]

Nearly two-thirds of steamboats in the southern interior took form in Pittsburgh, Cincinnati, Jeffersonville, Indiana, New Albany, Indiana, Louisville, and St. Louis. Not only were these river towns the only ones with foundries large enough to forge steam engines, but they had quick access to all the raw materials of riverboat construction. The Parsons and Newell boatyard in Jeffersonville advertised its services as far away as Mobile, and its rival, the Howard Shipyard in nearby New Albany, sent one-third of its boats to

TABLE 1

Steamboats in the southern interior, 1811–1860, by decade

Years	Tonnage	Number of steamboats built	Average boat size (tons)	Average longevity (years)
1811–1819	12,943	58	220.6	5.7
1820–1829	30,464	190	160.3	4.9
1830–1839	58,499	355	164.8	5.4
1840–1849	130,943	668	195.8	4.9
1850–1859	195,683	788	248.3	5.4
1860	23,275	110	211.6	5.2
Total	451,807	2,169	208.2	5.2

Sources: See Appendix A.

New Orleans and Mobile. There were no standardized plans for steamboats, so boatbuilders custom-made each boat, or even portions of boats, to individual requirements. Sometimes one company built the entire craft, while at other times boats took shape in stages in nearby locations. The price of boats varied immensely (with furnishings for the cabin being the most significant variable that inflated prices), but general figures, when expressed as a dollar amount per measured ton, fell from $125 between 1810 and 1819 to $100 for the decade of the 1850s.[32]

Despite the presence of large shipyards, steamboat construction was strewn along southern rivers, as 141 different towns manufactured at least one boat and 41 percent of boats for the southern interior took shape in the region. Typically, local merchants, bankers, or men with experience in the flatboat trade pooled their financial and technical resources, ordered engines from foundries, and then put them in boats they assembled on site. As demand for steamboat service spread from the major rivers into smaller streams, buyers across the Southwest ordered or built small boats that best suited the conditions of their local river systems. Businessmen in Mobile, for instance, built a steamer for the Tombigbee River in the hopes of exploiting trade to the state's interior. The appropriately named *Alabama* astounded veteran rivermen so much that when the 218-ton craft churned past two flatboats, one amused passenger wrote that the rivermen "exclaimed a Steam boat by G——d & then complimented us in the stile of Kentucky boat men on the Mississippi." Whether that salute was profane or respectful is open to interpretation. Local steamers like the *Alabama* usually connected their home port with New Orleans, Mobile, or another regional city and were noticeably smaller than craft built for the major rivers. Enterprising businessmen in tiny Bolivar, Tennessee, built the 104-ton *Native* in hopes of capturing the cotton trade on the Hatchie River and hauling it to Memphis. The Koun family of Shreveport, Louisiana, built a number of small, maneuverable riverboats that could thrive in the Red River's special conditions, and at least twenty locally built riverboats steamed up and down the Chattahoochee River prior to the Civil War.[33]

Although outsiders brought the first steamers to the South, after 1817 southerners owned most of the boats. Systematic analysis of owners' residence is not possible because few records survive, but anecdotal evidence is strong. Virtually all of the records that cite ownership of boats that operated in southern waters indicate local ownership. In the supposedly capital-starved South, it seems that money for riverboats was readily available. Most of the first southern entrepreneurs were rivermen, and Shreve, although not a native southerner, is typical of the veterans of the western waters who carefully calculated their opportunities and gambled that steamboat ownership was their best chance for wealth. Shreve started with a keelboat in 1807, which he took to St. Louis with a crew of ten men. Within three years he had made enough money carrying lead and furs that he was free of debt and able to "go hansomly into business." He invested his savings in steamboats. Anthony R. Gale followed Shreve's example. The native southerner went from flatboatman, to steamboat captain, to owner of the *Vesuvius* in 1816. "I have no doubt it will be a profitable business," he wrote a friend.[34]

Merchants and store owners also commonly purchased steamboats. John K. West and Francis Duplisses, both New Orleans merchants, bought the *Louisiana* in 1818. They were like countless entrepreneurs in southern river towns who were eager to exploit a perceived advantage in technology to make a profit. William Cage, for example, teamed with his business partner to buy a steamboat that could bring hogsheads of Louisiana sugar directly to his Nashville store. Entrepreneurs along the smaller rivers also recognized a moneymaking opportunity when they saw it. Little Rock store owners Ficklin and Rapley bought the *Ottawa* and used it to control costs and ensure supply. Since steamboats provided connections to regional, national, and international markets, they allowed merchants to offer a wider assortment of material at lower prices.[35]

Other members of the southern middle class also invested in riverboats. The men who formed the Natchez Steam Boat Company on July 4, 1818, included bank presidents, magistrates, attorneys, and the man who would become Mississippi's first state governor. The company purchased the *New Orleans* and the *Vesuvius* from the moribund Fulton-Livingston monopoly. In Nashville, seven of the twenty-three men who established the Farmers and Mechanics Bank invested in steamboats. The motives of such investors are more difficult to discern. It seems that white collar investors built, bought, or bankrolled steamboats in response to a perceived need since such boats usually serviced the cities of their owners. That was the case in Natchitoches, Louisiana. "Merchants and Planters" formed the Natchitoches Steamboat Company in 1836 because the old steamboat company had no competition and was "charging a higher price for freight than was customary." Steamers established deep ties with the local business communities; they were responsive to local needs and also brought economic benefits to their home port.[36]

Planters like Stephen Duncan of Natchez also became steamboat entrepreneurs. He invested in the *Walk in the Water* in 1826 in the hopes of reducing the price of shipping his cotton. Although it struggled to make a profit at first, the boat paid large dividends when managed properly and Duncan used it to bestow favors on his friends and business associates. Further downriver, twenty-four men, all specifically identifying themselves as "Planters," established a steamboat company near Baton Rouge. In a type of prospectus, they complained of the "extravagant" freight charges and irregular service of steamers. Planters used steamboats to ship their staple crops to market, wanted a cheap and reliable means to receive supplies necessary for their operations, and yearned for a way to bring control to their operations.[37]

Just as steamboat owners varied in experience and background, they used different methods to become part of the ownership class. Most commonly, a limited number of partners pooled their resources to buy a steamboat. If the numbers for the western waters as a whole apply to the South, then single proprietors operated around one quarter of southern riverboats, partnerships of two to five men owned approximately 40 percent, and groups of five or more owned 25 percent. Such diffusion of ownership had the convenient benefit of deflecting potential lawsuits. Establishing jurisdiction when partners lived in different states was no easy matter and muddled legal proceedings. The remaining 10 percent of western boats belonged to joint stock companies. At least seventy investors enabled the Natchez Steam Boat Company to be capitalized at $100,000. Similar companies ranged from the St. Stephens Steamboat Company in Alabama to the Natchitoches Steamboat Company in northern Louisiana. Such corporations typically sold shares for $50 or $100, limited the number of shares any one investor could hold, and established a president and board of directors.[38]

Although steamboats could be lucrative investments, they were also risky ones. Snags, fires, explosions, collisions, floating debris, and other hazards reduced the life expectancy of a Mississippi River steamer to about five years. The unlucky duo of Ficklin and Rapley, for instance, operated the *Ottawa* for a few months before it sank on the Arkansas River. Most owners had insurance for such contingencies, and it is not surprising that suits and countersuits over damaged or lost cargo crowded the dockets of southern state courts. Even experienced rivermen like Shreve could run into financial reverses. Despite his success in toppling the monopoly and building better steamers, Shreve was nearly bankrupt in 1822. He owed over $97,000 to thirty different creditors and had mortgages on his properties in Kentucky. Although Shreve was ultimately able to make money in riverboats, countless others were not.[39]

Despite such financial risks, residents of the Southwest poured money into riverboat construction, spending about $44 million between 1811 and 1860. Steamboats were the quintessential southern business: one that functioned well on a local level, augmented agriculture, but could not keep pace with the rest of the country. Riverboats' relatively inexpensive price tag and minimal capital requirements made them an attractive investment for southerners who were willing to take chances. Initial costs were comparatively low (a medium tonnage steamer might cost $20,000 to build), and other expenses, such as supplies, maintenance, and wages, were nominal and could be paid out over time. Steamboats possessed a number of advantages over railroads, a technology that only made significant inroads into the interior South after 1850. Unlike railroads, riverboats demanded no supporting infrastructure since the rivers and city levees were already in place, thus making it easier to raise the necessary capital. Nor did steamboat owners have to ask for right-of-ways or land grants. The first steamers required almost no government help and did not offend southerners who were wary of increasing state power, although eventually owners would seek public money for river improvements. Steamboats, moreover, generated immediate revenue and could be free of debt in a few years if operated properly and lucky enough to avoid explosions, fires, and snags. Low costs, quick profits, and the extensive southern river system meant that steamboats easily fit into the southern political economy.[40]

Steamboats also illustrate the limitations of southern industrial growth.

The lack of large industrial facilities limited engine production to St. Louis and Louisville and hampered the overall development of steamers in the South. Machinery varied widely in price, but engines and boilers for medium boats were about one-third of the overall price. Even though many engines were salvaged from wrecked and sunken boats, a significant amount of capital flowed out of the South to purchase machinery. And while riverboats might quickly turn a profit and were an attractive investment, white southerners preferred to put their money into a proven commodity: slavery. Table 2 shows that for every dollar southerners invested in steamboats between 1820 and 1859, they spent eleven on new slaves. The disparity was particularly acute during the heyday of the interstate slave trade in the 1820s and 1830s. In those two decades, the ratio of investment in slaves to steamboats was about twenty to one. Riverboats were a means to enhance slavery's profitability, and the amount of money invested in them never approached the amount that was sunk into the peculiar institution.[41]

TABLE 2

Estimated investment in interstate slave trade compared to southern steamboats

Years	Estimated value of slaves sold in the interstate slave trade	Estimated cost of steamboats	Ratio of investment in slaves to investment in steamboats
1820–1829	$57,381,000	$3,292,630	17:1
1830–1839	$143,298,000	$6,332,040	23:1
1840–1849	$73,968,000	$11,614,860	6:1
1850–1859	$157,527,600	$19,219,500	8:1
Total	$432,174,600	$40,459,030	11:1

Sources: Appendix A; Steven Deyle, Carry Me Back: The Domestic Slave Trade in American Life (New York, 2005), 140.

Even if southern investment in steamboats was a fraction of the money tied up in slaves, the pursuit of riverboats demonstrates a southern willingness to adopt new technology as a way to modernize slavery. The rapid spread of the cotton gin after 1800, the switch to steam-powered sugar mills in the 1820s, slaves working in iron foundries, increased reliance on watches and clocks, and eventually the spread of the railroad in the South demonstrate that technology could be reconciled with slavery. But it was only certain types of technology that could flourish in the South; machines had to augment southern agricultural production rather threaten it. Steamboats, like the cotton gin, were a perfect technology for the South because they made slaves more efficient and more valuable.[42]

Southerners in the Southwest became enamored with steamboats and invested heavily in them because they solved a number of problems. As design changes brought the boats in greater harmony with the environment, steamboating became one of the South's most noteworthy businesses and was part of a greater communication and transportation advance. The heavy southern investment in riverboats, even if it could not approach the money spent on slaves, placed the interior South on the cutting edge of technological development in the 1820s and 1830s. And as more and more steamboats thrashed across southern waters, they became the workplace for thousands of southern whites, free blacks, and slaves. These workers, as the next chapter reveals, faced grueling conditions of work but could also use the terms of their employment to unprecedented advantage.

TWO

WORKING ON OLD MAN RIVER

It seemed like business as usual on the *Western World* during its passage upriver from New Orleans to Cincinnati in 1852. The cabin passengers were enjoying their meals, the boat was making good time, and there was enough cargo to ensure a tidy profit. A few days into the trip, the steward had a suspicion that there was something not quite right about the passenger later identified as Robert. The steward was in a difficult position. Although Robert was "a shade lighter than a new saddle" and had "long dark hair" that was straight, it was not uncommon to see darker men who were classified as free and white according to the South's arbitrary system of racial profiling. If Robert was black or, worse yet, an escaped slave, he would be in violation of the racial protocols of cabin passage. But should the steward confront Robert and learn that he was a free white man, the boat's reputation would be damaged. The steward prudently shared his thoughts with the captain, who confronted Robert in the passenger's cabin. Several passengers came to Robert's defense and criticized the captain for unfairly singling out a white man. Despite a noisy protest, the captain seized Robert and brought him to the "calaboose" in Memphis.[1]

Once the captain returned to the boat, the passengers were shocked to learn that Robert was not a white passenger but an escaped slave. The biracial man had worked as a waiter on steamboats, learning how cabin passengers behaved and spoke. He put his knowledge to use in a bold bid for freedom that came undone just a few days before he would have set foot on free soil. Robert had eaten at the first class table during his stint on the steamer, a seemingly innocuous activity that was much more difficult than it appears at first glance. Pleasant conversation was just as important as good food, and Robert apparently created a false identity for himself that was convincing enough to fool the guests. One shocked passenger had no idea that Robert "had African blood in his veins" and judged the slave to have "more the appearance of the gentleman than the plebeian." Even the engineer was impressed with Robert's "very genteel deportment." But the fugitive was ultimately betrayed not by his interior but his exterior. One of the boat's employees probably scanned the runaway section of newspapers and spotted the telltale advertisement. It took a keen observer thoroughly familiar with the workings of a steamboat to realize that Robert harbored a past that could not be forgiven in the South.[2]

Robert's story provides a glimpse into the complexities of labor on a western river steamboat and the vagaries of race and slavery in the South. The *Western World*'s captain, steward, and passengers were trying to fit Robert in his proper place within the South's social order. A person's social identity could not always be reduced to simple categories of slave and free or black and white. Oftentimes observers had to triangulate what they knew of a person's personal history, appearance, and behavior to determine where a stranger stood on the various continuums. In this case, Robert had learned how to "be" white and free and crafted a new identity for himself: to be white, he had to behave white. Although he could control two of the three tests of social identity, he could not manage perceptions of his skin color.[3]

Work on steamers in the interior South both distorted and reflected southern notions of race and class. Whites worked the best jobs, like captain, pilot, engineer, or mate, and even the lowly position of clerk could be the path to upward mobility and a place in the middle class. Most workers, though, remained locked into readily identifiable groups on the main and boiler decks that had little sense of being part of a larger working class. African Americans inhabited some of the same physical space as whites, but formal and informal rules erected unseen barriers between the races. In the face of widespread discrimination, blacks found means to subvert the harsh realities of slavery and resist the peculiar institution. While individual slaves translated employment on the waters into personal freedom, steamers tended to entrench slavery by making slaves and their labor more valuable.

"GOOD LOOKING, FRANK, BRAVE, DARE-DEVIL FELLOWS"

Steamboats in the southern interior were a diverse lot, and so were their crews. An 1850 count of St. Louis steamboat workers revealed that 43 percent were native whites, 24 percent were Irish, 11 percent were Germans, 3 percent other whites, 6 percent free blacks, and 12 percent slaves. Small boats on the tributary streams might have ten workers, while the mammoth *Eclipse* employed 121 people. Captains, clerks, and sometimes pilots earned a yearly salary, but the rest of the crew drew wages by the month rather than the voyage, as was the practice on seaborne vessels. Most steamboat laborers could count on only eight or nine months of work, since low or frozen water prevented year-round operation. Wages also varied considerably and depended on the location and the particular boat. On average, though, a rough hierarchy emerged with pilots and captains earning the most money. Pilots, for instance, made about $150 per month through much of the antebellum period, which translated into yearly earnings of about $1,350. Clerks and engineers were next, followed by the second engineer and mate. Crew members who did most of the physical work earned significantly less, because their labor could most readily be replaced. Deck and cabin crew members earned $20 to $25 a month, or about $180 to $225 a year. Table 3 contains a more extensive listing of wages on western river steamboats.[4]

TABLE 3

Wages on western river steamboats

	1820–1829	1830–1839	1840–1849	1850–1860
Captain[a]	$1,000	$1,250	$1,250	$1,500
Clerk[a]	600	750	800	900
Pilot	60	150	125	150
Engineer	75	100	75	100
2nd engineer	50	50	50	50
Mate	50	60	50	75
Steward	30	40	40	45
Cook	30	40	40	40
Deck and cabin crew	20	25	22.50	25

[a]Annual salaries; all other figures are monthly wages.

Source: Adapted from Erik F. Haites, James Mak, and Gary M. Walton, *Western River Transportation: The Era of Early Internal Development, 1810–1860* (Baltimore, 1975), 141.

Captains were the visible representation of the steamboat. Although anyone with enough money could buy a boat and declare himself the captain, as a matter of course most captains had practical experience on the rivers or some type of mechanical background. The captain of the *Bueneta*, for instance, left Ireland at nineteen, traveled to Mobile, worked his way up to second mate, then first mate, and ultimately became a captain. George Washington Harris, who became more famous as the creator of Sut Lovingood, parlayed his apprenticeship in a metalworking shop into the captaincy of the *Knoxville.* Captains were responsible for the day-to-day operation of the boat. They had almost nothing to do with the actual navigation, but made decisions regarding when to leave, where to dock the boat, and served as the visible presence of management. Captains spent time in the pilothouse, inspected the cargo, and mingled with passengers in the saloon (the public portion of the main cabin that also served as the dining room for cabin passengers). They were known to keep the peace by putting particularly unruly or obnoxious passengers ashore or settling disputes that erupted between customers. A captain's authority on the boat was not absolute, as he could not overrule the decisions of the pilot, but in all other matters his word was final.[5]

Successful captains blended knowledge of the river, business sense, and the ability to charm passengers. One of the best was Thomas P. Leathers. A Kentucky native, Leathers started on the Yazoo River in 1836 and remained on the Mississippi until his death six decades later. Nicknamed "Old Push," he had the fierce demeanor of an Old Testament prophet: flashing eyes, shock of hair, full beard. Leathers, whose family supposedly possessed the powder horn and tomahawk of Tecumseh, was captain and owner of a string of boats named *Natchez,* and it was one of Leathers's boats that transported Jefferson Davis to Montgomery for the birth of the Confederacy. Davis returned the favor by seizing the boat and converting it into a troop carrier. After the war, the federal government arrested Leathers for being a Confederate spy. Even though President Andrew Johnson pardoned the captain, Leathers supposedly flew the "Stars and Bars" from the *Natchez* thereafter. Besides a stubborn determination, Leathers possessed an intuitive business sense. He made the *Natchez* more than a riverboat; it was an experience that catered to the high expectations of well-to-do customers.[6]

While a boat's captain found it difficult to separate his personal identity from his boat's reputation, the same could not be said for the pilot. Even though pilots were permanent crew members rather than temporary guides brought aboard for the navigation of a difficult portion of the river, they still moved from boat to boat in search of higher pay. Pilots were responsible for the actual direction of the steamboat once it was under way, and normally two were aboard at any one time. They rotated in four-hour shifts, in the hopes of keeping one of them alert, as they were the men with the greatest responsibility and also the most authority. Good pilots were hard to find, so owners and captains clamored to secure them to long-term agreements. Pilots specialized in one portion of a river but sometimes ventured into unknown waters because they possessed a general ability to interpret the signs of a river. This practice was more common in early steamboat days, but once steamboats became larger and more profitable the risks were not worth the rewards.[7]

Most early pilots were keelboat or flatboat men who built up knowledge of the rivers and their conditions. John C. Bush, for instance, first became acquainted with the Mississippi River by guiding a flatboat from Kentucky to New Orleans. In 1819 he learned to pilot a steamboat and made runs to Louisville, Natchez, and St. Louis. Once keelboats and flatboats became less common, clerks, mates, or other steamboat workers learned how to be pilots. A formal system of apprenticeship quickly established itself where cub pilots agreed to pay an established pilot a portion of their future wages in exchange for training. Cub pilots might train for two to three years before they were able to strike out on their own. In 1852, pilots on the western rivers formed their own association, which unionized their profession and had the practical effect of raising wages by limiting the number of men who became apprentices. The Steamboat Inspection Act formalized this system and conferred licenses on pilots after their apprenticeship. Pilots were among the few professionals in the antebellum South who were licensed.[8]

Learning the river was an immensely difficult task. Samuel Clemens, before he convinced Horace Bixby to teach him, figured it should be easy to be a pilot since all he had to do was "keep his boat in the river, and I did not consider that that could be much of a trick, since it was so wide." He quickly learned otherwise and later described a pilot's knowledge as comparable to learning by heart every house, every window, every light, and every sign on the longest street in New York. Bixby tested his student at every opportunity, and Clemens often failed. Once, when Clemens was brimming with confidence, Bixby casually asked if he knew the river's depth in the upcoming section. Clemens replied that he couldn't reach bottom with a church steeple. Bixby then planted the seed of doubt, "You think so, do you?" and strolled out of the pilothouse. Clemens did not know that his mentor had instructed the leadsman to call out fake river depths. As a crowd gathered to watch Clemens sweat, the leadsman's figures became impossibly shallow. Clemens panicked and shouted at the engineer to reverse the boat. Just then Bixby stepped into the pilothouse and the crowd broke into a chorus of laughter. Clemens learned to trust his knowledge.[9]

Thanks in large part to Clemens, pilots have become the most romanticized of steamboat workers. Clemens was more interested in telling a good story than in conveying the absolute truth, but his account is generally correct. The great knowledge necessary to be a pilot and their tremendous responsibility meant they commanded respect. Some pilots tried to cultivate a mystique through their clothes and demeanor. Clemens even wore a blue serge jacket and white pants when he was working, and Bixby was known for his impeccable dress. One awestruck passenger gushed that pilots were "usually good looking, frank, brave, dare-devil fellows with a great love of dress, jewelry and pretty girls." The truth is much harder to find because there are surprisingly few descriptions of antebellum pilots. Most certainly had a confident aura but were probably not the great showmen of popular myth.[10]

Clerks completed the crew on the hurricane deck and were third in authority behind the captain and pilot. They were responsible for a steamer's bookkeeping and served as the boat's business manager. In their offices on the boiler deck, clerks recorded names, freight, passengers, and wages in a series of books. They bargained with shippers, set freight rates, solicited cargo, and did whatever other tasks were necessary to turn a profit. A clerkship was a highly coveted position because it had none of the physical difficulties associated with other jobs and clerks could parlay their experience and connections into a spot in the mercantile houses of river towns. Henry Dumesnil, for one, used this path to achieve financial success. He served as clerk for ten different steamboats between 1837 and 1844 before landing a job in a store in Milliken's Bend, Louisiana. William Clark also used his clerkship to achieve financial success; besides earning $50 a month on the *Paul Jones*, Clark bought a share of the boat's bar, which was "quite profitable." Young men who aspired to be clerks typically had some type of apprenticeship as second, or "mud," clerk. They learned their craft but paid the price of having to deliver small packages or bags to wharves or plantations in all types of weather. Even these jobs were much sought after. When J. W. Gosen bought the *Autocrat,* he joked at receiving "seventy five thousand applications for the No 2 clerk's berth."[11]

Captains, pilots, and clerks—all of whom who were white, as on all other steamers in the United States—were part of an emerging middle class in the antebellum South. Class is probably best defined by a combination of income and attitude, and for the antebellum South the middle class was somewhere between poor farmers and planters. Professionals, ministers, educators, shopkeepers, and bankers were all men whose occupations were not far removed from captains, pilots, and clerks. But these steamboat workers were never wholly in the urban or rural worlds of the antebellum South. They helped bridge the two worlds, and the services they provided certainly made it easier for the middle class to thrive.[12]

"SUPPLE-LIMBED BLACK BOYS"

One level down, the boiler deck was home to the cabin crew, essentially a hotel staff transferred to a steamboat. Stewards, who had the most authority on this level, performed a variety of tasks. They purchased food for the boat from a networks of grocers, farmers, and planters. Stewards supervised the preparation and presentation of meals, made sure the cabin was clean, and sometimes planned activities for the passengers. Stewards were also responsible for waking the passengers, although they often delegated this obnoxious job to a cabin boy. On the early steamboats with no staterooms, stewards pulled back the curtain as a type of welcome to the breakfast table. If a steamboat had staterooms, a worker walked through the saloon ringing a bell and creating a "querulous and deafening clamor." Drowsy passengers stumbled out of bed, unable to stand the tumult. Stewards needed a variety of skills to be successful, including a sense of diplomacy. They were among the most visible of steamboat workers because they conveyed the captain's orders, enforced the rules of the boat, attended to the desires of the cabin passengers, and mollified angry or finicky customers.[13]

Most often native-born white men were stewards, although a few German immigrants, hired slaves, and free blacks served in that capacity. What was difficult for a white steward was sometimes impossible for a black one. While many white southerners might simply be annoyed at the authority of white stewards, they resented the power of African American stewards. That an African American person, whether slave or free, might be able to command a white man was contrary to the South's racial etiquette. An African American with power was something that most whites would not tolerate. One black steward learned this lesson when he admonished a passenger for violating the rules of cabin passage. Let the captain give orders, the man growled at the steward, "I'm not going to obey a *nigger* like you."[14]

Although stewards were a measure of a boat's quality, cooks were just as important to an overall evaluation of cabin passage. Superior boats were known to have good food, so talented cooks commanded higher wages than deckhands, roustabouts, firemen, waiters, chambermaids, and cabin boys. Each day they prepared three meals for passengers and crew, a job that began at three in the morning. The number of cooks depended on the size of the boat, with the largest vessels employing four cooks and a pastry chef and small steamers relying on one or two cooks. Cooking multiple meals for hundreds of people was no easy task, as one passenger on the *Indiana* learned in 1851. Celia Ricker was amazed at the huge stove (which consumed a cord of wood each day), the large pans of rolls, and the "nearly half a cow" roasting on the stove. The open flames, which were almost always burning, might have provided much-desired warmth in the winter but were oppressively hot in the summer. A cook's job was not done once he had finished the meal, since he had to scrub and store pots and pans. An eighteen-hour work day in a cramped kitchen was a cook's common lot. Most of them were white, although some were African Americans and the first known black to work on a steamer was Jacob, the black cook of the *George Washington* in 1816.[15]

Once cooks finished preparing a meal, the waiters brought it to the saloon. Most waiters were white immigrants or enslaved men. During meals they served food and drink to the guests, an exhausting chore that required them to constantly walk up and down the stairs to the kitchen. They set up the dining tables, complete with table cloths and place settings. This job was neither as easy nor as quick as it might sound. An English traveler watched two "supple-limbed black boys" bring out a twenty-foot-long folding table and set it for dinner, put chairs in their places, and set up the cutlery, dishes, glasses, and napkins. The chore took an hour. The waiters then served the guests and, when the meal was over, bussed the dishes and removed the table and chairs. By the time the two waiters had completed a few other tasks, it was time to bring out the table again. Their lot was typical. In between meals, waiters tended to the stoves that heated the cabin, brought out mattresses when the staterooms were overbooked, and cleaned the saloon (a task that might include scrubbing the floor). The continual work took its toll on the "sleepy waiters" and "heavy-lidded" slaves, who caught sleep in small bursts.[16]

Larger steamboats had porters and cabin watchmen. Porters carried the luggage of the cabin passengers to the boiler deck and checked it into the luggage room. They also tended to the personal freight of cabin passengers and helped unload baggage. Watchmen walked through the saloon, the ladies' cabin, and the guards during the night. They were on the alert for fires and other hazards. Porters and watchmen usually helped the waiters with their tasks, and so there was not always a clear separation of duties for the cabin crew.[17]

Cabin boys could be found on most steamboats and were employed doing all sorts of disagreeable tasks. Most were youths who hoped to become clerks, mates, or even pilots, and some had run away from home, perhaps lured by the romance of the river. John Anderson, for instance, fled when he was ten and stowed away on a steamer bound for New Orleans. He worked as the third cook and cabin boy and stayed on board a year before going to live with his brother. Such young boys were vulnerable to a myriad of calamities, but also learned to live by their wits.[18]

Chambermaids were usually the only women employed on steamboats. There might be one chambermaid on smaller boats and a handful on larger craft. They attended to the needs of the female passengers, but their most valuable duties were washing and cleaning. Chambermaids washed the linens from the dining tables and the bedding and towels from the staterooms. Sometimes they even cleaned the laundry of passengers and crew. It was physical, ceaseless, and thankless labor. One female passenger observed how the chambermaid "had a great deal to do" but also chastised her for being lazy. This privileged woman scarcely had an appreciation for the work that was involved. Chambermaids hauled water to the boiler deck and heated it before scrubbing the laundry. They then hung sheets, towels, tablecloths, and napkins out to dry in the ladies' cabin or on the verandah. Once the laundry was dry, the chambermaids ironed it. The small, heavy irons had to be continually reheated on a stove, rendering a tiresome chore even more difficult. Eliza Steele, traveling on the *Monsoon,* complained that the enslaved chambermaid was making the ladies' cabin too hot with her ironing. The chambermaid was probably even more uncomfortable, something unfathomable to Steele.[19]

Since the members of the cabin crew were visible representatives of the steamboat, they were expected to present a pleasing appearance. Stewards and waiters wore clean white shirts and sometimes white coats. Chambermaids wore long cotton dresses, aprons, and headbands or ribbons in their hair. Men and women had to keep reasonably clean and comb their hair. That most were of African descent only reinforced white assumptions that God created blacks to serve them. The cabin crew also had to develop an attitude of service and attention to detail. Many withered under the impossible demands of multiple passengers, but others developed important negotiation skills. Enslaved waiters, for instance, learned how to navigate their way through white society—a useful skill that might be employed in escape attempts. They eavesdropped on dinner conversations, learning how to behave as white passengers did. Waiters especially could imbibe stories, names, and information that could be put to good use during a run to freedom. In a very real sense, steamboat saloons functioned as etiquette schools for perceptive slaves who desired to earn more than just money.[20]

Stewards, waiters, porters, and chambermaids were constantly on call. Their labors seemed endless and, like the deck crew, they snatched fitful sleep at irregular intervals. The cabin crew normally slept on the floor of the saloon, ate leftover food, and had almost no opportunity for privacy. They were, moreover, subject to the whims of cabin passengers and could become convenient targets for bored or irritable travelers, who vented their frustrations on whichever cabin crew member was close at hand. When one enslaved steamboat porter inadvertently bumped a cabin passenger with a bag, the man turned around and thrashed him.[21]

Chambermaids faced a worse form of assault—sexual attacks. They frequently worked in isolation, so were not be able to fight off an attack or even signal for help. An empty stateroom, the officers' quarters, or a hidden nook in the laundry area were locales that provided enough privacy for a sexual assault. And while both white and black chambermaids faced this indignity, enslaved women were more vulnerable. Slaves were not allowed to testify against a white in court, and so lecherous passengers or crew members could strike with little or no fear of legal consequences. The song of enslaved firemen, complete with its sexual imagery, alluded to the vulnerability of chambermaids:

> I heard the captain say,
> Shove her up my lively lads and get her in the way.
> Shove her up, get her steaming hot,
> I will pay you fifty-dollars to pass the *Alex Scott.*
>
> (Chorus)
> But everybody knows, and everybody says,
> They know his tricks, they know his ways,
> From time to time and never late,
> They'll find him with the chambermaid.[22]

Although bartenders and barbers were not part of the cabin crew, they worked on the boiler deck, where they rented space for about $50 per month. The bar was a small room shoehorned somewhere near the saloon that merely housed and sold the liquor. A bartender's business was usually brisk, as only Quaker-owned boats refused to sell alcohol. Henry Humbright testified that he made a profit of $100 per month on the *Caddo* and would have made more had not an outbreak of cholera cut into his sales. A different bartender, who rented space on a New Orleans to Louisville boat, cleared $400 on one trip. "The amount of drinking on western steamboats is enormous," one traveler wrote. "Passengers are driven into the habit by mere listlessness."[23]

Only the largest boats had barbers, virtually all of whom were black, as was customary in the South. More often than not they were freemen, like the barber of the *Anglo Saxon* who purchased himself for $600. While men like this barber could work in a city, renting space on a riverboat had a number of advantages. Steamboat barbers had a monopoly, a consistent clientele, they might save money by convincing a sympathetic cook or steward to allow them to eat scraps, and they traveled the rivers for free. In fact, according to James Thomas, free black barbers like himself disliked working in land-based shops because they enjoyed the advantages found in being on the river.[24]

"I AM A LABORING MAN"

Most of a steamboat's workers toiled on the main deck, and the only skilled workers on this level inhabited the engine room. The engineer was responsible for keeping the machinery in good working order, maintaining power to the engines, and translating the pilot's orders into action concerning speed and movement. It was a difficult job that often drove engineers into a blasphemous rage. A system of bells connected the engine room to the pilothouse, and the rapid succession of signals to stop, back up, or move ahead slowly could be maddening. Broken shafts, cracked pipes, and mangled paddle wheels created emergencies that demanded attention. An engineer needed to be a jack-of-all-trades in order to fix the multitude of problems that bedeviled steamboats. He drew good wages (he might earn as much as the captain), but the hot, stuffy, greasy, and noisy conditions often magnified an engineer's frustrations. His job was a thankless one and he typically received blame for what went wrong—a boiler explosion—rather than recognition for a job well done. Engineers were easy targets for ridicule, as illustrated by John Robb's satires. Robb created the amusingly named Tom Bangall, an engineer who believed that "a steamboat wouldn't work without some swearing" and feared heaven because he would encounter all the people he had killed in boiler explosions.[25]

Few engineers had formal training, but most had a mechanical aptitude or interest. They learned their craft through trial and error on the steamboat's engine. Larger boats had apprentices, or strikers, who handled routine maintenance, such as oiling and cleaning the machinery. Strikers gradually learned to adjust and repair the machinery before supervising their own boat. The lack of formal training or a certification process is unthinkable today, but was a matter of course in nineteenth-century America. The absence of academic training meant that many engineers had a minimal understanding of the physical forces that caused boiler explosions, so they took unnecessary risks. Various steamboat inspection acts made river travel safer, but could not compensate for slipshod work practices and sheer ignorance.

Firemen, who had the most physically demanding job on a steamboat, worked for the engineer. The majority of firemen on boats below Louisville were rented slaves, although Irish immigrants and other poor white laborers also worked in the immense heat of the boiler room. Fredrika Bremer was captivated when she glimpsed firemen for the first time. The large steamer on which she rode had eight open furnaces and beside each one "stood a negro naked to his middle, who flung in firewood. Pieces of wood were passed onward to these feeders by other negroes, who stood up aloft on a large open place between them and a negro, who, standing on a loft stack of firewood, threw down with vigorous arms food for the monsters on deck." The slave on the woodpile sang out a stanza and the other firemen echoed a chorus, all in perfect time to their movements. The whole scene "was so accordant and well arranged, that it would have produced a fine effect upon any theater anywhere." Firemen also stoked the fires with long rods. The intense heat and constant motion was so arduous that they worked in four-hour shifts and usually refused to work for more than two successive voyages. Not only did firemen throw wood into furnaces, they helped load it on steamers. A recent German immigrant recalled that his stint as a fireman, besides being the hardest work he had ever done, was dangerous. Darkness, slippery riverbanks, and a tottering gangplank made a plunge into murky waters a common occurrence.[26]

Mates were the other supervisors on the main deck. They needed no special navigation or engineering skills but typically directed the deckhands and roustabouts. Most seem to have been members of the deck crew before being entrusted with a supervisory role. As the person primarily responsible for converting the captain's wishes into work for the deck crew, mates could be, as a longtime riverman remembered, "about the meanest set of people on earth." They needed a distinct physical presence and routinely used beatings to enforce discipline, to increase the pace of work, or to punish someone for sloppy work habits. Newspaper stories abounded with mates thrashing deckhands with clubs, hammers, knives, heavy hickory canes, or whatever object was handy. Mates were also legendary for their extensive and imaginative use of profane language.[27]

The deck was also the home of roustabouts and deckhands, unskilled laborers who often moved from boat to boat. Roustabouts, strong men who hauled freight on and off steamers, were the most visible workers on this level. The first roustabouts were white and had worked on flatboats or keelboats, but by 1860 most roustabouts on steamboats that traveled below Louisville were free blacks or slaves, while Irish immigrants dominated on the upper Ohio, Mississippi, and Missouri rivers. One English traveler going north from Mobile even saw Creek Indians working as roustabouts on his steamboat.[28]

A steamboat's arrival was the cue for roustabouts to stir from their studied nonchalance, stretch, and prepare themselves for the heavy work to follow. The placid scene quickly became a melee as "mates screamed and cursed as only Mississippi boatmen can" in urging roustabouts into a flurry of activity. The swarm of "black ants" lifted heavy bags of cotton seed onto the backs of fellow workers, carried boxes, and rolled hogsheads of sugar. Each roustabout wielded a cotton hook—"the unmistakable badge of his profession"—and worked with a partner to wrestle the four hundred-pound bales onto the steamer. The fleecy stuff tended to stick to the workers' clothes and hair, so that by end of the day they looked like they had rolled in gauze (an appearance that gave rise to the expression "cotton to," or be attracted to). Roustabouts also coaxed mules, horses, oxen, cows, sheep, turkey, geese, and ducks on and off boats. Particularly stubborn hogs had to be slung over one shoulder, and immovable animals provided "infinite fun" for bored passengers and observers who watched the proceedings. Roustabouts were even known to spur cattle forward by twisting or biting their tails. One amused observer noted that "it took an army of darkies a couple of hours to persuade" a drove of hogs to scuttle aboard a steamer. "It was pig *vs.* nig, and such a grotesque struggle I have never seen." Roustabouts clattered across the five-foot-wide gangplank, no mean feat in bad weather or when mud clung to shoes and boots and made the passageway dangerously slippery.[29]

Stopping at a farm or plantation magnified the difficulty of a roustabout's job. Once the captain lightly grounded the steamer in the mud, a roustabout splashed out and tied a line to a tree or pole. Narrow, winding, and soft paths made feet slip or sink into the soft earth. "Imagine a gang of forty or fifty men," a fascinated observer wrote, "engaged in landing boxes, casks, sacks of corn and salt, wagons, livestock, ploughs; hurrying, crowding, working in each other's way, sometimes slipping and falling, the last barrel tumbling down upon those below; and the mate driving them with shouts and curses and kicks as if they were so many brutes." He thought the work was dirtier and more demanding than any he had seen. Emergencies required even more exertion, such as the time when the *Robert J. Ward* got stuck on a sandbar, and the roustabouts "worked unceasingly at the windlass" through the night.[30]

The rough appearance of roustabouts matched the difficulty of their lives. The "variety of rags" that clad them were usually dirty, old, torn, and often second-hand. Some wore flannel shirts and coarse trousers, others had coats and vests but no shirts. Nails and edges tore up pants, while sacks and crates rubbed holes in shirts and jackets. "The roustabouts looked all of one hue, from their shoes to the tops of their heads," wrote a visitor the South. "Their coffee-colored necks and faces match their reddish-brown clothes, that had been grimed with the dust of everything known to man—which dust also covered their shoes and bare feet, and made both appear the same." The elements took their toll on the clothing and constitution of roustabouts, who worked outside in all kinds of weather.[31]

Deckhands, who were usually white, took cargo from the roustabouts and stowed it on the deck or in the hold. Like roustabouts, they were under the direct supervision of a mate. Most had experience on keelboats or flatboats, but their occupation became less desirable as time wore on, and it became more difficult to find native-born whites to serve as deckhands. In the last two decades before the Civil War, German and Irish immigrants took these low-paying and demanding jobs. Not surprisingly, most deckhands were young men and there was a high degree of turnover because of the exhausting work. Matilda Houstoun observed the "extremely severe" labor of the deckhands in bad weather during her trip to New Orleans. They were so worn out from packing freight and working the steamer off sandbars that several cabin passengers complained about the "cruel and tyrannical manner in which the Irish and Germans on board were treated." The captain ignored their intercession. Deckhands commonly switched to other boats or worked a variety of jobs, depending on their supervisors, the seasonal nature of work, or the pay. As one young Irish immigrant remarked, "I am a laboring man. Sometimes I work on the Levee, sometimes in the cotton yard, sometimes steamboating."[32]

A deckhand's work was "the hardest in the world," according to one laborer. Deckhands formed bucket brigade lines to pass freight to one another, moving so quickly and rhythmically it looked as if the cargo "burned their fingers." Steamboats that stopped at more than one location had to have a reliable means to retrieve all cargo bound for that farm or city, so deckhands balanced the dispersal of freight against its organization. Too much cargo on one side of the boat could force a noticeable list or produce difficulty in maneuvering. All cargo that was destined for one location had to be readily identifiable and easily retrieved at once. Deckhands also stacked the cotton sometimes as many as twelve tiers high, a particularly backbreaking task before the advent of steam-powered lifts in the 1840s. Like roustabouts, they were on call at all hours of the day and caught short naps while the boat was in motion. Other chores for deckhands included cleaning the deck, pumping water out of the hold, measuring the depth of the river for the pilot, taking turns as night watchmen, and cleaning animal waste off of the deck. This last task was especially disagreeable, and became so odious that deckhands complained about the "hogwash" that offended their nostrils. Although hogwash first described an obnoxious chore, it came to mean something ridiculous.[33]

"A YOUNG MAN'S JOB"

Roustabouts and deckhands faced perils that were seen and unseen. The "crushing work" led to health problems like hernias, strained or torn muscles, misaligned joints, and broken bones. Animals that refused to move could suddenly kick or bite. When oxen trampled one worker, "it was miraculous he was not killed," wrote an alarmed passenger. Mates regularly kicked and hit workers, sometimes knocking them overboard. Lack of meaningful rest was another danger for the deck crew. They rarely had extended or deep sleep, making them more susceptible to disease and more likely to have an accident. In warm weather the deck crew slept on the guards, and when it was cold they curled up near the boilers, an area they sarcastically called the St. Charles, after the sumptuous St. Charles Hotel in New Orleans. They flopped down on cotton bales or laid up on boxes in hopes of catching some fitful sleep before "the perpetually ringing bells" summoned them back to work. Undisturbed rest was an elusive dream for the workers, who sometimes moved slowly in order to preserve their strength. Some observers misinterpreted the lackadaisical pace for laziness. When it came time to roll three hundred barrels of lard aboard a steamer, one passenger judged the movements of the "lazy Blacks" to be "perfectly aristocratic and by no means hurried."[34]

Work could literally kill members of the deck crew. There were no safety measures to speak of on steamboats—no guard rails, policies for working in inclement conditions, or safeguards around moving parts. Proximity to the engines exposed firemen especially, but also roustabouts and deckhands, to death or disability from a boiler explosion. Gabriel, a slave rented out on the *Louisiana,* suffered an agonizing death when the steamer exploded and hot ashes scalded his lungs. Workers, though, often met their death in more prosaic ways. One enslaved roustabout drowned while transferring corn from one steamboat to another in rainy and windy conditions when he slipped and fell into the Mississippi River. Likewise, a deckhand on the *Bravo* drowned when the boat's windlass knocked him overboard. The number of close calls exceeded the deaths, and one deckhand wondered that he survived when a piece of iron fell on his head and nearly knocked him into the water. It is no coincidence that the life insurance for slaves who worked on riverboats was the most expensive in the antebellum South.[35]

Although steamboat labor could be cruelly harsh, it could also be a source of masculine pride for individual workers. Competition to see who could work harder, faster, or accomplish a specific task enlivened drudgery and led to impromptu contests of strength and skill. It also fueled a sense of camaraderie, or produced a "good deal of rivalry and fun," as a passenger on the *Eclipse* put it. Crew members sometimes had to cut wood for steamers, and such occasions quickly turned into competitions. As passengers cheered, workers attacked trees with axes and made "chips fly like hail." Axmen then positioned themselves four feet apart along the downed tree and attempted to be the first to cut through the log. "The contest was enlivened by drams administered at intervals and bets by passengers on their favorite chopper," remembered one passenger. Thomas Bangs Thorpe witnessed about sixty steamboat slaves during a wood stop. Passengers lined the guards to watch the "exciting physical contest" as firemen and roustabouts vied with each other to carry the most wood. While the mate urged on the men with swearing of "monstrous proportions" that either rendered him "really profane or simply ridiculous," the slaves worked with precision to bring the wood aboard. "Zephyer Sam" won the prize that day of "model darkie." The racial condescension of Thorpe is palpable, but his essential point is correct—steamboats workers strove to prove their worth through physical prowess in a way that validated their sense of identity.[36]

A masculine identity also emerged at meal time and during breaks between work. Crew members criticized their bosses, swapped stories, told jokes, sang songs, and amused one another with tales as they sat around on freight and boxes. Frederick Law Olmsted thought that such banter was "good-natured and jocose." Coarse language typically punctuated such wordplay. All hands, "even down to the little boys," one observer noted disapprovingly, "utter an oath almost every other word." Alcohol was also universal. It was not uncommon for crews to scoop whiskey out of pails or swig down a cup of grog. Many crews received liquor during their shifts rather than their off hours, probably to make the working conditions slightly more palatable. Even hired slaves were "merry with liquor," but the small portions prevented widespread drunkenness. Slaves on steamers knew that if they became intoxicated they could be sent back to their masters and be forced to endure severe punishment. Gambling was also endemic for steamboat workers, with craps being the favored game, although card games were also common. Henry Dumesnil left Louisville at age seventeen to be a clerk on a steamboat and used his skill at cards not only to earn more than his share of coffee, pecans, and cash but also to fit in with the crew.[37]

The raw masculine identity found on a steamer's main deck was connected to a lack of privacy and an emphasis on individual liberty. "It is a young man's job, full of violence and change, of coming and going," an observer recorded. Crew members had a bare bunk, supplied their own bedding, and carried few valuables since anything of worth could be easily stolen. Having no private space reduced a crew member's sense of identity with a particular vessel and contributed to his tendency to flit from boat to boat in search of higher wages or better conditions. George Forman, for instance, worked as a deckhand on three different steamers in less than a year. At the end of each stint, he collected his wages and walked away. This chronic rootlessness left even the better run steamers chronically short-handed and prompted Captain Thomas Leathers to have his brother scour Kentucky in order to find workers for the

Natchez. John Leathers promised to "hire you some good hands . . . and send them down for your boats for the season."[38]

Crews also gained a reputation for hooliganism in the various port cities, particularly in the dockside taverns. That deckhands and roustabouts could become incapacitated or die in the regular course of their work probably increased a sense of living for the pleasures of the moment. Sprees of crapulous revelry, though, could spiral out of control. A steamboat worker from the *Star of the West,* for instance, went ashore in Cairo, Illinois, for what would be his last time. The details remain uncertain, but after a confrontation in an infamously seedy tavern, someone shot the man in the temple and left him bleeding in the street. His boat mates returned to town the next day and forced the justice of the peace to arrest a suspect. Indeed, large groups of steamboat workers could be particularly unruly and present a threat to public order and scare local citizens. The problem seemed to be particularly acute in Natchez at the notorious Under-the-Hill, a lawless section of town near the water's edge. In New Orleans there were so many drunken and rowdy boatmen that local police made sport of beating them.[39]

"KILL THE D——D NIGGER"

The masculine identity was not a building block for a sense of working-class consciousness within steamboat workers. There were, for instance, no unions for roustabouts or deckhands. Not only were riverboat laborers rootless, they were fractured along skill and racial lines. The cabin crew believed themselves to be superior to the deckhands and did not mix with them. Waiters, the *St. Louis Globe-Democrat* reported, looked down upon roustabouts and deckhands "with sovereign contempt." Even within riverboat skill levels, racial identity kept crew members from mixing together unless the specific job demanded it. That white crew members had limited contact with black crew members was evident in something as simple as meals. A steward's "Grub pile!" shout was the cue for the crew to swarm around tubs and kettles for leftovers from the cabin. In deference to the South's racial caste system, white crew members went first and then African Americans picked through the rest of the food. Both groups piled food on shingles and fanned out across the deck to eat, whites on one side of the boat and blacks on the other in self-imposed segregation. Frederick Law Olmsted saw about ten black roustabouts, "excessively dirty and beast-like in their appearance and manners," eating leftovers as they sat on cotton bales. They passed around one knife, used splinters of bone or firewood as forks, drank from a common tub, and tossed their scraps and garbage in the river. Such intimate interactions—that is, the mingling of spit and sweat—did not occur across racial lines.[40]

Although there were instances of racial comity, the bulk of the surviving evidence points to a pattern of racial intolerance and harassment. Violence between blacks and whites was common, particularly after the exchange of sharp words. Alex Boss, who worked on the *Rubicon,* remembered how the boat's mate argued with a "sassy Negro deckhand" and clubbed the slave over the head and knocked him in the river. Almost anything could spark a confrontation. When a free black fireman on the *Western* refused to work past his usual shift, the captain attacked him with a club, lumps of coal, and a sledgehammer. After the captain put the fireman ashore without settling wages, the worker threw a rock at the steamboat. His impulsive action prompted the captain to run ashore with two revolvers and threaten to "kill the d——d nigger." The fireman seems to have escaped with his life, but racial violence was so common that it usually failed to elicit disapproval. An African American worker on the *Maid of Orleans* tried to eat with the white hands, but provoked a knife attack instead. The rough nature of the labor and the difficult working conditions were partly to blame for the tensions between whites and blacks. White workers feared and resented the competition of slaves and free blacks, who could be hired for less money. The white rivermen of New Orleans, according to an article in a southern newspaper, harbored "great antipathy" to slaves working on steamers because they held down wages. Even the abolitionist press sensed the racial animosity and used the issue to trumpet the free labor argument.[41]

"HARD WORK BUT A FINE LIVING"

Despite the racial tensions, a significant number of enslaved Americans sought out employment on steamboats in the southern interior because they judged the potential rewards to be greater than the risks. Hired slaves in the antebellum South generally enjoyed more opportunities than those who were not rented out, and working on a riverboat brought unique advantages. Black steamboat employees created a type of working fraternity on the western waters. The songs, gambling, jokes, banter, and meals were more than just expressions of working-class culture, they were an initiation into an ever shifting

48

community of uncommonly autonomous slaves. Besides gaining a set of like-minded colleagues, enslaved Americans on riverboats were able to make decisions that their masters might otherwise make for them. Henry Hawkins was one such person. Hawkins cleaned out steamers in New Orleans, and when he took sick after eating some old bread on the *Dime,* the slave took control of his medical choices. He elected to drink brandy mixed with cayenne pepper in addition to rubbing mustard on his calves and knees. When Hawkins passed away, his owner sued the steamboat owners for $1,500, making the implicit argument that the slave would not have died if the owner had made the medical decisions. Even if Hawkins made the wrong decision, it was *his* decision. The choice of medical care was merely one more arena where the shifting tug-of-war between master and slave was played out. Work on a steamboat increased both potential risks and rewards; as slave roustabout Joe Mayes remembered many years after the Civil War, it was "Hard work but a fine living."[42]

Escape was one of the decisions available to enslaved Americans working on riverboats. When the steamboat carrying William Wells Brown landed at Cincinnati, for instance, Brown picked up a trunk and carried it to the wharf. He blended in with the crowd and walked to freedom. Other escape attempts were more elaborate, as we saw from the chapter's beginning. Slaves who worked on the boiler deck gained crucial skills and, if they were keen observers of human behavior, learned how to blend into white society. People like Dennis, a waiter on the famous *J. M. White,* learned verbal and nonverbal cues that aided them in their quest for freedom. Free black steamboat workers were also such a nuisance, at least to white authorities, that several states in the southern interior passed legislation limiting their movement. Such efforts demonstrate how steamboats altered traditional perceptions of space, time, and law. Riverboats collapsed the distance and lowered the barriers between slavery and freedom. Enslaved Americans who crossed state lines challenged notions of which set of laws should govern their status. Travel in free territory might provide enough justification to warrant a lawsuit for freedom.[43]

Even though a noticeable number of enslaved steamboat workers struck out for freedom, the fact remains that the vast majority did not. There were never enough escapes to warrant undue concern for owners or to undermine the riverboat industry. That slaves ignored countless occasions for escape suggests that motivations other than a single-minded desire for freedom animated their existence. Work on steamboats gave enslaved Americans unparalleled opportunities to search for family members. As black river workers traveled from city to city, and sometimes shifted from boat to boat, they inter-sected with ever more circles of information. A well-timed question could lead to the reunion of families separated by the ravages of slavery. Milton Clarke, who was sold away from his family when he was six, was hired to a steamer in 1836. Clarke regularly visited New Orleans and made persistent inquiries about his sister. After about four visits to the Crescent City, Clarke found out where she lived and introduced himself to his long lost sibling. A slave named Catherine pursued a similar path to find her sister. Catherine began work as a chambermaid on a boat for $30 a month. She doubled her income through tips from passengers and profits from the sale of apples and oranges. As she saved money, Catherine relentlessly searched for her sister, who had been sold to Louisiana's cane country. She eventually paid for her own freedom and that of her sister. Employment on steamboats gave slaves access to a widespread kinship web and enabled them to stitch together tenuous relationships.[44]

Enslaved Americans who worked on steamers had another reason to re-main in chains: they had the ability to earn a fair amount of money. Massa-chusetts native Edward Russell was unfamiliar with riverboat customs during his trip up the Red River. A steward offered to brush Russell's clothes and then "asked 'a bit or so,' for doing it." Russell forked over the money, grum-bling that he would take care "not to get bit again." Everywhere they turned, it seemed that passengers were paying for extra services: thirty cents for tow-els, a dime for a shoeshine, or a half dollar for someone to carry their trunk. Thrifty workers could parlay such tips into a sizable savings. When William J. Anderson started working on a steamboat, his only requirement was to pay his master $25 per month. Anderson kept whatever else he made, and in ten years had saved $500. For those slaves who desired freedom but thought es-cape too daunting, steamboat employment was a slow but less risky alterna-tive. As one owner acknowledged about his slave who worked on a riverboat, "he can make a good deal [of money] for himself." The accumulation of cash not only affirmed and increased slaves' sense of independence, it loosened the bonds of servitude. Money might buy freedom, but could also purchase small freedoms—gifts, clothing, alcohol, or a treasured personal possession.[45]

Slaves working on steamboats were sometimes given remarkable latitude to shift for themselves. They got out from the watchful gaze of their masters and from the confining boundaries of power. Slaveowners created an elabo-rate "geography of containment" with their system of plantations, passes, slave patrols, and spot checks of slave quarters. Mobility was linked to liberty, and white southerners assiduously worked to prevent enslaved Americans from enjoying either concept. Work on riverboats created unprecedented opportunities for slaves to challenge these ideals. Jeff, who worked as a fireman on the *Liah Tuna,* had a pass of the kind that was "usually given to boys who run as deck hands on the river; permitting him to hire himself out on any steamer leaving New Orleans during a certain period of time or up to a certain time." Slaves frequently negotiated their own terms of employment and returned to their masters at irregular intervals. If enslaved Americans lived their lives in terms of local neighborhoods, then employment on riverboats cracked this concept wide open. And the ability to live outside the normal bounds of slavery, even if for a short time, loosened the shackles of the peculiar institution.[46]

There were limits to this mobility, however, and whites in the interior South created another system of containment to prevent slave escapes. Alert masters used the ability of steamers to transmit information quickly to foil numerous escape attempts. Advertisements in the *New Orleans Daily Picayune* consistently cautioned steamboat owners and operators to be on the lookout for fugitive slaves. One owner asked captains to watch for George, a fireman on the *Brilliant* who ran away. "Captains of steamboats are particularly cautioned," warned another advertisement. The steady drumbeat of similar notices provided captains, mates, and crew with ample reasons and cash incentives to be on guard for any suspicious activity. The second mate of the *Statesman* was one such sharp-eyed crew member. He spotted Louis Hughes sneaking out from behind hogsheads of sugar and told the would-be fugitive, "Why, I have a reward for you." The mate brought Hughes to the captain and verified that a $500 reward awaited the successful return of the slave. When an Alabama slave ran away in Mobile, the owner sent word to authorities in the river towns to be on the lookout for the escapee and send him on a steamer to Montgomery if discovered. Word via telegraph lines or in the columns of newspapers on steamboats traveled faster than most would-be runaways.[47]

Had an intolerable number of slaves working on steamboats run away, men like James Rudd would have stopped renting them out. Rudd, a Louisville businessman, hired out his slaves John, George, and Little Charley on at least six different riverboats. He did not have to feed or clothe the men and still collected anywhere from $20 to $40 per month for their labor. Those owners who needed an extra measure of security limited where their slaves could work, particularly by excluding them from going past Louisville or St. Louis. Masters who needed more financial incentive charged an extra dollar a day for boats

that neared free soil. At a time when male slaves hired out to work on plantations earned perhaps $10 to $12.50 per month, the lure of the steamboat for the
owner was clear enough. Hiring slaves to work on riverboats was a high risk,
high reward endeavor.[48]

Work on Old Man River brought benefits to select employees. For ambitious
whites, work as pilots, clerks, or engineers was a means to social and economic improvement through entry into the middle class. The majority of
riverboat workers, though, had dead-end jobs. Shot through with racial and
skill distinctions, these men failed to develop a class consciousness and often
lived their lives for the pleasures of the moment. And while racial tensions on
steamboats in the Southwest were often palpable, enslaved Americans who
worked on riverboats experienced more freedom than their friends and relatives stuck on plantations and farms. Just as riverboat labors had profoundly
varied experiences, so did passengers. As the next chapter shows, cabin passengers enjoyed sumptuous traveling experiences on the best boats while deck
passengers suffered in filthy and smelly conditions.

THREE

FLOATING PALACES AND HIGH-PRESSURE PRISONS

Aperson's first steamboat ride was often a memorable experience, and Tom, whose farm near Natchez yielded about a hundred cotton bales in 1855, was no exception. He feared the deadly power of riverboats and only a friend's urging and the desire to go to New Orleans and see the St. Charles Hotel, hear the children speak French, and see the "beautiful Creole Ladies with black eyes and Cinderella feet" convinced Tom to lay aside his fears. He rode his horse to the bluffs overlooking Natchez's waterfront, took a breath, and dismounted. The wharf was a crowded place during the spring, as ten or more steamboats might land on any given day. Scores of riverboats were lined up, their bows touching the shore and their smokestacks looking like blackened trees scorched by a wildfire. Roustabouts, passengers, and curious onlookers crowded the docks. Tom threaded his way through the throng at the riverfront, made his way toward one of the boats, bought his ticket, and strode across the stage, or permanent gangplank, and onto the main deck.[1]

Tom had boarded the *Natchez,* one of the most famous and recognizable boats on the Mississippi River. Its trademark golden bale of cotton, suspended between the two red smokestacks, glinted in the sunlight while six Native American warriors stood guard from those chimneys, ready to repel boarders. Tom brushed his way past the deck crew and excitedly sprinted up the stairs to the saloon. He had heard fabulous tales about the *Natchez's* main cabin and he was not disappointed at what he saw. Tom marveled at the "sumptuous architecture," the rich furniture, the marble tables, and the gilded Indian princess. After feasting on a "superb supper," he contentedly smoked a cigar. In the next few days he visited the bar, checked on the various cabins, strolled past the clerk's room, poked his head in the pantry, watched the scenery pass by, and flirted with some of the female passengers. His excitement grew as the

Natchez neared New Orleans, and Tom wondered at the towers, turrets, and spires. "It is worth a life time," he wrote, "to enter a great city in this style and behold it unrolling before your eyes like a gorgeous map."

Tom's experiences on the *Natchez* are probably what most modern Americans associate with antebellum steamboats: luxury travel similar to a Caribbean cruise. The *Natchez* was certainly a grandiose riverboat, but the social world of steamboats in the interior South was much more complex. Once riverboats evolved into their multi-layered form, they tried to establish and enforce an elaborate social geography of racial, social, and gender conventions. In democratic America, steamboat owners promoted the idea that cabin passage was a refined experience. Few riverboats lived up to expectations, and when status became a commodity, white travelers could buy their way into first class. Formal rules, however, still governed the interactions of men and women, as domestic values became integrated into the gritty world of steamboat travel. An African American, moreover, entered the saloon only as steamboat employee or the slave of a passenger. Like much of antebellum society, refinement and privilege on steamboats were unsteady and unpredictable.

"DOMESTIC ATLASES"

On southern steamers, passengers traveled on the main deck or in the cabin. Deck passage—a "very undesirable way of traveling," according to one traveler —attracted the majority of customers because it was one-fourth the cost of cabin passage. By the 1850s, a deck passenger could travel from New Orleans to Louisville for $3 (about $70 in modern currency). Particularly cost-conscious passengers decreased this price even more by agreeing to haul wood aboard. Many, however, shirked their duty. When the clerk walked through the main deck shouting, "wood-pile, wood-pile, where are the wooders?," deck passengers feigned illness, hid in the baggage, or skulked in the woods on shore. Those who did work could not keep up with the firemen (who carried a dozen cordwood sticks on their shoulder) and suffered the sharp stares and pungent words of the clerk. Deckers normally carried logs in empty salt sacks and stripped to the waist in hot weather during wooding, which took anywhere from thirty minutes to several hours. Rainy conditions lengthened the process and increased the misery when drenched clothes stuck to bodies and deckers slipped in the mud and tumbled down embankments. Cabin passengers watched in amusement at the whole process or sometimes "frolicked and jumped in the woods." The gulf between deck and cabin passage was probably most apparent during the wooding process.[2]

A significant portion of deck passengers were migrants, either foreigners arriving in the United States for the first time or American citizens moving west. The Irish and Germans were most noticeable, and captains offered discounted fares for large groups, which sometimes reached four or five hundred. Some of these throngs moved en masse from their embarkation in New Orleans to an upriver steamboat, while others made their way across Virginia to Wheeling and took passage down the Ohio River. Their tendency to cluster together fed into negative stereotypes and sparked resentment. A Pennsylvanian who shipped from St. Louis to Natchez learned these lessons firsthand. Henry Miller took passage on the *Alton* as a deck passenger. His trip would have been pleasant, he thought, had the boat not been so crowded. There were too many Germans and Irishmen, the "the lowest kind" of person, he wrote. All the Germans had pipes, he judged, and delighted themselves in rolling the smoke out of their mouths. At least they were quiet. The Irish were all "noise & agitation, tumult & disorder." Miller blamed it on their whiskey, "which they will always have as long as it lasts, which, however, is not very long."[3]

American migrants also gravitated toward deck passage. Some went overland across Virginia to a town on the Ohio River, such as Wheeling, Huntington, or Guyandotte, while others traveled across Kentucky or Tennessee until they reached one of the tributaries that fed into the Mississippi. From there, they loaded slaves and supplies on flatboats and steamboats. One planter bound for Mississippi set off from the Cumberland River on a steamer that carried his sixty slaves and a year's worth of provisions. I. A. Conn followed a similar plan when he decided to move from Kentucky to Lake Providence, Louisiana. Conn bought eight hundred acres of land along the Mississippi River and wrote his uncle William to bring thirty "good hands," mules, and other useful material. The younger Conn argued against a land journey, which was "a great undertaking" when compared to the three-day steamboat trip. Conn's only concern was coaxing the slaves to move to Louisiana, so he advised his uncle to give them plenty of whiskey on the trip and watch them carefully when the steamer stopped for wood.[4]

Whether or not they owned slaves, "domestic Atlases" like the Conns carried "their own little world on their shoulders." Migrants packed "household stuff, kettles, dogs, implements of husbandry, and all the paraphernalia of the backwood's farm" into wagons and also moved any horses, mules, and cattle they might have available. They could ride steamers to just about any of the scattered regions west of the Appalachians: Louisiana, Arkansas, Texas, Missouri, Kansas, Iowa, and beyond. In 1832, the steamers *Volant* and *Reindeer* brought nearly four hundred migrants to Crawford and Washington counties in Arkansas. Migrants provided a steady income for steamboat owners but also left their cash in river towns. St. Louis seems to have been especially favored. Even by 1827 the *Missouri Gazette* reported that once migrants stepped off the steamboats, they bought wagons, mules, food, and clothing. "Business brisk," was its curt judgment.[5]

Slave traders—men who specialized in buying slaves, transporting them to labor-hungry regions, and selling them for a profit—found steamers to be especially useful. River cities like Louisville, Memphis, St. Louis, Vicksburg, Natchez, and New Orleans became important hubs for their business. Traders established offices in all these cities, either scouring the local area for slaves to buy or establishing slave pens that incarcerated enslaved Americans until their purchase. Calvin M. Rutherford, a slave dealer based in New Orleans, used steamers to communicate within his burgeoning commercial empire. He dispatched letters on steamers to his various agents, instructing them about buying slaves and arranging for financial backing. Rutherford then waited in New Orleans for the arrival of the new purchases, who might be shipped down the river for only $3. On at least one occasion he used a steamboat to retrieve a slave from an unsatisfied buyer. Steamers, in short, were a quick and efficient way to coordinate the commerce in human beings.[6]

Traders so commonly shipped slaves on riverboats "that no one, not even the passengers, appear to notice it, though they [the slaves] clank their chains at every step." It is not true that no one noticed the presence of coffles on steamboats, but southerners especially became inured to the sights and sounds of suffering slaves. Enslaved Americans became just another form of freight, as Daniel Chapman Banks revealed. When Banks traveled from Louisville to New Orleans on the *Manhattan* in 1822, he kept a diary in which he laconically listed thirteen slaves alongside the tobacco, lard, flour, whiskey, pork, hoops, and sheep. Some steamers even had special modifications to accommodate the interstate slave trade. The *Uncle Sam* had two parallel chains that ran the length of the main deck and were bolted down. Like tentacles, twenty-five short handcuffs extended from each chain.[7]

Such journeys were often hellish ordeals for the slaves. They languished in the freight room or on the guards. Conditions in the deck room were filthy, according to William Wells Brown. Property of a slave trader, Brown remembered that it was "almost impossible to keep that part of the boat clean." Since potential escapes were as close as diving over the boat's edge, traders normally kept the enslaved Americans in chains day and night. One horrified English passenger was appalled at the "wretched and disgusting" treatment of a coffle of slaves on his steamer. The presence of chains meant slaves remained in their own filth and excrement because they could not perform "the ordinary functions of cleanliness." The physical conditions were appalling, but the psychological toll may have been even worse. As the slaves were forced aboard the steamer, they fully realized that they would probably never see their families and homes ever again. Some desperate bondservants tried to flee or, worse, kill themselves. Brown, who later used a steamboat to run away, recalled how one agonized woman, when separated from her husband and children, jumped overboard and drowned herself. Other slaves tried to distract themselves from their present circumstances, at least if Abraham Lincoln is to be believed. Lincoln boarded the *Lebanon* in 1841 for a trip to St. Louis and saw a dozen slaves chained together "like so many fish upon a trot-line." The enslaved Americans, who played the fiddle, danced, sang, told jokes, and played card games, were "cheerful and apparently happy." The genuine affection that the slaves had for one another was a means of commiseration as they came to terms with their harrowing new circumstances.[8]

"A SCENE OF FILTH AND WRETCHEDNESS"

Deckers, whenever possible, staked their claim to a small part of the freight room on the steamboat's main level. More often than not, they grumbled at not being able to find enough floor space to stretch out. Experienced passengers (boatmen in particular) hung hammocks in a crazy-quilt pattern. Besides cargo and domesticated animals, this dark, cheerless room normally had a few dim lanterns, several lice-ridden bunks bolted to one wall, and a long sheet iron stove. Tobacco juice stains and animal excrement were ground into the "smeary dirty deck." Most occupants thought the room looked more like a stable than anything else. Deckers prepared their own meals since food was not included with their passage, and those with some measure of foresight or the wisdom to listen to good advice brought bacon, bread, crackers, boiled ham, or cake with them. Animal waste, human body odor, food, and freight mingled together and created a "peculiar odor" that caused the room to smell like a combination of a stable, a poorly ventilated locker room, and a kitchen.[9]

Nor was the "high-pressure prison" a place suited to quiet reflection. The tromping of heels and scraping of chairs from the saloon's floor reverberated throughout the freight room. The engine's roar and the boat's constant movement caused horses, cows, and mules to protest. Constant neighing, mooing, oinking, and clucking served as background noise to the deckers. Boatmen swapped "wondrous tales and horrible Indian stories," bragged about their accomplishments, told bawdy jokes, laughed uproariously, passed a bottle or jug, and seemed to be constantly gambling. Some deckers sawed on a fiddle for most of the day, plucked a Jew's harp, sharpened their knives, or spat tobacco juice on the stove just to hear it hiss. The "rumpus" from the deck could be so loud that it drowned out the noise of the engine and disturbed the cabin passengers, forcing the captain to dispatch a clerk to quiet the crowd.[10]

Captains contributed to the "comfortless and cheerless" conditions of deck passage when they oversold space. They made extra money without compromising the sources of their most important revenue: freight and cabin passengers. It was normal to see several hundred deck passengers crammed on a boat; the three hundred deck passengers on the *Indiana* "had not room scarcely to sit down." The tight conditions forced many deckers outside the freight room. They "had their choice of freight for beds" and could be seen using hogsheads, barrels, cases, cotton bales, boxes, rolls of leather, and cotton bale-rope for shelter or comfort. These outside deckers faced their own share of problems: weather that was too hot, too cold, or too wet; pesky bugs that attacked them; and roustabouts or deckhands who forced them to give up a comfortable place on a cotton bale or elsewhere.[11]

Deckers most likely used the small toilet facilities that were available for the crew, and it takes little imagination to believe that such accommodations were disgusting. One traveler discovered that the toilet room contained only a barrel of water and a chunk of yellow soap chained to a tin basin. A report from the secretary of the Treasury concluded that the main deck "generally presents a scene of filth and wretchedness that baffles all description." Poor sanitation and minimal opportunities for hygiene created unhealthful situations. One traveler in deck passage noted the epidemic of something he called "Running off from the Bowels," an unpleasant affliction that was also known as "River Sickness." Cholera raged through deck passage in waves, claiming the lives of untold numbers of passengers. Whereas deaths in deck passage were commonplace, they were unusual in the cabins.[12]

Other dangers lurked in deck passage. Crime was prevalent and ranged from robbery to shirkers who managed to avoid paying for their passage. When one captain confronted three deckers who owed money, they jumped him. One man punched the captain and tried to gouge out his eye. When the captain retaliated by choking the man and shaking him until "he was black in the face," one of the freeloaders stabbed the captain in the arm while the other almost bit off a finger. The fight ended when the first mate beat the deckers to a pulp and threw them on shore. A lack of privacy tempted thieves, as Edward Jarvis learned. He was in deck passage when a would-be robber cut the pockets of a sleeping flatboat owner. Another man stopped the theft, but two other men tried to steal a coat. The captain threw all the miscreants off the boat. Fights were common, and a plantation overseer watched with amusement as two deck passengers on a passing steamer threw their coats aside and wrestled one another. An unexpected plunge into the river cooled both their tempers.[13]

Death might come suddenly to deckers. The *John L. Avery* was steaming up the Mississippi River in 1854 when it snagged and sank forty miles south of Natchez. The resulting scramble to get off the boat magnified the tragedy because deckhands had stacked hogsheads of sugar so tightly that an impenetrable barrier hemmed in the deckers. Eighty or ninety Irish immigrants drowned. On a different occasion a passenger who agreed to load wood slipped overboard and was sucked under the paddle wheel, never to be seen again. Such occurrences were not unusual. There were virtually no precautions for safety—guard rails and warning signs were unknown—so people traveled at their own risk. On one boat, at least, it was a "standing joke" at the breakfast table in the main cabin to ask the captain "how many of his [deck] passengers had been missed since the night before."[14]

The gendered expectations of the antebellum South failed to take hold on the rough planks of the main deck. Women might find some partial privacy in the back of the cargo room behind crates or barrels, but had no guarantee that they would remain hidden. Sleeping for extended periods or being separate from friends or family invited trouble. Nor were women on the deck shielded from the vulgar customs of deckhands or roustabouts. When a deckhand on the *Martha No. 2* insulted a female immigrant from Germany, her husband and two sons retaliated. The captain banished three crew members from the boat, but ten of their friends attacked the Germans with hammers and wrenches from the engine room. The deckers fought back with knives. When crew members finally broke up the fight, three deckhands were grievously injured, the husband had broken ribs, and one son had suffered a fractured skull. Preserving the virtue of a female decker could exact a heavy price.[15]

The main deck of a steamboat failed to integrate the domestic values that were found in the saloon. Despite the presence of women and children, deck passage was a masculine world. Violence was commonplace and deckers sometimes directed their aggression at captains and crews, since there was no effective means to voice their grievances. On "several" occasions, according to a report in the *New Orleans Daily Delta,* deck passengers took control of large boats. Apparently fed up with their meager conditions, on one occasion the deckers "devastated" the boat, "maltreated" the captain, and committed acts that violated standards of law and order. Intense physical work also helped define the masculinity of deck passage. Loading wood, preparing food, and sharing space with roustabouts meant that there was little or no opportunity to create a feminine enclave that was similar to the ladies' cabin.[16]

Not only did deckers travel in squalor and face an increased risk of death, they suffered a supreme indignity in the South: being reduced to the same level as blacks. In the South's race-conscious society, whites identified their place by assuming slaves were inferior, so it was insulting to be lumped together with enslaved Americans. Samuel J. Peters was forced to take deck passage on the *Heroine* because it was the only boat that could get to Bladon Springs, Alabama. He particularly resented sitting next to chained slaves, a circumstance that made the trip "very unpleasant." Deckers who sat on a crate of dry goods next to a coffle of slaves learned they were an afterthought in the South's structured world. Slaves might have been used to being treated as just another commodity, but whites were less likely to encounter such treatment. Roustabouts, most of whom were black on the Deep South riverboats, might even order a white deck passenger away from freight. A slave directing a white person upended the racially stratified South.[17]

"THE BEST BOATS"

Cabin passengers were literally and figuratively above deck passengers. They spent most of their time on the boiler deck, and the large room on this level, called the saloon or the main cabin, was a public space that also doubled as the dining room. The size of the saloon, obviously, reflected the size of the boat. Most early main cabins were no longer than forty or fifty feet, but by the 1840s saloons stretched two hundred feet or more. Mammoth boats of the lower Mississippi, such as the renowned *Eclipse,* had saloons that were as long as a football field. But these corridor-like main cabins were no more than twenty feet wide on the larger vessels and even smaller on little boats. The main cabin of the *Crystal Palace,* for instance, was typical of a mid-sized boat. It stretched two hundred feet in length but was only seventeen and a half feet wide. By 1830, staterooms lined the outer two walls of most saloons. Reputedly named after various American states, these six-foot square rooms had, at a minimum, two doors (one which opened to the saloon and the other to the promenade deck), two berths fastened to a wall, and a mirror.[18]

The saloon was the primary location for social interaction on the boiler deck, and activities there varied immensely. Anton Reiff passed a pleasant evening listening to singing, while other passengers were busy dancing, talking politics, playing cards, and swapping stories. On another boat, earnest conversation turned to "steam-boats, liquors, black-land, red-land, bottom-land, timber-land, warrants and locations, sugar, cotton, corn, and negroes," observed Frederick Law Olmsted. Introspective passengers read newspapers and books or wrote letters (if the boat wasn't shaking too badly). Drinking was so common that one visitor tut-tutted that "whiskey is used just as freely as water. All [passengers] drink." Astonished Europeans added the chewing and spitting of tobacco to the list of ubiquitous and iniquitous steamboat activities. It was "incessant," wrote one English tourist who saw Americans coat the carpet with expectorations when they were not spitting in the cabin's stove. Bored passengers even shot deer, bears, turkeys, geese, and alligators. If a clergyman or a particularly pious passenger was aboard, he could organize church services on Sunday mornings, and even though some boats prohibited gambling on Sundays, usually the Sabbath was merely another day of traveling.[19]

Steamers quickly gained reputations, and the best indicator of a boat's quality was word of mouth. Savvy travelers arranged their trips around the schedules of what became known as "the best Boats." Charles Minor's potential visit to St. Louis was in jeopardy because the *J. M. White, Peytona,* and *Sultana* were not going to the city and he could not pinpoint the schedules of the *Harry of the West* or the *Princess.* He was unwilling to travel on a boat of dubious reputation. Cabin passengers like Minor self-consciously chose a vessel like the *Sultana* so "that they may be less thrown into contact with ruder travelers." Those who found themselves on an "unendurable" boat sacrificed time and money in favor of comfort and switched to a vessel like the *Magnolia,* with "large state rooms, excellent fare, pianos, etc." A definite hierarchy of riverboats emerged, and passengers who knew the river, or who solicited good advice, could avoid irritation and anguish. An Englishwoman traveling on the Tombigbee River was wise enough to learn that the *Orline St. John* was the only way to travel. "In the first class Boats," she noted with a mixture of satisfaction and relief, "you pay an extra passage but you avoid the rush & rabble that throng the smaller & poorer Boats."[20]

The best boats used the opulence of their grand saloons to attract attention and customers. Owners were so competitive in making their boats visually overwhelming that even today's most inventive Las Vegas promoters might blush. The *Eclipse,* which sensibly balanced political sympathies by placing statues of Andrew Jackson and Henry Clay on opposite ends of the saloon, featured elaborate frescoes of diamonds, acorns, and oak leaves painted on the walls and ceilings. An English tourist ranked the boat equal to Niagara Falls and the New Orleans levee as one of the three wonders of the United States. On the *Eclipse,* as on other fine boats, intricate scrollwork adorned doors, transoms, and ledges. Visitors were willing to pay a higher ticket price to marvel at the brightness of gas lights, admire gilded columns, turn crystal doorknobs, tread on plush Brussels carpeting, sit in mahogany chairs, listen to grand pianos beneath sparkling chandeliers, and study the heavens through etched glass skylights. Emblems like a golden eagle on the pilothouse or golden balls suspended between the ninety-five-foot-high smokestacks added to the stunning appearance, and the opulent excess gave rise to the style known as steamboat gothic. One visitor even commented on the "beautifully decorated" public restrooms on his steamer. Upon seeing the interior of the best saloons for the first time, most visitors were overwhelmed. "The view is really gorgeous!," is the only thing one dumbfounded New Yorker could think to write.[21]

The best boats, not surprisingly, provided a sumptuous dining experience. Slave waiters "were perfectly trained to their duties" and their easy air made meals agreeable. Women were first to find a place at the table, and then the men followed once the steward rang a bell. Guests could always drink coffee or tea, and sometimes wine from crystal tumblers. Opaque river water waited in glasses, and guests usually let the sediment settle lest they drink mud and prove the old river adage that the person who drank water on a steamboat would soon grow corn in his stomach. Stewards brought fine china laden with food that ranged from the mundane (biscuits and crackers) to the esoteric (alligator steak and oysters), but was usually of a great variety and fresh. Guests on the best boats raved about their food. "I have never lived better in a hotel than I have here. We have a great variety of dishes, & well cooked," gushed Edward Russell. Even the best boats sacrificed quality for quantity. Meals relied heavily on meats and were a pretentious display, meant to impress the passenger, much like the entire steamboat experience.[22]

Pleasant staterooms were another noticeable feature of the best boats. They were slightly larger than on ordinary vessels and featured soft mattresses, fine furniture, and sometimes a basin for water. Passengers were not slow to notice such high-class appointments. Anton Reiff thought the marble washstand, sofa, mirror, lamp, and two chairs in his stateroom appreciably improved his travel experience. Top-notch boats reserved a few double-sized staterooms exclusively for families, while the *Jacob Strader* even had hot and cold running water in select cabins.[23]

Captains of famous boats like the *Eclipse* or *Natchez* understood that travel was more than just being conveyed from one point to another, it could become an experience. They wanted their steamers, in essence, to be mobile four-star hotels. One satisfied guest looked back on his trip and concluded with satisfaction that nothing could compare with a steamboat for "comfort and pleasure." And since Americans equated comfort with social progress, riverboats were an exemplar of human advancement. Passengers on the best boats imagined they were staying in a palace or playing a part in a fairy tale. Indeed, the phrase "floating palace" filtered into writing so frequently that it became a cliché. In the South, a region of the country where white residents made self-conscious parallels to medieval Europe, the comparison to a palace had special resonance. European carpeting, paintings, and furniture (even if they were replicas) provided access to a world that most travelers had visited only in books. The marble-topped tables, intricate scrollwork, statues, frescoes, and gilded surfaces transported passengers to a world where they became lords and ladies. The best boats catered to elite expectations by allowing passengers to purchase noble status, if only for a short time. Even European tourists were not immune to the charms of riverboats. High-end steamers were just as good, if not better, than the clipper ships that brought European tourists across the Atlantic Ocean. Lady Emmeline Stuart Wortley, daughter of the Fifth Duke of Rutland, described the *Autocrat* as an "enchanted castle" that seemed to float on the clouds. The best boats were places where passengers could imagine themselves in a better life—even if just for the duration of the voyage—where they were wealthy, powerful, and without worries.[24]

Wealthy southerners who traveled on the best boats found that their experiences meshed nicely with their assumptions of a hierarchy and privilege. Slaveholders and other well-to-do whites stood atop a pyramid, with poor whites and immigrants further down the scale, and African Americans at the bottom. The symbolic superiority of cabin passage was not lost on Joseph Ingraham when he commented that cabin passengers were "high above all the freight, and all the 'disagreeables' of those parts of the boat where the hands and the emigrants stay." Wealthy European travelers quickly picked up on the condescension that filled the saloons. When Matilda Houstoun heard someone yell man overboard, the cabin passengers rushed to the windows. They quickly lost interest when they learned "it was *only one of the deck passengers*," and *not* one in whom [they] were deeply interested." Besides revealing callousness, such grim humor captures the disdain cabin passengers harbored toward deck passengers. Occupants of the cabins created and inflated a sense of separation between themselves and the lower level. Demonizing deck passengers was a way to achieve a degree of self-definition as someone who had attained at least some degree of refinement. An English traveler captured the sentiments of many southern cabin passengers when he referred to deck travelers as "the scum of the population."[25]

"FILTHY OLD RAT-TRAPS"

Few steamers attained the status of best boats; most were unpretentious vessels that specialized in hauling freight rather than catering to passengers. The faux finishes, poorly painted walls, grimy carpeting, rickety furniture, and shoddy carpentry in their saloons betrayed pathetic attempts to create a luxurious environment. Even steamers with better-than-average furnishings became disappointments once thousands of passengers trooped through them. Customers wore down carpeting, nicked furniture, spat on walls, and broke glass. Men so doggedly whittled down chair arms, railings, and guards that it caused one alarmed French woman to conclude "nothing is sacred against their knife blades." The public restrooms on steamers were so dirty and poorly stocked that clean ones prompted comments from astonished passengers. Guests commonly had to fetch their own water from the river (no easy task on a moving steamboat), wash their faces with a public bar of soap, dry themselves with the one dirty towel, and use the community comb hanging from the mirror. The combination of noise, smoke, smells, and motion produced headaches and even vomiting in less hardy passengers. When William Fairfax Gray boarded the *Heroine* at Vicksburg, he could not help but notice that it was a "sorry old boat." Only the attentive officers and an accomplished black steward prevented the trip from being a total disaster. There were also the worst boats—"the very filthiest of all filthy old rat-traps," in the words of John James Audubon. The saloons of these neglected and dirty craft held no charms for passengers who expected a more inviting travel experience. Margaretta Sanders was one such dissatisfied customer. She criticized the *Nicholas Biddle* as the "dirtiest place" she ever stayed, even worse than an execrable tavern in Ghent that assaulted her senses and haunted her memory. Her mood did not improve when she transferred to the "vile and filthy" *New York*.[26]

Not surprisingly, the dining experience on bad steamboats was grossly inadequate. Overwhelmed or inattentive cooks routinely ruined meals, resulting in food that was "greasy and nasty," according to Audubon. Charles Dickens, who had almost nothing good to write about his journey through America, compared the cornbread on his steamer to a pin cushion. Poor service compounded the badly prepared cuisine. When one patron on the *Gallant* wanted coffee instead of tea, the waiter took the cup, flung the tea to the carpet, and then poured coffee into the empty vessel. For passengers who expected at least decent food and service, steamboat meals on bad boats were a miserably monotonous experience.[27]

Disagreeable staterooms on mediocre boats tested the endurance of even the most patient traveler. Passengers complained about mattresses that felt like "an armful of sticks sewed up in a sack," pillows filled with corn shucks, shabby furniture, walls "black with tobacco juice," leaky ceilings, and loud neighbors. Matilda Houstoun's stateroom was so dreadful that it "almost made me wish myself back again among the pigs of Cincinnati." Captains who were not attuned to the desires of their customers placed no restrictions on the amount of animal cargo they took aboard. The result could be a "Noah's Ark" that featured a deafening cacophony and "anything but agreeable odors" for cabin passengers.[28]

Bad staterooms were better than none at all. Greedy captains on bad boats deliberately oversold cabin capacity, forcing unfortunate passengers to sleep on cots or mattresses littered throughout the saloon. Passengers were wedged so tightly that knees dug into strangers' stomachs, feet kicked heads, and it became impossible to walk through the public area after ten p.m. without stepping on someone. Exhausted passengers snored like hogs, remembered

one traveler, while Frederick Law Olmsted only recalled being packed in between men who emitted "an exceedingly offensive smell." Female passengers
never had to sleep in the saloon, but occasionally had to crowd three people
into a two-berth cabin. Overcrowding, bad food, horrible smells, and obnoxious noises made cabin accommodations on bad boats resemble deck passage. Such terrible conditions were deeply offensive to travelers who paid extra
money for relief from democratic modes of travel.[29]

"THERE IS IN THE WEST A REAL EQUALITY"

Travel in cabin passage, at first, created a de facto hierarchy that appealed to
travelers, southern and otherwise. A ticket on an early steamboat was quite
expensive and few people could afford the $80 fare from New Orleans to Fort
Pickering, near present-day Memphis. Fewer still could spend another $45 to
continue to Louisville. The high expense of those tickets—the equivalent of
paying $1,800 in modern currency to travel from New Orleans to Louisville—
put the first steamboats out of the reach of most Americans. The best boats
tried to maintain this sense of exclusivity, but the flimsy hierarchy of western
steamboats could not survive the onslaught of changing market conditions.
The intense competition and large number of boats made prices plummet. On
the eve of the Civil War, cabin passengers paid only $15 to travel from New
Orleans to Louisville, a cost of perhaps $400 today. Prices were so reasonable
that one traveler was astonished to learn that his passage from New Orleans to
Cincinnati included food. At the cost of one dollar per day, he concluded that
riverboat travel was "literally cheaper than staying at home." Since most passengers traveled shorter distances, from New Orleans to Natchez, say, steamboat passage was within reach of a wider spectrum of people.[30]

Customers expecting a refined traveling experience were usually disappointed if they did not secure passage on one of the best boats. European
travelers in particular commented on indecorous cabin passengers. Charles
Latrobe complained that meals on steamboats consisted of "a shove to the
table, a scramble, and a shove from the table," while one of his countrymen
merely groused that he would prefer to share the saloon with pigs rather than
Americans. On another boat, a "beastly drunk" passenger stumbled into the
wrong stateroom and vomited all over another guest's clothes. Even southerners noticed crass practices like women spitting over the rail and men not using

serving utensils. During a miserable trip on the Ohio River, a grumpy Texan endured the company of "not very refined" cabin passengers.[31]

Gentility did not exist if it could be purchased with a ticket for cabin passage. Owners compensated by creating a strict set of rules to govern shipboard conduct, to protect their investment, and to attract customers of the better sort. Even owners of the first steamboats, where the high price vetted potential customers, encountered uncouth behavior. A broadside for the *Vesuvius* and *Aetna* reminded potential passengers that "cleanliness, neatness and order, are necessary" on the boats. Paying customers were not allowed to smoke in the main cabin, and those who were so unrefined as to lie down in their berths while wearing boots or shoes paid a $1.50 fine. Card games had to cease at ten p.m. and passengers needed to take care lest they "injure the furniture or the boats." The captain, moreover, had the authority to put ashore any passenger who was a "nuisance" if the majority of his fellow passengers voted for banishment. In setting up these expectations, the boats' owners noted that the need for decorous behavior "must be obvious to all." Had the expectations been so obvious, of course, there would have been no reason to post the broadside in the first place. Posters emblazoned with rules were universal on steamboats, and, it seems, universally ignored. As Frederick Olmsted archly observed, "there was a placard of rules forbidding smoking, gambling, and swearing in the cabin, and a close company of drinkers, smokers, card-players, and constant swearers."[32]

An apocryphal story about steamboats illustrates the tension between refinement and market conditions that created opportunities for anyone to purchase exclusivity. A German prince supposedly refused to sit at the dinner table with a pig farmer. The nobleman requested a private dinner in his cabin. The captain went a step further and, when the steamer stopped next to an island, ordered a table set up on land for the prince to dine alone. When the prince obliged, the captain cast off and shouted that his now former passenger would have to make due by himself. While not literally true, the story conveys an important understanding of steamboat travel: passengers must be ready to accept social inferiors or face rejection and ostracism. Steamboat travel became democratized in a way that mocked pretentious travelers.[33]

Stories of the kaleidoscope of humanity on steamers became standard fare in the day's travel accounts and letters. While it was an exaggeration that "nearly every nation on the face of the globe has its representatives" aboard a

Mississippi River steamer, the variety of people was astonishing to Americans expecting insularity. "Wolvereens, Suckers, Hoosiers, Buckeyes, and Corn-crackers" mixed with slave traders, gamblers, farmers, politicians, planters, judges, tourists, and ministers. Passengers mingled with strangers from across the country and globe when steamboats annihilated differences of time and space. A Frenchman correctly summed up the ability of riverboats to break down geographic and social barriers by noting, "There is in the West a real equality."[34]

"PUT ON A CABIN FACE"

Steamboats, at least the best boats, tried to create an artificial world where travelers could be divorced from reality for a short time. Reality, however, was too stubborn to be wished away. Laughing and conversation from the saloon easily penetrated the paper-thin stateroom walls. Whistles and bells were even more disruptive of rest. But it was the engine's monotonous throbbing that was "peculiarly disagreeable." An engine working at full capacity could be so loud—one traveler likened it to "a sort of huge behemoth who had been chained down on the lower deck"—that it drowned out normal conversation. Boats, particularly smaller ones, shook so badly that guests could not read or write, let alone enjoy a meal. Environmental factors could be even more vexing. Heat was an issue, especially in the summer. Furnaces, boilers, and chimneys heated stateroom floors to the point where passengers scorched their feet if they did not wear shoes or slippers. The summer sun that baked the steamer's roof was so intense in the Deep South that passengers seared their hands on the ceiling while climbing into their berths. Small cabins became oppressively stuffy on warm nights, making sleep virtually impossible. Travel in cold weather was also a nuisance. The heat from the engine and the stoves was poorly distributed, so temperatures ranged from too hot to freezing cold. Noise, vibration, and extreme temperatures could destroy the ambience of boats and make travel a nightmarish experience. Boats that grounded in low water, were stuck in ice, or snagged on river obstructions might spend hours, days, or even weeks helplessly idle.[35]

Boredom also plagued steamboat travel, particularly if the steamer tarried unusually long to take on wood or freight. Conversation soon reached its natural limits, many faces remained the same, and confinement to the same room grew tiresome. In desperate attempts to escape the narrow confines of the saloon, passengers visited the pilothouse if possible, walked around the guards, observed the firemen, and studied the alligators swimming in the river. When the tedium and constant social interaction wore down public facades, passengers shed the mask of civility and lashed into one another. Smoldering annoyance flared into shouting matches, threats, and fights. Eight days into his trip to St. Louis, a Louisiana slaveholder on the *George Collier* watched a bad joke escalate into a passionate dispute. Only some hasty mediation prevented a duel. Likewise, Anton Reiff recorded a pleasant night of singing, dancing, and political discussions one week before he almost ended up dueling over places at the dinner table. Boorish and obnoxious guests became insufferable and, when combined with the tedium of steamboat travel, abraded the veneer of gentility. Charles Latrobe's rant captures the annoyances associated with steamboat travel:

> heated in body and mind by confinement and disappointment, you are peevish as a pea-hen; that the society is decidedly ill-bred and vicious— further you have no books—the cabin is crowded—the machinery wants constant repair—the boilers want scraping. This hour you get upon a sand-bank; the next you are nearly snagged—drift-wood in the river breaks your paddles—the pilot is found to be a toper,—the engineer an ignoramus,— the steward an economist,—the captain a gambler,—the black fire-men insurgent, and the deck passengers riotous.[36]

Cabin passengers in southern steamboats were locked in an artificial and superficial world, one that matched the tawdry riverboat furnishings. Men and women were constantly sizing up one another, comparing, and making judgments based on outward appearances. After Reiff's dispute, he dared not betray his inner turmoil. Even though he did not enjoy his meal, Reiff "put on a Cabin Face" so that none of the passengers would think him weak. This emphasis on outward appearance stressed public perception of the individual as a means of defining one's place in society, in this case the small world of the steamboat.[37]

"CLUBS IS TRUMPS"

Gambling was a perfect distraction in this artificial world, as men took on new identities. Passengers gambled on nearly every southern steamboat, with brag, three-card monte, euchre, and poker being the games most frequently mentioned. Men (women were not allowed to participate) crowded around smoky tables, passed packs of dirty cards, spat tobacco juice on the floor, and swigged shots of whiskey. Darkness hardly slowed down the gaming frenzy; stewards brought candles to the gambling tables and the players might spend the whole night making bets and exchanging money. A traveler on the *Daniel O'Connel* managed to break off from the gambling at midnight only to wake at five o'clock to shouts of *"Clubs is trumps."* Others literally fell asleep at the gambling tables, scattering torn, bent, and folded cards amid the tobacco ashes and expectorations.[38]

Residents of the emerging Southwest loved to gamble and, as Joshua Rothman has argued, their risk taking was not unlike participation in the speculative market economy, complete with opportunities for quick gains and stunning reversals. Land purchases, slave sales, and investment in railroads were, in a real sense, legal speculation common throughout the South. Planters who just cashed in their cotton crop or slave traders who recently sold a coffle of bondservants might try to magnify their earnings at the poker table. The thrill of risk reinforced one's sense of masculinity in a very serious form of play. Boredom also drove men to the gambling table; there simply were few other activities that were of enough interest to fill the hours. That a steamboat was a "world of strangers" also lured men to games of chance. Passengers were constantly entering and leaving riverboats at various stops, so the social world of the antebellum steamer was a crazy, ever-shifting kaleidoscope of humanity. The anonymity of travel on western waters gave men the opportunity to transcend their mundane lives and take on new identities as they crossed into a world of play. What was prohibited or discouraged at home might suddenly be a temptation too alluring to resist. The sharp talk around the table, the thrills associated with risk taking, and the intensely competitive atmosphere made the riverboat gaming table a place where amateurs could show their skill and affirm their masculinity.[39]

Not all men were innocents aboard, and the stereotype of the riverboat gambler has some basis in fact. Most gamblers on the Mississippi River and its tributaries were novices, but enough professional gamblers existed to attract the attention of travelers and generate a number of tall tales. These blacklegs—the universal insult directed toward a professional gambler—numbered in the hundreds by 1858, according to an article in *De Bow's Review*. Some traveled alone, but others operated in groups of two or three and worked together to fleece unsuspecting rubes. According to myth, riverboat gamblers used gold stickpins and other jewelry as ready sources of cash, and wore shiny vests, striped cravats, and frock coats. The truth is less certain, and gamblers did not dress so audaciously because they did not want to call attention to themselves. They hoped to blend in with the crowd and frequently posed as planters, attorneys, physicians, or businessmen. Gamblers wanted to be perceived as respectable people with money. One "river shark" was so effective in his disguise that his fellow passengers guessed that he was a lawyer, physician, or divinity student. These confidence men often stayed in hotels along the river towns, looking for prospective victims, particularly farmers who had just sold a crop and had wads of cash in their pockets. Should the potential victims board a steamer, the gamblers followed and sometimes tipped the steward to share quarters or be put in an adjoining stateroom. The seemingly innocent conversation that followed was not only a way to gain trust, but served as intelligence gathering for the gambler.[40]

The masking of one's identity violated notions of fair play, and the criminality of stealing from men who viewed gambling as a type of masculine competition only enhanced the hatred of blacklegs. Once a professional was unmasked, the situation became frighteningly unpredictable. One planter who suspected that his loss of several hundred dollars was not by chance secured a fresh deck, put a pistol on the table, and announced he would shoot any man whom he suspected of foul play. He lost no more money. Gamblers might have to flee, fight, use fast words to ease themselves out of a tight spot, or face the consequences. One professional, who refused to return money unfairly won from deckhands, supposedly had his neck tied to the boat's piston rod. When the captain started the engine, crew and passengers alike laughed as the man lunged forward and back in a desperate effort to keep from being decapitated. Professional gambler George Devol, whose romanticized narrative makes for interesting reading, claimed he reveled in delivering headbutts to dissatisfied players and sometimes flashed his gun, which he nicknamed Betsy Jane.[41]

Since gamblers operated on society's margins, they often recruited fellow outsiders and had little trouble persuading enslaved Americans to help them. Devol admitted that he paid roustabouts to vouch for his identity as a planter. While new passengers crowded the guards to say goodbye, Devol stationed "some old 'nig'" nearby with instructions to yell out, "Good-bye, Massa George; I's goin' to take care of the old plantation till you comes back." Devol also paid African American bartenders to verify his new identity and keep his cards for him. When he ran up against a particularly skilled player, Devol asked if the barkeep could bring a new deck of cards. The accomplice cheerfully provided a supposedly fresh pack that Devol knew were "my old friends." Enterprising African Americans, including the future governor of Louisiana, P. B. S. Pinchback, not only earned money as confederates of gamblers but also learned valuable lessons in how to invert traditional relationships of power. Slave culture had developed a rich tradition of trickster tales where the weak outwitted and humiliated the strong. Allying with a blackleg was one way enslaved Americans could use secret knowledge and play unsuspecting whites for the fool.[42]

Professional gamblers were successful enough to inspire cautionary tales and whispers to be on guard against charlatans. The *Philadelphia Inquirer,* for instance, printed a story in which it warned that untold numbers of people who took passage on Mississippi River steamers were never heard from again. "The midnight gambling, the fierce quarrel, the dirk, the sullen [sudden] plunge of the ghastly cor[p]se, with heavy weights attached" were the dire consequences that befell anyone who dabbled in games of chance. Another widely circulated story lugubriously recounted how a Kentucky farmer gambled away a fortune while his wife slowly died in their stateroom. Indeed, tales drifted from boat to boat, made their way into newspapers, appeared in books, and became as much a staple of river travel as the boat's whistle. Experienced travelers became so perceptive at spotting professionals that it was not uncommon for blacklegs to slink off a riverboat once they could not separate the supposed fools from their money. While these stories counseled riverboat passengers to shift for themselves, another set of rumors reassured travelers that authority figures would restore fair play to gambling. Stories abounded of captains evicting professional gamblers from steamboats, lashing them to the paddle wheels, or even nailing their ears to the deck. In all likelihood, blacklegs rarely earned the fabulous sums of legend (since such winnings would attract too much attention) but probably earned enough money to avoid having to find gainful employment.[43]

The legends surrounding riverboat gamblers helped deflect criticism of games of chance and enshrined gambling as an acceptable behavior for cabin passengers. It was only the professional, the man who cheated by controlling chance, who could have no place on a steamboat. Ordinary travelers, who entered the gambling environment on a par with other competitors, were almost celebrated by the ritualistic cleansing of the cheaters. As long as one was not a professional who violated the written or unwritten rules, then the behavior was tolerated or celebrated. Risk taking was one way to project masculinity and prove worth to strangers. There are no known accounts of gambling in the ladies' cabin or of women participating in games of chance. Women might play cards, but they could go no further, since doing so would signal a challenge to the day's gender conventions. Gambling provided a marker between male and female culture.

"THE 'HOLIEST OF HOLIES'"

Although steamers failed to maintain effective class arrangements, they were more successful in reinforcing gender norms. The first western steamboats followed the pattern of eastern boats and designated a public space as the ladies' cabin. Once saloons became the norm, the ladies' cabin moved to the rear of the boiler deck, a location that shielded women from the heat and noise of the boiler room. Arrangements varied, but many boats had foldable partitions, a permanent wall, or sliding doors that separated the saloon into men's and women's cabins. By the 1850s some steamers no longer relied on walls but trusted that the carpeting in the ladies' cabin would be enough of a contrast with the wooden floor of the men's cabin to enforce standards of propriety. A separate space for ladies reinforced the idea that women needed protection from the masculine world of the southern steamboat. Women who traveled in public could maintain their private roles without transgressing the conventions of respectable womanhood. Just like nineteenth-century railroads, steamboats created public domesticity within their midst by creating a haven for women.[44]

Not only did women have their own preserve, but they enjoyed better accommodations. The *General Bernard Pratte* had a sumptuous men's cabin with ornate doors, glass chandeliers, and French mirrors, but boasted that its ladies' cabin was "still more elegantly furnished and fitted up." Fine tables, imported carpet, rocking chairs, sofas, and a piano gave that fashionable room a touch of home. Ladies' cabins, typically one-third the size of the men's saloon, were "more tastefully adorned" because, presumably, women would either treat the furnishings with more respect or could better appreciate the increased refinement. Not only was the public space better, but ladies' staterooms were often superior as well. An advertisement for the *W. R. McKee* boasted that its ladies' rooms were seven feet by seven feet and contained luxurious hair mattresses with soft covers. Such nice surroundings were designed to reflect the morality of travelers and uphold the notion that women needed special accommodations to ease the rigors of travel.[45]

The ladies' cabin was not truly separate, but served more as a permeable space that regulated behavior and shielded women's virtue in a public and masculine environment. Married men slept in the ladies' cabin with their wives, while single men could enter during the day and only at the invitation of a female passenger. Women came and went in the male portion of the saloon, but usually did not tarry at nighttime and were not allowed in male staterooms. Children typically stayed in the ladies' cabin with their mothers, reinforcing the notion that women were guardians of the next generation. Overbooked steamers stretched the comfortable fiction that the ladies' cabin was a moral guardian. Should there be a shortage of ladies' accommodations, the steward or captain forced men out of their staterooms. Such arrangements were usually disagreeable for all parties. The men ended up sleeping on cots in the saloon while the women lost that small sense of protection a room in the ladies' cabin provided. Miriam Badger Hilliard chafed at the "discomfort" she endured by having her stateroom "midway down the gentleman's cabin." She stayed there two nights before moving to a stateroom in the ladies' cabin.[46]

The ladies' cabin was typically quieter than its counterpart for males, particularly if it was protected behind a wall or partition. There was much less drinking, spitting, or swearing than was found in the men's cabin. One passenger described the chief amusements as "nonsense, flirtation, and music," a revealing contrast to the discussions of cotton prices, slave sales, and politics that went on in the men's cabin. Not all ladies' cabins were sanctuaries of peace and quiet. A British visitor who stayed aboard a steamer with his wife complained about unsupervised children who were "so riotous and undisciplined" that they tormented passengers who dared to correct them.[47]

Perhaps the most common activity in the ladies' cabin was flirtation, and bachelors competed to secure the coveted invitation to this "holiest of holies." Tom, the Natchez bachelor farmer, found it a thrill to be admitted to the ladies' cabin during his voyage upstream. His "good fortune" meant that he could pass the time "quite charmingly" by flirting with women and playing with children. Another unmarried man not only strolled on the promenade deck with several young ladies but captivated them at night by playing his flute. Most men spent only a few hours a day in the ladies' cabin, and it appears that boats enforced at least a nominal separation of men and women. Marg Sanders, for instance, was disappointed when the clerk chased the men out of the ladies' cabin at sundown, thereby ending a friendly game of whist. On the surface, at least, it seemed as if steamboat captains served in loco parentis with their efforts to protect the chastity of young women traveling alone.[48]

It is impossible to determine how much playful behavior blossomed into sexual activity; nineteenth-century Americans, even in their private correspondence, were reluctant to comment on such matters. There are a few examples of women and men who pushed the boundaries of propriety. The captain of one southern steamer ousted a nighttime guest from a woman's stateroom, but token enforcement could not prevent amorous trysts. It is unknown how many saloons were abuzz with rumors of late night indiscretions. Nor is prostitution mentioned, meaning that it was infrequent, carefully hidden, or ignored. The author of a traveler's guide to western riverboats did broach the topic, albeit in a roundabout fashion, when he alluded to "shocking depravity" on a few steamers. He was confident that the good morals of passengers would prevent further instances of "a subject so disgusting to every virtuous mind."[49]

That riverboats did not live up to expectations to guard a woman's virtue is not as important as what passengers believed. Captains successfully convinced travelers that steamers provided protection for women in ways that reinforced emerging middle-class notions of domesticity and Victorianism. Stagecoaches and flatboats, for instance, had no regard for the separation of women from men. Southern railroads usually did not have separate cars for women, but might have a ladies' compartment that provided some measure of distance from men. On riverboats, by contrast, women in cabin passage found refuge from unwelcome or harmful contact with obnoxious philanderers. The ladies' cabin regulated public interactions and brought order, comfort, and familiarity to a woman's travel experience. It mediated the tension between the very masculine world of the steamboat and the need for women to inhabit the public space. The creation of a woman's enclave also preserved the comfortable fiction that women did not engage in sexual activity outside of marriage. But had men behaved in a fashion expected of upper-class cabin passengers, then no protection from indecorous or amorous habits would have been necessary. The creation of a ladies' cabin and the rules meant to govern behavior within it were a tacit recognition of the difficulty that men had in restraining their baser impulses.[50]

"NEGROES EXCEPTED"

Even if class conventions faltered and separation of men from women was un-even, steamboats were successful in enforcing racial order. African Americans were allowed to enter the saloon under two circumstances: as workers or as slaves. Blacks who worked on the boiler deck spent their free time elsewhere, normally with other African American crew members. Most boats traveling in southern waters allowed slaves on the boiler deck, as long as they were under supervision. As one New Yorker crudely phrased it "We have now niggers of all grades as most [white southerners] have a servant or two." The enslaved Americans combed their owners' hair, assisted them in dressing and undress-ing, and put away clothes. One master was even "tucked up in Bed by a Sooty wench!!!," perhaps a veiled reference to sexual exploitation. Another owner would not allow his three slaves in the saloon but forced them instead to re-main on the verandah outside his stateroom. They slept on luggage beneath a blanket in a cold, driving rain. Southern whites expected to see African Americans in menial roles, so the rules governing saloons reinforced societal notions of white superiority and reflected the nonchalance regarding slavery. The presence of slaves in the saloon had the potential for the opposite ef-fect on northerners and foreigners, as they might draw negative conclusions about the peculiar institution based on the exploitation of the slaves. As James Huston has noted, personal or sustained contact with the horrors of slavery convinced many northerners as to the iniquity of the peculiar institution.[51]

Southern steamboats prohibited free blacks from entering the saloon un-less they were part of the crew. Most African Americans could not afford the price of cabin passage anyway, but racial prejudice cemented racial exclusion for those with enough money to buy a ticket. In this case, the harsh racial hierarchy trumped the demands of the marketplace. Since exclusion served as a tangible reminder of presumed African American inferiority, allowing free blacks in cabin passage would have been one small indicator that they were equal to whites. As one traveler keenly observed, riverboats were open to all who could pay, "negroes excepted. A coloured man, however well educated or wealthy, dare not show his nose in the saloon, he must confine himself to the deck, with the deck hands and deck passengers." William Johnson, a free barber in Natchez, experienced this discrimination firsthand. Johnson mixed to some degree with white society in his hometown and possessed the financial means to travel in cabin passage on any steamer. His records indicate that whenever he paid steamboat passage for himself or his family, those prices were in line with deck travel. At one point the frustrated Johnson prevailed upon a friend to persuade the captain of the *Maid of Arkansas* to change the racial policy. The captain reiterated that the rules of the boat prevented Johnson from attaining a stateroom. He "Spoke of Prejudice of the Southern people," Johnson wrote in his diary, but since the captain was a businessman, he "was Compelld to adopt those Rules." By enforcing racial segregation, the captain of the *Maid of Arkansas* fell into line with other public forms of travel in the South during the nineteenth century.[52]

Even if a riverboat's accommodations, food, and circumstances were bad, they compared favorably with other methods of travel in the antebellum South. One irritable traveler found the bad food and disgusting accommodations on his "horrid little boat . . . paradisiacal after the staging [i.e., riding in a stagecoach] of the last three days." Early southern railroads offered less comfort and seclusion than steamers. Showers of sparks and smoke blew through the passenger cars, sometimes setting customers' clothes on fire, passengers sat on large benches, and individual cabins were unknown until after the Civil War. But travel in the artificial world of a Mississippi River steamboat was a difficult experience by modern standards. Deck passengers were scrambled together in decidedly unrefined conditions without regard for race or gender. While steamboat owners tried to sell exclusivity, privilege, and refinement, their product was often inferior. Even though class distinctions tottered unsteadily, gender and racial conventions prevailed. Women received both condescension and exalted status, being treated as weak creatures who needed protection. African Americans, moreover, had no success in breaching the bulwarks of racial separation. Steamboats in the Southwest, then, were very much a reflection of southern society. And while steamboats in the southern interior put millions of white people in motion, they also upended the lives of Native Americans in the South. As we shall see in the next chapter, riverboats accelerated the drive for Indian land and became central to transporting Native Americans to Oklahoma.[53]

FOUR

INDIAN REMOVAL

It took the better part of a cold and rainy October 29, 1837, for the Alabama Emigrating Company to pack approximately 1,500 Creek Indians and their slaves onto the steamboats *Farmer, Black Hawk, Far West,* and *Monmouth.* The federal government had contracted with the company to move the Creeks to "Indian Territory." This deportation was part of Andrew Jackson's policy of Indian Removal, whereby the federal government forced Native Americans to trade their valuable lands east of the Mississippi River for relatively uninviting land in what would become Oklahoma. The Creeks who boarded those four steamers in 1837 had just arrived from Mobile, Alabama, where they had been waiting in an internment camp for some of their people to return from the Second Seminole War. Steamboats brought them from Mobile to a spot just south of New Orleans, railroads shuttled them around the city to avoid a cholera epidemic, and then they began to file back on boats. Dave Barnett, a Creek aboard the *Monmouth,* recalled how, when the convoy shoved off after sunset, most of his people did not want to start the journey at night. But the crew, whom Barnett judged to be fortified by whiskey, insisted on leaving immediately. To make matters worse, the small boats were hopelessly overcrowded, with at least five hundred people shoehorned onto the 135-ton *Monmouth.*[1]

As the four steamers churned upriver, the wind picked up, whipping the rain and reducing visibility. At Prophet's Bend, a tricky stretch of river twenty miles north of Baton Rouge, the *Monmouth's* pilot apparently steered the vessel into a one-way channel reserved for descending vessels. Alarmed Creeks saw lights bearing down on them and screamed in panic. The steamer careened suddenly but still crashed into the middle of the *Trenton,* an empty sailing vessel in the tow of the *Warren.* The *Monmouth* broke apart, with one large chunk floating downstream and another slipping beneath the water.

Men, women, and children screamed as they scrambled to the upper decks to buy time for the other vessels to circle around and rescue them. Those who were thrown into the river's strong current swam to shore, clung to bobbing chunks of wood, or slipped below the water's surface. Daylight revealed a ghastly scene, as both the *Monmouth* and *Trenton* were complete wrecks. Even worse, numerous bodies had washed ashore. Survivors gathered what dead they could find and hastily buried them in riverside graves. Perhaps 311 people —including two crew members and thirty-two African Americans enslaved to the Creeks—perished. Presumably the survivors were loaded on the other steamboats and continued their journey upstream. It was the deadliest transportation accident in U.S. history prior to the explosion of the *Sultana* in 1865.[2]

Between the army, the Alabama Emigrating Company, and the operators of the *Monmouth,* there was sufficient blame to share and negligence to shoulder. The army's reaction, however, reveals the underlying callousness of the whole removal process, as officers barely mentioned the accident in their correspondence. When John Page successfully brought the survivors to Fort Gibson, he laconically remarked that "the movement with the exception of the disaster on board the Monmouth has been a very pleasant and agreeable Emigration." Indeed, the army spent more time and effort sorting out suspected overcharges for removal than it did in examining the poor decisions that led to the accident.[3]

Even though Indian Removal is usually associated with a land journey, the majority of Native Americans traveled all or part of the way to Oklahoma in steamers. The federal government used one of the day's best technologies to bring order, hasten the removal process, control the Native Americans, and reduce difficulties associated with relocating large groups of people. Steamboats not only changed the removal process, but they revealed dominant cultural attitudes toward technology. The reliance on steamers helped convince whites that the exile process was humane since it was conducted in a supposedly efficient and superior manner. Steamboats also helped define the cultural and geographical terrain of Jacksonian America. Shallow-draft steamers penetrated the smaller rivers of the Southwest in the 1820s, accelerating migration, adding value to land, and bringing whites into more frequent contact with the Native Americans. What was once relatively remote Indian land became valuable and appealing once steamboats could carry cotton to market and bring goods to far flung settlements. Steamboats gave shape to and made possible economic exploitation and theft of Indian land. The area that became "Indian

Territory," by contrast, had no such value, as low river levels prevented consistent riverboat service. Native Americans could be safely dumped into that space with little fear that whites would covet the land. Steamboats, in effect, became a technological expression of American expansion.[4]

"STEAMBOATS, WITH HUNDREDS OF INTRUDERS"

Indian Removal was the eventual outcome of a policy toward Native Americans that was confused, contradictory, and patronizing. Actions vacillated between expansion with honor, extermination, civilization, and removal. By the 1820s, the major Native American groups remaining in the South—Cherokees, Creeks, Choctaws, Chickasaws, and Seminoles—had adopted aspects of white culture with various degrees of enthusiasm and success. Never nomadic, these so-called Five Civilized Tribes learned to reside in log cabins or frame houses, dress like their white neighbors, and raise corn and livestock. Some owned slaves, a fair number sent their children to schools operated by Christian missionaries, and the Cherokees published a newspaper. The tribes also began to centralize authority. Both the Cherokees and Choctaws wrote constitutions and elected leaders, most of them of mixed Native American and white ancestry.[5]

Such steps toward assimilation did not satisfy most whites, as Native Americans could never do enough to substitute for the imprimatur of race. President James Monroe advocated removal in 1817, and by 1821 Native Americans had surrendered territory in much of Florida, Alabama, and Mississippi and parts of North Carolina, Georgia, Kentucky, and Tennessee. It was not enough. When southern state legislatures began asserting control over the Native Americans, it was clear that confrontation was imminent. Tribal leaders turned to Washington for protection, but their hopes were misplaced. President Andrew Jackson vigorously pursued a policy of complete eviction, explaining that it was the only way to preserve the Native Americans. In 1830 the Indian Removal Act gave him the authority to remove Native Americans from their homes and force them to Indian Territory across the Mississippi River.[6]

Steamboats helped propel whites into the southern interior, bringing them in ever increasing contact with Native Americans. The resulting friction put pressure on Indians to cede their land. Much of Creek land, for instance, straddled the Chattahoochee River in eastern Alabama and western Georgia. On February 6, 1828, the *Steubenville* reached the Chattahoochee's fall line, and four months later a surveyor had laid out the streets that would become the city of Columbus. Augmented by the federal road that passed through town, Columbus's population swelled to two thousand people by 1832. This handy confluence of water and land transportation transformed the city into a gateway to Creek lands. No longer did whites mainly transit through Creek territory, they stayed. Using Columbus as their starting point, at least fifteen hundred squatters infiltrated Creek territory after 1828, while whiskey sellers, traders, and speculators infested the region. The Chickasaws and Choctaws also witnessed the intrusion of steamboats into their land in northern Mississippi. In the early 1820s, steamers penetrated the Yazoo Delta and, by the end of the decade, made regular runs up the Tallahatchie River. The aptly named Cotton Gin Port on the Tombigbee also grew in size during this time—thanks to steamboat trade—and became a jumping-off point for whites looking for fertile farmland. Access to riverboat traffic made the land more valuable and thus more desirable to whites, who, in turn, pressured their state governments to confiscate Native American land.[7]

This relentless push of steamers into trunk rivers accelerated white settlement by expanding access to cheaper and better goods, and by providing reliable and efficient shipping of cotton. As steamers penetrated Indian lands, white settlement coiled around the Native Americans and began to squeeze. There is no question that Indian Removal would have taken place without riverboats. Cherokee lands, for instance, contained gold and lay out of direct contact with steamboats, while much of Seminole land was inaccessible to riverboats. But, taken as a whole, steamboats carried white settlers into a wider settlement arc and the resulting abrasion between whites and Native Americans not only fueled the calls for Indian Removal, it accelerated the process.

Riverboats also helped define what was to become Indian land once the federal government decided to remove the Native Americans. Congress designated public space west of the Mississippi River as "Indian Territory" in order to facilitate the long-term social, political, and economic development of the United States. Removal forced Native Americans onto land that was of minimal value to the federal government and white citizens alike. Part of the lack of desire for the "Indian Territory" lay in its arid condition, but its low worth also stemmed from the lack of access to steamboats. Fort Coffee, just across the Oklahoma line, was the effective limit of steamboat service on the Arkansas River, and access to it was out of the question in dry months. The "Great Raft," a naturally occurring obstruction, prevented steamboats on the

Red River from going any further than Natchitoches, Louisiana. No other river linked the Oklahoma Territory to the east, lending to the perception that it was unfit for white habitation. A senator grasped this essential point during the debates over removal—even if he had a shaky grasp of steamboat geography—when he argued that moving Cherokees to Indian Territory was foolish, since "Steamboats, with hundreds of intruders, can ascend the Arkansas [River] into the heart of the Indian country." He predicted that once riverboats brought whites to the area, the Cherokees would have to move to an even more remote location. Although the senator was correct that Indian land was hardly secure, he overestimated the ability of steamboat designers to overcome environmental obstacles. The low waters of the Arkansas River and the raft in the Red River served as barricades to keep steamboats and white settlement out.[8]

As the senator implied, steamboat service was firmly linked to civilization in the public's mind. After removal took place, the *North American Review* captured this idea when it observed that steamboats have "built up large and wealthy cities, and placed within their reach all the means of comfort, all the elegances of refinement, and every blessing, social, religious, and literary, enjoyed by the inhabitants of the seaboard." By implication, the absence of riverboat access stunted social growth. Just as land in Indian Territory could not be tamed through civilization that came on the decks of steamboats, so too should Native Americans be placed outside the civilized realm. Steamboats, then, were a not just an expression of Americans' cultural superiority, but were another indicator that Native Americans were unfit to be proper stewards of the lush lands of the American South.[9]

"A WRETCHED AFFAIR FROM BEGINNING TO END"

Once the federal government began the removal process, steamboats became central to the whole undertaking. It appears that at least 35,700 Native Americans, or roughly 60 percent of the 60,600 involved in removal, traveled all or part of the way to Oklahoma in riverboats. This number, of course, is not intended to be a definitive tally but serves as a reasonable estimate that is based on letters and reports of the army officers, government reports, and newspaper accounts. A discussion of the sources is found in Appendix B, while table 4 shows the breakdown by tribe.[10]

TABLE 4

Steamboat removal by people group

	Choctaw	Creek	Chickasaw	Seminole	Cherokee	Total
Total number of Indians removed	14,000	19,600	5,000	5,000	17,000	60,600
Number of Indians removed on steamboats	10,935	13,784	3,576	4,222	3,224	35,741
Percentage of Indians removed on steamboats	78.11	70.33	71.52	84.44	18.96	58.98

Sources: See Appendix B.

The Choctaws were the first to face removal, and they signed over a wide swath of 11 million acres that sprawled across northern Mississippi in the 1830 Treaty of Dancing Rabbit Creek. The officer in charge of moving the Choctaws was no supporter of removal by water and wrote his superior that land journeys were "the cheapest conveyance, and most acceptable and profitable to the emigrants." Steamboats' dependence on water levels, he added, would force removal to take place so late in the agricultural cycle that the Choctaws would not be able to grow crops their first year in Oklahoma. Ecological conditions forced a change in plans when severe rains turned the roads into quagmires but increased river levels. Army officers marched the four thousand or so Choctaws to Vicksburg in November 1831, but faced the coldest winter in recent memory as temperatures plunged to single digits, snowstorms raged, and ice chunks threatened river traffic. The 1832 removal was little better, as the Choctaws moved west during a nationwide cholera epidemic and the close quarters on board only magnified the problem. The few Choctaws who removed the next year faced no unusual difficulties.[11]

Almost 11,000 of the 14,000 Choctaws removed in 1831, 1832, and 1833 (or about 78 percent) traveled all or part of the way to Oklahoma in a steamboat. The army dispersed them along the various rivers, lest they overwhelm steamboat landings or towns. About 3,300 Choctaws were dumped off at Arkansas Post, a point about thirty miles up the Arkansas River from its junction with the Mississippi, and nearly 3,500 went to Rock Roe (present-day Clarendon, Arkansas) on the White River. Migrants who traveled to these two points avoided the treacherous Mississippi swamps but still faced a 230- or 250-mile trek across Arkansas. Nearly 1,700 Choctaws traveled up the Ouachita River to Ecor de Fabre (present-day Camden, Arkansas), a long water route that left a 150-mile land journey to Oklahoma. The remaining 2,500 Choctaws went up the Arkansas River to Little Rock or beyond and faced the shortest overland march. While the short trips to Rock Roe or Arkansas Post might seem trivial because they left migrants with substantial land marches, both of them shaved time and difficulty from the overall removal process. Even the reduction of one hundred miles—a two-day steamboat trip—saved about a week of walking overland. The use of steamers for Choctaw removal was effective enough for the army to assume that further removals would take place mainly on the water rather than on land.[12]

At about the same time the Choctaws signed over their ancestral lands, the Creeks did the same. Although the government planned for an orderly transfer, zealous white squatters ran the Indians out of their villages. Massive land fraud ensued, war erupted, and the government was so bold as to enlist some Creeks to fight in Florida against the Seminoles. By 1836, though, the army began removing the Creeks. It was, as Anthony F. C. Wallace observed, "a wretched affair from beginning to end." The army contracted with the Alabama Emigrating Company, a firm that had no incentive to protect Creek lives. Huge refugee camps in Memphis and Mobile caused starvation, disease ravaged the migrants, and cold temperatures compounded the problems.[13]

Almost 14,000 Creeks (70 percent) removed via water, with most marching from eastern Alabama to either Montgomery or Memphis before boarding a steamer, although a few boarded boats in northern Alabama at Gunter's Landing (present-day Guntersville) on the Tennessee River. Those who went via Montgomery steamed down to Mobile, went over to New Orleans, and then ascended the Mississippi River. Upon reaching the Mississippi, about 8,300 Creeks disembarked at Rock Roe, while another 210 landed at Arkansas Post. The remaining 5,200 Creeks traveled on steamers to Little Rock or beyond.

While the army botched the Choctaw and Creek removals, it did much better transporting the Chickasaws. Their proximity to Memphis and relatively small population (about 5,000 people) simplified arrangements. A. M. M. Upshaw, superintendent of the Chickasaw removal, met regularly with the Native Americans and reported that they "petitioned to go by water." Although it is impossible to know if Upshaw accurately represented Native American attitudes, he nonetheless contracted with Simeon Buckner to transport the

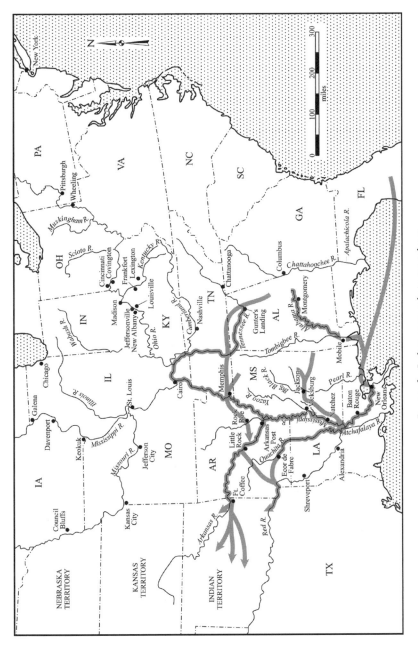

Routes for Indian removal via steamboat

Chickasaws from Memphis to Fort Coffee in Indian Territory. But when the Chickasaws reached the Mississippi, they learned of the *Monmouth* disaster and a "good many" refused "most positively to go on the boats," despite the army's efforts. The soldiers took several Indians on short river trips for reassurance, but 1,500 still insisted on marching across Arkansas. Nearly 3,600 of the 5,000 Chickasaws involved in removal (about 72 percent) traveled by steamboat from Memphis to Fort Coffee, a trip that took ten days.[14]

Cherokees were least likely to remove via steamers, even though Winfield Scott, who directed the removal of the Cherokees, preferred to use riverboats. The dry summer of 1838 reduced the Tennessee and Arkansas rivers to mere trickles, so only about 3,200 (19 percent) boarded flatboats at Ross's Landing in eastern Tennessee and floated to Muscle Shoals. After crowding into railroad cars for a short trip around the rough water, they boarded steamers once more and traveled to Little Rock or beyond. John Ross was one of the few who took this route, as he purchased the *Victoria* with the express purpose of bringing the old, sick, and physically incapacitated Cherokees to Oklahoma. For many of his people who walked the Trail of Tears, the parched conditions turned land removal into a death march.[15]

In contrast, the Seminoles were most likely to be shipped west on steamers, as just over 4,200 (84 percent) went via water, and further research will probably indicate that all of them traveled on riverboats. Their great distance from Indian Territory—and their fierce resistance—made a land journey impractical, if not impossible. While the Second Seminole War raged, the government used steamboats to move troops and supplies to the battle areas and then remove captives from the region. The Seminoles, who tended to travel in smaller numbers than the other Native Americans, were under armed guards for their journey across the Gulf of Mexico to New Orleans. They typically waited in army barracks before transferring to riverboats, and all of them traveled up through Little Rock or beyond once they left the Mississippi River.[16]

The steamers used for Indian Removal varied greatly and ranged in size from the tiny 71-ton *Farmer* to the mammoth 483-ton *Brandywine*, but typically were about 150 tons. Most were rented as is and, except for the removal of small groups of Seminoles, carried only the Native Americans, the soldiers, and the crew. The last-minute nature of army decisions and the reluctance of steamboat captains to abandon their normal trading practices meant that government officials took what was available. While the steamers were not the top of the line, they were not the antiquated wrecks that some critics alleged.

The average age of riverboats used for removal was just over two and a half years, typical for a river system where the average life a steamboat was about five years.[17]

The army expanded the carrying capacity of steamers by towing flatboats and barges. Such vessels normally carried freight, so carpenters modified them by building up to four stone hearths for cooking and heating, erecting temporary partitions to bisect the cargo rooms, and adding large side doors for ventilation. While it was common for steamboats to tow flatboats or barges, it was unknown for whites to travel in them; Choctaws, Creeks, and Cherokees became the equivalent of baggage.[18]

"IN ORDER TO PREVENT DESERTIONS"

Steamboats held great possibilities for making the removal process efficient, relatively humane, and orderly. The most obvious advantage was limiting overland travel, which not only greatly reduced the physical difficulties of slogging forward on wretched roads, but also simplified the logistics of food and shelter. Land travel across Arkansas in the 1830s was a trying experience in good weather and execrable in bad weather. According to one officer, the journey through "a country little settled, and literally impassable to any thing but wild beasts" was bound to prevent migrants from moving forward with any consistency or adequate food. It appears that Native Americans on boats, unlike those on land, did not suffer from lack of food since the riverboats carried sufficient provisions for the entire journey. Native Americans cooked their meals on the stoves within boats during the day or on shore when the boats stopped at dusk. On one such occasion, a steamboat clerk on the *Alpha* watched the women swarm onto the riverbank. They toted bundles containing cooking articles and tents, brandished axes in one hand, and tucked papooses under their other arm. The women chopped trees, made fires, and used sticks to broil meat over the flames. Soon the bank "looked like a little village." Steamboats also shielded Native Americans from the harmful effects of bad weather, particularly during the Choctaw removal. Some Native Americans who traveled on steamers had shelters that blocked the wind, and thus were able to keep round-the-clock fires so as to stay warm. Those who traveled on land had no such advantages.[19]

The army also used steamboats to control Native American behavior. Once the Indians boarded, they were essentially prisoners and the army dictated the pace of removal. There could be no stragglers and no escapes until the boat tied up at night or stopped for wood. Runaways were a significant problem for land marches, as was keeping the Indians moving forward. A veteran of Indian Removal who complained that it was difficult to maintain "regularity" because the Native Americans tended to walk where and when they pleased recommended using steamers as much as possible. Native Americans, though, proved to be resourceful and occasionally escaped during removal by water. After Lieutenant Edward Deas loaded 543 Creeks on flatboats at Gunter's Landing, a terrible storm forced the boats to land. Sixteen Indians bolted, but Deas recaptured all but one of them. Once the group boarded the *Black Hawk* on the other side of Muscle Shoals, Deas took several precautions to prevent escape. At one point the steamer landed on an island in the middle of the Mississippi River "in order to prevent desertions," and he later refused to allow the boat to stop at Memphis lest some Creeks wander off and visit Chickasaw country.[20]

Another defiant behavior that the army addressed with steamers was what one officer politely termed "dissipation." Whiskey dealers sometimes trailed land deportations, and Native Americans were known to become drunk and belligerent. Captains like George Washington Harris, who helped transport Cherokees to Muscle Shoals, typically stopped in areas away from known liquor sellers. Indian agents even prevented Native Americans from leaving the boats if a threat was nearby. Such precautions did not ward off all vice. The 210 Creeks on the *Nome* were able to procure alcohol when a flatboat moored alongside the steamer one night. Indian agents destroyed the contraband once they discovered the situation. Likewise, when a group of Cherokees stopped for the evening near Gunter's Landing, the army forced the Native Americans to set up camp on an island thirty yards from shore. The water was a paltry barrier. Several determined Cherokees made it to town, drank whiskey, and started fighting locals. One Indian barely avoided an axe blow to the head before the military intervened to restore order. For the most part, though, the army used steamboats to keep Native Americans away from alcohol. Officers adopted the attitude that riverboats could elevate Native American character through the denial of potential temptations.[21]

"A STATE UNFIT FOR HUMAN BEINGS"

Steamboats, though, did not live up to their promise during the removal process primarily because army officers seemed to have a casualness toward protecting the Indians' health and welfare. Native Americans languished for weeks or months in refugee camps near Memphis, Vicksburg, Mobile, and Little Rock while hapless officers secured steamboats or waited for rivers to rise. Had the Indians been traveling overland, they would have continued their journey; the camps essentially negated one of riverboats' greatest advantages: speed. Bored, frustrated, and angry Indians sometimes lashed out at local residents. Whiskey sellers clustered around the camps, contributing to widespread drunkenness. Poor shelter against the elements and abysmal sanitation not only increased misery but endangered health. Half-naked children in rags squatted around fires while their mothers tried to stitch raggedy clothing together. Memphis, with its population of only 663 in 1830, was flooded by waves of Native Americans. Alexis de Tocqueville passed through the town during his American sojourn and saw Choctaws encamped near the Mississippi River. It was December 1831 and a bitterly cold winter caused snow to linger on the ground and huge ice chunks to bob in the river. The Choctaws had almost no protection against the Siberian conditions. The scene was so pitiful, de Tocqueville wrote, that "never will that solemn spectacle fade from my remembrance." Six years later, more than three thousand Chickasaws gathered at Memphis during their deportation. Instead of facing harsh weather, they incurred the wrath of local residents who grew angry at the "troublesome visitors."[22]

The Creeks near Mobile inhabited arguably the worst refugee camp. While about seven hundred men served as warriors and guides during the Second Seminole War, the army brought at least three thousand of their kin and tribal members to Fort Morgan, Alabama, on Mobile Point in March 1837. Unusual circumstances prevented the army from moving the Creeks in a timely fashion. The massive movement of Indians along the White River had stripped that area clean of provisions and the waters of the Arkansas River were too low for steamboats. As they waited, the camp's public health degenerated into a "deplorable" state. At least 117 Creeks died between March and mid-July, and there was no hope that conditions would improve. Finally, by the end of July 1837 the army moved the Creeks to a new refugee camp at Pass Christian, Mississippi. Their health improved at the sprawling three-mile-long camp because of better sanitation facilities and in spite of the army's physicians. One doctor dismissively blamed the Indians' mortality on "an excess of provisions." In concluding they "eat too much," he lamely explained away the army's negligence. By September the Creek warriors in Florida were reunited with their kin, the Arkansas River had risen, and the whole encampment was made ready to leave for the Indian Territory. It was part of this group that boarded the *Monmouth*.[23]

Removal on the water also rubbed against Native Americans' connection with the land. The Indians enjoyed outdoor activity, particularly hunting, and such exertions were important touchstones for the community. As one frustrated army officer phrased it, his charges preferred to "hunt and loiter" rather than march westward. Although the practice was in decline by the 1820s, Choctaw men used prowess in hunting as a demonstration of their ability to tap into spiritual power. Ball playing, usually in the form of a game like lacrosse, was another important way for males to display their masculinity. Being cooped up in steamboats disrupted the ability of Native Americans to continue physical activity of all types, as many officers understood. Edward Deas, when he accompanied a party of Creeks on a steamer, noted that the boat made lengthy stops so the Indians could "exercise, the want of which to people of there [*sic*] habits is the greatest objection to transporting them by water." What Deas did not understand is that removal on steamboats virtually eliminated the pleasure associated with being on the land. A few stops to "exercise" were hardly a substitute for a physically active way of life, just as the arid earth of Oklahoma was an unequal trade for land east of the Mississippi River.[24]

A more serious—and visible—problem was overcrowding. The 98-ton *Reindeer,* 118-ton *Cleopatra,* and 136-ton *Talma,* for instance, left Vicksburg in 1831 with at least five hundred Choctaws on each vessel. The boats were too small to accommodate the Native Americans, as four army doctors pointed out. The physicians, who were involved in the Creek Removal, thought a 150-ton vessel that carried more than 375 passengers endangered the health of all on board. Such overcrowding was distressingly common for removal by water. White migrants on steamers, particularly those new to America, could also be packed tightly on the main deck of steamers, of course. The three hundred deck passengers on the *Indiana,* for instance, "had not room scarcely to sit down," but evidence indicates that whites did not suffer from the same magnitude of overcrowding found in Indian Removal. Pre–Civil War riverboats on the Mississippi River in the 1830s averaged 310 tons and typically carried a total of 250 passengers. Steamboats used in Indian Removal averaged 188 tons and carried an average of 494 passengers. Even considering the use of towed flatboats and keelboats, Native Americans were packed more tightly than whites, suggesting a disregard for their basic dignity, health, and safety.[25]

The Creeks suffered the most from overcrowding, probably because the government surrendered control of the removal to the Alabama Emigrating Company. Once the government agreed to a flat fee, it eliminated any incentives to preserve the Creeks' welfare since the company could cut costs by renting fewer boats and cramming together as many Indians as possible. While the Chickasaw, Choctaw, and Cherokee removals typically saw three hundred to five hundred Native Americans per boat, steamboats carrying Creeks might have one thousand or more passengers spread between the one steamer and the barges it towed. For instance, twelve hundred Creeks filed onto the 232-ton *Farmer* on October 13, 1836, and fifteen hundred more Creeks boarded the 156-ton *John Nelson* and its pair of flatboats two weeks later. Overcrowding became so closely associated with Creek removal that it prompted protests in the press and army. A report from the *New Orleans True American* described how the "avaricious disposition to increase profits" led to overloading. Basic considerations for "safety, comfort, or even decency" were ignored as "the poor creatures [were kept] in a state unfit for human beings." Army doctor J. M. Woodfin echoed this sentiment when he called for a standard of "seven superficial square feet to every Indian." Sufficient space was "absolutely necessary" to protect the Native Americans' health. Such guidelines were ignored more often than not, and overcrowding made removal by water for the Creeks a variation of the middle passage, where an ethnic minority was jammed together during a forced deportation.[26]

Overcrowding caused a cascade of problems that often made removal by water a hellish journey. Sanitation was a significant issue, particularly since accommodations for human waste were minimal and probably entailed privies and the use of the river as a sewer system. An army officer who criticized his government for forcing nearly naked Choctaws to march barefoot in the snow described his concerns about one boat's sanitation. The "disgusting sight" of people "leaving their evacuations in every direction through the whole range of the cabins and decks" was burned into his memory. Another officer only commented that keelboats had the "necessary fixtures" to "preserve cleanliness and pure air in the interior of the Boats." While he claimed that the "Boats are cleaned out every night after stopping," daily purification was the exception rather than the rule.[27]

Inadequate sanitation, of course, fueled the transmission of disease and was a problem not only on steamboats but most everywhere in nineteenth-century America. The close quarters and lack of proper hygiene made all riverboats particularly susceptible to outbreaks, but the overcrowded conditions on steamers were a drastic change for Native Americans that probably rendered them more susceptible to contamination than whites. Doctor C. Lillybridge, a New York physician, shivered alongside a group of Cherokees as they traveled to Little Rock. Sickness ravaged the group. One Indian named Henry Clay coughed uncontrollably. Young Squirrel's daughter had a headache and fever. Stand Watie (apparently the same individual who later fought for the Confederacy) was barely alive. James Williams had an inflamed spleen. The group landed at Tuscumbia, Alabama, where rain poured down all night as they waited for a steamboat to arrive. Lillybridge saw an increase in colds, influenza, and coughs in the ensuing days. The army, of course, was not responsible for controlling the weather, but it was liable for creating conditions that would preserve the health of the Native Americans. On this score, it was deficient.[28]

Cholera was the worst destroyer of Native American lives during removal by water. The second Choctaw Removal of 1832 occurred during a worldwide pandemic where the deadly bacteria raced across the United States and claimed the lives of untold numbers of Americans. Contracted by ingesting contaminated water or food, cholera causes severe vomiting and massive diarrhea that leads to dehydration. The mysterious disease was so prevalent along the inland river system that wood sellers abandoned their yards, creating an eerie spectacle for riverboats moving along the rivers. So many people died on steamers, one officer learned, that boats seldom stopped "without burying some person." Even before the Choctaws reached the Mississippi River, cholera ravaged them in the close quarters of the refugee camps in Memphis and Vicksburg. Overcrowding, poor sanitation, and lack of a varied diet combined to create a situation where the six hundred Choctaws waiting for a steamer at Vicksburg had about fifty cases of cholera a day. The disease snuffed out so many lives that a number of Choctaws refused to board a steamer and insisted on a land trip. The army took virtually no steps to minimize the disease's effects on Native Americans. Using steamboats to remove Native Americans was an obvious way to intensify the epidemic, but apparently no thought was given to delaying the removal until the scourge had passed.[29]

Another problem associated with removal on steamboats was burial rites, and here the army was oblivious or indifferent to cherished Native Americans beliefs. Creeks, for instance, typically interred their loved ones under the earthen floor of their houses. They included a number of important goods, a knife perhaps, to protect the dead in the spiritual realm. When a Chickasaw lost a husband or wife, the surviving spouse wept over the grave twice a day for a month, while the Choctaws also engaged in elaborate rites. The hurried pace of removal by water often prevented such important rituals and only served to underscore white disdain for traditional Indian practices, and the Creeks, at least, sensed it. A number of them refused to board a steamer in Memphis in 1836 not only because of the boat's unsanitary conditions but because they feared "being thrown overboard when dead." Even when the removal process slowed to allow a land burial, such occasions hardly reflected sensitivity to Indian funerary practices. One Creek child who died on the *Black Hawk* was unceremoniously "buried in the afternoon at the wood landing" before the boat hurried forward. While some army officers realized that granting the normal funeral rites for each Indian was too time consuming, others did not comprehend the importance of funeral customs for Native Americans. When a number of Creeks were entombing their loved ones during the transfer from Mobile to Pass Christian, a huge storm blew in and pelted them for two days. Soldiers tried to persuade the Indians to take shelter from the rain, but they refused, "saying it would spoil their physic." The officers could not fathom why the Creeks were getting soaked, while the Creeks could not understand why they could not inter their loved ones in peace.[30]

"WRONGED AND MISERABLE SAVAGES"

Not only did steamboats change the ways in which removal occurred, they revealed prevailing white racial attitudes. Indians clustered on riverboats or huddled together in refugee camps were a type of curiosity or amusement for whites. Like visitors to a zoo, spectators paid money to catch a glimpse of the Creeks before their banishment to Oklahoma. Steamboats "constantly" left Mobile with tourists "in order to visit the point and give the 'pale faces' an opportunity of witnessing the ball plays and war dances etc. of the captives," wrote one visitor to the area. White guests in a new hotel near the camp strolled past and bet on the Indian games. Whites could also be disdainful of the Native Americans, especially as they compared the Indians to the standards of American culture. The presence of four hundred Seminoles packed in a barge annoyed one steamboat passenger. He disparagingly described the women as being "as hideous as any hags that could be imagined." This contempt for Native American beauty was similar to another white passenger's disdain. James Moore commented on the Indians' lack of sophistication and foolishness when they tried to mimic white society. He found it both amusing and sad that a group of Creek Indians traveling on a barge played cards "and swore profusely in English." Contempt for Native Americans sometimes shaded into naked hostility. Crews of riverboats seem to have been especially malicious toward the Indians. It was enough of a problem that army officers or Indian agents sometimes insisted on remaining on steamers during removal. A. M. M. Upshaw defended what seemed to be a bloated payroll by explaining to his superior that he was "confident that the Indians might suffer if they did not have an Agent along." In a very real sense, whites could achieve a sense of self-identity by asserting their cultural superiority over the Native Americans. Part of this perception stemmed from an assumption that only an advanced civilization could produce something as wondrous as a steamboat.[31]

Curiosity about Indian captives dated back to European colonization of the western hemisphere, but George Catlin popularized public displays of Indians in the 1830s. Catlin tapped into a desire to see an exotic culture, perhaps before it disappeared. The popularity of Indians on display continued late into the century and reached its apotheosis in Buffalo Bill Cody's Wild West Show. Such shows had multiple meanings, but conveyed the message of racial triumph and were a way to display an enemy who had been tamed. Even the Javanese Village at the 1893 Columbian Exposition mirrored the pageantry of the wild west shows. Such late-century displays of racial arrogance were descended from the same tree that produced the desire to see Native Americans before they were banished to the West.[32]

Even though such distressing racial attitudes were common in the nineteenth-century United States, most Americans never completely abandoned the idea that Indians were humans who should be accorded as least a minimal level of decent treatment. Southern whites created a counter-narrative that ignored most of the obvious problems associated with removal on riverboats. Newspaper accounts of the removal process consistently reported that Native Americans were satisfied with their kind treatment, despite abundant evidence to the contrary. Many of the Chickasaws who were herded to Memphis in late 1837 were almost eager to board the "commodious" steamboats, if one report of the *Memphis Enquirer* is to be believed. The paper noted how the army graciously attended to the Indians' desires during the well-organized emigration. Likewise, a Little Rock paper reported that a party of Choctaw Indians supposedly expressed "much satisfaction with the arrangements which have been made for their comfort." Such self-congratulation was not limited to the media, as army officers frequently commented on the humane nature of the removal process. An officer for the Creek removal remarked that the "Indians . . . appear to be well satisfied in all respects," while another soldier discussed how "comfortably accommodated" his charges were. Officers certainly had a vested interest in presenting the best possible interpretation of removal, but this self-assurance also became an opportunity for white Americans to soften the edges of an inexcusable process. Although white racism provided the most powerful justification for Indian Removal, many people still needed reassurance that Indian Removal was not *too* exploitative. If removal could be presented and perceived as relatively humane, then lip service could be paid to the basic dignity of the Native Americans. As the *Memphis Enquirer* argued, even though the "wronged and miserable savages" were "cheated out of their lands," the "officers who accompany them are humane and kind, and hesitate not in commiserating their unfortunate wrongs." Steamboats, since they were a supposedly superior form of transportation that mitigated suffering, became crucial for whitewashing removal and mediating the tensions between Native American humanity and their cruel treatment.[33]

The ease with which steamboats moved passengers, freight, and produce perhaps allowed white Americans to entertain a plan as audacious as Indian Removal. Whether or not such thinking entered into the minds of those who re-imagined a South without Native Americans, steamboats became the preferred means to carry out the removal process. Riverboats were, in short, a tool to help reorder the South's ethnic landscape. In a country where steamers were considered to be a hallmark of superior civilization, technology held out the promise of quickly and easily achieving racial separation in Jacksonian America and affirming white identity; they symbolized the tremendous gulf in cultural assumptions between whites and Native Americans. But such ideals never fulfilled their promise. Steamboats magnified the poor decision making and callous neglect that were the sinews of Indian Removal. The result was a ghastly process where Native Americans were not just treated as an inferior race but were hauled around like baggage, with little regard for preserving their cultural identity. In a variation of manifest destiny, the federal government used steamboats to bring order to the geographic and racial dimensions of antebellum America. Some of the difficulties associated with removing Native Americans on riverboats, namely explosions and the spread of disease, made river travel dangerous for whites as well. Speed, as will be seen in the next chapter, made steamboats both exciting for the benefits they brought and frightening for the dangers they created.[34]

This painting depicts well the various levels, activities, and people associated with steamboats of the lower Mississippi River. On the *Gipsy*, roustabouts roll barrels off the guards while well-dressed cabin passengers loll on the boiler deck. Above them can be seen the texas deck and the pilothouse. Deck passengers crowd the *Grand Turk* and cabin passengers wave from the hurricane deck. The furnace is visible on the boat behind the *Gipsy*, and an African American man carries baggage onto the vessel. The levee is a picture of commerce, from men making business deals, to vendors selling fruit, to draymen moving freight.

Giant Steamboats at New Orleans, by Hippolyte Sebron, 1853, oil on canvas, 48 x 72 in., Newcomb Art Gallery, Tulane University, Gift of D. H. Holmes Company, New Orleans. Photo by Owen Murphy.

Early western steamboats like the *General Washington* were small crafts that combined elements of keelboats, flatboats, and sailing vessels. Although the *General Washington* had a paddle wheel, engine, and smokestacks, it also possessed a bowsprit. Other contemporary boats employed sails to augment their steam engines.

From the Collection of the Public Library of Cincinnati and Hamilton County.

Built in 1848, the *Grand Turk* shows the evolution of steamboat design. Like most riverboats in the southern interior, the wide guards of the main deck were ideal for stacking cargo and wood, while the high chimneys allowed more opportunities for sparks to burn out and enclosures protected the paddle wheels from river obstructions. The second, or boiler, deck housed the main cabin and private staterooms, while the hurricane deck was one level higher. This particular boat did not have a texas deck, so the pilothouse sat on the hurricane deck.

From the Collection of the Public Library of Cincinnati and Hamilton County.

In this undated drawing, cabin passengers watch as slaves and roustabouts load cotton bales on a steamboat. The roustabout standing on the cotton bales on the steamer's deck has a cotton hook in his left hand. Such stops might take as long as four hours.

Courtesy W. S. Hoole Special Collections Library, University of Alabama.

As this photo of the ladies' cabin in the *Planter* demonstrates, Victorian propriety governed behavior and accommodations in the ladies' cabins on western steamboats. Only women, their husbands, and children were to stay there, while single men could be invited to socialize for limited time periods. The chief amusements were reading, writing, social conversation, and card games like whist and bridge.

From the Collection of the Public Library of Cincinnati and Hamilton County.

Steamboats with a reputation for speed typically earned more business than their slower rivals, so captains of boats in the Southwest used a variety of methods to attract attention. Impromptu races were common, as was the tendency to start fast from a port. Both practices courted disaster because of imperfect boilers and inadequate knowledge of physics. The explosion of the *Moselle* in 1838 galvanized public opinion for federal regulation of steamboats. The resulting legislation, which proved to be ineffective, was the first federal effort to regulate a transportation industry.

From the Collection of the Public Library of Cincinnati and Hamilton County.

River obstacles like snagged trees inhibited steamboat traffic on the rivers of the southern interior. Once Henry Shreve invented a snagboat to tear out snags or snap them off, river travel became safer and more economical. As superintendent of the western rivers, Shreve directed efforts to tear up snags, remove sandbars, build wing dams, blast away underwater boulders, remove riverside trees, and dig cutoffs to straighten the rivers. Probably more than any other individual, Henry Shreve changed the environment of the interior South.

From the Collection of the Public Library of Cincinnati and Hamilton County.

Steamboats of the southern interior became a crucial link in the chain that connected cotton producers to their customers in the North and Europe. Cotton planters along the rivers of Alabama built long chutes so that their slaves could slide the bales downhill to a waiting steamboat. Roustabouts and deckhands might spend several hours loading cotton from one plantation. Captains often bought firewood during such stops.

Courtesy Alabama Department of Archives and History, Montgomery, Alabama.

Some steamboats, known as cotton boats, specialized in hauling cotton bales from plantations to cities like New Orleans or Mobile. This photograph shows the *Era No. 2* hauling several thousand cotton bales from the Red River region to New Orleans. Steamboats commonly carried so much cotton during plucking season that the bales prevented sunshine from reaching the cabins and forced passengers to burn lamps night and day. Setting new records for hauling cotton was also a point of pride for steamboat captains.

From the Collection of the Public Library of Cincinnati and Hamilton County.

Steamboats fueled urban growth, as evidenced by this 1859 photograph of the New Orleans levee. During the peak times of the 1850s, a hundred or more steamers might be lined up in the Crescent City. Not only did riverboats enhance the businesses of grocers, draymen, and tavern keepers, they created new forms of commerce, like wood sales, boat construction, and boat resupply. In 1860, steamboats created an estimated $18 million worth of business in the Southwest.

From the Collection of the Public Library of Cincinnati and Hamilton County.

FIVE

SPEED AND SAFETY

he *Moselle* immediately earned a reputation as a fast boat. During its first month in service, it established two new speed records, including a sparkling run from St. Louis to Cincinnati in two days and sixteen hours. In keeping with its fame, on April 25, 1838, the *Moselle* shot out of the Cincinnati wharf and darted upstream a half mile to a timber raft, where it picked up two families of German emigrants. The new passengers, unfamiliar with American riverboats, took twenty minutes to amble aboard the steamer, now teeming with 280 passengers. By necessity, the paddle wheels remained idle while the last of the Germans found their accommodations. But quiet paddle wheels meant that no fresh water was pumped into the boat. The chief engineer, always conscious of making sure the *Moselle* started with jaw-dropping speed, kept the steam pressure high. While this extra burst of pressure was good for show, it was extremely hazardous because the sudden influx of steam that sprayed against the hot boiler walls when the wheels started again needed an outlet, and too often it was a crack in the boiler, a weak spot, or a seam rather than a safety valve. When the engineer re-engaged the paddle wheels, it was the last decision he ever made.[1]

The *Moselle*'s side paddle wheels turned twice before an explosion that sounded like "a mine of gunpowder" tore the boat to shreds. All four boilers burst simultaneously and rocketed skyward in a ball of steam, smoke, and splinters. Chunks of flesh, splintered wood, and twisted metal cascaded down in a ruinous quarter-mile circle around the boat's carcass. The chief engineer, who supposedly had made the rounds in Cincinnati's beer halls earlier in the afternoon, was immediately decapitated. The captain's lifeless body was hurled against the prow of another steamer before sliding into the Ohio River. Passengers suffered all manner of gory deaths. One man bled to death on the wharf's cobblestones, a huge splinter shoved into his head from one ear to the other. Another passenger shot one hundred yards into the air and bored a hole through the shingles of a house, his body half in, half out. An emigrant dazedly peeled off his clothes, only to take the skin off with them. He collapsed and died, looking more like a three dimensional anatomy chart than a human being. All told, at least eighty people perished that day and another fifty-five were missing, probably blown to bits. Thirteen more people were badly injured. This deadliest entry in a string of recent steamboat accidents made national headlines.[2]

Reaction to the *Moselle* tragedy was immediate. Steamboats had exploded before, of course, but this particular accident was not only especially gruesome but could have been prevented. The city of Cincinnati created a committee to study the matter. Once word filtered out that the engineer may have been drunk and the steamer may have been racing, there was outrage. One correspondent in the *Southern Literary Messenger,* confusing the sad ending of the captain with the engineer, said he would have "execrated" the captain's memory except that his "head was blown off his shoulders by the first column of steam from the exploding boiler." George Carvill wrote to his sister in London that the *Moselle* disaster was particularly scary because it was a new boat and was the fifth accident in three months. Even though the United States was "proverbial for Steam Boat explosions," he was concerned that too many pleasure trips turned into death excursions. There was enough concern to prod the federal government into action, and soon after the *Moselle*'s victims were laid to rest Congress passed a law to regulate steamboats, the first such American legislation of a transportation industry.[3]

The *Moselle* explosion illustrates the paradoxes and tensions inherent within the shift to a new technology. Steamboats promised to improve society, and their speed became a marker of humankind's ability to harness natural elements in the service of progress. Captains staked their reputations on their boats' ability to outrun a rival and races became a measure of success and reputation. The greatest steamboat races took place in the Southwest, mainly because of geographic constraints. But the emphasis on speed had a distressing byproduct: explosions. Southerners, and Americans more generally, had to choose whether they valued speed and convenience over safety. In most cases, they valued the former and found ways to cope with the latter. Riverboats also carried on another type of murderous work: spreading cholera and yellow fever through the South. Between explosions and epidemics, then, riverboats challenged prevailing notions of a good death. Steamers were too important to the fabric of society to ignore, so Americans developed ways to accept, regulate, and explain away their deadly nature.

"OUR BOAT SHOOTS OFF LIKE AN ARROW"

There is no doubt that speed was thrilling to Americans of the early nineteenth century. In a time when a galloping horse was probably the swiftest mode of transportation, riverboats excited the imagination because they were so fast. Indeed, it was to a "race horse" that steamboats were most often compared. While most people expected downstream travel to be rapid, the ability to go upriver at unprecedented speeds was even more exciting. A passenger marveled at how his St. Louis steamboat "shot up the strong current of the Mississippi, and, turning above the town, dashed by the wharves with a velocity frightening to behold, but which seemed peculiarly exhilarating to both crew and passengers." It is no coincidence that a famous consortium of riverboats running between New Orleans and Louisville was called the Lightning Line.[4]

Speed was a tangible measure of humankind's progress. As riverboats conquered natural forces—moving upstream, reshaping the rivers, defying time—they completely altered conceptions of the possible. The proliferation of steamboats meant that people had to reconsider what was a long distance. "A family in Pittsburg[h] consider it a light matter to pay a visit to their relations on the Red River, at the distance of 2000 miles. An invitation to breakfast at a distance of seventy miles, it is no difficulty to comply with," wrote one tourist. When a New Yorker visited New Orleans he sensed this infatuation with convenience born of speed. A merchant on the levee locked his desk and told his employees he was going to Vicksburg, "just as coolly as he informs them of an absence to dinner." Technological achievements led to self-congratulation and self-assurance.[5]

A fascination with speed, convenience, and connectivity increased southern consciousness about time. The first steamboats did not run on regular schedules, and so passengers might or might not have to wait long when transferring to another boat. A visitor to a Memphis tavern was amused at the fuss of southern passengers. Every day "impatient" travelers bustled into the tavern wanting to know when the next steamer departed for New Orleans. The owner usually told them a boat would depart in a few hours, but the vagaries of travel sometimes stretched that figure to five days. It was no wonder that the tavern was "turned into [a] head quarters of discontent." Travelers waiting for a specific boat, often one of the best boats, were the most likely to be frustrated. One woman camped out on her hotel veranda waiting for the *Niagara*. Whenever she heard a whistle, she scooped up her satchel, shawl, book, and gloves and ran down the stairs to the steamboat landing. She was disappointed over fifty times (she claimed), eventually giving up and trudging back to her room "with a racking headache, sad, gloomy, and weary with disappointment."[6]

As captains competed for business they became more attentive to departing at a particular hour, rather than sometime during the day. Packet boats had definite departure times and advertisements trumpeted a boat's punctuality. It is true, as Mark Smith has argued, that southerners adopted clock time, but in the case of steamboats, at least, it was a fitful embrace. Exasperated northern and European travelers frequently learned that the riverboats in Dixie did not run on time. A northerner acidly observed, "It would be entirely inconsistent with the free and independent spirit of the people to be bound down to hours and minutes." Some of these delays were due to faulty technology, but southern steamboat captains manipulated expectations of clock time. Their favorite tactic to drum up business was to pretend to look busy, raise a head of steam, and make it appear as if they were preparing to shove off. The bustle created a buzz and convinced wavering passengers to hurry aboard the boat lest they miss its departure. One veteran traveler advised novices to ignore the smoke, steam, and noise, as they were merely "a pleasant fiction of the Captain's; they are merely firing up, as the finale of advertising stratagems." His boat was supposed to leave at five in the evening, and then the delay was pushed back to nine the next morning, then ten, and the boat finally left in the afternoon.[7]

Whether steamboats were laggard or punctual, their speed brought fame—and business—to their captains. Fast boats made headlines and attracted passengers who believed they would have to spend less time in transit between towns. The *A. L. Shotwell* started racing mainly "with the view of proving her speed and capacity as a matter of business reputation," thought the editor of the *Louisville Daily Democrat*. Discussions of times, speed records, and steamboat races filled the newspaper columns, levees, counting houses, barbershops, and taverns. Word of mouth was often a boat's form of advertisement.[8]

There were several ways a steamboat could establish its reputation for speed, all of which enhanced the probability for calamity. Captains frequently tried to make a dramatic departure from the wharf or dock, as the *Moselle* did on its last run. Steamboats on such "brag trips" raised steam quickly and departed suddenly. "Our boat shoots off like an arrow," wrote an enthusiastic steamboat passenger, "She is the swiftest craft I have ever seen." The rapid departure helped create the perception that a steamboat was fast and worth the price of a ticket.[9]

Steamboat owners also realized that being first at something, usually a product of speed, was an important element in drumming up business because the resulting notoriety would generate debates, arguments, and rumors. When Captain Peyton Key of the *Belle Key,* for instance, arrived in Louisville, he had difficulty attracting freight to his vessel because two other boats bound for New Orleans were already loading. With another southbound boat easing into the levee, Key had a flash of inspiration: he announced that he would steam to New Orleans with no way freight or passengers (meaning he would stop only for wood). Since Key promised to arrive in the Crescent City in less than five days, passengers canceled their other arrangements and flocked to his boat. Key made good on his promise and even passed the other two vessels that left ahead of him, ensuring that he could have the pick of freight when he arrived in New Orleans. Another famous publicity stunt involved the supposed kidnapping of Zachary Taylor. When it became known that the president-elect would travel upriver on a series of steamboats, Captain Thomas C. Coleman Jr. decided to take action. Coleman outraced the *Tennessee,* the official steamboat, to Taylor's plantation and announced that his *Saladin* would carry the president-elect to Vicksburg. When members of Taylor's escort party learned of the shenanigan, one supposedly drew a pistol and accused Coleman of kidnapping the president-elect. Coleman allegedly replied that Taylor was riding on his boat without permission but that he was reluctant to kick out such an important person. When Taylor learned of the prank he laughed it off, suggesting that his perturbed entourage have a drink with the captain and forget about it. People did not forget, and the incident won Coleman much acclaim—and business.[10]

"TAKE US IF YOU CAN"

Racing and holding the speed record between two towns were more noteworthy ways to establish the perception that a boat was fast. Captains were particularly sensitive about their boat's reputation, which merged with their own identity. The quality of a boat might be measured in many different ways, but speed was the most prestigious and tangible. Speed became an obsession, and the boat with the fastest time on the river between two cities "held the horns" until a rival could knock the champion off its pedestal. Somehow antlers became the trophy for the fastest boat, perhaps through the association of a deer being a swift animal or through the ancient connection between horns and prowess. In its pilothouse, the *A. L. Shotwell* proudly displayed a large set of gilded deer horns with pink ribbons suspending a silver plate that warned rivals to "Take us if you can." Such ornaments were a type of traveling trophy and would have to be surrendered if a rival did indeed win a race. Other captains posted markers along the rivers to mark their locations during a contest. The captain of the *Buckeye State* nailed signs where his boat was at the twelve-, twenty-four-, and thirty-six-hour marks during one of its fast runs. Not unlike modern mile markers, these signposts became navigational tools. The three-day marker for the *A. L. Shotwell* became a regular feature on maps of the Mississippi River, illustrating that captains held these achievements in such high regard that they found multiple ways to honor a fast boat. When passengers saw such markers, they were reminded of the tangible and intangible benefits of traveling on a speedy steamer.[11]

The easiest way to hold the horns was to win a race, and most contests were impromptu tests of masculine pride. The captain of the *Franklin,* for instance, started rubbing his neck when he saw the captain of the *Phillips.* When that unsuspecting captain asked what was wrong, his rival sarcastically said he strained it "looking back for you on the last run we made up" to Louisville. The race was on and bets were placed. Most races happened when a boat threatened to pass a rival. These pell-mell sprints took place over short distances, normally to a specific woodyard or town. Captains might lose their heads during the heat of the moment. In 1821 the captain of the *Napoleon* forgot to stop at Donaldsonville, Louisiana, because he was racing the *Post Boy.* Only when the boat reached Natchez did the captain realize he forgot to trade Enoch Pepper's 205 barrels of flour for Antoine Peytavin's sugar. In most cases, though, captains did not forsake business during contests, so racing boats stopped to load or unload both passengers and freight. They also stopped to take on wood, although particularly savvy captains reduced the number of scheduled stops and took wood from flatboats rather than shoreline woodyards. The few premeditated races that occurred between boats attracted coverage in the press and wagers in the saloons. Most of them turned into long-distance stop and go endurance contests that lasted up to four days.

Judging by the amount of money wagered on steamboat races, often as much as $10,000 for well-known boats, they were important cultural events.[12]

Races absorbed the efforts of the crew, excited the passions of the passengers, and attracted the attention of residents along the rivers. The "excitement produced by it [racing] is the most powerful that can be conceived," wrote one electrified participant. Passengers flocked to the boilers and cheered, whistled, shouted, and sometimes chanted to keep up the spirits of the firemen, whose checkered shirts became drenched with perspiration. In a particularly close contest, the deck passengers were known to crowd the front of the boat in the hopes of giving it a competitive advantage by reducing the drag in the water. Roustabouts rolled barrels of oil, turpentine, or tar to the massive furnaces, broke them open, and flung the incendiary material into the roaring inferno. Other passengers rushed to the rails to catch a glimpse of the rival boat, which was sometimes so close that people could have jumped into the other vessel. Steamers were even known to bump one another or become locked together. When one boat pulled alongside its rival, "The cries and noise with us then became indescribable. Captain, officers, crew, servants, passengers, firemen— all were gathered on our guards, insulting by voice and gestures" the people on the other boat. When these shouts were added to the hissing valves, pounding pistons, and thunderous paddle wheels, the whole scene was deafening and the atmosphere intoxicating. Close races gripped the attention of residents along the rivers, and when two closely matched boats sped past it sent a buzz of excitement through towns. People left their work and lined the riverbank to cheer, and perhaps catch a glimpse of an explosion.[13]

Even the boats seemed to come to life during a race. Captains swore that supple boats were faster than tight ones, so they commonly loosened the hog chains during a race. Freed from such restrictions, steamboats throbbed up and down in time to the driving pistons, sometimes as much as two feet according to river legend. Nails popped loose, seams cracked, and wood groaned under the convulsive shockwaves. The huffing boats—"roaring and snorting like angry hippopotami"—only contributed to the carnival atmosphere.[14]

Steamboat racing occurred in all areas of the country, but captains in the Southwest were most willing to risk the lives of their passengers and crew in the pursuit of pride. Geography dictated much of this obsession with speed. The distance between, say, New Orleans and Louisville was so great that holding the horns on that run brought attention from across the country. Even steaming between Natchez and St. Louis was a greater feat than bouncing along the shorter rivers of the east. The frozen rivers of the upper Midwest also prevented year-round racing and inhibited competition.

The 1853 race between the *Eclipse* and the *A. L. Shotwell* demonstrates how steamboat racing was a means to establish a captain's name and a boat's reputation; more than just business or a few bets were at stake when these boats raced. The *J. M. White* held the horns for the New Orleans to Louisville run, and the prestigious honor attracted competitors. When word spread of the impending race between the *Eclipse* and the *A. L. Shotwell*, residents along the Mississippi and Ohio rivers supposedly bet anywhere from $8,000 to $40,000. Speculation on who would win was so intense that Mark Twain later joked the captain of the *Eclipse* "left off his kid gloves and had his head shaved." The boats left New Orleans three days apart and their competition became the all absorbing passion of river residents. Crowds in New Orleans, Natchez, Vicksburg, Memphis, and Louisville cheered, sang songs, threw hats in the air, waved handkerchiefs, and occasionally fired cannons when either of the boats passed. Telegraph lines flashed between cities with news of the boats' times. According to a New Orleans newspaper, the race was "the engrossing topic of conversation in all parts of the city. At breakfast time, dinner table, and tea table, it was the absorbing subject of discourse."[15]

Deciding which boat won the race and who would collect on their bets, however, became a problem because the boats did not leave simultaneously and there was no standard time in the United States. When it arrived in Louisville, the *A. L. Shotwell* claimed it had covered the 1,455 miles in four days, nine hours, and twenty-nine minutes, improbably one minute ahead of its rival. That one minute difference was later stretched to five, but in either case there was no consensus as to who had won the race. The dispute played out in the newspapers, in a contest that pitted personal honor, evidence, and reputation. The owners of the *A. L. Shotwell* argued that an impersonal force, in this case a watch, should decide the winner. It was clear to them that a watch was an impartial recorder that could reconcile the fact that the boats left at different times. The owners of the *Eclipse* argued that technology was not perfectly accurate. The "slower the watch, the faster the boat" was their rebuttal. They accused their rivals of falsifying time—a public lie that could be confirmed by independent witnesses. This public challenge was a search for vindication and a defense of reputation by unmasking a falsehood, or showing the difference between the truth and a public persona.[16]

The *Eclipse*'s owners wanted both sides to nominate referees who could decide the matter. In other words, a man's word was to be valued over an impersonal piece of technology. When the owners of the *A. L. Shotwell* recommended that bettors on their boat should select the referees, the owners of the *Eclipse* exploded in anger. They argued that "honorable men" could plainly see that a "great wrong" had taken place and accused their opponents of wanting to perpetuate a lie. After the owners of the *A. L. Shotwell* refused to submit to an independent arbiter, the captain of the *Eclipse* gathered his own witnesses and published their accounts in the newspapers. The owners of the *A. L. Shotwell* followed suit, and eventually the issue faded away and most bettors agreed that no money should change hands. In an elaborate ceremony in Louisville, the *A. L. Shotwell* received the horns from the captain of the *J. M. White* and held them until the famous race between the *Natchez* and the *Robert E. Lee* in 1870. While we will never know who won the 1853 contest, we can infer that steamboat racing married personal reputation, competition, and a mania for speed into a potent combination that captured the public's imagination.[17]

"THAT SUBTLE AND TERRIBLE AGENT, STEAM"

Racing, although it could cement a boat's reputation for speed and enhance a captain's honor, was one of the most dangerous activities on the river. Hanging weights on the safety valve—universally known as the death hook—and tossing incendiary materials in the furnaces strained boilers to their maximum capacity. Not surprisingly, explosions and fires were closely associated with racing. The early morning accident of the *Ben Sherrod* in 1837 was one of the most notorious. It was steaming upriver about thirty miles north of Natchez when its captain decided to overtake the *Prairie*. In between throwing pine knots into the furnace and soaking the coal with rosin, the firemen took liberal tugs from whiskey jugs. The intense heat ignited nearby cordwood, which caused some whiskey barrels to explode. While flames raced through the boat, the boilers exploded, as did the forty barrels of gunpowder in the hold. What the eight explosions did not destroy, the fire did. Flames torched the tiller ropes, rendering the vessel unable to steer to shore. Passengers, most of them still in their night clothes, wildly ran through the decks looking for some way to escape the inferno. Most of them leaped into the Mississippi's murky water, desperately looking for barrels, casks, doors, splintered beams, or any type of flotsam to which they could cling. The death toll was unclear because the ship's register burned up, but at least 170 people perished that night.[18]

Even if steamboats on southern waters did not race, they were hazardous. Western steamboats were four times as likely to explode as their eastern counterparts, and their detonations also were much more deadly. Western boats were not only larger and carried more passengers, but they were equipped with high-pressure engines, which were necessary to overcome the strong currents of the Mississippi River. High-pressure engines blew up with more force than the low-pressure engines found in the East. With most of the western riverboats prowling the waters of slave states, steamboat explosions, while a national issue, had special resonance in the Southwest. And conditions on southern rivers, including muddy water pumped into boilers, frequent stops at plantations, and difficulties in overcoming the swift currents, created special difficulties for southern riverboats and added danger to steamboat travel. In retrospect it is clear that boilers were most often to blame for explosions. They had no pressure gauges, so engineers had to guess as to when the steam was too hot. The paddle wheels also pumped water into the boilers, and so when they were idle water levels could become dangerously low. Should the steamer raise steam too fast upon departure, cold water pumped against the red-hot boiler walls could cause them to burst. Many boilers were also cast imperfectly, having cracks or weak spots. When steam pressure became particularly acute, as during a race for instance, the walls might not be able to withstand the stress. Steamboats also had atrocious safety practices, from wood stacked too close to the furnaces to carrying kegs of gunpowder.[19]

Even though explosions were less numerous than other types of accidents, their calamitous results proved irresistible to editors trying to sell newspapers. Explosions made for good copy, and the more lurid the details, the more pain and suffering, the better. Press coverage of the 1849 explosion of the *Louisiana* at the New Orleans wharf was reprinted in countless newspapers and periodicals because it described the destruction to human bodies in a sensational way. While an unnamed New Orleans newspaper story regretted that it would be "utterly impossible to describe all the revolting sights which met our view," it certainly tried. A long and detailed story shocked and attracted readers with the following catalog of horrors: blood curdling screams; legs, arms, and trunks scattered on the levee; a beheaded man whose entrails were oozing onto the cobblestones; a "shockingly mangled" woman who was missing one leg; and a large man whose skull was crushed so badly it looked like someone painted his face red. Such accounts became so widely read that people could almost imagine themselves part of an accident. When an English geologist recounted the *Helen McGregor*'s explosion, one would almost think he was aboard. Simon Ferrall wrote that "the dead were shattered to pieces, covering the decks with blood; and the dying suffered the most excruciating tortures, being scalded from head to foot. Many died within the hour; whilst others lingered until evening, shrieking in the most piteous manner." He took his description from newspaper accounts.[20]

Newspapers were not the only ones to cash in on the misfortune of others. James T. Lloyd published his immensely popular *Lloyd's Steamboat Directory and Disasters on the Western Waters,* a compendium of misery and woe complete with over twenty woodcuts of steamers in various stages of fragmentation. In his foreword, Lloyd even apologized for charging two dollars rather than one for his volume, noting that it was the "laborious research" and not the titillating subject matter that dictated the increased cost. The "laborious research" involved collecting newspaper stories and publishing them verbatim with no attribution as to their sources.[21]

Judging from letters and newspaper stories, another part of the fascination with disaster stories was the power of the detonation itself. A large measure of riverboats' appeal came from their ability to harness one natural force to overcome another. But explosions demonstrated that humans could never completely control the mysteries of steam. Powerful consequences resulted when steamboats were shattered "to atoms." Written accounts consistently described the immense ability of explosions to defy physics and gravity. Bennett Barrow of Louisiana wrote in his diary that the explosion of the *Clipper* in 1843 tossed "some persons nearly a mile [and] others threw walls &c. one man threw Bakers hotel wall." Not only did the explosion of the *Red Stone* shoot bodies four hundred yards into a plowed field, but its boiler cut down a tree. Huge chunks of metal hurtling hundreds of yards and cutting swaths of destruction were staples of steamboat destruction stories. This ability of steamers to completely defy the natural laws was morbidly attractive. There was a certain amount of respect that such powerful forces could be harnessed on a daily basis mingled with the fear that such forces might suddenly slip out of control. The "explosive force of that subtle and terrible agent, steam," proved to be an irresistible lure.[22]

Salacious newspaper stories stoked public fears about riverboat travel and contributed to the "bias of the spectacular," that is, a tendency to focus on the heart-wrenching accidents while forgetting about the thousands of mundane trips. Travel on western riverboats, while it became safer over time because of improved technology and government regulation, was still a risky proposition by modern standards. Approximately 1 percent of all western steamboat round trips between 1811 and 1851 ended with some type of accident—a collision, fire, snagging, or explosion. Even worse, from 1816 to 1848, 185 western riverboat explosions claimed the lives of 1,433 people. During those same years, an estimated 9.3 million passengers traveled on western boats, resulting in a fatality rate of 155 deaths per million passengers. By way of comparison, the fatality rate per 1 million passengers for U.S. airlines from 1990 to 2009 was 0.12. By one measure, at least, riding an antebellum western steamboat was over a thousand times riskier than boarding a modern airliner—and if deaths from collisions, fires, and snaggings were included, the fatality rate for riverboats would be even higher. Even if steamboat travel was a dangerous endeavor, it was probably safer than traveling on an antebellum train. Comparative figures are difficult to ascertain, but one widely published report noted that from 1853 through 1859, 903 railroad accidents killed 1,109 people. Potential passengers had good reason to be wary about traveling on antebellum railroads or steamboats.[23]

"CHIEFLY THROUGH THE AGENCY OF STEAMBOATS"

Besides catching fire and exploding, steamboats threatened public safety in other ways. Collisions were numerous enough to warrant concern and attention. Most such accidents happened at night, particularly because early riverboats did not have warning lights and there were no clear rules for right-of-way in shipping channels. Most collisions were minor matters, as when the *Vicksburg* sideswiped the *Pennsylvania*. A young Samuel Clemens testified that timbers crashed and decks swayed while the two boats rubbed against one another. Occasionally collisions were severe enough to cause fatalities, particularly because, as was the case for the *Louisiana* and the *Belle of Clarksville*, "all the passengers were in their berths asleep" at three in the morning. According to one passenger who escaped by swimming, the accident sheared off the upper decks from the *Belle of Clarksville*, killing about forty people, most of whom were trapped in their staterooms.[24]

Steamboats also imperiled the public health by hastening the spread of dangerous contagious diseases, such as cholera and yellow fever. Cholera arrived in the United States in 1832 as part of a worldwide pandemic and again in 1848. The mysterious disease reached Cincinnati in late 1832, and a cook employed on a packet between that city and Louisville brought the scourge to the South. From Kentucky, it spread along the western waters to the major towns of the interior South, reaching the capital of Arkansas on the *Little Rock* in May of 1833. Even though southerners did not understand cholera's causes, they associated it with steamboats. "Scarcely a boat on the river is free from the disease," reported one paper. Although relatively safe on her Louisiana plantation, Rachel O'Connor told her brother that "the cholera has commenced again. Reports say that it is raging in New Orleans and on each side of the Mississippi all along the coast, and of course on board the steam Boats." A Natchez resident echoed O'Connor's suspicion about steamboats being incubators of the disease when he reported, "We have some cases of cholera on the *Boats*[,] indeed every Boat that goes up [river] loses some of her passengers." Despite these alarms, southerners do not seem to have avoided riverboat travel in great numbers. Extant newspapers show that steamers were the primary source of information about the disease's spread, and people fled from epidemic centers on riverboats.[25]

If cholera was a national problem, then yellow fever became a sectional one. While the 1793 epidemic in Philadelphia is perhaps most closely associated with the disease, the 1853 yellow fever outbreak was the deadliest in the years before the Civil War. Approximately ten thousand people perished from the disease that year in New Orleans alone. The disease, of course, is spread by female *Aedes aegypti* mosquitoes that carry the virus from human to human, like malevolent flying dirty needles. In areas where frost does not kill off mosquitoes in the winter, yellow fever can be a year-round problem.[26]

Yellow fever also became linked to steamboats in the public mind. After the 1839 epidemic, Dr. John W. Monette concluded that the black vomit (so-named because yellow fever victims hemorrhage internally and throw up dark blood) spread through the South "chiefly through the agency of steamboats." Writing in the *Western Journal of Medicine and Surgery,* Monette theorized that the boats carried bad air that then infected people as they rushed aboard. Just as in the case of the cholera epidemics, there appears to have been no concerted effort to limit or stop steamboat traffic. River commerce was too fundamental to the southern political economy to bring it to a halt.[27]

"MY VERY SOUL MELTS WITHIN ME"

The disturbing tendency of boats to blow up, catch fire, collide, or spread disease threatened to undo public faith in the efficacies of steamboat technology and raised concerns about the negative consequences of speed and convenience. Steamboats could be particularly alarming because they posed such a public and emotional threat to nineteenth-century American notions about a good death. At least for the middle class, dying became an art where people had to prepare for their hour of death and willingly give up their souls when the time came. Sudden or calamitous death, particularly one away from family members, represented a profound challenge to these assumptions. As one southerner commented after a friend died on the *Henry Clay,* "death though awful in any shape, seems doubly so when sent in such a sudden and terrible form."[28]

The publicity surrounding steamboat accidents hints that southerners, like other Americans, struggled to reconcile the unpredictable nature of riverboats with the benefits they bestowed. At least in peacetime, steamboat accidents were the sites where people sorted out their feelings about sudden, calamitous death on a large scale. Newspaper accounts praised citizens who helped in times of need and damned those who exhibited less noble tendencies. After the *Woodsman* exploded, the *New Orleans Picayune* complimented the citizens of Bayou Sara, Louisiana, for "the attentions they gave to alleviate the pain of the suffering and dying." The desire for people not to perish alone and for their bodies to be identified and buried dominate accounts of deaths associated with steamboats. The public display of bodies, as when victims from the *Pennsylvania* explosion were laid out in coffins in front of Memphis's Rainbow Hotel, caused observers to weep. After the *Louisiana* exploded in New Orleans, "the numerous unknown, unclaimed bodies were laid out on the levee, for their friends or relatives to identify and remove." In these very public places, relatives worked through their private struggles with death.[29]

Relatives went to great lengths to provide a good death for their loved ones, to undo some of the psychological damage that came from death in a steamboat accident. When the four boilers of the *Pennsylvania* exploded south of Memphis and killed perhaps one hundred people, Samuel Clemens rushed to the scene. Clemens might have been one of the victims had it not been for a dispute with his mentor pilot, William Brown. Although Clemens remained in New Orleans when the big steamer paddled upriver, his younger brother Henry was aboard as a mud clerk, a position of promise rather than profit. Henry owed his place on the boat to his older brother, a fact not lost on the man who would make his living writing as Mark Twain. When the elder Clemens arrived in Memphis on the steamer *A. T. Lacy,* he learned that Henry lay in the Memphis Exchange. With mattresses flung hastily on the floor and the smell of linseed oil lingering in the air, the Exchange was converted into a temporary hospital for the survivors of the *Pennsylvania* explosion. Henry had been blown into the air while asleep, landed on a boiler, and then been crushed beneath falling debris. He managed to crawl into the water, where woodhawks and deckhands on the *Kate Frisbee* were fishing out survivors. Samuel Clemens remained at his brother's bedside for the next five days, praying "as never man prayed before" that Henry would live. When Henry finally slipped away after a week of suffering, Samuel sent a terse telegram to a relative in St. Louis, "Henry Died this morning leave tomorrow with the Corpse." Samuel Clemens did what he could to provide his brother with a portion of the good death.[30]

Clemens was not unique in trying to honor family members who became victims of steamboat accidents. When Walter Nicol put his family aboard the *Piney Woods,* he did not suspect that it would be the last time he would see them alive. Upon learning that his wife, two children, sister, two sisters-in-law, brother-in-law, and two family slaves perished after the steamboat burned, he wrote, "my very soul melts within me." Nicol and his father-in-law rented a schooner and plunged time after time into the inky depths, searching for the bodies. Performing love's last heartbreaking errand for a week, they hauled out thirteen corpses but failed to find Nicol's wife, Jane. That Nicol ended his prolific diary with "what a sad, sudden, and awful change" suggests that he struggled to make sense of his wife's terrible death.[31]

"MAKES LITTLE DIFFERENCE TO AMERICANS PROVIDED THEY CAN GO FAST"

The specter of sudden death or dismemberment—that they would be denied a good death—caused some southerners to fear river travel and expect the worst when a loved one boarded a riverboat. W. F. Weeks put it succinctly in writing to his friend: "accidents to steamboats are so common now that ones safe arrival is a matter of congratulations." Fear of their own demise or the death of others forced a few southerners to forsake riverboat travel altogether. After one accident, a potential riverboat traveler concluded that it was "most prudent to take our chances at home." Rachel O'Connor of Louisiana was so rattled by recent steamboat explosions that she made five of her slaves walk home from her brother's plantation rather than ride a riverboat.[32]

Such people were in the decided minority, and it might be surprising that the rate, deadliness, or publicity of accidents had no apparent effect on the number or volume of passengers on southern steamers. Even as some people wrung their hands over steamboat calamities, their neighbors were crossing the gangplank for another voyage. After a riverboat accident that claimed eighty lives, a correspondent thought the event was "somewhat discouraging to travelling on our Rivers." In the next sentence, though, he mentioned that acquaintances who were visiting would return to Kentucky in steamboats. Outside observers attributed the curious mingling of concern and nonchalance to a general acceptance of risk. A Frenchman who accompanied Napoleon III to America in 1836 noted that the threat of an exploding riverboat "makes little difference to Americans provided they can go fast." The English geologist George Featherstonhaugh came to the same conclusion. Steamboat explosions were so frequent that they have created "a general indifference."[33]

There is some truth to the observation that southerners, and Americans more generally, attained a measure of grudging acceptance of the dangers associated with riverboat travel. The "talk of accidents, past, present, and to come, was in every one's mouth," according to one Ohio River traveler. Newspapers in southern river towns printed and reprinted long and short accident stories from around the region. One southerner's diary, for instance, listed explosions with as much fanfare as the weather. "Explosion of the S. B. Knoxville" ran one typical entry. Explosions were a topic of conversation in parlors, saloons, and street corners. In a very real sense, there was no escaping the discussion of steamboat accidents. Outpourings of shock and distress after an accident—or nervous words uttered before travel—served to defuse tensions and restore faith in steamboats.[34]

Residents of the southern interior used gallows humor to deal with the fears and stresses associated with river travel. Many jokes about explosions involved a passenger's location, as the ladies' cabin was commonly considered to be the safest part of the boat since it was not immediately above the boilers. One well-worn gag about the likelihood of an explosion during a race is worth quoting in full:

"Do you believe in predestination?" said the captain of a Mississippi steamer to a clergyman who happened to be traveling with him. "Of course I do." "Well, I'm glad to hear it." "Why?" "Because I intend to pass that boat ahead in fifteen consecutive minutes, if there be any virtue in pine-knots and loaded safety-valves. So don't be alarmed, for if the boilers ain't to burst they won't." Here the divine began putting on his hat, and looking very much like backing out, which the captain observing said, "I thought you said you believed in predestination, and what is to be will be." "So I do; but I prefer being a little nearer the stern when it takes place."[35]

Captains even laughed off the potential for an explosion, as a Missouri resident learned. When William Conn took a stateroom next to the ladies' cabin, the "Capt asked me in a joke if I was afraid he would blow me up." Such humor was a way to acknowledge the very real threat of travel on a southern steamboat while refusing to change behavior.[36]

"AS SAFE AS SLEEPING IN ONE'S BED"

Not everyone thought the dismal safety record of steamers was a laughing matter, and a relatively small number of southerners joined the growing chorus of Americans who voiced a measured criticism of riverboats. Some concerned citizens criticized reckless captains who endangered innocent bystanders. With some justification, the son of Henry Clay noted in his diary that the "Dreadful loss of life" aboard a steamer near St. Louis was due to "criminal racing." A later observer widened the web of blame to include "sober, quiet, decent citizens" who lost control of their senses in the heat of the moment. They were just as much to blame for the scourge of racing as riverboat captains and owners. In a few cases, nervous passengers intervened during a race in the hopes of putting a stop to the danger. During the contest between the *Franklin* and the *Phillips,* female passengers on the latter boat asked their husbands to persuade the captain to stop racing. Their entreaties failed. What critics lamented most was the passion for speed. The *Little Rock Arkansas Gazette* warned, "So long as speed, without regard to safety, is the only object, the public ear will continue to be pained by the recital of the end of 'crack steamers.'" After the *Pennsylvania* exploded, another editorial wanted civilization to slow down. Under the heading "The Steam Demon" a Louisiana writer wondered if "the use of steam is worth the price, in life and limb, bereavement and sorrow, that is paid for it."[37]

As these examples attest, there was enough public concern to do something to regulate the steamboat industry. Even though explosions were a national issue, southern states took the lead in regulation, as Alabama, Louisiana, Kentucky, and Missouri passed laws between 1826 and 1836. The Alabama law, which mandated an annual inspection and certification for riverboats, was like other state legislation in that it applied only to intrastate commerce. Since most of Alabama's riverboats did not cross state boundaries, the law seems to have been relatively effective. In Louisiana it was the explosion of the *Lioness* that prompted the legislature to act. Roustabouts had stowed several kegs of gunpowder in the cargo hold and when unsuspecting crew members lit candles so they could rearrange the freight, the boat was blown to splinters. That Louisiana senator Josiah Johnston was one of the fifteen dead brought attention to steamboat regulation and galvanized public opinion that something needed to be done. Louisiana's law was relatively ineffective because, as written, it did not apply to interstate commerce. In general, state legislation was ineffective in taming the dangers associated with steamboats.[38]

While some southern states moved forward, the federal government also began examining steamboat accidents. However, in the face of laissez-faire assumptions about government regulation, social inertia, and ignorance regarding the cause of the problems, Washington was slow to act. Congressional committees and the Treasury Department first turned to men who had practical experience in navigating steamers on the western waters. Not surprisingly, the captains and mates testified that riverboats were essentially safe and needed little or no regulation. In 1824 the captain of the *Rob Roy* noted that while it would be useful to have safety valves for the boilers, sheer numbers proved that steamboats did not need formal regulations. He pointed out that over 1 million people had traveled on steamers but only fifty-six of them had perished in a steam explosion. Eight years later Henry Shreve made a similar argument to a House committee, stating that steamboat explosions killed few people when compared to other vessels or even drowning accidents.[39]

To its credit, Congress did not merely rely on steamboat captains for evidence, but also turned to the Franklin Institute. Founded in 1824, the Franklin Institute was dedicated to the diffusion of scientific knowledge. A study of something as prominent as steamboats was an opportunity for the young organization to carve out a niche for itself. Through a series of four reports, the Franklin Institute did more to confuse than to clarify. The first report was massive, technically complex, contradictory, and probably went unread. The other reports were not much better, and the congressional committee sided with Shreve and his fellow captains by concluding that it was best to defer to "the sound discretion of those concerned" rather than to legislate "the particular kind of machinery to be employed." Congress claimed it could not keep up with a rapidly changing technology but did understand that faulty boilers were usually to blame for explosions. As a result, it recommended that inspectors should examine riverboat boilers on a regular basis, but the issue faded away.[40]

It took a number of highly publicized explosions on both the eastern and western waters, primarily the *Moselle* disaster, to bring steamboat regulation back into public debate. The resulting Steamboat Act of 1838 was a halting first step that emerged as a series of compromises between Congress and the steamboat industry. Riverboat owners and captains were leery of intrusive legislation, but also realized that something had to be done or they risked losing public confidence. Under the terms of the law, all steamboats had to be licensed and agree to periodic inspections of the hull, boilers, and machinery. When a boat was stopped, the captain had to open the safety valve to keep the pressure down, and all craft had to replace twine tiller ropes with iron rods or chains. The law imposed fines or imprisonment for negligent crew members and made it easier to establish fault in lawsuits.[41]

Southerners welcomed this federal intervention. A Mobile newspaper predicted that the new law would make steamboat travel "as safe as sleeping in one's bed." It could not have been more wrong; the 1838 law was a dismal failure in preventing accidents. It did, however, reassure the public that something was being done to make riverboat travel safer, lay the groundwork for future steamboat legislation, and gently prod the industry to make self-corrections. Between a comprehensive law in 1852 and incremental safety features, steamboats became a much safer means of travel. One of the most important additions was "the doctor," an independent pump that brought water into the boilers even if the paddle wheels were not turning. Other commonplace changes included nighttime running lights, life preservers, and fire hoses. The 1852 law also required licenses for pilots and engineers, created a steamboat inspection service, and gave power to inspectors to revoke licenses. Legislation and industry self-correction contributed to a noticeable reduction in steamboat accidents in the decade prior to the Civil War.[42]

Southerners also tried to reassert human agency in the midst of steamboat calamities, particularly before the two major steamboat acts. There was a prevailing sentiment in the southern interior that savvy travelers could avoid steamboat accidents if they were prudent. With some exaggeration, one observer concluded, "In every case where a boiler bursts it is fair to infer that it proceeded from neglect, until the contrary shall be proved." A Missouri resident, taking in the explosion of the *Oronoko* and the *Moselle,* concurred. He would not be deterred from steamboat travel, he wrote his sister, because "both the affairs were caused by gross negligence and ignorance." Potential travelers merely had to take care to "select a vessel in which the captain and mate, engineers and pilots, are well known to the public to be skillful and trust-worthy persons." In other words, riverboat travelers could greatly reduce the prospects of becoming a casualty statistic by gravitating to boats with good safety records. It was not the technology that was the problem, according to the prevailing view, merely the misapplication of it. Steamboat captains were quick to reassure the public that they operated their vessels in a safe manner, and advertisements trumpeting safety equipment became more prominent.[43]

The public's fascination with steamboat speed existed in tension with the need for responsible safety measures. For some, there is no question that speed was king. After all, as a German traveler archly observed, "The life of an American is, indeed, only a constant *racing,* and why should he fear it so much on board the steamboats?" For those southerners who could not completely ignore their fears, Captain Edward T. Sturgeon of the *Eclipse* demonstrated how to reconcile contradictory impulses when he took on critics who insisted he subjected his passengers to "appalling dangers." Even though he famously raced against the *A. L. Shotwell,* Sturgeon denied the obvious by writing, "The Eclipse never engaged in a race with any boat whatever, and she never will while under my command." Instead, "trials of speed," where the captain took on no freight, stopped at prominent points, and arranged for fast wooding, shielded his customers from danger. Perhaps people believed that Sturgeon was in a hurry rather than racing, but his reassurance provided a way out of the trap that speed endangered safety. His words did not fall on deaf ears. The *Eclipse* remained one of the most popular and profitable steamboats until 1860, when it was damaged beyond repair during a collision. Speed, although worrisome, was too intoxicating to resist. Rivers that were free from obstructions also contributed to the mania for speed. As the next chapter reveals, residents of the Southwest welcomed federal efforts to reshape the western waters and, in so doing, helped bring extensive ecological change to the region.[44]

SIX

THE NATURE OF IMPROVEMENTS

In August of 1829, Henry M. Shreve began an ambitious effort to reshape the environment of the Mississippi River valley. He steered the *Heliopolis* toward Plum Point, a dangerous section of the Mississippi River about fifty miles north of Memphis, near Fulton, Tennessee. Regarding this portion of the river, *The Navigator*, a published guidebook for western boatmen, warned travelers about a sandbar that funneled traffic to the western side of a riverbend, where a forest of underwater snags menaced steamboats. This area, warned the book, is "one of the most dangerous places in low water between the Ohio [River] and New Orleans." These snags and the others that infested the western waters were created when the river cut a new channel. Some snags were trees left standing when the waters changed course, while others were whole trees, their roots still clutching a mass of earth, that were washed into the river. As the heavy root masses absorbed water, they sank and embedded themselves on the river bottom. The river's current stripped away leaves and smaller branches, making the skeletal trees more difficult to see and thus more deadly to flatboats and steamers. Such snags were often divided into two types: planters (trees firmly rooted in the riverbed, usually not visible above the water) and sawyers (trees that bobbed up and down in the water, often pointed upstream). Sawyers were so named because as they moved with the current, it looked as if their branches were sawing the water. Planters were the more dangerous of the two because of their invisibility and their solidity. Between them, sawyers and planters presented rivermen with fearsome obstacles. Shreve, though, went to Plum Point not with a sense of dread like most rivermen, but with the confidence of subduing it. He set out, in essence, to show that man could conquer the worst river obstacles that nature had to offer.[1]

The *Heliopolis* was no ordinary steamboat; it was the first successful snag boat. Shreve designed and built it with federal money but assumed the financial risk in case it flopped. The *Heliopolis* did not disappoint and became the prototype for U.S. snag boats for the rest of the nineteenth century. It had two hulls, each about 125 five feet long and about 30 feet wide. Each hull had its own engine, boilers, and paddle wheel, making the boat both maneuverable and powerful. Two tiers of beams connected the hulls together, like a catamaran. The front beam, called the snag beam, was at the waterline. A sheet of iron encased the two-and-a-half-foot-thick bar, making it virtually indestructible. A twenty-foot-high windlass towered over the waterline, and a series of rollers ran from the snag beam to the vessel's aft. The *Heliopolis* drew five and a half feet of water, allowing it to operate in the dry season when snags and other hazards were readily apparent.[2]

Employing tactics suggestive of an enraged bull, the *Heliopolis* raised a full head of steam and bashed into a snag, hoping to knock it free from the river bottom or snap it off and render it harmless. In either case, workers then looped chains around the loosened snag and used the windlass to haul it up on deck, where they sawed it apart. Thus dismantled, the root clump sank harmlessly to the river bottom while the trunk and limbs floated on the surface. Stubborn snags required several shots, and those too far below the surface to pummel might be yanked out of the mud with chains and hauled on deck. The *Heliopolis*, Shreve exulted after a bruising eleven-hour first day, "far exceeded my most sanguine expectations" by removing all the snags at Plum Point. It then steamed to Islands 62 and 63 near the confluence of the Arkansas and Mississippi rivers, another important juncture point for the regional and national economy. The two islands funneled navigation—and snags—into a narrow channel that was almost as dangerous as Plum Point. The snags were no match for Shreve's machine, and the area was soon safe for navigation. Shreve worked for seven more months, racking up unprecedented results: the *Heliopolis* removed 1,548 snags, including forty-seven in one day, and yanked out one monster that was 160 feet long, three and a half feet in diameter, and weighed at least sixty tons. When the Captain of the Engineers examined Shreve's results, he was surprised to learn that places like Plum Point were so safe that steamboats could navigate at night. This first season was just the start, as snag boats continued to patrol the rivers through the end of the century and beyond.[3]

Probably more than any other person, Henry M. Shreve changed the ecology of the interior South before 1860. As superintendent of western rivers, he and his successors blasted away rocks, scraped sandbars, dug cutoffs to straighten rivers, clearcut trees, and generally busied themselves at a host of activities that were part of a larger effort to conquer the unruly portions of the natural world and align them with human settlement. Steamboats, as the leading edge of this assault on nature, were the embodiment of a nineteenth-century American ethos that glorified technology for its supposed ability to restructure the natural world. And while it seemed that the Army Corps of Engineers might be able to bend the environment to do its bidding, such was not the case. New snags appeared, riverbanks caved in, sandbars shifted, sheets of ice entombed steamers, low water grounded vessels, and the Mississippi River cutoffs did not yield the expected results.[4]

The concerted effort to transform the environment is also revealing of how residents of the southern interior formed their identity and regarded their place in the nation. Regional lobbyists made the case that the Mississippi River system was crucial for interstate commerce and national economic growth and that the federal government had the obligation to improve the interior. Their stance, moreover, placed them at odds with a growing sentiment in the coastal South to resist federal authority. The federal improvements program and attitudes toward nature are a way to understand regional identify formation and the differences of opinion within the slave states.

Even though such improvements, as they were optimistically called, brought rapid ecological change to the Mississippi River valley in the first half of the nineteenth century, the everyday activities of steamboats were probably more transformative. Riverboats consumed enormous quantities of wood and led to deforestation. Trees provided solidity to the Mississippi's shoreline, and their absence allowed the river to wash away more of the bank than ever before. River pollution rose to new levels as steamboat captains, crews, and passengers used the waters as both a garbage dump and a sewer system. In short, not only did southerners consciously alter the environment through the improvements program, they unknowingly changed it through pollution and the depletion of wood supplies.[5]

"SHOUTING, YELLING, AND RUSHING BACKWARD AND FORWARD"

More than a few riverboat travelers presumed that steamboats represented the triumph of American ingenuity over natural forces. One described the great noise of rushing water, the columns of smoke, and the showers of sparks that looked like meteors. He was thrilled at the idea that steamboats had conquered the mightiest river on the continent. There was "a proud consciousness of the power of the dark hull beneath your feet, which plunges, thundering onward," and added "to the majesty and wonder of the time." Passengers frequently remarked on the contrast between the artificial world of a riverboat and the natural world that glided past in the background. The peripatetic Timothy Flint wondered at the disparity between the mahogany tables, rich carpeting, and splendid mirrors of his "floating hotel" and the "wild and uninhabited forest . . . the abode of only bears, owls, and noxious animals." The several Mississippi panoramas captured this tension between humankind and nature. These traveling exhibitions were especially popular along the East coast and consisted of large canvases, stitched together, wound on spindles, and unrolled to simulate a steamboat voyage. John Banvard, who advertised his panorama as being three miles long, was just one of many landscape artists who hoped to capitalize on peoples' curiosity about the natural world that was vanishing as steamboats crowded the western rivers. Between the drowsy reverie of Flint and the commercial hucksterism of Banvard, steamboats were part of an American tendency to see technology as extending society and civilization into an untouched space. These tales of using machines to fulfill humankind's promise to subjugate the natural world—what David Nye has called second creation stories—explained and validated expansion.[6]

Such progress, however, came at a price. A group of Cincinnati residents noted that even as steamboats built up cities and brought "every blessing, social, religious, and literary," to the West, "[s]uch magnificent results could not reasonably be expected, without some accompanying evils." These evils were, at best, inconvenient and, at worst, fatal. Western steamers faced problems common to other river systems: sandbars, ice, jagged rocks, and the like. However, the environment of the western rivers, and the peculiar machinery of the boats themselves, made travel on the Mississippi River and its tributaries among the most dangerous activities in the United States during the first half of the nineteenth century. Snags were ubiquitous in the western waters but unknown on most other American rivers. Reading the river (looking for ripples that might reveal a hidden snag or knowing how much a sandbar might have shifted) was more difficult in the West than elsewhere because water levels were capricious and the waterscape was constantly shifting.[7]

Snagging was, by far, the most common steamboat accident on the western waters. The estimated fifty thousand snags in the western rivers sank more boats and destroyed more cargo than any other hazard. Fittingly, the *New Orleans*, the first steamer on the Mississippi River, snagged after it tied up for the night at a woodyard two miles above Baton Rouge. The river dropped sixteen inches overnight, impaling the boat on a stump. When the captain used the capstan to heave the boat off the snag, he only gouged a hole in the hull. The *New Orleans's* snagging was unusual in that it took place when the boat was stationary. As boats increased in size and speed, snaggings became more dramatic and huge logs splintered paddle wheels, ripped through guards, and sometimes tore into the deck cabin or engine room. Snags to the guards or paddle wheels were nuisances more than anything else because they did not compromise the vessel's seaworthiness. Those that pierced the hull were more serious and often created an explosive shock that sent the entire boat into a panic. Not only were people "shouting, yelling, and rushing backward and forward" but there "were a great number of horses and mules on board, and they became dreadfully frightened and commenced rearing, kicking, plunging and snorting furiously." Longtime steamboat worker Alex Boss remembered the immense damage to the *Rubicon* when it hit a snag. Smokestacks toppled over and crashed onto the roof of the pilothouse, the off-duty pilot was thrown out of his bunk, and the boat careened out of control. Carpenters and crew packed gunny sacks and canvas around the snag, delaying the flow of water into the hull while the captain steered for the riverbank or a sandbar. Once the vessel ran aground, passengers and crew could exit safely and the freight could be offloaded to another riverboat.[8]

Few snags caused significant loss of life. The main problem was damage to cargo. The great shock from a snag might send cargo like cotton, boxes, casks, or even live hogs into the river. Unless the water was extremely low, the cargo either sank or floated downstream and was often beyond recovery. Even if the freight could be found, water damage was often irreversible. James Alexander sadly noted after his steamboat snagged near Memphis that he lost his entire cargo of coffee, sugar, and dry goods. If an owner like Alexander paid for insurance, then he would not be liable for damages, but if he did not, then he was responsible for replacing lost or damaged items. The loss of an uninsured boat could easily cause financial ruin for its owner. These difficulties made the price of snagging immense; from 1822 to 1827 (the years immediately prior to the river improvement campaign) the loss of property on the Ohio and Mississippi rivers from snags was $1,362,500. Snagging was so frequent that it gave rise to the expression to hit a snag, or to run into unforeseen difficulties.[9]

Waterfalls and rocks were other natural phenomena that threatened technology's fulfillment of nature's promise. The Falls at Louisville were the most obvious barrier, as steamers could chance a voyage over them only in stages of high water. The Falls necessitated two fleets of steamers, one upriver and one downriver, and also nourished Louisville's commerce through the unloading, overland transportation, and loading of cargo. Other natural obstacles, such as Muscle Shoals in Alabama, the Grand Chain of Rocks on the lower Ohio River, the rapids near Alexandria on the Red River, and the Harpeth Shoals on the Cumberland River also inhibited traffic and commerce. Boats striking rocks might either have holes gashed in their hulls or run aground, literally hitting rock bottom.[10]

"PROTECT OUR AGRICULTURE AND OUR INTERNAL COMMERCE"

The problem of riverboats lost to natural hazards on the western rivers was so salient that residents along the western waters asked the federal and state governments to tame the environment. Southerners initially adapted steamboats to the environment, but came to realize that they had to adapt the environment to steamboats. In 1819 a joint committee from the states of Ohio, Kentucky, Virginia, and Pennsylvania commissioned Magnus Murray to draw a map of the most dangerous obstructions in the Ohio River. No tangible plans came from the commission, but concern over how the environment inhibited economic growth dominated the committee's recommendations. Not only was the loss of property from snags a problem, but the "painful spectacle" of steamboats "locked up for the want of a sufficient depth of water" was a serious hindrance to the region's development. That low water happened at just the time residents wanted to move their crops to market made the situation dire. Other states beholden to the river for their economy went even further. Louisiana, for instance, spent about $490,000 on internal improvements between 1800 and 1833, mainly building levees, removing obstructions, dredging streams, and digging canals. The state had its own snagboat and the Board of Works relied on slaves, some of whom were provided by the state penitentiary and the Baton Rouge jail, to do most of the work. Tennessee and Arkansas were other states that implemented improvement programs, but such efforts were usually sporadic and chronically underfunded.[11]

Perhaps the most notable state project to coordinate economic development was a canal to bypass the Falls of the Ohio at Louisville. The Kentucky state legislature chartered the Louisville and Portland Canal Company in 1825 with authority to sell stock and build a two-mile-long canal. The project was a fiasco from the beginning. Cost overruns delayed construction and triggered an infusion of federal money to finish the project. When the canal opened, the locks were small and crooked, rocks gashed holes in steamers, and mud, debris, and ice often hindered passage. Even though the company paid dividends to its investors, the canal failed to live up to its promise to circumvent natural obstacles. Most steamers either stopped on one end of the Falls or chanced passage over the rocks in high water. The Louisville and Portland Canal project was an unsurprising result of a southern state government that was neither predisposed enough to continue funding significant river improvements nor wealthy enough to have done so even had the political will been there.[12]

While state efforts to promote interstate commerce by subduing the environment sputtered along, the federal government was tiptoeing toward a western river improvements program. Washington was somewhat favorably disposed to internal improvement projects that would increase interstate economic activity, so in 1820 Congress appropriated $5,000 for a survey of the Ohio and Mississippi rivers with a view to improve navigation. After a trip down the Ohio and Mississippi, army engineers Simon Bernard and Joseph G. Totten laid out a plan that became the basis for improvement projects in the Southwest. They recommended a canal at Louisville, wing dams to channel the current and scour away sandbars, removal of the Grand Chain of Rocks, and snag elimination. Although they realized that labor would be continual because the river channel constantly changed, Bernard and Totten thought "machines can be contrived to raise them [snags], or to break or saw them off."[13]

Four years later Congressman Robert Pryor Henry of Kentucky introduced a measure to appropriate $75,000 for snag and sandbar removal, arguing that in order to "protect our agriculture and our internal commerce," the federal government had to act against the "stationary pirates of the Ohio and Mississippi." Henry's bill fit comfortably in this Whiggish sensibility that an improved infrastructure would boost economic growth. Improvement projects also flowed from the unhappy consequences of the War of 1812. The British exposed America's shabby infrastructure, and in 1819 Secretary of War John Calhoun proposed a comprehensive program to improve roads and waterways. The improvements bill won easy approval.[14]

Many residents of the interior South apparently thought that Henry's bill did not go far enough. As early as 1829 they sent petitions to Washington asking for more action to remake the western rivers. Steamboat captains, citizens of Louisville and St. Louis, and the legislatures of Missouri, Louisiana, Arkansas, Alabama, and Tennessee were among those who pressured the federal government. While one petition mentioned military necessity and another the loss of lives, the most common justification for federal aid was commercial improvement. They framed their argument around the Constitutional questions of interstate commerce and whether the federal government should pay to promote the general welfare. Louisville residents, for instance, wanted snags removed so that valuable merchandise and produce had a better chance to arrive in New Orleans unharmed. Citizens in eastern Tennessee voiced a desire for their products to "have egress to the best markets," while the legislature of Alabama thought improvement to Muscle Shoals would increase land values in the area.[15]

Southerners along the country's interior rivers believed that a stubborn natural environment stood in the way of material prosperity. They shared this attitude with residents of the Midwest, who also petitioned the federal government to spend more money on internal improvements. Steamboats changed assumptions about trading patterns and the desirability of the federal government to connect the emerging regions of the Midwest and Southwest. Starting in the mid-1820s, petitions from residents along the Great Lakes and major western rivers poured into Congress. Americans in the Mississippi River valley, to a large extent, saw their future prospects knit together around steamboat commerce. On this score, the intersection of technological improvement and environmental factors trumped political alliances. In general terms, the two major parties divided sharply over the issue of internal improvements. Whigs, under the leadership of Henry Clay, typically wanted the federal government to pay for roads, canals, river improvements, and the like. The Democrats, who ultimately rallied around Andrew Jackson, usually opposed such measures. Congressmen from the West, regardless of party affiliation, tended to vote for internal improvements if they thought it advanced their local interests.[16]

The relative comity between residents of the Mississippi River valley stands in stark contrast to the tension between slave states of the southern interior and the Atlantic coast. Petitions from the Southwest were arriving in Washington at about the same time that Vice President John Calhoun left that city and returned to his home state of South Carolina. Calhoun had retreated from his nationalistic pronouncements as secretary of war and was now the leading advocate of states' rights. He published *The South Carolina Exposition*, which argued that a state could nullify a federal law, and led the movement in South Carolina to nullify the Tariff of 1832. Congressmen from South Carolina also vociferously opposed internal improvements that would have benefitted the slave states along the Ohio and Mississippi rivers. Besides their philosophical opposition to increased federal power, they were reluctant to spend tax dollars on projects that did not directly benefit them. Residents of the southern interior, for their part, overwhelmingly opposed nullification and adopted a different view of the utility of federal power. Slave states in the Southwest were forming, at least for the time being, an identity centered around their river system that marked them as western *and* southern. The federal government, whether through driving out Native Americans or improving conditions for commerce, had a place in this identity. Federal promotion of interstate trade was not only vital to the economy of the southern interior, but helped nurture the idea that southerners were safest when they were working within government rather than confronting it. Calhoun's disciples, though, had at least one thing in common with lobbyists in the southern interior: slave labor was the foundation of economic prosperity. The slaveowners of South Carolina looked to the Atlantic Ocean as their thoroughfare, while their counterparts in the Mississippi River valley wanted to build an economic network that stretched inward and outward.[17]

"MONSTER SNAGS SO FIRMLY EMBEDDED IN THE SAND"

Henry's law made an improvements program the purview of experts, in this case the officers of the U.S. Army Corps of Engineers. In 1802 Congress established the U.S. Military Academy at West Point to provide military and engineering training for army officers. West Point cadets learned much more about engineering than military tactics so that the country could put them to work on civil defense projects. The Corps of Engineers at first concentrated on building forts, mapping the young nation, and exploring the continent before shifting to road and bridge construction. Improving the western rivers was a natural extension of these activities.[18]

Alexander Macomb, chief engineer of the U.S. Army, directed the first federal improvement projects on the western waters. He sent Major Stephen H. Long to tackle the sandbars, and also instituted a public contest to design a snag removal machine. Advertisements in newspapers across the country offered a prize of $1,000 and the potential for a government contract. It seemed like the perfect manifestation of the young democracy: any man could win despite his station in life as long as his idea was superior to all the others. Nearly one hundred designs poured in from across the country, although most entrants lived near the Ohio or Mississippi rivers. Plans were a curious mix of human, animal, natural, and steam power that ranged from the ridiculous (a floating dam pulling underwater plows) to the sophisticated (a double-hulled steamboat that anticipated Shreve's design). The contest revealed a confidence that Americans could create a machine to overcome just about any natural obstacle. Steamboats, after all, had conquered the mighty currents of the Mississippi, and so now residents along the western rivers looked to overcome other environmental factors that hindered movement or commerce. The plans, moreover, expansively addressed more than just snags. William Wainwright, for instance, proposed a "mud tortel for remooveing the sand and gravel and erth of off aney Bar or Shoel or islands shuts in the River of Ohio or Missippi," in essence a large scoop shovel. In one form or another, entrants proposed every activity that the superintendent of western rivers would implement. The federal improvements program reflected the American impulse to use technology to control the environment.[19]

John Bruce won the contest with a singularly unimpressive plan to mount a windlass on a machine boat. Workers would lower an iron claw from the windlass, attach it to a snag, and then turn a capstan in the hopes of pulling up or breaking off the snag. While his design held potential, it certainly did not hurt matters that Bruce was an ardent supporter of Henry Clay. Bruce's letter, in fact, contained more testimonials from influential people than specific plans to defeat the snags. That his design beat out superior plans, including ones from the first superintendent of western rivers and a future member of the Topographical Engineers, suggests that rather than being an open process, Bruce won on the basis of political connections. He quickly signed a contract in which he promised to remove obstructions at least ten feet below the low-water stage in order to make the channel safe for navigation.[20]

Bruce, though, was a schemer. He interpreted the contract so narrowly that he picked his way down the Ohio River, removed a few snags, sawed off the tops of others, and did not even attempt work on the Mississippi River. Nor did he touch any snags in the busiest portions of the river, sawyers that could have been chopped down from sandbars. When word filtered back to Washington that Bruce's progress was less than desirable, Macomb sent Samuel Babcock to look over Bruce's shoulder. Babcock, who had just been court-martialed for faulty construction of Fort Delaware, was a poor choice. He had no experience with western rivers, and when he proclaimed that Bruce had made the river safe for navigation, forty steamboat owners confronted Bruce in Louisville. Macomb then sent Captain William Chase to clean up the mess, and he found shocking violations of the contract.[21]

Southerners, like Americans in general, did not stand in awe of a river that had created forests of snags, but believed they could re-order the natural environment. William Poyntz, a Kentucky steamboat captain, wrote to Clay that Bruce had been negligent in his duties. Poyntz was confident that some-one who was "acquainted with the navigation and the river" could remove the snags and logs. A group of steamboat pilots and owners concurred, saying that Congress had appropriated enough money to master the rivers. They suggested that the Corps divide the rivers into sections and rely on "good pilots" to point out the dangerous obstructions. It was not that the western waters rebuffed the best that John Bruce could offer, but that Bruce was not resource-ful or honest enough to meet the problem head-on. Between complaints about Bruce and petitions to the federal government, westerners living near the riv-ers forced Washington to respond to their desires. The improvements program showed their tenacity to shape the environment to suit the dictates of emerg-ing agricultural production, commercial relations, and geographic mobility. It also revealed a river-centric conception of social and economic development. Residents of the Southwest believed that the network of western rivers was central to their existence.[22]

While Bruce was busy writing angry screeds to the secretary of war, Henry Shreve received the appointment as superintendent of western river improvements. Like most of the entrants in the 1824 contest, Shreve was well acquainted with the whims of the Ohio and Mississippi rivers through labor and experience. He thus approached his job with a single-minded practical-ity rather than the perspective of a scientific expert. Shreve was open to ex-periment to find what worked, rather than studying the physics, geology, and hydrology in search of a solution. He inspected Bruce's work and proclaimed it negligent and incomplete, and declared that Bruce was unable to accom-plish the task at hand. Shreve then fired Bruce, took over the improvements program, and sent out laborers to accomplish what Bruce should have done. But human efforts were rather pitiful in the face of the tremendous obstacles. Shreve quickly learned that he could cover only six miles a day as he worked his way down the Ohio River removing snags and steamboat wrecks. The work was not only "extremely laborious and somewhat hazardous," but the "bilious fever, ague and fever, mosquetoes, extreme heat, etc." plagued his men. Shreve, like most southern riverboatmen, still limited his vision to the application of muscle rather than steam power to rid the rivers of obstacles.[23]

By late 1827 Shreve realized that he had to use technology to soften the environment to the degree that steamboats would not be so beholden to natural constraints. As he put it later, "nothing short of the power of steam could be successfully applied in breaking off and raising monster snaggs so firmly embedded in the sand." The sheer number of snags and their size gave him good reason to rethink the degree to which he could tame the western rivers through human toil. Even if Shreve's axmen could cut down sawyers sprouting from sandbars in the Ohio River, they stood no chance of making a dent in the Mississippi River snags. He proposed to spend $20,000 on his snag boat prototype, arguing that it would be cheaper and more efficient than manual labor. But the obstacles were so daunting—a waterlogged tree could weigh several thousand pounds—as to cause experienced rivermen to think Shreve's plan absurd. A number of them wrote to the War Department complaining that "*All machinery, whatever, whether used by lever or steam power*" was a "*useless expenditure of time and money.*" In their eyes, Shreve was but another Bruce. Even Shreve acknowledged the opposition to his boss, noting that "public opinion has been much against the practicability of effectually removing the obstructions" to navigation. He was savvy enough to convince "respectable and experienced Steam Boat Masters" to write letters and send testimonies to Washington that a forceful application of steam was the only way to deal with the snag problem. In other words, while Americans agreed that man should alter the environment to serve his purposes, it was a matter of debate as to how much could be accomplished and whether or not the result would justify the cost.[24]

The *Heliopolis* was the tangible expression of this impulse to apply technology to subdue nature. After its first year in operation, Shreve sent an official account to Macomb that was too outlandish to be taken at face value. Hoping to avoid a repeat of the Bruce fiasco, the chief engineer sent Captain Richard Delafield to verify Shreve's claims. Delafield completely vindicated Shreve, writing that the boat worked "admirably well" and made the waters so safe that riverboats now routinely ran at night through what had once been dangerous water. The *Heliopolis*'s success discredited Shreve's critics and, at least for the moment, answered questions as to whether or not people could use technology to accomplish their purposes. The government responded by building the *Archimedes,* the *Eradicator,* and the *Henry M. Shreve* and then spreading them out along the Ohio, Mississippi, Missouri, Arkansas, Cumberland, and Red rivers.[25]

The snag removal project was massive, relying on both human and machine efforts. Incomplete reports show that between 1830 and 1837 Shreve's men tore up at least 6,700 snags, a figure that is less a testament to their raw physical labor than an indication of the western rivers' dynamism and power. In order to create that many snags, the rivers were more than just sluggish streams wending their way to the Gulf of Mexico. The fact that the improvements program was seasonal—that is, based on water levels—showed that natural forces were still difficult if not impossible to overcome. Up to six hundred men labored alongside the snag boats, cutting back brush and trees along the riverbanks or hacking apart snags in dry riverbeds. This combination of machine power and raw human muscle completely changed the underwater conditions of the western rivers. For instance, in a two-mile stretch of the Ohio River near the Louisville and Portland canal, axmen piled twelve hundred cords of snagged wood on the bank. High water and low water came to resemble one another: free of obstacles and able to support enormous amounts of shipping. Like much technological interaction with the environment, the snag program was intended to nullify nature's extremes, rendering it safe and predictable. Shreve's snag boats made a tangible difference in just a few years, as losses from snags, both in terms of numbers and lost property, declined immediately and insurance rates dropped by half.[26]

The good showing of the snag boats convinced Congress to sink over $3 million into remaking the western rivers. Andrew Jackson, usually known for his fiscal discipline, signed all river improvements bills that crossed his desk, including one that spent $100,000 clearing the Cumberland River from western Kentucky to Jackson's Hermitage plantation. Jackson, in fact, spent more money on internal improvements than any other antebellum president, and the heyday of improvements came during his eight years in office. Jackson's largesse allowed Stephen Long to experiment with several techniques below the mouth of the Green River, near Henderson, Kentucky. He used hand-powered piledrivers on flatboats to set parallel rows of posts halfway into the Ohio River's center. Long then filled the space between the posts with brush to create a wing dam. Since the dam was angled 45 degrees downstream, it channeled the river into a smaller area, strengthening the current and scouring the riverbed. Sand and gravel collected against the dam, solidifying it enough so that it lasted for more than four decades. More importantly, Long's dam worked well enough that the Corps of Engineers built several more on the western rivers, including one on the Cumberland River near Smithland, Kentucky. The Smithland dam was a more ambitious project to alter the waterscape, since it was sixteen feet high, thirty feet wide at the base, and a half-mile long. At one point, workers quarried three hundred tons of limestone rock per day and hauled it to the dam. The Army of Corps of Engineers put natural forces to work against one another in order to create a safer environment for river traffic.[27]

Shreve went to the mouth of the Ohio to work on the Grand Chain of Rocks, a two-mile-long stretch of underwater boulders. The Grand Chain was hazardous enough that steamers traversing that portion of the river often hired special pilots to pick their way through the rocks, some of which were forty feet long and twenty feet wide. During the low water seasons of 1829 and 1830, Shreve's men attacked the rocks with sledgehammers, crowbars, drills, and blasting canisters. By project's end, they had hauled out 225 boatloads of rock (3,375 tons), much of which they reconfigured into a wing dam. Shreve, in essence, changed not only the shape of the rocks but their function, converting them from fearsome obstructions to benign channel deepeners.[28]

The most ambitious improvements project was the effort to destroy the Red River Raft. The raft—how it acquired its name is unclear—was not a raft at all but a series of naturally occurring logjams that blocked 150 miles of the Red River in northern Louisiana. Although the area held excellent potential for cotton cultivation, it remained disconnected from the Southwest's commercial web because the raft acted as a barrier to repel settlement and trade. In April 1833 Shreve and his laborers attacked the Great Raft, and by the spring of 1838 they finally removed the last of it and rammed the logs into a side channel. Their victory was short-lived, as spring freshets and snow melts washed more trees into the Red River and in 1839 another raft appeared about fifty miles north of the recently established town of Shreveport. Below the new raft, however, a startling transformation occurred. Speculators and settlers poured into the area, bringing vast numbers of slaves with them. Cotton became king as these immigrants forced slaves to carve "extensive plantations" out of reclaimed land. A region that was once remote and passed over for cultivation quickly looked like the rest of the plantation South.[29]

The improvements program was a smashing success when measured against the expectations of whites in the southern interior. River commerce (the subject of the next chapter) boomed and steamboat traffic soared. Despite these astounding gains, efforts to overcome the environment and promote interstate steamboat commerce crested in 1837 and, with two notable exceptions, thumped along spasmodically, with no consistent funding or results until after the Civil War. With funding limited, the Corps of Engineers concentrated on snag removal for the Mississippi River system. As the mania for improvements receded—in many respects there was not much left to do to make the waters safe for steamboats—regional identities shifted and political partisanship sharpened.[30]

"TAMPERING WITH A DANGEROUS SUBJECT"

Residents of the interior South believed the snag boats, wing dams, and tin boxes of gunpowder were put to good use because they yielded incontrovertible results. It was unclear if other improvement projects—river cutoffs and clear-cutting the banks—actually improved the waterscape. The Mississippi River is notorious for its long loops that coil back and forth. These bends made steamboat river travel significantly longer than a straight trip and also complicated navigation because pilots had to veer from bank to bank as they followed the deepest portion of the channel. Straightening the river would, in theory, save on travel time, transportation costs, and reduce accidents by simplifying navigation. The Mississippi had, in effect, straightened itself in select places, and several naturally occurring cutoffs left behind oxbow lakes. Shreve, however, wanted to improve upon nature's pitiful efforts.[31]

In 1829 Shreve dug a cutoff about two hundred miles above Natchez, but it was an abject failure. From the sketchy sources that are available, it appears that he used human muscle to dig a "small ditch" that was not large enough to divert the river. Shreve learned from his mistake and two years later put machines to work in an effort to alter the river's course. He steamed the snagboat *Heliopolis* to Turnbull Bend, a curious section of river. The Mississippi River made a long C curve, with the Red River flowing into the Mississippi at the northwest turn and the Atchafalaya River flowing out at the southwest turn (except at low water, when it sometimes flowed into the Mississippi). After characteristically "felling all the timber in the vicinity," Shreve eased the boat's bow on the shore and built two "scrapers of large size," each with two lines running to two windlasses. One windlass pulled the scraper into the earth while the other extended the arm, similar to biceps and triceps in the human arm. The scrapers also used a natural force—the river's current—to wash away scraper loads at a rate of four tons per minute. It took two weeks to scratch out a canal ninety-two feet long, seventeen feet wide, and twenty-two feet deep. On January 28 Shreve let water into the ditch, and within five days the force of the river increased the canal to a half-mile in width and deepened it to a level equal to the rest of the river. Upon becoming the river's main channel, this cutoff shaved eighteen miles from river travel. One contemporary estimate thought steamboats would save annually $28,800 on wood, wages, and time.[32]

Shreve wanted to lop off five more bends in the Mississippi River, but the Corps of Engineers restrained him because such efforts were not spelled out in the river improvements act. The squelching of the cutoffs program probably arose from concerns about disrupting the flow of three rivers as much as from constitutional scruples. One observer thought Shreve was "tampering with a dangerous subject" because a mass of water passed through the area in four minutes instead of four hours. He worried that the increased velocity would force a rise in water along the lower Mississippi and put too much strain on the levees. An 1853 government survey confirmed this conclusion, and the Army Corps of Engineers made no more cutoffs on the Mississippi River until Franklin Delano Roosevelt was president. Shreve tried to do too much to complete nature's work and triggered a backlash. Digging cutoffs did not yield the expected or desired results in the same way that snag or sandbar removal did.[33]

American efforts to straighten the Mississippi River and its tributaries were not unique. In 1809 Johann Tulla, a German engineer who is memorialized as "The Man who Tamed the Wild Rhine," proposed a series of cuts in the Rhine River to make it more amenable to navigation. Germans made over twenty cuts in the Rhine between 1817 and 1878. These cuts seem to have been more effective than the cuts in the Mississippi, even if they took more time to reveal their results. Tulla's cuts relied mainly on human muscle (up to three thousand men labored at each stage) and took an average of nine years of digging to establish each of the new channels. As was the case in the United States, Germans assumed that this conquest of nature was a mark of the moral advance of humankind.[34]

Whether Shreve's cutoffs added to humankind's reputation was a matter of some debate. The cut at Turnbull Bend was "deservedly unpopular," a government study noted, because it "removes the evil from one point to throw it with aggravated force and effect upon another." Sandbars appeared regularly at the Red's mouth, making the navigable channel only twenty yards wide by 1843. As the sandbars grew, the Red River increasingly flowed into the Atchafalaya. Local residents saw the potential in an invigorated Atchafalaya River and pressured the state government to remove a floating raft of trees, logs, and branches that obstructed navigation for thirty miles. Once the Louisiana state engineer started work in 1840 on this project, the Atchafalaya became a major distributary for the Mississippi River. As one New Orleans paper phrased it on the eve of the Civil War, "Unless something is done to prevent the Red river from seceding, New Orleans will lose a large amount of valuable traffic." In the short term, at least, it looked as if commerce from the fertile Red River valley would no longer travel through the Crescent City.[35]

The loss of revenue from the Red River was the least of New Orleans's worries. As the Atchafalaya gained strength, it slowly captured the Mississippi. If unchecked, this development would eventually divert the Father of Waters away from New Orleans and Baton Rouge, leaving them to sit on brackish estuaries. A number of devastating floods, most notably the 1927 inundation that caused so much damage, further weakened the Mississippi's flow in its historic channel. When Shreve made the cutoff at Turnbull Bend, he wound the geologic clock forward several centuries, forcing the Army Corps of Engineers to act quickly to prevent further diversion. In short, the Corps once again had to impose order on a disorderly river system and spend $30 million to build a series of dams called the Old River Control Structure.[36]

"VERY MUCH PILLAGED BY THE STEAM BOATS"

Shreve and his men changed the Mississippi's riverscape in another controversial fashion. With the zeal of a revival preacher, Shreve begged for permission to cut down trees within a hundred yards of the riverbanks. As he explained, denuding the shores was "one of the most important parts" of making the river safe for navigation because it removed the "first cause of the formation of snags." In Shreve's mind, the rivers were almost alive—"the alluvial banks are continually throwing their heavy forests into their channels"—and cutting trees minimized potential dangers. He did have a point. The rushing waters of the Mississippi especially, but also other rivers, scoured lower banks and undercut the shore. John James Audubon saw nature's power firsthand while traveling the Missouri River: "The banks themselves, along with perhaps millions of trees, are ever tumbling, falling, and washing away from the spots where they may have stood for and grown for centuries past."[37]

For Shreve, trees along the banks were not part of a verdant forest but were barriers to safe navigation because they were potential dangers. Not only did trees become snags when riverbanks eroded, but they "perpetually obstructed" the shores to such an extent that they prevented flatboats from landing. In a bit of imaginary reasoning, Shreve added that even if flatboats managed to find a safe bit of shoreline, they were "liable to be sunk by the trees falling on them." The river was safer for everyone, according to Shreve, and felling the trees "preserved the banks." Cutting down trees was a way to forestall environmental change, make riverboat commerce safe, and impose order on the landscape. Shreve's opinions were at odds with most residents along the rivers, who came to see trees as a commodity to be exploited rather than a nuisance to be controlled.[38]

The total number of trees that government employees removed will never be known, but it was immense. Presumably they did not fell *every* tree in areas that seemed to be in danger of eroding, just those large enough to obstruct navigation. Shreve's axmen fanned out along the banks and doggedly chopped down at least 40,872 trees between 1832 and 1837, despite being forced to cease operations for two seasons between November 1833 and September 1835. Government crews hacked down another 80,000 trees between November 1842 and July 1845. If the axmen worked inland to Shreve's standard of one hundred yards, they cleared along the shoreline for over fifty miles.[39]

What became of this wood is unclear, but in late 1832 the government sold timber on the banks of the Mississippi, and some of the wood probably ended up in the snag boats' furnaces. After 1832 there are no surviving records of government wood sales, so it appears that chopping the trunks into firewood was too laborious and most of the trees were wasted. As Shreve explained in 1836, the "trunks & tops float off on the surface of the water & never become dangerous to navigation," while the stumps sank to the riverbed if the land eroded. He acknowledged that his critics attacked the program for wasting timber, but dismissed the wood as being of little value because it was cottonwood and sycamore. In a supreme irony, as the cutting crews were tossing freshly cut trunks into the Mississippi River, Shreve expected to spend $8,000 on wood for the *Heliopolis* and the *Archimedes* snag boats.[40]

The number of trees that fell at the hands of Shreve's axmen was paltry when compared to the timber that became fuel for steamboats. Riverboats were voracious consumers of wood; exactly how much they burned is impossible to say, but a reasonable estimate can be calculated. Table 5 shows the steady rise of wood consumption in the years before the Civil War. Between 1815 and 1860, southern steamers burned wood from perhaps 22,392,023 trees, enough to cover 583 square miles of land, an expanse equal in size to the city of Houston. Even given that these figures are reasonable estimates and subject to modification, it is clear that riverboats burned massive amounts of trees.[41]

TABLE 5

Estimates of wood consumption by southern steamboats

Years	Tonnage	Estimated cords per day per ton	Estimated days per year in operation	Estimated total cords consumed	Estimated trees consumed	Estimated square mileage
1815–1819	17,095.5	1/1/20	90	76,930	51,287	1.34
1820–1829	141,966.5	1/1/12	100	1,183,054	788,703	20.54
1830–1839	274,326	1/1/10	128	3,511,373	2,340,915	60.96
1840–1849	565,804.5	1/1/8	130	9,194,323	6,129,549	159.62
1850–1859	994,311.5	1/1/8	141	17,524,740	11,683,160	304.25
1860	119,013.5	1/1/8	141	2,097,613	1,398,409	36.42
Total	2,112,517.5			33,588,033	22,392,023	583.13

Sources: See Appendix D.

While the great commercial assault on southern timber was still to come, steamers rapidly depleted southern forests. Shreve's clear-cutting and the number of trees burned in steamboat furnaces was just the start. The boats themselves were mostly made of wood, the foundries that cast the engines burned wood, and, as steamboats added value to forested lands, more migrants moved in and cleared trees. Travelers along the southern rivers in the early days of riverboats could not help but notice the wooded banks. As one Mississippi River traveler wrote in 1835, "The background wood, wood, wood!" But even in that decade the backdrop to river travel was changing. As early as 1830 a Virginian visiting southwestern Tennessee commented on how the land was "very much pillaged by the Steam Boats." Nine years later, a writer in the *Southern Literary Messenger* agreed after traveling from Cincinnati to Louisville. He was appalled at the "nakedness of the banks" that came at the expense of increased riverboat traffic. By the time of the Civil War, the "steamboats and locomotives" had "burnt off the forests" around Memphis, wrote another steamboat traveler. The image of vast stretches of stumps scarring the land anticipated the sight of deserted buffalo carcasses littering the prairie or strip mines gouging the earth.[42]

It seems that few southerners, and Americans generally, perceived the heavy demand placed on forests to be a problem. D. J. Browne was one of the handful of Americans who pointed out that the increased consumption of wood created environmental troubles. Writing in 1832, he worried that even though steamboats used so much wood, "no one ever seems to feel that our forests are not inexhaustible." There is no evidence that southerners heeded Browne's pleas, and, instead of wringing their hands over the effects of deforestation, they rejoiced that steamboats took something that was "not only useless, but an obstacle" and, "with something like magical influence, has turned them into objects of rapidly increasing value." Sales of wood to steamboats became an important business in the interior South and woodyards popped up along the riverbanks. Trees got in the way of agricultural development and would have to be removed to make way for progress. Steamers merely made the eradication of trees more profitable.[43]

"THE SEWER OF A HUNDRED CITIES"

The deforestation along the southern rivers created ecological difficulties. Thomas J. Halderman, a steamboat captain on the Arkansas River, ridiculed Shreve for wasting the government's money on clearing trees. Felling trees caused a "direct injury" to the banks, he explained, which washed away much faster. Halderman was correct in this case. The Mississippi River had shifted its course for millennia, depositing silt in some places and shaving away banks in others. Land along the river was notoriously unstable and trees were one of the few means of bringing solidity to the banks. Both the natural current and steamboat waves undermined these fragile shorelines, causing more and more of the scarred landscape to crash into the rivers. In one particular case, after the crew of the snagboat *Archimedes* cleared trees along a section of the Mississippi, the river washed away enough riverbank acreage to produce three hundred cords of wood. Instead of complaining about changes to the land, the angry landowner submitted a claim for damages, only underscoring the tendency to see the land in terms of dollars that could be earned rather than as a resource to be protected. Removing trees on the banks—whether done by Shreve's men, wood sellers, or plantation slaves—actually increased river obstacles. The number of snags washed into the river does not seem to have declined with clear-cutting, but more stumps than ever before found lodging on the riverbed and became particularly problematic during low water.[44]

Caving in banks increased the sediment load in the rivers, particularly the Mississippi. Coupled with the steady increase in the height and length of levees along the lower Mississippi, much more sediment remained in the river rather than spread out along the countryside. More sediment within the river raised its bed, prompting a government dredging program in the late nineteenth century. Dredging the shipping channels, though, failed to address the long-term consequences of sediment build up. The result, in part, was the disastrous 1927 flood.[45]

Another complication of deforestation was the destruction of animals' ecosystems along the rivers. The rapid depletion of timber destroyed nesting grounds, boroughs, and food supplies for insects, birds, mammals, and amphibians. Not only did animals face scarcer resources, but the increased steamboat traffic brought human contact on a daily basis. While much of the interaction between passenger and creature was benign, significant numbers of people used steamboats as hunting platforms. Steamboat travelers and employees continued the practice of rivermen on flatboats and keelboats, who regularly shot animals for sport and food. Indeed, a French visitor on the *Vesuvius* in 1817 shot an alligator, a turkey, and a rattlesnake during his voyage upriver, and a crew member killed a deer. The turkey and deer ended up on the boat's table. Steamboat passengers regularly brought guns with them while traveling, and the practice of using riverbanks as a shooting gallery continued through 1860 and probably beyond. After about 1825, most travelers killed animals for amusement and did not bother to use them as food or collect them as trophies. Any creature could become a target, although alligators are mentioned most often in travelers' accounts, presumably because they were exotic and dangerous. Such hunts, if they can be called such, were very public displays meant to affirm the hunter's masculinity and power, even if they did not showcase his ability to track game.[46]

Riverboats also contributed significantly to the pollution of the western waters. Pollution was already a problem before steamers and would have increased without them—one passenger correctly observed that the Mississippi was "the sewer of a hundred cities"—but riverboats concentrated populations on and around the waters. And they were populations oblivious to the harmful effects of dumping waste into the environment. There are no direct references to the disposal of human and animal sewage, but presumably roustabouts or deckhands swept animal droppings into the river, deck passengers and crew relieved themselves directly from the guards, and stewards emptied chamber pots into the waters. Wooding stations, too, probably had their fair share of human waste left behind during lengthy refueling stops. Food waste, though certainly not as unsanitary, also found its way into the rivers. "The refuse of every thing that remains after dinner, and the other meals, bread, meat, &c. is thrown into the river," noted one traveler. When a novice cook tried to feed leftovers to an elderly deck passenger, the captain cursed him and flipped the food into the Arkansas River. Business considerations—not having deck passengers get something for nothing—triumphed over kindness, and the river was the worse for it.[47]

Hasty burials also degraded the environment, particularly when the cholera and yellow fever epidemics clustered deaths in riverboats. The disposition of the corpses varied significantly, but it was fairly common to dump them into the river or hastily inter them in riverside graves. One fireman on the *Constitution* traveling from Natchez to New Orleans said bluntly, "I saw men perishing every minute about me . . . and thrown into the river like so many dead hogs." At other times, crew members sewed those who had succumbed to yellow fever into blankets and rolled them overboard. One captain told a passenger that "he noticed here and there bodies stuck in snags, or moving up and down with the sawyers." Decaying bodies, when combined with human and food waste, turned the western waters into something of a toxic stew. Americans moving overland in the nineteenth century were known for "trashing the trails," that is, dumping vast amounts of garbage as they moved across the landscape. Travelers on the watery inland trails betrayed the same disposition to strew trash upon their environment.[48]

The struggle to make the Mississippi River and its tributaries conform to humankind's expectations was part of a larger American effort to impose order on the landscape and align it with human purposes. Steamboats were the leading edge of this effort, and the long but successful day at Plum Point convinced Shreve, at least, that the proper application of technology increased the value, utility, and beauty of the natural world. "Instead of a forest of snags," he explained in a public letter, "there remained a beautiful sheet of water, uninterrupted by the former tenants." Nature was not so much to be admired as to be completed. Another writer articulated the southern (and American) notion that the land itself must be organized for productive ends. Thirty years ago, he wrote in 1844, "the valleys, and plains, and hills, traversed only by savages, were an unproductive waste." Now, thanks to riverboats, the land along the former Red River Raft was civilized. But these changes came at a cost that went largely unnoticed in the nineteenth century. The waters became more polluted and the shorelines more barren. Instead of chugging past a verdant backdrop, the steamboats roiled fetid waters that flowed through a scarred landscape.[49]

The improvements program for the western rivers also strengthened the sense of a regional identity for the interior South and set it in opposition to the coastal slave states. While John Calhoun was blustering against the powers of the federal government, residents of the interior South were asking Washington to rip out snags, destroy the Red River Raft, and place wing dams in the western waters. They did so because their particular vision of political economy needed the federal government to promote interstate commerce. With the waters rendered relatively safe for travel and commerce, steamboats nourished economic growth in the interior South and helped give rise to the Cotton Kingdom. Riverboats, as the next chapter demonstrates, not only created new types of business in the Southwest, they helped power an international age of cotton.

SEVEN

THE RISE OF THE COTTON KINGDOM

Tyrone Power was perturbed that his steamboat trip was taking so long. The boat stopped constantly to take on cotton, a laborious process that chewed up precious time, limited progress down the Alabama River to twenty miles a day, and was, in the words of another passenger, "a great bore." But one night when the riverboat stopped at the base of a 150-foot-high bluff, the English traveler's mood turned from annoyance to wonder. Roustabouts pushed cotton bales into a semicircle barricade on the steamer's bow. Deckhands extended the gangplank to shore, where it stopped just short of a rickety wooden slide that snaked its way down the hill. Huge bonfires on the summit revealed a spectacular scene. "[B]lack half-naked devils," joking and yelling at one another, stirred to their work. They attacked a pile of cotton with restrained fury, dragging bales to the slide and letting them go. Bale after bale came hurtling down in quick succession. The moment a bale struck the barricade on the steamer, roustabouts dug their cotton hooks deep into it and yanked it away. They dragged the fleecy bundle to the boat's aft, stacked it on the pile, and began the process anew. Occasionally a bale bounced off the slide into the trees, hopped into the river, or crashed over the cotton bale wall, "breaking stanchions and railings, and scattering passengers to the berth deck." Roustabouts scrambled up the hill or splashed into the water, tracking down stray bales and hauling them to the riverboat. Once all the cargo was safely aboard, roustabouts retracted the gangplank and found a comfortable place to rest. As the boat eased away from the bank and churned away, Power reluctantly admitted the amazing scene was "worth the delay we paid for it."[1]

Although such scenes were memorable, it was the mundane activities of steamboats that made them central to economic development in the Southwest. Riverboats were an immediate boon to staple crop production because they increased the profitability and relative efficiency of farms and plantations, allowed for better transportation of products, reduced the costs of farm materials, opened up new avenues of information, enhanced the value of slave labor, and provided windfall profits for residents along the river who sold wood to passing boats. These activities, at least until 1850, made steamboats crucial to cotton production in the interior South and helped create an international age of cotton. Riverboats also boosted urban growth and created new forms of commercial exchange, and their movement along the western waters connected the markets of the Southwest and Midwest.[2]

"LOADED TO THE GUARDS"

Before steamboats came thrashing upon the scene, flatboats limited cotton production. Residents along the rivers of the interior South normally flagged down passing flatboats during harvest season, but it was a hit and miss proposition. In 1810 a cotton planter near Natchez, for instance, shipped 200 cotton bales on "Henderson's barge" and another 104 bales on James Rust's flatboat ten days later. While most flatboatmen were honest, enough were not to give farmers pause whether or not to entrust their treasure to strangers. Many planters preferred control to convenience, so they built their own flatboats or coordinated transportation with neighbors. If there were not enough trusted friends or younger sons to man the flatboats, then "their own Negroes, or occasionally a few hired Indians" were used as muscle. Cotton producers who built and then manned their own boats lost time that was better spent working in their fields. Small cotton producers faced more disadvantages in shipping their crops—they could not spare workers or afford to hire strangers. Not only did flatboats often leak and damage the cotton, but they could carry no more than 100 to 150 bales, a puny number when compared to steamboats. Flatboats limited agricultural productivity and profitability by restricting the shipment and sale of staple crops.[3]

Perceptive southerners shifted their business to riverboats as soon as practicable. William Kenner is a case in point. He was a shrewd New Orleans factor and commission merchant who handled the business affairs of planters up and down the Mississippi River. Kenner saw the *New Orleans* arrive in 1812 and immediately realized that he should begin shipping cotton on the boat. He wrote to Stephen Minor, a wealthy Natchez planter, that he had spoken "to Mr. Roosevelt on the subject of taking down your cotton next trip." Kenner added that he was sending a shipment of oysters to Natchez, certainly a highly unusual delicacy away from the Gulf coast and one that would probably spoil on a keelboat going upriver. It is a measure of Kenner's dissatisfaction with the flatboat trade that he switched to the unproven *New Orleans* for the movement of Minor's most valuable product. So many farmers followed Minor's example that the Ohio Steam-Boat Navigation Company's managing agent in the South estimated the Natchez to New Orleans cotton shipments to be more profitable than the entire Hudson River trade. Jasper Lynch begged company officials for another steamer to be put into the water "as one boat does not bring down one fourth of the cotton."[4]

Steamboats had significant advantages over flatboats when it came to hauling agricultural products. They could stop just about anywhere along the riverbank, could operate in low water, had a much greater cargo capacity, and made several round trips in the time it would take a flatboat to make one journey. The *New Orleans* and other early boats carried up to four or five hundred bales of cotton, a significant increase over flatboats. There was so much demand for their services that crew members braced the guards with logs to prevent cotton bales from tumbling into the river. The advent of hog chains around 1830 greatly increased the size and capacity of riverboats. Wide guards were perfect places to stack cargo, and carrying huge amounts of material became a badge of honor, as ambitious captains bragged that their steamboats were "loaded to the guards." Soon it became common to see thousands of cotton bales heaped upon steamers. Before the Civil War the famous *Sultana* normally carried 3,500 bales, while in 1837 the *John Randolph* once hauled 5,000. Captains constantly pressed their crews to load more and more cotton and bragged when they outdid a rival. Hog chains notwithstanding, it was not uncommon for guards to dip so low that riverwater rippled against the lowest bales. Boats hauling massive amounts of cotton were an impressive sight. Tyrone Power "saw one monster come groaning down the stream, looking like a huge cotton-bale on fire. Not a portion of the vessel remained above the water, that could be seen, excepting the ends of the chimneys: the hull and all else was hidden by the cotton-bags, piled on each other, tier over tier, like bricks." So much cotton crowded the deck that only a small alleyway allowed passengers to move about. Bales commonly blocked the windows and doors on the boiler deck so completely they prevented sunlight from reaching the cabins and forced passengers to burn lights day and night.[5]

The cotton trade was so immense and became so lucrative that some steamboats specialized in hauling the staple. They possessed flared guards and extra high smokestacks so the sparks would burn out before falling on the bales. The *Ozark* was one such cotton boat, and its owners promised it would "pay strict attention to the calls of the planters." Cotton was so closely associated with steamers that bale capacity, rather than tonnage, became the standard measure. When the owners of the *Lamplighter* tried to sell it in 1837, they stressed the cotton capacity. It meant nothing to describe the *Lamplighter* as a 200-ton boat; it meant everything to call it a 1,200-bale boat.[6]

The ease with which producers could ship cotton on steamboats fueled the demand for farms and plantations in the Southwest, which increased the tempo of slaves' forced migration. Carving a plantation out of the woods was tremendously difficult and taxed slaves' bodies to the limit. Masters relied on young slaves, particularly men, to do the hard work of clearing land, erecting buildings, and breaking the soil. Between the first voyage of the *New Orleans* and the secession of South Carolina, at least 875,000 African Americans became part of one of the largest forced migrations in American history. This second middle passage became a building block for the Cotton Kingdom by destroying slave families. A significant number of these slaves would have moved even without the invention of steamboats, of course, but the majority of these bondservants were clustered along the region's rivers. As steamboats moved up and down the Mississippi, Tombigbee, Yazoo, and Red rivers, they made river bottom land more attractive in a number of ways. Steamboats accelerated the cultivation of cotton and thus deepened the need for enslaved Americans in the southern interior. During his trip up the Alabama River, Thomas Nichols learned firsthand how steamboats enhanced the value of slave labor. Nichols spoke with a planter who had just returned from New Orleans with four or five families of slaves destined for his new plantation along the river. Given the nature of the New Orleans slave market, the slaves Nichols saw almost certainly grew up in the Chesapeake.[7]

Steamboats quickly and easily meshed with the rhythms of plantation life. Cotton picking could be a bottleneck in production—farmers typically grew more cotton than they could harvest—and white fields unleashed a flurry of activity. Enslaved Americans worked long hours picking the same field over and over again since the cotton continued to ripen for weeks. They hauled, ginned, and baled the cotton. Once the cotton was stamped into fleecy blocks, slaves slipped bags around the bales and used rope to tie the package together. Someone, perhaps the overseer, then weighed the bales and marked them with the initials of the planter. Long, hard days were the norm during cotton season. "Today I have been helping weigh and mark Cotton to send down by the Cotton Plant," scribbled the exhausted overseer of a plantation in southern Arkansas. After the overseer recorded the weight of the bales, slaves carted them to the riverbank in a wagon. The process was repeated until all the cotton had been processed. Slaves on Bennett Barrow's plantation in Louisiana, for instance, made the five-mile journey to Ratliff's Landing at least six times in November 1836, bringing 845 bales to the water's edge. Many large plantations had warehouses along the river where cotton could be stored until a steamboat arrived. These shed-like structures had wooden slats on the ground to prevent the cotton from becoming dirty or wet. Warehouses provided minimal protection against the elements, so planters tried to ship their cotton as soon as possible. Often a few trusted slaves remained with the bales—sometimes chopping wood to sell to steamers—and flagged down the first riverboat that churned by. Steamboats increased agricultural productivity by allowing planters to manage labor more effectively. Riverboats, simply put, freed bondservants to work a staple crop rather than build a flatboat and transport it.[8]

The amount of cotton that riverboats brought to New Orleans underwent spectacular growth. In 1816, a time when steam was just becoming known, steamboats carried 37,000 bales to the Crescent City. Six years later the figure was 161,000, it climbed to 428,000 in 1830, and reached 923,000 in 1840. It was "an almost every day occurrence," wrote one New Orleans resident, "that a cargo of 2,500 to 3,000 bales is landed." The situation in Mobile was similar, as the city received 103,065 bales in 1830 and 440,102 a decade later. As one visitor to the city deduced, "The cotton crop is the basis of all the business of the place."[9]

Cotton was not the only cash crop that benefited from contact with the steamboat trade. Sugar and tobacco plantations also reaped substantial benefits. Whereas cotton producers relied on riverboats to send cotton in one direction—to New Orleans or Mobile for reshipment to northern mills or English markets—other producers sent their products up and down the rivers. Steamboats literally changed the direction of the United States' internal trade. No longer did molasses, for instance, have to travel through New Orleans, up the Atlantic seaboard, and across the Appalachian Mountains. Two-way river traffic on steamboats enabled planters to plug into regional markets and ship their products to Omaha, St. Paul, Louisville, Pittsburgh, or virtually anywhere in between. In 1817 Germain Musson sent seventy hogsheads of sugar from his

Louisiana plantation to Cincinnati, and fellow planter James Dalzell shipped his three hundred barrels of molasses directly to Pittsburgh on the *Saxon* thirty-eight years later. Dalzell's direct connection with Pittsburgh was not the norm, and the necessity to offload products at Louisville made merchants and commission agents liaisons between southern planters and northern buyers.[10]

The iron and hemp industries also underwent steady growth thanks to the advent of steamboats. In Tennessee, the Western Highland Rim (the craggy hills west of Nashville) held rich deposits of iron ore that attracted entrepreneurs who built a ring of blast furnaces. By the time of the Civil War, Tennessee was one of the South's leading producers of iron ore and riverboats on the Cumberland carried virtually all of it away, mainly to Pittsburgh. Iron entrepreneurs James Winchester and Thomas Yeatman purchased riverboats not only to carry their products but to bring in the necessary supplies to keep their smelters running. The hemp industry—centered mainly in Tennessee, but also found in Missouri—relied on steamboats to reduce transportation costs and increase profit margins. Perhaps just as significantly, riverboats used much rope, which was often purchased directly from manufacturers when boats stopped to take on freight.[11]

While steamboats generally aided the plantation economy, they also enabled slaves in riverfront plantations and towns to test the limits of their enslavement through escape attempts. Exact numbers are impossible and estimates are notoriously unreliable, but thousands of fugitive slaves rode the decks of steamers to freedom. John Warren is one example. He labored on a Mississippi cotton plantation, where he secretly learned to read and write. Warren fled to Memphis after attacking the overseer and wrote a pass for himself indicating he could work in the city. He quickly found employment on a steamer and used the opportunity to escape to Canada. However, the risks and hardships—one Arkansas slave waded forty miles through swamps before stowing away on a steamer—deterred most enslaved Americans from making escape attempts. And, as discussed earlier, masters effectively used steamboats to foil escape attempts.[12]

"CONFIRMS ALL MY PREJUDICES AGAINST COTTON CARRYING STEAMERS"

The transportation of staple products on riverboats was reliable and efficient, but problems were not unknown. Captains were responsible for protecting their cargo from the elements while in transit, and the slipshod efforts of roustabouts or mates might reduce a product's value, particularly cotton, since it was not packed in such a way as to resist the elements. Stephen Douglas, the Illinois politician, learned this lesson the hard way. He controlled a plantation in Mississippi that his wife inherited. When his overseer sent eighty-six bales of cotton on the *Pearl Plant* in 1852, Douglas alleged that roustabouts negligently threw some of his bales onto the riverbank to lighten the steamer. When the cotton reached New Orleans on a different riverboat, a witness said that it looked like it had been rolled in the mud. Such complaints were common. One planter groused that roustabouts soiled his cotton when they trampled on it with muddy feet, and another learned that heavy rains drenched his bales. It was a tiresome chore to sort out blame in such cases, particularly when unscrupulous captains altered bills of lading. The Toledano and Taylor firm in New Orleans cautioned one of its clients to write an exact description of his cotton and seal the envelope. "[T]he Boats are so very fond of having Bills of Lading sent by them *open and unsealed* that they have full chance to alter them to their own mind without our having any knowledge to the contrary," they warned.[13]

Fire, not water, was the chief threat to commodities on riverboats. Michel Chevalier, a French national who traveled in the United States, was horrified that steamboat passengers sat on bales and smoked. Cigar ash should have been the least of his worries; cinders from smokestacks were a menace, as were the torches steamers used to light the night sky. A number of horrific blazes consumed not only the cotton but the boats as well. When Joseph Ingraham visited New Orleans he woke in the middle of the night to panicked cries of fire. He ran to his window and saw wild red flames devour two mammoth steamers laden with cotton. Although a quarter of a mile away, Ingraham felt the rush of hot air on his cheeks as he saw flaming bales of cotton spinning in the air and shooting into the river. The sizzling and spangling of sparks created a remarkable scene. The burning of the *Charles Belcher* created an equally memorable spectacle in 1854. It arrived at Vicksburg early in the morning, laden with five hundred bales of cotton, seven hundred hogsheads of tobacco, and a huge quantity of pork. Another steamer arrived at the levee, and sparks from its torches set the cotton on the *Charles Belcher* ablaze. Flames then leaped to five other boats, including the *Natchez*, which had 2,500 bales of cotton aboard, before consuming produce stacked on the levee. Frightened passengers leaped out of cabins, only to learn that lard, oil, and liquor had turned the river into a sheet of flame. Burning cotton bales bobbed next to blackened corpses. When the last fires had been extinguished, the toll was almost incomprehensible. The *Charles Belcher, Mohican, Natchez, Liah Tuna, Crescent,* and *Saxon* were complete wrecks. Fire claimed the lives of at least thirty African Americans and caused perhaps $1 million in property damage. One eyewitness grimly wrote that the incident "confirms all my prejudices against cotton carrying steamers."[14]

Despite such dangers, residents of the Southwest preferred to use steamboats to transport agricultural commodities. At a cost of one or two dollars, a farmer could send a cotton bale to New Orleans or Mobile, where factors or cotton brokers handled all other arrangements. The costs for such services were reasonable, particularly when the cotton market was strong. James Jordan, for instance, sent ninety-one bales of cotton to Mobile, where Rives, Battle, and Company arranged for its sale. The 45,220 pounds of cotton grossed $2,826.25. After deducting $264.52 for freight, drayage, wharfage, weighing, storage, fire insurance, and the commission, Jordan still had a handsome profit.[15]

"CLEARING THE TIMBER OFF THE RIVER BANK
IN ORDER TO MAKE A WOOD YARD"

Steamboats enhanced the profitability of plantation agriculture in a number of other ways. They increased the value of hired slaves by expanding the scope and value of rental markets. No longer were slaves leased out only within walking distance of their homes. Steamboats allowed masters to send their bondservants to distant locales and increased the interdependence between plantation and town. Henry Summers was one owner who took advantage of the flexibility that riverboats provided. Summers normally hired out three slaves to a tobacco factory in New Orleans. When work at the factory ceased, he added to his income by sending the men via the steamboat *Emperor* to cut sugar cane. Steamers also maximized the value of slaves by allowing planters to shift labor, or potential labor, in a timely fashion. When a particular task was time sensitive, steamers were the natural means to bring in extra hands. Rachel O'Connor swallowed her scruples about her bondservants traveling on riverboats and allowed five of them to go by water so that they could reach her brother's plantation in time to chop cane.[16]

Steamers also nourished farms and plantations as part of "an interior commerce of immense proportions," according to a government study. Surviving receipts reveal that riverboats brought salt, lard, pork, peas, corn, figs, and raisins to pantries; soap, washtubs, candles, mattresses, and bed rails to houses; and rope, nails, grindstones, ginning bags, saws, and cotton gins to farms. Planters wrote to their factors or contacted mercantile houses directly. In either case, riverboats stopped at plantations and communal landings to deliver a medley of materials. One overseer recorded how the *Cotton Plant* made regular stops at his plantation. On December 13, 1848, it left twenty sacks of salt, and a month later it deposited lumber. Ten sacks of salt and two barrels of tar arrived ten days after that. Riverboats also carried the food that sustained the slaves, with barrels of mess pork from Cincinnati finding their way to plantations alongside sacks of corn. The low cost of shipping wheat, flour, and livestock from northern farms enabled planters, if they wished, to devote more land to staple crops rather than food production. Steamboats, as one guidebook for emigrants concluded, were "an invaluable acquisition for the inhabitants" of the Mississippi River valley because of their ability to support the plantation economy.[17]

Residents of the southern interior also took advantage of the voracious appetite of steamboats for wood. The arrival of the *New Orleans* in the West converted trees from nuisance to commodity and marked the beginning of the southern timber industry. For planters moving to virgin land, wood sales were a way to pay expenses before staple crop production became profitable. Newcomers were clearing land as a matter of course, but they dispatched gangs of slaves to prepare it for sale rather than merely burning it. One young planter near Natchez earned $12,000 in wood sales alone during his first year in Mississippi. The next year he sold $10,000 worth of wood and raised eighty bales of cotton. Had the planter taken a steamboat to visit the New Orleans slave markets, he could have traded his wad of cash for sixteen slaves. For a few planters, wood sales reached extreme amounts. Isaac Franklin's woodyard, located at the confluence of the Mississippi and Red Rivers, raked in from $10,000 to $20,000 annually from 1846 to 1850. Perhaps not all the proceeds came from steamboats, but the yard's location is suggestive that the majority did.[18]

Wood sales to steamboats were a perfect fit for plantations because felling trees and chopping them into pieces did not require consistent or constant activity. Owners could dispatch slaves to cut firewood during times of slack activity in the fields and then recall those slaves when labor demands spiked. Harriet Martineau remembered seeing groups of slaves, "most of them nearly naked," chopping wood on the banks of the Mississippi. The work was difficult, but probably no worse than many other tasks that slaves faced. Enslaved

Americans sometimes manned woodyards in round-the-clock shifts, with the night shift lighting huge bonfires to catch the attention of passing steamers. Some slaves even preferred wood preparation, especially if they were allowed to fish driftwood out of the river, an activity much easier than wielding an axe. Other enslaved Americans found a measure of freedom as lumberjacks. They typically were away from the main work activity of the plantations and, more importantly, out from under the watchful eyes of the masters and overseers. A number of slaves even worked partial days. One traveler along the Mississippi was surprised to learn that a particular slave had to prepare one cord of wood a day and then "whatever he does after that was for himself."[19]

Small producers also benefitted from wood sales. They might own land or, more commonly, squat on it until the owner chased them away. Samuel Davis decided to seek his fortune as a woodhawk, as the proprietors of small wood-yards were commonly called. Davis moved to Breckinridge County, Kentucky, along the Ohio River, and was immediately excited by his prospects. Even the hard work—"I have been for two days past clearing the timber off the river bank in order to make a wood yard"—did not dint his enthusiasm. He reported that steamboats regularly passed by and that he expected his yard to thrive. William Johnson, the African American barber in Natchez, made enough money from his woodyard near Natchez that he could hire a white overseer to watch the property and pay whites and rented slaves to cut the wood. Indeed, rumors of easy profits attracted so many people that one 1832 estimate figured there were 4,400 woodhawks along the southern rivers. The presence of so many woodyards naturally fueled arguments, and when competing yards were too close to one another, "the rifle settles the dispute."[20]

Steamboat passengers rarely used kind words to describe men like Samuel Davis. They were "tall, lanky, unwashed men, with clay-coloured faces, look-ing for all the world as though they had been made out of the same mud that dyes the Mississippi waters," clucked one cabin passenger. Their homes varied in size and quality, but most seem to have been drafty and small. Edward Jarvis wandered through one woodhawk's home in 1841. The walls of the one-room building were about sixteen feet per side and enclosed a fireplace. The only furniture inside were two beds and a trundle. Jarvis noticed that this and most of the other woodhawk homes were so poorly built that he "could see through them from the river." Woodhawks normally raised some corn on the land they cleared and depended on wild game to supplement their diet. They bought everything else from passing steamers or flatboats.[21]

Particularly savvy wood sellers loaded flatboats with forty or fifty cords of wood and moored them in the middle of the river. As riverboats passed, workers threw a rope to the boat and deckhands lashed the flatboat to the steamer's side. Firemen and roustabouts jumped into the flatboat and pitched the wood aboard the steamboat, "the Mate helping them by swearing as hard as he can." While the crew worked, the captain negotiated a price and the mate made sure the cordage was correct by measuring the wood with a long pole. Once the crew finished its work and the captain settled the bill, a deckhand cut the rope and the flatboat floated free. The steamer hardly slowed down during the process. The woodhawk then pushed the flatboat to his yard, replenished it, and poled back into the river to wait for the next customer.[22]

Between 1820 and 1850, steamboats were crucial to the cotton boom in the southern interior. They hauled staple crops, increased plantation productivity, enhanced the value of rental slaves, carried farm supplies, and provided windfall profits through wood sales. Steamboats helped create the age of cotton in the mid-nineteenth century. American cotton exports rose from next to nothing in the 1790s to two-thirds of the world's raw cotton supply by 1860. Beginning at least in the 1840s, bales shipped to New Orleans and Mobile (mainly on steamboats) comprised about 40 percent of all cotton produced in the United States. This white gold ignited industrial revolutions in England and the United States, sustained the American merchant marine (based mainly in the free states along the Atlantic coast), provided profits to northern banks and insurance companies, and created international trade networks. Cotton was, like oil today, the world's single most valuable commodity. Growers in the Atlantic slave states did not need steamboats to produce the fleecy staple, but their counterparts in the southern interior came to rely on riverboats to an unthinkable degree. Steamboats in the interior South influenced the direction of world commerce.[23]

"THE ENTIRE WHARF FRONT WAS A DAILY SCENE OF BUSINESS LIFE AND ACTIVITY"

A steamboat's arrival in a city unleashed a hive of activity. The whole wharf, particularly in a large city like New Orleans, seemed to be "alive with a ceaseless maelstrom of motion." While one part of the crew tied the mooring lines to the wharf, roustabouts strained to unload the cargo. Workers at each other's heels rolled barrels, carried boxes, hoisted bags of corn on their shoulders, and dragged cotton bales as they tromped across the stage. Roustabouts dropped their loads into one of the several thousand drays, or low, heavy carts. The draymen cracked their whips or swore at their mules, and the drays clattered away to find the proper warehouse, mercantile store, or connecting steamer. Slave traders jostled their way through the tumult, searching for coffles of enslaved Americans that their business partners had forwarded to them. Passengers worked their way off the boats, eager to find relatives or explore the town. Dockworkers struggled to load boats that were busy disgorging their freight. "[C]lerks, porters, draymen, hackmen, stevedores, deck-hands, passengers, and loafers" swarmed past cotton bales, mounds of corn sacks, piles of tropical fruits, and heaps of hogsheads. The sound of hoofs, wheels, and voices was punctuated with the hiss of escape pipes, clamor of bells, roar of engines, and clank of cranes. On New Orleans's four-mile-long levee, the noise associated with this "commercial beehive" was deafening.[24]

Commission agents and factors were on hand to sort through the bewildering array of southern bounty. They directed dock workers to cluster barrels together and throw a tarp over them if necessary to ward off the rain. At any time, amazed observers saw "Pork without end; as if Ohio had emptied its lap at the door of New Orleans. Flour by the thousand barrels." Other agents marked cotton with flags. Damaged bales went to a pickery, where it cost $2.50 for pickers to pluck the bad cotton from the bale and try to repair or clean the rest. Draymen hauled the good cotton to a cotton press, where slaves shoved a bale under a compressor. As the iron sheet crushed the bale, other slaves cut the binding ropes and then tied new ones around the cotton. Suddenly the bale was one-third its original size, looking "ragged as a beggar," and ready for shipment to a cotton mill. This display of rhythmic precision took thirty seconds.[25]

Harried clerks, in the meantime, faithfully tracked the arrivals and dispersals. Over the course of three days in June 1856, one employee of the Bowling Cotton Company recorded the arrival of cotton from Shreveport, Paducah, St. Louis, Memphis, Louisville, Galveston, Jefferson, Bayou Sara, and Vicksburg. He documented the arrival of an average of 470 bales a day from June 14 to July 17. For the first ten days of September, the average shot up to 1,800 bales a day. Between the bales stacked along the levee and the draymen clip-clopping along with cotton bound for the presses or the pickery, clumps of cotton floated in the air. Along the waterfront it looked "as if it had been snowing large flakes."[26]

Even though cotton was king, trade of all types grew as the number of steamers increased. In 1814, twenty-one riverboats brought 67,500 tons of freight to the Crescent City. A decade later, 436 steamers hauled 136,240 tons of cargo. Those figures rose to 1,958 and 542,500 by 1841. Between 1830 and 1840 New Orleans, according to a government report, had the fastest growth of any American city, rising to fourth in population. More impressively, its port was the third busiest port in the world. Although it is impossible to determine how much of this development was directly attributable to steamboats, the chief of the U.S. Bureau of Statistics was convinced. Steamboats, he wrote in 1888, caused a "large increase" in the Crescent City's river trade. Clearly, the lack of riverboats would have stunted New Orleans' growth.[27]

Along the western rivers, St. Louis was second to New Orleans in commercial growth and trade volume, thanks in large part to its location at the confluence of two major rivers. St. Louis stood at the intersection of three trade orbits—Midwest, Far West, and South. The first riverboat docked at St. Louis on August 2, 1817, an event the *Missouri Gazette* incorrectly hailed as "the day of small things." It was impossible, the paper apologetically explained two years later, to believe that steamers could carry material from Philadelphia or New York to St. Louis. As steamboat traffic increased (over 250 different boats touched St. Louis's rocky shores in 1847), citizens poured money into steamboat investments. Local residents had $4,747,000 tied up in boats that transited through their city. Riverboats mainly carried coffee, salt, sugar, glass, and luxury goods from New Orleans and Louisville, slashing prices as much as 75 percent. Lines of "floating palaces nearly two miles in length" received flour, whiskey, pork, hemp, flax, beef, corn, skins, buffalo robes, iron, and other products from Illinois, Missouri, and beyond. St. Louis served as an important gateway to the West, and with the growth of river traffic on the Missouri River, a place as distant as Montana was connected, if tenuously, to New Orleans and Pittsburgh.[28]

Louisville's economic growth also stemmed from environmental conditions, in this case the Falls of the Ohio. The Falls were impassable in low water and risky in high water, forcing steamers to offload their cargo so draymen could lug it around the obstruction. Essentially, Louisville was tied to two fleets of steamers—one in the waters above the city and the other below—and the break in river traffic served as a steady means of employment for countless draymen, freight handlers, warehouse owners, and wagon drivers. As early as

1828, according to the *Western Monthly Review,* nearly two hundred steamboats serviced the city and were one of its primary sources of wealth. Even after completion of a canal around the Falls in 1835, the area was "lined with hacks, omnibuses, wagons, drays and all kinds of vehicles, hauling passengers and freight to and from the boats arriving and departing." The waterfront teemed with activity. "Stores, barrooms, lodging-houses and groceries lined the river front," remembered one visitor, "and, what with steamboatmen, flatboatmen, passengers, teamsters and stragglers, the entire wharf front was a daily scene of business life and activity." One of the tavern owners was Jim Porter, also known as the Kentucky Giant, who became an object of curiosity for travelers. Porter, who also drove a hack, was seven feet, eight inches tall and kept an eight-foot-long rifle behind the counter of his store. Visitors to Louisville gawked at Porter and had their friends stand next to him. When Charles Dickens saw Porter walking down the busy Louisville wharf, he said the man looked like "a lighthouse walking among lamp-posts." Even if the Kentucky Giant was a curiosity, the dependence of the Louisville economy on steamboats was not.[29]

New Orleans, Mobile, St. Louis, and Louisville were not the only towns that grew as a result of steamboat traffic. Regional entrepots like Memphis, Vicksburg, Natchez, and Montgomery prospered greatly from their connection to the riverboat trade. The web of small rivers in the South meant that most cotton producers had at least inconsistent access to riverboat transportation. Thanks to small steamers, producers in fairly remote regions could ship cotton at a low cost and also receive the necessary farm supplies. The *Native* and the *Hatchie Planter,* for instance, moved the fleecy staple down the Hatchie River to Memphis. That city became a collection point for cotton grown in western Tennessee, northern Mississippi, and northern Alabama. Slaves transferred bales from the small riverboats to the large Mississippi boats for their trip to New Orleans. Similar scenes were played out in Vicksburg, Natchez, and Montgomery, and the amount of cotton shipped through these regional centers is noteworthy. In 1843, for instance, riverboats hauled about 100,000 bales out of Memphis, 75,000 out of Vicksburg, and 50,000 out of Natchez. Three years later steamboats carried 57,000 bales from Montgomery, a city that had to keep building bigger and better wharves to handle the growing trade. Steamboats, in other words, helped unite rural and urban in an impressive commercial web.[30]

BROWN SUGAR, ALMONDS, BROOMS, ROPE,
AND DRIED BEEF TONGUES

Besides accelerating the market economy in the interior South, steamboats created new businesses. They were a major employer, even if many of the workers were enslaved Americans. Riverboats based in the Southwest paid out over $7 million to roughly ten thousand employees (or, if they were slaves, to their masters) in 1860. Mates, deckhands, and members of the cabin crew pumped much of this cash into river towns. For those slaves who never saw their wages, their owners kept the money and spent it in a variety of ways, while those bondspeople who retained some of their earnings likely distributed part of it in places like Natchez and New Orleans.[31]

Riverboats also contributed to the economy of the southern interior with their enormous consumption of wood. Steamers burned up to thirty cords a day, and in 1860 that amounted to perhaps 2.1 million cords of wood. With captains paying anywhere from $1 to $5 per cord (with $2 to $3 being the norm), southern steamers bought about $5.2 million worth of fuel in 1860, making wood sales a silent but important business along the major rivers. In a fairly typical transaction, the captain of the *Robert J. Ward* paid $250 for one hundred cords of wood at a Louisiana plantation. One traveler spied woodyards every four or five miles along the Mississippi River, and southerners sometimes purchased riverfront land for the sole purpose of harvesting wood.[32]

Other southerners capitalized on the fact that riverboats constantly needed refitting and supplies. The owner of a shipyard in New Orleans testified that it took more time to refit a boat than it did to build it new. He employed thirty-five to forty people to tear out rotted wood, apply new caulk, and paint boats so they could attain the best insurance rating. In Louisville, workers in the Jefferson Foundry grated water wheel flanges, repaired bolts, patched boilers, and replaced the force pump arms. New Orleans alone had six shipyards devoted to the maintenance and repair of steamboats, an industry that provided hundreds of jobs. Riverboats also consumed massive amounts of supplies and were constantly buying material from grocers, small producers, and planters. Buckner and Hughs of Louisville, for example, sold buckets, sperm oil, charcoal, soap, butter, potatoes, mackerel, corn meal, pickles, mustard, rice, cheese, knives, forks, brown sugar, almonds, brooms, rope, dried beef tongues, and many other items to steamers. Not only did steamers buy corn, turnips, and potatoes from small producers like William Johnson, they bought fresh produce at plantations, particularly when tied up for wooding. In 1860, steamers on the western waters spent perhaps $5.5 million on repairs, refitting, and replenishing, money that brought tangible economic benefits to towns, small landowners like Johnson, and planters.[33]

Steamboats also consumed the products of the slaves' informal economy. Across the South, enslaved Americans tended gardens, raised chickens, caught fish, or made small products on their own time that they sold. The *Alpha,* a steamer that plied the waters of the Attakapas River in Louisiana, routinely relied on slaves for flour, ham, lard, coffee, tomatoes, and other groceries. Slaves also made good use of steamboats to dispose of stolen items. Charles Brown bought pilfered food, silver spoons, and jewelry from his fellow slaves and sold them to passing steamers. Many of the boats' purchasing agents were African Americans, and they probably asked no questions regarding the origin of such items. The steady interchange along the river established commercial networks between slaves bound to plantations and their brethren who had breathtaking mobility on the rivers. Such trading webs connected farms, towns, and steamers in a complex arrangement that facilitated not just the flow of material goods but the transfer of information. The slave who sold eggs to a steamer obtained information and made personal connections that might be put to other uses.[34]

In the four decades prior to the Civil War, steamboats probably paid out a remarkable $289 million on wages, wood, repairs, and stores within the southern interior. As table 6 shows, riverboats were a significant boost for the southern economy and an important southern business. They created new commercial exchanges, animated economic life along the rivers, and opened opportunities for southerners to become integrated into the market economy. Steamboats grafted capitalistic practices onto the slave-based economy by creating markets where none had existed a few years earlier, accelerated the pace and quantity of cash and credit transactions, and gave southerners the opportunity to diversify their economic practices. As floating engines of capitalism, steamboats created commercial exchanges where none had existed just a few years earlier.[35]

"REVOLUTION IN WESTERN COMMERCE"

This economic whirlwind caused the unification of the West as a marketplace and region, at least until 1850. Consumer goods moved along western waters in the age of keelboats, but the proliferation of riverboats slashed shipping

TABLE 6

Estimated costs associated with southern steamboats in selected years

Year	Wages	Wood	Repairs	Stores	Year total
1820	$452,100	$240,684	$24,288	$297,897	$1,014,969
1830	1,565,150	954,304	59,202	1,083,365	3,662,021
1840	2,796,420	1,720,692	79,078	1,942,358	6,538,548
1850	5,756,790	3,728,437	210,276	4,078,647	13,774,150
1860	7,100,550	5,244,032	277,380	5,308,170	17,930,132
Grand total					
1815–1860	$114,617,795	$83,655,086	$5,315,944	$85,257,339	$288,846,164

Sources: See Appendix E. The grand total figures represent all years between 1815 and 1860 inclusive, not just those listed in the table.

charges and made products more affordable. This "revolution in Western commerce" meant that John Minor could satisfy his appetite for the finer things of life. The Natchez planter sent a barrage of letters to his factor in New Orleans requesting oysters, oranges, wine, champagne, brandy, olives, fresh raisins, chocolate, and "fine thick cotton stockings." Low freight rates allowed James Sproule in Louisville to advertise that he received men's clothing from New York on a weekly basis. As the South shook off its isolation, southerners greedily bought the same types of products that were available elsewhere in the United States. Ice from Minnesota, a commodity that would have melted in a flatboat, became a regular feature in the Southwest. Steamboats expanded the array of consumer goods to such an astonishing degree that Ann Jennings was disappointed when she went to Philadelphia. Jennings, a Nashville native, hoped to bring home the latest bonnets and impress her friends. Nashville had the same fashions as the East—thanks to steamboats—and Jennings came home empty-handed. As an influential western periodical observed, the steamboat brought "a little Paris, a section of Broadway, or a slice of Philadelphia" to people along the western waters.[36]

Thanks to riverboats, the markets of the Southwest and the Midwest were united and became increasingly interdependent. Lead shipments out of the Midwest topped $14 million between 1823 and 1848 and were the single most important factor in developing the Upper Mississippi's river trade. Other commodities, such as wheat, furs, and pork, also found their way southward on steamers. Return voyages brought products like agricultural equipment, fruit, stoves, military supplies, and trade goods that nourished frontier settlements in Illinois, Wisconsin, Iowa, Minnesota, and South Dakota. Up through about 1850, the Mississippi was the great thoroughfare of western trade.[37]

The vast majority of white southerners were uncritical of the economic changes that steamers wrought. Residents along every sluggish stream in the interior South hungered for steamboat service because they equated the arrival of a riverboat with progress and commerce. Southerners near the White and Black rivers in Arkansas hoped that riverboats would touch their waterfronts, while an editorial in the *Montgomery Republican* ecstatically extolled the benefits of regular steamboat traffic. The river, which used to be "silent and unprofitable . . . now bears to its bosom the products of every quarter of the globe." Whereas one steamboat used to supply the needs of the area, now five chugged up and down the river but still struggled to keep up with demand. "What a wonderful change in commercial affairs has taken place within four or five years in Alabama!" the paper trumpeted. The arrival of the season's first boat on the Upper Bigbee River in Alabama was cause for celebration. "Whenever a steamboat whistles," a local resident confessed with perhaps too much candor, "we break for the landing and Japhet never searched for his daddy with more avidity than we hunt for oysters. When we find the precious package, we know we shall ejaculate, Eureka! Eureka!" Reaction to the advent of steamboat traffic in Bowling Green, Kentucky, was similar. When the *United States* unloaded its goods in January of 1828, one observer wondered if all those goods could be purchased. They were. Local residents were so keen to maintain riverboat service that local businessmen pressured the state legislature to improve the Green River. Steamboats were so directly associated with progress that lack of effective riverboat service was a sign of backwardness. When James Norman Smith flinched the first time he tried oysters, his companions gazed at him incredulously and wondered where he had been living. Smith explained that he hailed from Maury County, Tennessee, "And as Their was at That [time] No Steam Boats or Barges coming up to Nashville or the Cumberland River—No Fresh Oysters were ever Seen There." Smith's sheepish account betrayed a lack of sophistication that came from living in an area cut off from riverboat access.[38]

But if southerners uncritically accepted the connection to an ever-widening arc of markets and ideas, they were less enthusiastic about the by-products steamboats brought to southern cities. Free blacks, rented slaves, and white laborers crowded levees, boat repair facilities, and the countless taverns near the waterfronts. White southerners blamed free black steamboat workers for creating conditions dangerous to the public order. One correspondent to the *New Orleans Picayune* thought he put his finger on the problem when he noted that free black stewards used their training and influence "to prevail upon our [slave] stewards to abscond," while another writer blamed the escape of three slaves on free black steamboat workers who "seduced" the unwitting slaves. Once steamboat employees were "aping the fashionable dress and manner" of polite society, whites had to find methods to prevent the erasure of the differences between white and black, slave and free. Complicating the situation was the increasing political clout of riverside towns. In larger cities like New Orleans and St. Louis, working-class whites became involved in gang activity and violence near election time. If the sustained steamboat traffic brought a measure of stability to the southern economy, then side effects such as urban growth enhanced tension between town and country and fed into the uncertainty of southern politics.[39]

Steamboats were such a powerful force that they altered the shape of not only the southern economy, but the world economy. What was a new and unproven technology in 1811 quickly became a necessary element of the Cotton Kingdom. By the 1830s, steamboats had become the workhorses of the economy in the southern interior, as they enhanced the value of slaves, raised plantation productivity, and provided new sources of revenue for planters. These planters were increasingly enmeshed in a global system of commerce that cotton came to define. As riverboats connected merchants to regional, national, and international markets, they brought wealth, population, and political power to the Southwest. Steamboats also created new markets in the southern interior, and it was no accident that *De Bow's Review,* the leading southern magazine on commercial matters, featured a riverboat as one of the images on its cover. When a foreign observer noted, "The circulation of steamboats is as important to the welfare of the west, as the circulation of blood is to the human frame," he understood how riverboats helped create a slavery-dominated western economy. The transcendence of the steamboat, however, was short-lived. As we shall see in the next chapter, the advent of the railroad shifted American trade patterns, helped unite the South, and brought the golden age of steamboats to and end.[40]

EIGHT

STEAMBOATS IN DECLINE

Once Henry Shreve was forced out as superintendent of western rivers, he moved to St. Louis, where he had purchased farmland in anticipation of his retirement. Shreve, then in his mid-fifties, built a mansion and turned his energy to his estate. The old riverman, however, could not completely disengage himself from steamboats, as his son-in-law managed several craft and Shreve invested in others. He was perceptive enough, however, to realize that the day of the steamboat was waning and the time of the railroad was dawning. In 1849 Shreve joined with several other investors to incorporate the Missouri Pacific Railroad Company. The company's grandiose name advertised its equally ambitious designs: to build a railroad from St. Louis to the West coast. Forty years earlier Shreve had made the technological jump from outdated flatboats to steamboats, and now he was moving one last time.[1]

Shreve did not live to see the growth of the Missouri Pacific, one of the first American railroads west of the Mississippi River. In 1855, four years after Shreve died, the Missouri Pacific connected St. Louis with Jefferson City. Merchants in the capital city welcomed the railroad, seeing it as a way to expand the town's steamboat trade. The city's most prominent hotel, in fact, latched on to the mania and reinvented itself as the Pacific Railroad Hotel. For its part, the railroad returned the embrace and chartered three steamboats to connect with the railroad and bring passengers and freight to Kansas City on Tuesdays, Thursdays, and Saturdays. Passengers walked from the train depot to the steamboat landing via a canopy-covered boardwalk. Ritcherdson's Express Company soon matched the Missouri Pacific, arranging for four riverboats to intercept passengers at the Jefferson City landing. Business was brisk, a riverboat pilot remembered, as thousands of people and tons of freight now took the rail shortcut to Jefferson City. This direct route was the prime virtue of the Missouri Pacific, as it shaved hours from the riverboat trip from

St. Louis to Kansas City. The heyday of the Jefferson City landing was short-lived, as the Missouri Pacific eventually connected St. Louis with Kansas City and ultimately put the waterfront out of business. With the completion of the 1874 Eads Bridge over the Mississippi River, the railroad showed its impressive mastery of environmental obstacles and cemented its role as the reigning transportation technology.[2]

The Missouri Pacific illustrates a number of important interactions between steamboats and railroads. Even though it was obvious that railroads could overcome environmental constraints that steamboats could not, most of the first railroads in the interior South were intended to be auxiliaries for the riverboat trade. Railroads and steamboats coordinated their schedules and riverboats initially benefitted from the inroads of the iron horse. By the late 1850s, though, residents of the Southwest pursued railroad construction with such great vigor that the iron horse greatly corroded riverboat traffic. More ominously, the growth of railroads and canals in the North greatly reduced steamboat traffic between the southern interior and the Midwest. Residents of the Southwest, as a consequence, shifted their self-perception from southern and western to only southern. In the process, they looked to themselves rather than the federal government to coordinate and promote economic development. The growing confinement of steamboat traffic within the interior South helped prepare the region to accept secession.

"LITTLE BUSTLE IN OUR STREETS"

If steamboats proved their merit in overcoming one natural force—river currents—they proved deficient in coping with others. Snags, the Falls of the Ohio, and the Grand Chain of Rocks provided difficulties for riverboat navigation, but the federal government proved fairly effective in combating these obstacles. Other natural phenomena proved to be less tractable and contributed to the perilous conditions on western waters. Icy rivers were a seasonal problem as far south as Memphis. When Anton Reiff woke up "nearly dead" from the temperature being "two hundred below zero," he learned his steamboat was frozen solid in the Ohio River. He and some of his fellow "Arctic Explorers" made the best of a bad situation by visiting local farmers and going skating. Reiff was fortunate that his boat soon broke loose. Passengers on the *Cornelia* fared much worse. In 1852 the boat was locked in the Ohio River's icy grip for four weeks. When food ran low, the captain announced that all passengers must "ship for themselves." Most travelers scattered and hiked overland, some up to two hundred miles, but the Carvill family remained on the boat. Father and son tromped through the snow, hunting rabbits to survive. When they could bear their glacial prison and high protein diet no longer, the whole family hiked to a cabin and stayed with some relatives of Daniel Boone before taking a sleigh to the nearest town. As these stories illustrate, wintry conditions could bring commerce to a freezing halt. Steamboat crews rarely tried to chop up the ice and usually had no choice but to wait until it thawed. Floating ice chunks were also a nuisance because the larger ones could pierce particularly fragile hulls. Steamboats could not to conquer all that nature had to offer.[3]

Conditions for mid- to late summertime travel were vexing in a different way, as streams evaporated and sandbars shifted irregularly, particularly on the Mississippi's tributaries. Groundings were so common in the dry season that John James Audubon, who was floating down the Ohio on a flatboat, nonchalantly remarked at "having Seen Steam Boats almost every day fast on Sand Barrs I have taken no particular Notice of any of their Names & Positions." Residents along the Ohio River saw a bonanza in the captive audiences aboard riverboats. Men and boys rowed out to stranded steamers, offering apples for sale or charging a fee to liberate the passengers from their temporary prisons.[4]

Steamboat owners used strength and ingenuity to cope with low water. The usual first course of action was to lighten the riverboat in hopes that it could float free, as one steamer did when it grounded one hundred miles south of Louisville on a day hot enough to "roast a salamander." In this case, the crew's sweaty five hours paid off. If lightening the boat failed, crew members tried kedging. They sank an anchor deep into the riverbottom behind the boat, and, as they strained against the capstan, the captain reversed the engine in hopes of popping the boat free. Another method, known as walking, involved using spars or long poles angled like paddles on either side of the boat. A cable connected to the winch then pulled the spars in the hopes of lifting the boat over the obstacle. Other steamers looped a cable around a tree and turned the capstan to drag the boat forward. When all else failed, captains either waited for another steamer to pull them free, abandoned ship, or waited for the river to rise.[5]

Dry conditions tested the patience and endurance of the passengers and crew alike. The "half starved" and crotchety cabin passengers in stranded steamers scolded one another in fits of anger. Boats might be stuck for hours, days, or even months. The unpredictability of natural conditions forced customers to make hard decisions. Some transferred to other boats, but there was no guarantee as to accommodations and cabin passengers might find themselves sleeping on the saloon's floor or in the deck room. Travelers could also walk to the nearest town, as Charles Peter Grizzard's family did when their boat was stuck near Selma. The men formed a line on the steep bank and "passed up the Womenkind." They then dragged their baggage one quarter of a mile through a cornfield under the hot sun before boarding an omnibus, where they had to pay for their own passage. Patience, comfort, and opportunity were factors that passengers weighed as they tried to reassert control over their travel experience.[6]

As the water dried up, so did business in river towns. The "absence of steamboats at the wharves—the scarcity of cotton, the unemployed draymen to be seen in the shade, quietly waiting for a job—and at night the unlighted counting rooms, all give indication that the business season is over," concluded one small-town newspaper. Even large ports on major rivers felt the effects when low water reduced riverboat traffic. Coleman Rogers in Louisville complained to his friend in Lexington, "In consequence of the steam Boats being generally in lower trade, we have but little doing, and but little bustle in our streets." When low water grounded boats, havoc ensued in the economy of the southern interior, as when an 1855 drought reduced the Alabama River to a mere stream. Shipping prices spiked to $5 per bale, tempting desperate planters to build flatboats. The paralyzed riverboat trade brought financial ruin to overextended southerners like W. N. Smith, who had given William P. Gould generous terms for a loan. When the drought struck, Smith called in his loan, apologetically explaining that these "extra-ordinary times of low rivers have caused an oppressive demand for money"—but Gould was unable to pay up. By contrast, planters had to act quickly when the rains came. A rapid rise in river levels could undercut cotton prices, as one factor warned a cotton planter. Sell now, McDowell, Withers, and Company warned Hugh Davis, before "the rivers get up and large quantities [of cotton] arrive with its restless owners." Men like Hugh Davis, who once saw the steamboat as their economic savior, grew weary of being a slave to natural conditions.[7]

"FOR THE CONVEYANCE OF COTTON BALES TO THE RIVER"

The inconveniences associated with steamboats—scraping over sandbars, shooting out of the mud, and paralyzed commerce—made it clear that another technology was necessary to move passengers and freight across the Southwest. By 1830, Americans had already turned to railroads to overcome the liabilities of other forms of transportation. The first railroads were in the more densely populated states along the Atlantic coast, but residents of the southern interior were also interested in the new technology. For those southerners who lived on the tenuous edges of riverboat service, railroads seemed to be the answer because they did not depend on meteorological or environmental conditions for their vitality. The iron horse, moreover, could extend into regions untouched by steamboat traffic and travel in a straight line where rivers meandered back and forth. They were faster, too. A report in the wake of the *Moselle* explosion captured the optimistic potential of railroads. They were destined to do more for southern commerce than steamboats, the report predicted, because "ice in winter, low water in summer, [and] a circuitous and tedious route at times, interfere with [the] precision and accuracy" of riverboat travel. Railroads held out the promise of mastering the environment rather than working within its constraints.[8]

Given the obvious inadequacies of steamboats, one might think that railroads garnered enthusiastic support within the interior South. To a degree, they did. A few visionaries pushed for a railroad that would connect Mobile with the Ohio River, while others promised great benefits from a track running northward from New Orleans. Residents of the Southwest exhibited no sense of urgency, however, in taking on such schemes, and their rail companies constantly labored under the disadvantages of low capitalization and heavy debt. It can be argued that the general economic malaise after 1837 and the emphasis on buying slaves hamstrung capital investment into the railroad industry. Such objections are exaggerated; southerners along the Atlantic seaboard were capable of promoting, funding, and building railroads. In 1840 the seven slave states bordering the Atlantic Ocean had 28 percent of the country's track (796 of 2,808 miles), whereas the southern interior contained a woeful 5 percent (139 miles). A decade later, the picture was not appreciably different. Coastal southern railroads had 22.3 percent of the country's track (2,015 of 9,030 miles), while lines in the Southwest still languished at 4.7 percent (425 miles). Judging from these figures, residents of the southern interior had the capacity to build railroads, they just chose not to do so.[9]

The most telling explanation for this disparity is the effectiveness of the river trade in the Southwest. Even though the problems associated with steamboat traffic were well documented, southerners retained a stubborn

loyalty to steamboats and originally envisioned railroads west of the Appalachian Mountains as complementing river traffic rather than competing with it.
The first southern railroad west of the Alleghany Mountains, the Tuscumbia,
Courtland, and Decatur Railroad, is a case in point. Completed in 1832, the
forty-three-mile-long line shunted freight around Muscle Shoals, facilitat-
ing the flow of cotton out of northern Alabama. In the 1840s, southerners
completed other lines that jabbed out from rivers into the back country from
Vicksburg, Montgomery, Port Hudson, and New Orleans. All of them merely
augmented steamboat service. One Mississippi resident argued that it was
"common sense" to build a railroad into the interior "for the conveyance of
cotton bales to the river, merchandize to the country, and passengers to and
fro." As late as 1850, residents of the southern interior envisioned a transportation network with steamboats as the dominant partner. Conversely, southerners along the Atlantic coast did not enjoy the same useful river system
and wanted a transportation network that favored railroads. By 1850, rail lines
connected Richmond to Raleigh, Goldsboro, and Wilmington; Charleston to
Columbia, Athens, Atlanta, and Chattanooga; and Savannah to Atlanta. While
it would be presumptuous to describe southern railroads along the Atlantic
coast as forming a network, they were certainly more interconnected than the
scattered scars that marked the map of the Southwest.[10]

The decision to rely on steamboats until the 1850s made logical sense for
residents of the southern interior. Railroads were expensive to build whereas
steamboats were not. The rivers were navigable long enough to allow significant commerce to take place. Steamboat operators did not have to contend
with the divisive political debate that plagued railroad construction. Nor did
riverboat owners have to face sticky issues like right-of-way or construction
and engineering problems. Steamboats remained a proven investment that
normally brought immediate returns, while railroads could be risky and typically were slow to pay dividends.[11]

Until the early 1850s, railroads in the Southwest expanded steamboat traffic
by opening up new markets. Railroads brought freight and passengers from
relatively isolated counties to riverside wharves and carried finished goods
and passengers on the return trip. Planters were overjoyed to be able to move
cotton quickly and cheaply on railroads rather than having to haul the staple
overland on bad roads. The cost of moving cotton from inland Mississippi
near the Big Black River dropped from $4 a bale to $1 once rail lines were
fully operational. Vicksburg received 40,000 bales from interior Mississippi

counties in 1847 and more than doubled that total to 98,000 six years later. In similar fashion, the West Feliciana Railroad hauled cotton from Woodville, Mississippi, to the steamboat landing at Bayou Sara, Louisiana.[12]

Most historians assume that railroads quickly eclipsed steamboats in importance, but that was not the case in the interior South. Disentangling the relative strength of the two technologies is tricky because almost no antebellum steamboat records survive and railroad company records are spotty and inconsistent. The best that can be done at this time is to estimate through ton-miles, tonnage transported, and number of passengers, based on surviving evidence. When comparing through ton-miles for passengers and freight, railroads were an inconsequential factor for the political economy of the Southwest until the second half of the 1850s. In the southern interior in 1849 (the first year for which comparative data is available), table 7 shows that steamboats handled 878 times as much freight and 107 times as many passengers as railroads, when measured in miles shipped. Estimates of tonnage hauled on riverboats and railroads reveal a similar (if less one-sided) picture, and can be found in table 8. In 1840, steamboats in the Southwest hauled about twelve times as much freight as railroads, and about ten times as much a decade later. Even though all of these figures are only reasonable estimates, the trends are clear: until the late 1850s, railroads of the interior South were still intermediate carriers that primarily hauled cotton and other agricultural products to steamboat landings.[13]

"THE BOAT STOPS AT ALL THE RAIL ROADS"

Even if southern railroads were unable to make an appreciable dent in steamboat traffic on the western waters before 1850, that trade was shifting dramatically. As east-west rail and canal networks spread north of the Ohio River, cotton and other produce that steamboats had previously carried to New Orleans went eastward. Starting about 1840 traffic from the Ohio to the Mississippi declined; midwestern corn, wheat, and flour that previously had been marketed through New Orleans now found its way to Chicago or other northern cities. In the twenty years before 1860, the value of midwestern products arriving in New Orleans dropped from 58 to 23 percent of total receipts while upriver freight to the Midwest also suffered a decline.[14]

As river trade started seeping away from southern cities, their residents looked to railroads to staunch the flow. What touched off the orgy of railroad

TABLE 7

Steamboat and railroad output in selected years

	1849		1855–1856		1859	
	Ton miles (thousands)	*Pass. miles (thousands)*	*Ton miles (thousands)*	*Pass. miles (thousands)*	*Ton miles (thousands)*	*Pass. miles (thousands)*
Steamboats, Southern Interior	2,119,284	703,080	2,085,102	691,740	2,489,589	825,930
Railroads, Southern Interior	2,414	6,560	49,581.8	45,840.5	166,945.77	171,001.6
Ratio Southern Interior SB: Southern Interior RR	878:1	107:1	42:1	15:1	15:1	5:1
Railroads, Entire South	81,092.94	53,339.67	420,477.2	203,069.9	573,282.65	423,478.29
Ratio Southern Interior SB: Entire South RR	26:1	13:1	5:1	3:1	4:1	2:1
Railroads, US	347,016	468,149	1,903,952	1,756,053.8	2,577,682.2	1,879,616.4
Ratio Southern Interior SB: US RR	6:1	2:1	1:1	1:3	1:1	1:2

Note: Southern interior: KY, TN, MO, AL, MS, LA, TX.

Entire South: KY, TN, MO, AL, MS, LA, TX, DE, MD, VA, NC, SC, GA, FL.

Sources: See Appendix F.

building in the interior South was not only concern over the inadequacies of steamboats, but the relative loss of commercial revenue to other regions of the country. After all, residents of the Southwest recognized the limitations of steamboats by the 1820s and could have pursued railroads as vigorously as residents of the Atlantic coast. James De Bow was the most enthusiastic railroad booster in the southern interior. Compiler of the 1850 census and a resident of New Orleans, De Bow published a monthly journal that commented on

TABLE 8

Steamboat and railroad freight hauled, 1840, 1850, and 1860

	1840	1850	1860
Steamboats in the southern interior (tons)	1,016,532.00	2,665,435.50	3,748,925.25
Railroads in the southern interior (tons)	85,068.00	260,100.00	2,992,068.00
Ratio SB:RR	11.95:1	10.25:1	1.25:1

Note: Southern interior: KY, TN, MO, AL, MS, LA, TX.

Sources: See Appendix F.

southern agricultural and economic matters. *De Bow's Review* was brimming with reports, letters, and statistics explaining why southerners should invest in and build railroads. In a series of articles starting in the late 1840s, De Bow trumpeted the need for railroads for New Orleans, Mobile, Jackson, Vicksburg, Memphis, Louisville, and Shreveport. In his vision, railroads would supplant steamboats as the dominant means of transportation and commerce in the Mississippi River valley.[15]

De Bow's influence is difficult to measure, but by the early 1850s residents of the southern interior no longer viewed railroads as mere appendages to the river trade. Where an earlier generation of citizens in Bowling Green, Kentucky, hailed the arrival of steamboats in 1828 as their economic salvation and lobbied the state legislature for river improvements, twenty-five years later their children made sure that the Louisville and Nashville Railroad ran through their town. Lines in the Southwest shot up to 16 percent of the national total (4,889 of 30,626 miles) by the time South Carolina seceded. The most astounding growth was in Tennessee, which went from having nine miles of track in 1850 to having 1,253 miles ten years later. By contrast, even though the slave states along the Atlantic coast doubled their railroad mileage, their percentage of the national rail total shrank to 19.5 percent (5,976 miles).[16]

Railroad backers in the southern interior after 1850 had more urgency and were more effective at securing funding. Over time, they altered their conception of what the iron horse should do, as they no longer merely envisioned railroads as the handmaidens of steamboats. Rail lines now competed with rivers and had the potential to begin a commercial revolution in the Southwest. When it was completed in January of 1860, the Great Northern ran between New Orleans and Memphis and provided an alternative to steamboat traffic. Likewise, workers began laying rails on the north side of Mobile in 1852 and nine years later the city was connected with Columbus, Kentucky, on the Ohio River. Another railroad that provided direct competition with river traffic was the Louisville and Nashville. Coupled with a railroad running northeastward out of Memphis, the L&N allowed shippers to bypass the Ohio River entirely.[17]

Railroads—both northern and southern—sliced into the steamboat trade. In 1856, the ratio of freight (when measured in through ton-miles) shrank to 42:1 in favor of steamboats and the number of passengers decreased to 15:1. Three years later the figures were 15:1 and 5:1. Shippers (who valued cost) remained somewhat committed to steamboat traffic, while passengers (who valued time) switched wholeheartedly to railroads. The absolute tonnage also moved in the same direction. Tables 7 and 8 show that even though riverboats handled over ten times as much freight as railroads (when measured in absolute tonnage) in 1840 and 1850, that ratio was nearly even by the time Abraham Lincoln was elected president.[18]

As these figures make clear, railroads made substantial inroads into the steamboat trade in the 1850s, particularly in the last few years of the decade. Riverboats, though, were still an important part of the southern economy and would remain so for the next several decades. The majority of cotton and other southwestern produce still reached market on the decks of steamers rather than in the confines of a rail car. Increased mileage did not automatically translate into a high volume of freight shipped via rail. The five hundred-mile-long Mobile and Ohio Railroad, for instance, had only twenty-five engines and 361 freight cars in 1860. Freight cars had a capacity of eight to ten tons per car, but most were loaded far below capacity. Most trains, therefore, had payloads well under 150 tons, a figure way below what was normally shipped on one steamboat. Although railroads had obvious advantages in speed and ability to operate year round, they did not eclipse riverboats in bringing produce to New Orleans until 1883–1884. Steamboats, although giving way as the central force in the political economy of the southern interior, were hardly moribund in 1860.[19]

Cotton became the mainstay of the fading steamboat industry in the 1850s. Even though railroads siphoned off some of the fleecy staple to the Midwest, riverboats still carried most of the cotton produced in the Southwest to Mobile or New Orleans. In 1840–1841, about 812,000 bales arrived in New Orleans,

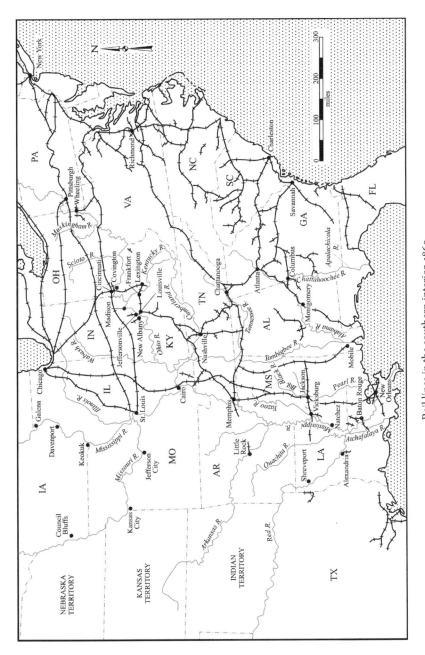

Rail lines in the southern interior, 1860

and that figure increased to 1,431,000 fifteen years later. Not only did the overall number of cotton bales increase, but the ratio of cotton's value to the rest of the river trade rose. In 1849–1850, receipts for cotton were valued at 43 percent of the produce received at New Orleans. A decade later they stood at 59 percent, in part because farmers shifted their perishable produce to railroads. Even though trade carried on steamboats on the western waters advanced in the 1850s, it lost much business to railroads and became heavily dependent on cotton. What had once been a thriving inter-regional steamboat trade was giving way to regional commerce, primarily cotton.[20]

Steamboats were able to cling to business by adjusting their commercial activities to coordinate with the railroads. We have seen how steamboats operated in conjunction with the Missouri Pacific, and such agreements became commonplace. A line of four boats operating out of Memphis connected with the Memphis and Charleston Railroad, while ten steamers coordinated their schedules with the Illinois Central Railroad on the north side of the Ohio River. At least one railroad even built riverboats as a means to extend its commercial reach. The Baltimore and Ohio constructed seven steamers to take passengers and freight from Wheeling to Louisville and all points in between.[21]

Once railroads gained strength, steamers had to be more conscious of altering their schedules to maintain business, particularly passengers. In 1855 the *Natchez* promised that it would deliver passengers "in time to connect with the Cars to Jackson," while the packet service between New Orleans and Mobile timed its movement to coordinate with rail service in both cities. For passengers with connecting service on steamboats, such scheduling was welcome. But for those who would not be taking the cars, waiting for railroads was just one more maddening delay associated with riverboat travel. "The Boat Stops at all the Rail Roads Coming to the Cumberland or Ohio River," wrote an irritated James Norman Smith in 1859 as he traveled from Nashville to Memphis. He was obviously put out that at each stop he had to "wait a Long Time for Passengers" to switch conveyances. In a similar fashion, a traveler ascending the Mississippi River in early 1860 noted how his steamer stopped in Vicksburg at seven in the morning and waited over four hours for the arrival of a late train. Steamboats were put in a bad spot. Southern railroads operated with a relatively high regard for time, but delays were inevitable. Waiting for the cars was one more measure of riverboats' relative decline and one more reason for passengers to forsake river travel.[22]

"THE UNION OF THE SOUTH & WEST"

John Calhoun unknowingly anticipated the results of this shift in southern trade patterns. In 1845 he addressed several hundred delegates in Memphis, Tennessee, at the first southern commercial convention. Telling his listeners what they wanted to hear, Calhoun argued that the steamboat converted the western waters into a great inland sea and implied that the federal government should remove river obstructions. In a later clarification, he proposed that the states levy tonnage duties to pay for improvements. Calhoun was trying to balance states' rights with a nod to potential federal activity. While he conceded the federal government had the right to conduct internal improvements, he denied that it should do so. Besides setting his sights on the presidency, Calhoun was trying to "remove the only barrier, that remains between the union of the South & West."[23]

By the late 1840s, residents of the southern interior were turning away from asking the federal government to improve the western rivers and, by extension, promote economic development. The work of snag removal sputtered along, but the western rivers had undergone enough improvements that the issue faded from public consciousness. As long as the superintendent of western river improvements kept the waters free of obstructions, most residents of the Southwest were satisfied. As we have seen, their sights were increasingly set on building railroads. The debates within the southern commercial conventions reflected this shift in sentiment. In Memphis, delegates mixed calls for river and harbor improvements with discussions of railroad building. Fourteen years later, in Vicksburg, there was no talk of federal help for clearing the rivers, only the need to build a transcontinental railroad through the South. Starting in Charleston, it would run through Montgomery, Vicksburg, Shreveport, and Marshall, Texas, before continuing to the Pacific Ocean. The iron horse would be, in the words of one enthusiast, a "powerful instrument to combine and strengthen the South" and promote the region's "commercial independence."[24]

The growth of northern railroads ruptured a trade pattern that worked in relative harmony with the natural world. Steamboats had made rivers the easiest avenues for commerce for the southern interior, but the extension of railroads across the land challenged this idea. As residents of the Southwest worked to link rail lines with cities like Atlanta, Charleston, and Richmond, they no longer thought of themselves as southern and western, just southern.

The fraying of intersectional commerce, due in part to the rise of the Great Lakes economy, also contributed to extremism in both the North and South. Southerners increasingly put their faith in cotton production and, as a result, became even more defensive about threats to slavery. De Bow, who initially cheered Calhoun's call for river improvements, retreated from any efforts that might promote trade between the Southwest and Midwest. In 1850 he sketched out a plan of southern self-sufficiency that asked southerners to stop buying northern products. This plan of southern economic development was intended to protect slavery from northern attacks. The most pressing issue of the 1859 commercial convention in Vicksburg was not railroad construction but the reopening of the Atlantic slave trade. The strangulation of the riverboat trade was one more factor that sharpened sectional differences and helped bring on the Civil War.[25]

That riverboats inhibited railroad development by asserting sway in the southern interior until the late 1850s had important consequences. Southern railroads fell behind their northern counterparts in the 1840s, argues James A. Ward, a time when steamboats were still very powerful. By the time southerners decided to invest heavily in rail, they were "technologically a decade behind the rest of the country." Southern railroads were deficient in construction, rail, motive power, and rolling stock. The South, moreover, possessed one-third of the nation's track but employed only one-fifth of the nation's railroad workers. Railroads in the Southwest were still struggling to realize their full potential when hostilities erupted in 1861.[26]

The interior South made a Faustian bargain with steamboats: cheap and relatively efficient transportation in exchange for a low-power economy that required minimal administrative expertise. A thriving steamboat presence nullified many of the arguments for an expansive rail network in the Southwest. Indeed, no rail network was really necessary because the dominance of the steamboat trade meant that river and rail would have to be integrated. But when it came time to fight a war for independence, southerners west of the Appalachian Mountains were in no position reap the benefits of an efficient rail system. The interior South had built inferior railroads that it was still learning to coordinate. And while it cannot be argued that the Union triumphed by 1865 because of southern steamboats, the South's inability to effectively use and administer its rail system was a serious problem in the Confederacy.[27]

Steamboats exerted a powerful but sometimes hidden influence on the course of southern history. The Southwest's thriving riverboat trade inhibited railroad construction and nourished trade with the Midwest. The growth of northern railroads and the problems associated with steamboat travel eroded steamboat commerce and spurred the drive to lay track in the southern interior. As residents of the interior South built railroads that connected them to the Atlantic coast, they also became less beholden to the Midwest and increased the likelihood of a war over the future of slavery. Steamboats helped create, and their demise helped undo, the Cotton Kingdom.

MARK TWAIN'S ODYSSEY

The beginning of 1882 was not kind to Mark Twain. He invested money in a bogus watch company, his stock portfolio was slipping, he poured money into home renovations, and the critics were unkind to *The Prince and the Pauper,* his latest book. Twain was also having difficulty finishing what would become *The Adventures of Huckleberry Finn* and needed a distraction before he could plunge back into work on the novel. He decided to visit his boyhood home and the portions of the Mississippi where he had been a pilot. The trip was partly an invitation to reminisce about the past but was also an information gathering foray for what would become *Life on the Mississippi,* a strange conglomeration of a book. Twain, his publisher, and a stenographer traveled by train to St. Louis and then rode steamboats south to New Orleans and north to St. Paul. He piloted the *Gold Dust* on the way downstream, dined with Joel Chandler Harris and George Washington Cable, met up with his mentor Horace Bixby in New Orleans, and spent three days in Hannibal, Missouri, where he grew up. It was, Twain thought, one of the best trips of his life.[1]

Time's inexorable march had changed much of the world that Twain remembered. In two decades parts of the river had become unrecognizable, as tow heads (small new islands) appeared, other islands completely disappeared, and parts of the Mississippi had changed course. "It was," he lamented, "like a man pointing out to me a place in the sky where a cloud had been." Worse yet, steamboat traffic on the great river had dwindled to insignificance. In St. Louis there were perhaps "Half a dozen sound-asleep steamboats" at the levee, a far cry from the solid mile of boats that used to line the shore. Travel on the "lonesome Mississippi" was nothing like it had been in its heyday. During Twain's final trip, he rarely saw two steamboats on the river at the same time. The status of the pilot declined in direct proportion to the river trade, thought Twain. Snag removal, nighttime lighting, and excellent charts made piloting almost as easy as driving a stage. Worse yet, pilots now had to wait in the pilothouse while freight was loaded and sometimes had to wear uniforms. "The government has taken away the romance of our calling; the Company has taken away its state and dignity," complained Twain. The culprits for this distressing new reality were railroads and bridges over the Mississippi. It was no coincidence that Twain spotted locomotives almost the whole way from St. Louis to St. Paul.[2]

Twain's account, while generally true, was also a wistful remembrance. While he acknowledged Charles Dickens's criticisms of Mississippi River steamboats, he also argued that Americans thought that riverboats were floating palaces. Judged by the standards of American society, steamboats were magnificent, thought Twain, because they were better than anything found in Baton Rouge, New Orleans, or St. Louis. Prior to 1860, riverboats transported passengers to a new and marvelous world; they created a sensual traveling experience. The 1882 boats were merely pre-war steamers caked with layers of dirt. Steamboats were dying of neglect. Clearly nostalgic, Twain made sweeping generalizations that gave too much credit to antebellum boats and discounted the charms of their post-war counterparts. Riverboats, although in serious decline in 1882, were still an economic force in the Southwest.[3]

Steamboats, although they helped make the antebellum South, did not die with the Civil War. The war itself was highly disruptive of steamboat commerce, as both the Union and Confederate governments initially set up blockades of riverboat traffic in 1861. While conditions eased by the end of the year, one reporter still thought the St. Louis levee was as quiet as a graveyard. Boat owners started making a profit again in 1862 when the federal government contracted with riverboats to haul war materiel and troops. As the Union asserted control over more and more of the western waters, commerce revived to pre-war levels.[4]

Confederate surrender and Federal demobilization removed the primary source of steamboat revenue, and peacetime trade continued to shift to the railroads. The only commerce that showed a significant revival was the cotton trade below Memphis, but even then, boats were getting smaller and changing in character. Owners started building towboats and barges to haul raw materials and imperishable items and largely abandoned the passenger trade by the end of the century. The stunning post-war growth of the railroad was largely responsible for this "slow paralysis" of river transportation. Steamboats even ceased to be steam-powered boats when they shifted to more powerful and efficient diesel engines.[5]

As Twain noticed during his trip, the number of steamboat workers was rapidly declining. African Americans still worked on the post-bellum boats, but the intense labor held few charms for the freemen. Mobility was one of the greatest advantages for slaves working on riverboats, but emancipation allowed freedom of movement for all African Americans. Steamboat workers no longer had tangible benefits denied to other blacks. While race relations hardly improved in post–Civil War America, at least black steamboat workers were able to bargain for better wages and challenge horrendous working conditions in court.[6]

The great irony is that arguably the most famous steamboats came from the post-bellum era, when steamboats were fading away. On April 27, 1865, the fifth incarnation of the *Sultana* entered the collective memory when it exploded while carrying more than 2,000 Union soldiers recently released from southern prisons. This largest maritime accident in American history killed over 1,700 people, at least 1,100 of whom were soldiers. Another boat carrying a pre-war name, the *Natchez,* lost to the *Robert E. Lee* in the country's most famous steamboat race in 1870. Both vessels became wharf boats within eleven years. The third *J. M. White* took to the waters in 1878, but the opulent boat burned to the waterline eight years later. By 1900 famed boats like these were quaint anachronisms.[7]

Steamboats faded from the Southwest at the same time that the Lost Cause and the moonlight and magnolias myths took hold in the New South. Interpreting the antebellum South in the most favorable light possible, these romantic visions stressed the benign nature of the peculiar institution, the chastity of women, the nobility of slaveholders, the justness of secession, and the faithfulness of slaves. Steamboats were a regular feature in paintings and drawings that depicted pleasant plantation scenes, particularly those sold by Currier and Ives. Works that depicted a steamboat race, a woodyard, and the Mississippi River during peacetime stressed the power and majesty of riverboats. In the hand of Currier and Ives's Frances Flora Bond Palmer, who never visited the South, the riverboat was not just a symbol of progress but also a place of romanticism and excitement. These sentimental paintings emerged at the same time that Twain's dinner guest Joel Chandler Harris published his Uncle Remus stories, a batch of tales that emphasized the compassionate nature of slavery, and Thomas Nelson Page wrote about a mythical pre-war South that was governed by the laws of chivalry. The selective remembrance of steamboats, then, fit well with the moonlight and magnolias myth that was becoming so popular among the eager readers of Harris and Page. Indeed, the steamboat gothic style fit comfortably with the notion of southern slave owners being lords and ladies of their realms. But just as sanitized versions of slavery forgot about Nat Turner's rebellion, brutal whippings, and half-naked slaves, southerners forgot the nastiness of deck passage, the segregation of cabin passage, the ecological devastation, the groundings on sandbars for days, the explosions, and other gritty steamboat realities. Even Mark Twain, who was rarely accused of sentimentalism, succumbed to the hazy memory of riverboat days. Twain to some degree, but others more particularly, shifted their emphasis to cabin passage on the best boats, riverboat gamblers, races, calliopes, tall stacks, and gently gliding past plantations of faithful slaves. Boats moving lazily up and down the river fit with ideas of an aristocratic antebellum South that was not in a hurry. It was an image that was attractive in a New South ever more dependent on railroads and increasingly unsure about the social manifestations of freedom.[8]

Riverboats are still firmly associated with the romanticism of the antebellum South. Most modern-day steamboats (even that term is incorrect, for they now use diesel engines and the paddle wheels are just for show) offer short pleasure cruises, buffets, gambling, and Dixieland bands. Not unlike plantations that are now tourist sites, today's boats make conscious associations to the golden age of steamboats and the glories of the antebellum South. Between plantation tours and riverboat excursions, there is ample evidence that Americans are skilled at crafting a highly romanticized version of the past. The messy reality that steamboats entrenched slavery, exploited African American labor, and were central to Indian Removal does not resonate with most Americans. A more fitting way to remember riverboats is not as pleasure craft for wealthy planters but as crucial components for the rise of the Cotton Kingdom.[9]

APPENDIX A

ESTIMATES OF STEAMBOAT CONSTRUCTION, TONNAGE,

AND LONGEVITY ON SOUTHERN RIVERS, 1811–1860

I compiled a database of southern steamboats by going through William M. Lytle and Forrest R. Holdcamper, *Merchant Steam Vessels of the United States, 1790–1868: Documents of the United States and Other Sources,* rev. and ed. C. Bradford Mitchell, with assistance of Kenneth R. Hall (Staten Island, 1975), also known as the Lytle List, and recording information about each steamboat that was listed as having a town in the southern interior as its home port. For this study, that meant Alabama, western Florida (Apalachicola), Kentucky, Louisiana, Missouri, Mississippi, Tennessee, eastern Texas (mainly Galveston), and western Virginia (Wheeling). Arkansas had no entries in the Lytle List. The database is limited to the boats built between 1811 and 1860, inclusive. The Lytle List has the following information: name, tonnage, year built, construction location, home port, disposition (sunk, explosion, retired from service, etc.), and year the vessel passed out of service.

After compiling the initial alphabetical list, I could then reorganize the material by any of the main categories. Two of the most useful measures were number of boats and tonnage, essentially a measure of the steamboats' potential carrying capacities. I reorganized the boats by year and then proceeded to calculate each year's number of boats/tonnage. To make calculations on a large scale, if a boat was lost or built in a year (say 1825), it was considered to be in service for six months, and was calculated as half a boat. If a boat passed out of service the same year it was built, it was not included in this estimate. Boats that passed out of service in an unknown year were considered to be afloat for one half of a year. Number of boats/tonnage thus became rolling figures that depended on the previous year's amount.

In Erik F. Haites, James Mak, and Gary M. Walton, *Western River Transportation: The Era of Early Internal Development, 1810–1860* (Baltimore, 1975), the authors used a different method for determining a particular year's tonnage and the number of boats. They calculated the number of boats/tonnage each year by subtracting the boats/tonnage that went out of service and adding the boats/tonnage that came into service. Such a method assumes that boats that went out of service did not operate at all in a given year and that new boats operated the whole year. For the basis of comparing southern steamboats to all western steamboats only, I followed their method. All of the other number of boats/tonnage figures for the rest of the book relied on my own method.

APPENDIX B

CHOCTAWS, CREEKS, CHICKASAWS, SEMINOLES, AND
CHEROKEES REMOVED BY STEAMBOAT, 1830–1843

T hree sources provided the bulk of the raw numbers regarding Indian Removal. Letters and reports of the army officers responsible for removal gave some insight into how many Native Americans were shipped westward. Government agents filled out enrollment reports and tracked the number of Native Americans involved in removal. But not all agents exercised due diligence in reporting their activities. A Senate investigation on Indian Removal, *Correspondence on the subject of emigration of Indians . . . in five volumes,* 23rd Cong., 1st sess., 1834, S. Doc. 512, serial 244, also yielded important information. The *Little Rock Arkansas Gazette* provided a steady stream of information. Numerous steamboats packed with Native Americans stopped at Little Rock, and it is likely that the paper's publisher received reports directly from the officers who were shepherding the Indian refugees. A small portion of the material for this study flows from two secondary sources. Grant Foreman's *Indian Removal: The Emigration of the Five Civilized Tribes of Indians,* 2nd ed. (Norman, 1953), although deeply flawed in many respects, contained useful caches of information. A recent report from the American Native Press Archives at the University of Arkansas at Little Rock (Amanda L. Paige, Fuller L. Bumpers, and Daniel F. Littlefield Jr., *The North Little Rock Site on the Trail of Tears National Historic Trail: Historical Contexts Report* [Little Rock, 2003]) also brought together an impressive array of material. Although concentrated on the movement of Native Americans through Little Rock, it provides much material about the larger removal process.

The sources usually provided estimates rather than exact counts. This is especially true with the numbers from the *Arkansas Gazette,* which comprises less than a quarter of the material at hand. For instance, the January 25, 1832, issue of the paper announced that the *Reindeer* arrived with "about 500 Emigrating Choctaws." If the materials gave a range of Native Americans, the lower number was used unless there were compelling reasons to believe the larger figure. Moreover, the statistics emerged from more than one source, and were usually on a par with one another. For example, Nathaniel Smith reported that he put eight hundred Cherokees on a steamer on July 14, 1838. When the group arrived in Little Rock, the *Arkansas Gazette* reported the figure as seven hundred to eight hundred. Determining the total of Native Americans transported in steamboats involved culling, balancing, and aligning sources. Overestimates were probably more common than underestimates, and so the numbers presented in this study are intended as a guide. It is certain, though, that some sources were overlooked, and it is likely my total lacks a 1,500-person contingent of Creek Indians that could not be adequately documented. Government records indicate that 3,100 Creeks waited in a refugee camp near Mobile in 1837. Surviving records verify the movement of 1,600 of these people on steamboats, and it is almost certain that the remainder traveled on a riverboat. Also, the totals do not include 3,349 Cherokees who moved themselves on steamers between 1830 and 1837 rather than face the rigors of coercive deportation. Further research will undoubtedly modify the numbers.[1]

APPENDIX C

The estimated accident rate of western steamboats was calculated from figures in Erik F. Haites, James Mak, and Gary M. Walton, *Western River Transportation: The Era of Early Internal Development, 1810–1860* (Baltimore, 1975), 130–31, 142–43, 160–61. I took the number of riverboats from each year (1811 to 1851) and multiplied it by the estimated number of round trips per year (3 from 1811–1819, 5 from 1820–1829, 8 from 1830–1839, and 10 from 1840–1851). That total (77,587) was the number of round trips between 1811 and 1851. In those same years, there were 995 steamboat accidents on the western waters, according to Louis C. Hunter, *Steamboats on the Western Rivers: An Economic and Technological History* (1949; reprint, Mineola, N.Y., 1993), 272. The accident rate was thus 0.013 percent.

To estimate the fatality rate from boiler explosions, I first estimated the number of passengers who traveled on western steamboats between 1816 and 1848. Using figures from Haites, Mak, and Walton, *Western River Transportation*, 130–31, 142–43, 160–61, I multiplied each year's tonnage by the average number of trips per year (3 from 1816–1819, 5 from 1820–1829, 8 from 1830–1839, and 10 from 1840–1848) by the average number of upstream passengers per ton per trip (0.30 from 1816–1819, 0.35 from 1820–1829, and 0.40 from 1830–1848). To calculate the number of downstream passengers, I multiplied the upstream passenger figures by 0.75, as per Haites, Mak, and Walton. Adding the upstream and downstream passenger figures yielded an estimate of 9,317,668 passengers on western riverboats between 1816 and 1848. I then compared the number of passengers to the number of fatalities (1,443) found in

Hunter, *Steamboats on the Western Rivers*, 287. The estimate of riverboat passengers might be overstated since passenger traffic in the late 1840s declined when railroads became a competitive force, and so the fatality rate might be even higher.

APPENDIX D

ESTIMATES OF WOOD CONSUMPTION BY SOUTHERN
STEAMBOATS, 1811–1860

According to a contemporary estimate, land along the Mississippi River yielded eighty to one hundred cords of firewood per acre, so this study will assume that one acre contained sixty good-sized trees.[1] The formula for computing the shoreline space was 100 (yards inland) x 1760 (yards in a mile) divided by 4,840 (square yards in an acre) = 36.36 acres per mile of shoreline. Then, 36.36 x 60 (estimated trees per acre) = 2182 (the number of trees along a one-mile section of river, one hundred yards deep). 120,872 trees divided by 2,182 = 55.39 (miles of shoreline).

The estimate for cords consumed is based on computing the volume of wood consumed by southern steamboats. Appendix A describes the calculation of tonnage for southern boats. Wood consumption was derived from the tonnage of a single year, divided by the ratio of cords to tonnage, times average running time per year, estimates that are taken from Erik F. Haites, James Mak, and Gary M. Walton, *Western River Transportation: The Era of Early Internal Development, 1810–1860* (Baltimore, 1975), 143–46.

APPENDIX E

The estimated number of workers was calculated by using the tonnage figures from Appendix A, dividing that number by 220 (the representative tonnage size), and then multiplying it by 19 (the typical crew size for a 220-ton boat). See Erik F. Haites, James Mak, and Gary M. Walton, *Western River Transportation: The Era of Early Internal Development, 1810–1860* (Baltimore, 1975), 140–42, for crew information. Payroll amounts were calculated by determining the number of boats each year, again from Appendix A, and then multiplying those figures by the average payroll expenses for each decade ($5,320 until 1819, $6,850 for 1820–1829, $13,610 for 1830–1839, $12,265 for 1840–1849, and $15,720 for 1850–1860). See Haites, Mak, and Walton, *Western River Transportation*, 140–42.

Estimating the value of wood sales involved taking the yearly figures from Appendix A divided by the average of cords per day per ton (one cord for each 20 tons before 1820, one cord for each 12 tons between 1820 and 1829, one cord for each 10 tons from 1830 to 1839, and one cord for each 8 tons thereafter) and then multiplying those figures by the average price for one cord of wood ($2.25 per cord prior to 1830 and $2.50 per cord thereafter). See figures from Haites, Mak, and Wilson, *Western River Transportation*, 144–46.

The estimates for repairs and stores are based on Haites, Mak, and Wilson, *Western River Transportation*, 136–42, multiplied against figures from Appendix A. Haites, Mak, and Wilson estimated that repairs cost 12 percent of a boat's original purchase price, while the estimate for stores were 30 percent of the total cost of stores, wages, and fuel.

APPENDIX F

T he figures for steamboats are discussed in Appendix A. To calculate the ton-miles and passenger miles, I followed Erik F. Haites, James Mak, and Gary M. Walton, *Western River Transportation: The Era of Early Internal Development, 1810–1860* (Baltimore, 1975), 11, which relied on the material from *Report of the Secretary of the Treasury on the Statistics and History of the Steam Marine of the United States,* 32nd Cong., 1st sess., 1852, S. Exec. Doc. 42, 113–14. That material is based on figures reported in the January 1849 issue of the *Western Boatman.* The railroad numbers are taken from the tables in Albert Fishlow, *American Railroads and the Transformation of the Ante-Bellum Economy* (Cambridge, 1965), 326, 328, 337. Fishlow does not discuss why he chose 1849, 1855–1856, and 1859, nor does he specify if 1855–1856 was twelve calendar months, although it appears so. For comparative purposes, I used 1855 steamboat numbers, instead of the higher 1856 numbers. Where the material on Missouri, Delaware, and Maryland was not specified in terms of passenger-miles or ton-miles, I calibrated the figures using total receipts for each state as a ratio of the regional receipts and applied them to the mileage figures. All figures in the tables, therefore, are reasonable estimates and not exact figures, but the trends that emerge are clear enough.

Estimating tonnage followed a similar vein. Henry Varnum Poor estimated that railroads in the United States hauled 5,500,500 tons of freight in 1851 and 18,750,000 seven years later (*New York Times,* May 31, 1869). Using mileage figures from 1850 and 1860, that would mean a ratio of just under 612 tons of freight per mile. I used the 612 figure and multiplied by the amount of track in the interior South in 1840, 1850, and 1860. The steamboat figures were based on tonnage for a specific year (as outlined in Appendix A), multiplied by the average carrying capacity for upstream trips, average carrying capacity for downstream trips, multiplied by the number of round trips per year. After the 1830s, the carrying capacity of southern steamboats was greater than their tonnage (because of design characteristics). The figures are from Haites, Mak, and Walton, *Western River Transportation,* 143, 157–60. For the record, they are 1840: 1.60 carrying capacity upstream and half that for downstream, with ten round trips per year. The 1850 and 1860 figures are 1.75 carrying capacity downstream and half that for upstream, with twelve round trips per year.

These figures need to be regarded with caution. The tonnage of southern steamboats is clear enough, but estimates of through tonnage, carrying capacity, and round trips per year are just that, estimates, and subject to the problems of collecting data for subjects with limited or contradictory records. The carrying capacity of riverboats, for instance, is based on travel between New Orleans and Louisville. Since many steamers traveled a shorter distance, it is quite likely that southern riverboats carried more freight than the figures that I have calculated. Basing the tonnage for railroads on Henry Varnum Poor's numbers is also not without complications. Poor helped compile figures for the *American Railroad Journal,* so presumably he had access to accurate information. But he might have also inflated the numbers to make the railroad industry look good. Calculating tonnage on the basis of mileage is imprecise and assumes no regional differentials. It is quite likely that railroads in the southern interior carried less freight than other lines in the United States because of the lower population density, the ways in which slavery inhibited demand for consumer goods, and the lack of a standard gauge. Thus the figures presented in chapter 8 quite probably overestimate the amount of tonnage carried on southern railroads. Moreover, these figures are measurements of potential freight and passengers. Not every train or steamboat was filled to capacity, but both had economic incentives to be reasonably full. Haites, Mak, and Walton, *Western River Transportation,* 158–60, estimates that riverboats were typically 75 percent or more full.

FREQUENTLY USED ABBREVIATIONS

DBR	*De Bow's Review*
DU	Perkins Library, Duke University, Durham, N.C.
FHS	Filson Historical Society, Louisville, Ky.
HNOC	Historic New Orleans Collection, New Orleans, La.
IRL	Inland Rivers Library, Public Library of Cincinnati and Hamilton County, Cincinnati, Ohio
JAH	*Journal of American History*
JER	*Journal of the Early Republic*
JSH	*Journal of Southern History*
LHQ	*Louisiana Historical Quarterly*
LSU	Hill Memorial Library, Louisiana State University, Baton Rouge, La.
LSUS	Noel Memorial Library, Louisiana State University at Shreveport, Shreveport, La.
NARA	National Archives and Records Administration, Washington, D.C.
TSLA	Tennessee State Library and Archives, Nashville, Tenn.
TU	Special Collections, Howard-Tilton Memorial Library, Tulane University, New Orleans, La.
UNC	Southern Historical Collection, University of North Carolina, Chapel Hill, N.C.
UTX	Center for American History, University of Texas at Austin, Austin, Tex.
WHMC	Western Historical Manuscript Collection, University of Missouri, Columbia, Mo.

NOTES

1. Unless otherwise noted, the description of the *New Orleans* and its voyage for this and the next paragraphs is from J. H. B. Latrobe, *The First Steamboat Voyage on the Western Waters* (Baltimore, 1871); J. H. B. Latrobe, *A Lost Chapter in the History of the Steamboat* (Baltimore, 1871); George L. Norton to James A. Henderson, June 6, 1911, and H. Dora Stecker to George M. Lehman, July 7, 1911, both in *New Orleans* (Steamboat) Collection, 1911, Historical Society of Western Pennsylvania, Pittsburgh, Pennsylvania; Jay Feldman, *When the Mississippi Ran Backwards: Empire, Intrigue, Murder, and the New Madrid Earthquakes* (New York, 2005), 104–31, 148–53; Mary Helen Dohan, *Mr. Roosevelt's Steamboat: The First Steamboat to Travel the Mississippi* (New York, 1981); James M. Powles, "*New Orleans*: First Steamboat Down the Mississippi," *American History* 40 (June 2005): 48–55; Charles W. Dahlinger, "The *New Orleans*," *Pittsburg Legal Journal* 59 (October 1911): 579–91; F. Van Loon Ryder, "The 'New Orleans': The First Steamboat on Our Western Waters," *Filson Club Historical Quarterly,* 37 (January 1963): 29–37; "First Western Steamboat," *Waterways Journal,* November 7, 1896, 8; "On the Old Missouri," *Waterways Journal,* December 13, 1902, 3. Steamboats (and boats in general) are usually described by their tonnage, which is a rough measure of volume. More tonnage usually means more cargo capacity unless the boat or the engine is unusually heavy. The *New Orleans* at 371 tons could not carry 371 tons of freight because of its weighty engine.

2. The size of the paddle wheels is conjecture based on the size of the wheels on the *Vesuvius,* which was of the same design. See Edouard de Montulé, *Travels in America 1816–1817,* trans. Edward D. Seeber (Bloomington, 1951), 102.

3. Lydia Latrobe Roosevelt's younger brother J. H. B. Latrobe wrote the only primary account of the *New Orleans*'s maiden voyage. His writings, referenced in note 1 above, are based on family stories that were written down sixty years after the fact. They are much romanticized but contain some useful information.

4. Feldman, *When the Mississippi Ran Backwards,* 126 (quotation); Frederick Brent Read, ed., *Up the Heights of Fame and Fortune, and The Routes taken by the Climbers to become Men of Mark* (Cincinnati, 1873), 65.

5. Titian Ramsay Peale, May 19, 1819, journal entry, as quoted in Michael Gillespie, *Come Hell or High Water: A Lively History of Steamboating on the Mississippi and Ohio Rivers* (Stoddard, Wisc., 2001), 13 (quotation); Michael Allen, *Western Rivermen, 1763–1861: Ohio and Mississippi Boatmen and the Myth of the Alligator Horse* (Baton Rouge, 1990), 37–39.

6. James Lal Penick Jr., *The New Madrid Earthquakes*, rev. ed. (Columbia, 1981), 4–8, 76–82; Margaret Ross, "The New Madrid Earthquake," *Arkansas Historical Quarterly* 27 (summer 1968): 90–91.

7. Latrobe, *First Steamboat Voyage*, 31 (quotation); Mrs. S. Kussart, *Navigation on the Monongahela River*, comp. and indexed by Richard T. Wiley (n.p., 1971), 367; Thomas H. Cox, *Gibbons v. Ogden, Law, and Society in the Early Republic* (Athens, Ohio, 2009), 47–48.

8. *Aggregate Amount of each description of Persons within the United States of America, and the Territories thereof, agreeably to actual enumeration made according to law, in the year 1810* (New York, n.d.), 1; "Historical Census Browser," http://fisher.lib.virginia.edu/collections/stats/histcensus/index.html, University of Virginia, Geospatial and Statistical Data Center; "Fast Facts," www.census.gov/history, U. S. Census Bureau. The largest southern towns in order were: Baltimore, New Orleans, St. Louis, Louisville, Richmond, Mobile, and Memphis.

9. James Mak and Gary M. Walton, *Western River Transportation: The Era of Early Internal Development, 1810–1860* (Baltimore, 1975), 130–31.

10. Ari Kelman, *A River and Its City: The Nature of Landscape in New Orleans* (Berkeley, 2003), 50–68; Ari Kelman, "Forests and Other River Perils," in *Transforming New Orleans and Its Environs*, ed. Craig E. Colten, 45–63 (Pittsburgh, 2000); Thomas C. Buchanan, *Black Life on the Mississippi: Slaves, Free Blacks, and the Western Steamboat World* (Chapel Hill, 2004); Carl A. Brasseaux and Keith P. Fontenot, *Steamboats on Louisiana's Bayous: A History and Directory* (Baton Rouge, 2004). For steamboats on the western waters, see Louis C. Hunter, *Steamboats on the Western Rivers: An Economic and Technological History* (1949; reprint, Mineola, N.Y., 1993); Haites, Mak, and Walton, *Western River Transportation*; Allen, *Western Rivermen*; Adam I. Kane, *The Western River Steamboat* (College Station, 2004); Paul F. Paskoff, *Troubled Waters: Steamboat Disasters, River Improvements, and American Public Policy, 1821–1860* (Baton Rouge, 2007); and Herbert Quick and Edward Quick, *Mississippi Steamboatin': A History of Steamboating on the Mississippi and Its Tributaries* (New York, 1926). For examples of works that favor the importance of railroads over steamboats, see William J. Cooper and Thomas E. Terrill, *The American South: A History*, 3rd ed. (New York, 2002); Bradley G. Bond, *Political Culture in the Nineteenth-Century South: Mississippi, 1830–1900* (Baton Rouge, 1995); Jonathan Daniel Wells, *The Origins of the Southern Middle Class, 1800–1861* (Chapel Hill, 2004); and Richard M. Follett, *The Sugar Masters: Planters and Slaves in Louisiana's Cane World, 1820–1860* (Baton Rouge, 2005).

11. Zadok Cramer, *The Navigator: Containing Directions for Navigating the Monongahela, Allegheny, Ohio, and Mississippi Rivers*, 7th ed. (Pittsburgh, 1811), 31.

CHAPTER ONE

1. *Nashville Gazette*, June 9, 1819 (quotation); Byrd Douglas, *Steamboatin' on the Cumberland* (Nashville, 1961), 7–9; Jonathan Kennon Smith, *Genealogical Abstracts from Reported Deaths, the Nashville Christian Advocate, 1897–1899* (Jackson, Tenn., 2002), 104.

2. Account Book of Winchester and Hall, 1819–1824, James Winchester Papers, TSLA; Walter T. Durham, *James Winchester: Tennessee Pioneer* (Gallatin, Tenn., 1979), 228; James Wallace Hammack Jr., *Kentucky and the Second American Revolution: The War of 1812* (Lexington, Ky., 1976), 30–31, 47–53; William M. Lytle and Forrest R. Holdcamper, *Merchant Steam Vessels of the United States, 1790–1868: Documents of the United States and Other Sources*, rev. and ed. by C. Bradford Mitchell,

with assistance of Kenneth R. Hall (Staten Island, 1975), 48. Winchester's company eventually paid $18,650 for the *Cumberland*.

3. Steamboat Cumberland Receipt, November 23, 1822 (cargo quotations), and Sterling M. Banner to Winchester, Hall and Company, September 2, 1822 (final quotation), Account Book, 1819–1824, both in James Winchester Papers, TSLA. Grog was an alcoholic beverage usually made of rum or beer.

4. *Nashville Whig*, March 7, 1816, as quoted in Kristofer Ray, *Middle Tennessee, 1775–1825: Progress and Popular Democracy on the Southwestern Frontier* (Knoxville, 2007), 120 (first quotation); John Summerville to Thomas E. Sumner, June 30, 1818, John Sumner Russwurm Papers, TSLA (second quotation); Anita Shafer Goodstein, *Nashville, 1780–1860: From Frontier to City* (Gainesville, 1989), 35; Douglas, *Steamboatin' on the Cumberland*, 9–13.

5. Arthur Augustus Thurlow Cunynghame, *A Glimpse at the Great American Republic* (London, 1851), 129 (quotation); Alice Morse Earle, *Stage-Coach and Tavern Days* (1900; reprint, New York, 1997); Oliver W. Holmes and Peter T. Rohrbach, *Stagecoach East: Stagecoach Days in the East from the Colonial Period to the Civil War* (Washington, D.C., 1983); Jack Larkin, *The Reshaping of Everyday Life, 1790–1840* (New York, 1988), 224–26; George Rogers Taylor, *The Transportation Revolution, 1815–1860* (New York, 1951), 15.

6. Ari Kelman, *A River and Its City: The Nature of Landscape in New Orleans* (Berkeley, 2003), 52 (first quotation); David Crockett, *The Autobiography of David Crockett* (New York, 1923), 126–28 (second quotation); Erik F. Haites, James Mak, and Gary M. Walton, *Western River Transportation: The Era of Early Internal Development, 1810–1860* (Baltimore, 1975), 165–69; Edouard de Montulé, *Travels in America 1816–1817*, trans. Edward D. Seeber (Bloomington, Ind., 1951), 97; John James Audubon, *John James Audubon: Writings and Drawings* (New York, 1999), 19–20; Michael Allen, *Western Rivermen, 1763–1861: Ohio and Mississippi Boatmen and the Myth of the Alligator Horse* (Baton Rouge, 1990), 66–80; W. Wallace Carson, "Transportation and Traffic on the Ohio and the Mississippi before the Steamboats," *Mississippi Valley Historical Review* 7 (June 1920): 26–38; Leland D. Baldwin, "Shipbuilding on the Western Waters, 1793–1817," *Mississippi Valley Historical Review* 20 (June 1933): 29–44.

7. Allen, *Western Rivermen*, 69–73; Kelman, *A River and Its City*, 51; Haites, Mak, and Walton, *Western River Transportation*, 12–26; Herbert Quick and Edward Quick, *Mississippi Steamboatin': A History of Steamboating on the Mississippi and Its Tributaries* (New York, 1926), 12–19; Baldwin, "Shipbuilding on the Western Waters," 29–44; James Hall, *The West: Its Commerce and Navigation* (1848; reprint, New York, 1970), 130; Louis C. Hunter, *Steamboats on the Western Rivers: An Economic and Technological History* (1949; reprint, Mineola, N.Y., 1993), 33. Inventive New Orleans residents built a "horse boat" in which horses walked on a type of treadmill that turned a set of paddle wheels. It left for Louisville with great hopes, but it ended in failure when "some twelve to twenty horses were used up on the treadwheel," and the trip was abandoned (*New Orleans Gazette*, July 23, 1807, as quoted in Mak, Haites, and Walton, *Western River Transportation*, 17).

8. Montulé, *Travels in America*, 101; Adam I. Kane, *The Western River Steamboat* (College Station, 2004), 44–58.

9. James S. Buckingham, *The Slave States of America*, 2 vols. (London, 1842), 1:262 (first quotation); Bazil Kiger to Caroline Kiger, October 1, 1852, Kiger Family Papers, UTX (second quotation); Alfred A. Maass, "Daniel French and the Western Steamboat Engine," *American Neptune* 56 (winter 1996): 39; Edwin Adams Davis and John C. L. Andreassen, eds., "From Louisville to New Orleans

in 1816: Diary of William Newton Mercer," *JSH* 11 (August 1945): 394; Hunter, *Steamboats on the Western Rivers*, 21–24, 121–80; Haites, Mak, and Walton, *Western River Transportation*, 68–71.

10. Hunter, *Steamboats on the Western Rivers*, 85–89, 171–75; Kane, *Western River Steamboat*, 63–64.

11. Hunter, *Steamboats on the Western Rivers*, 85–89, 171–75; Kane, *Western River Steamboat*, 63–64; Charles Preston Fishbaugh, *From Paddle Wheels to Propellers* (Indianapolis, 1970), 15–17.

12. Joseph Suppiger, Salomon Koepfli, and Kaspar Koepfli, *Journey to New Switzerland: Travel Account of the Koepfli and Suppiger Family to St. Louis on the Mississippi and the Founding of New Switzerland in the State of Illinois*, trans. Raymond J. Spahn and ed. John C. Abbott (Carbondale, 1987), 121 (first quotation); Hunter, *Steamboats on the Western Rivers*, 84 (second quotation); Mark Twain, *The Family Mark Twain*, vol. 1, *Life on the Mississippi* (New York, 1935), 56–61.

13. Hunter, *Steamboats on the Western Rivers*, 91–94; Kane, *Western River Steamboat*, 111–12; Haites, Mak, Walton, *Western River Transportation*, 134–48, 157–60. The upstream carrying capacity (which was smaller because boats had to carry more firewood) moved from 55 tons to 315 tons in the same period.

14. Hunter, *Steamboats on the Western Rivers*, 70, 90–91, 394–96; Twain, *Life on the Mississippi*, 33; Thomas C. Buchanan, *Black Life on the Mississippi: Slaves, Free Blacks, and the Western Steamboat World* (Chapel Hill, 2004), 9; Language of the River, http://riverlorian.com/languageoftheriver. htm, Jerry Hay.

15. William Kenner to Stephen Minor, January 20, 1812, Minor Collection, UNC (first quotation); Adam Rothman, *Slave Country: American Expansion and the Origins of the Deep South* (Cambridge, 2005), 81; Zadok Cramer, *The Navigator: Containing Directions for Navigating the Monongahela, Allegheny, Ohio, and Mississippi Rivers*, 11th ed. (Pittsburgh, 1821), 13; *New Orleans Monitor*, March 5, 1812, as quoted in Charles W. Dahlinger, "The *New Orleans*," *Pittsburg Legal Journal* 59 (October 1911): 587; *Louisiana Gazette*, February 12, 1812, as quoted in Ethel C. Leahy, *Who's Who on the Ohio River and Its Tributaries* (Cincinnati, 1931), 308; Thomas G. Andrews, *Killing for Coal: America's Deadliest Labor War* (Cambridge, 2008), 34–38; Scott Reynolds Nelson, *Steel Drivin' Man: John Henry, The Untold Story of an American Legend* (New York, 2006), 7 (final quotation). Reynolds wrote about the switch from wood to coal, the transformation of steel from precious metal to an everyday commodity, and the ascendance of nitroglycerin over gunpowder. My point is that steamboats caused as much of a leap in both perception and practice.

16. Maass, "Daniel French," 29–36; Mrs. S. Kussart, *Navigation on the Monongahela River*, comp. and indexed by Richard T. Wiley (n.p., 1971), 375–76; U.S. Congress, House, Department of the Treasury, *Report on the Internal Commerce of the United States 1887*, William F. Switzler, part 2 of *Report on the Commerce and Navigation of the United States*, 50th Cong., 1st sess., 1888, H. Exec. Doc. 6, serial 2552, 193; Albert A. Fossier, *New Orleans: The Glamour Period, 1800–1840* (New Orleans, 1947), 30; "Commencement of Navigation," *Waterways Journal*, November 7, 1896, 8; Benjamin Henry Latrobe to Robert Fulton, March 1, 1814, 115/B8, Maryland Historical Society, Baltimore, Maryland (microfiche ed.); Edith McCall, *Conquering the Rivers: Henry Miller Shreve and the Navigation of America's Inland Waterways* (Baton Rouge, 1984), 16, 96–113, 128–31; "Political Portraits with Pen and Pencil: Henry Miller Shreve," *United States Democratic Review* 22 (February 1848): 160–64; Caroline S. Pfaff, "Henry Miller Shreve: A Biography," *LHQ* 10 (April 1927): 194–98.

17. *Louisiana Courier*, March 11, 1812, as quoted in Kussart, *Navigation on the Monongahela River*, 368 (first and second quotations); Dunbar Rowland, ed., *Official Letter Books of W. C. C. Claiborne, 1801–16*, 6 vols. (Jackson, Miss., 1917), 6:1 (final quotation); Dahlinger, "The *New Orleans*," 588.

18. Leahy, *Who's Who on the Ohio River*, 304; *Pittsburgh Commonwealth*, May 15, 1816, quoted

in Dahlinger, "*New Orleans*," 590; Thomas, *Travels through the Western Country,* 62; Committee of the House or Representatives, Territory of New Orleans, January 18, 1817, as quoted in Morrison, *History,* 209–11 (quotation).

19. Jasper Lynch to Dominick Lynch, July 25, 1816, September 10, 1816, October 25, 1816 (quotation), Letter Book of Jasper Lynch, Oneida County Historical Society, Utica, New York; *Pittsburgh Commonwealth,* May 15, 1816, as quoted in Kussart, *Navigation on the Monongahela River,* 376.

20. Photostat, *The Heirs of R. R. Livingston and R. Fulton v. H. M. Shrieve* [*sic*], Hardin Collection, LSU (quotation); Kelman, *A River and Its City,* 58–59; McCall, *Conquering the Rivers,* 152–53; Thomas H. Cox, *Gibbons v. Ogden, Law, and Society in the Early Republic* (Athens, Ohio, 2009), 88–91. The Letter Book of Jasper Lynch is surprisingly silent on the ruling.

21. Maurice G. Baxter, *The Steamboat Monopoly: Gibbons v. Ogden, 1824* (New York, 1972), 29–68, Cox, *Gibbons v. Ogden,* 152–60.

22. Taylor, *Transportation Revolution,* 56–62; Daniel Walker Howe, *What Hath God Wrought: The Transformation of America, 1815–1848* (New York, 2007), 203–42; Daniel Feller, *The Jacksonian Promise: America, 1815–1860* (Baltimore, 1995), 22–25; John Lauritz Larson, *The Market Revolution in America: Liberty, Ambition, and the Eclipse of the Common Good* (New York, 2010), 31–32; William J. Peterson, *Steamboating on the Upper Mississippi* (Iowa City, 1968), 196–226; William E. Lass, *Navigating the Missouri: Steamboating on Nature's Highway, 1819–1935* (Norman, 2008), 85–112; Alan D. Watson, "Sailing under Steam: The Advent of Steam Navigation in North Carolina to the Civil War," *North Carolina Historical Review* 75 (January 1998): 29–68; Ruth Cowan Schwartz, *A Social History of American Technology* (New York, 1997), 108; Carroll Pursell, *The Machine in America: A Social History of Technology* (Baltimore, 1995), 76–77.

23. Logbook of Natchez Landings, 1835–1837, Logbook of Natchez Landings, 1839–1840, Natchez Trace Steamboat Collection, UTX.

24. Logbook of Natchez Landings, 1835–1837, Logbook of Natchez Landings, 1839–1840, Natchez Trace Steamboat Collection, UTX.

25. U.S. Congress, Senate, *Petition of a number of citizens of Louisiana, praying for an alteration in a mail route,* 26th Cong., 1st sess., 1840, S. Doc. 274, serial 358, 1 (first quotation); R. W. Esthlin and Company to Peter Hickman, April 30, 1855, Bryan-Hickman Papers, WHMC (second quotation); George Campbell Childress to Rebecca Childress, August 1, 1845, George Campbell Childress Papers, UTX; De Lassus Diary, July 8, 1836, entry, LSU; Hall, *The West,* 128; Leonard V. Huber, "Beginnings of Steamboat Mail on Lower Mississippi," *American Philatelist* 74 (December 1960): 187–200; Richard R. John, *Spreading the News: The American Postal System from Franklin to Morse* (Cambridge, 1995), 90–92; David Henkin, *The Postal Age: The Emergence of Modern Communications in Nineteenth-Century America* (Chicago, 2006), 3.

26. William Kenner to John Minor, May 23, 1817, and June 10, 1820 (quotation), Kenner Papers, LSU; "National Character of Western People," *Western Monthly Review* 1 (May 1827): 137.

27. *Natchez Courier,* September 24, 1852 (quotation); Philip Graham, *Showboats: The History of an American Institution* (Austin: Univ. of Texas Press, 1951), 28–30; Penelope M. Leavitt and James S. Moy, "Spalding and Rogers' Floating Palace, 1852–1859," *Theatre Survey* 25 (May 1984): 15–21.

28. *Mississippi Free Trader and Natchez Gazette,* March 9, 1850 (quotation); Graham, *Showboats,* 205; Leavitt and Moy, "Spalding and Rogers' Floating Palace," 15–20; Gregory J. Renoff, *The Big Tent: The Traveling Circus in Georgia, 1820–1930* (Athens, 2008), 11–32.

29. Unidentified newspaper clippings from January 5, 1838 (first quotation), and November 30, 1838, in "Iron Men—Wooden Boats," vol. 1, Joseph Merrick Jones-Donald T. Wright Steamboat

Collection, TU; "National Character of Western People," *Western Monthly Review* 1 (May 1827): 26 (remaining quotations); Michael O'Brien, *Conjectures of Order: Intellectual Life and the American South, 1810-1860*, 2 vols. (Chapel Hill, 2004), 1:472-525. Earlier generations of historians tended to regard the antebellum South as resistant to change, but recent interpretations argue for an imperialist, modern, and interconnected South. For able summaries of the literature, see Peter Kolchin, "The South and the World," *JSH* 75 (August 2009): 565-80, and Anthony E. Kaye, "The Second Slavery: Modernity in the Nineteenth-Century South and the Atlantic World," *JSH* 75 (August 2009): 627-50.

30. David E. Nye, *American Technological Sublime* (Cambridge, 1994), xv (first quotation), 56-58; William B. Dewees, *Letters from an Early Settler of Texas*, comp. by Cara Cardelle (Louisville, 1852), 11 (second quotation); Ebenezer Stedman as quoted in Craig Thompson Friend, *Along the Maysville Road: The Early American Republic in the Trans-Appalachian West* (Knoxville, 2005), 252 (third quotation); Mell A. Frazer, *Early History of Steamboats in Alabama* (Auburn, 1907), 4. For more discussion of technology and its relation to accepted American values, see Leo Marx, *The Machine in the Garden: Technology and the Pastoral Ideal in America* (New York, 1964); John F. Kasson, *Civilizing the Machine: Technology and Republican Values in America, 1776-1900* (New York, 1976); and David Nye, *America as Second Creation: Technology and Narratives of New Beginnings* (Cambridge, 2003).

31. Hall, *The West*, 128; Fossier, *New Orleans*, 30; George H. Yater, *Two Hundred Years at the Falls of the Ohio: A History of Louisville and Jefferson County* (Louisville, 1979), 34-35; Hunter, *Steamboats on the Western Rivers*, 12-20, 105-6; John Hebron Moore, *Emergence of the Cotton Kingdom in the Old Southwest* (Baton Rouge, 1988), 157-58; Walter Prichard, Fred B. Kniffin, and Clair A. Brown, eds., "Southern Louisiana and Southern Alabama in 1819: The Journal of James Leander Cathcart," *LHQ* 28 (July 1945): 752-53; Schwartz, *Social History of American Technology*, 69-92, 112-18. See Appendix A for a discussion of how the number and tonnage of southern steamboats was calculated.

32. Fishbaugh, *From Paddle Wheels to Propellers*, 10-11, 34; Hunter, *Steamboats on the Western Rivers*, 106-11; Haites, Mak, and Walton, *Western River Transportation*, 137; Walter Havighurst, *Voices on the River: The Story of the Mississippi Waterways* (New York, 1964), 62.

33. Prichard, ed., "Journal of James Leander Cathcart," 858 (quotation); Lytle and Holdcamper, *Merchant Steam Vessels*, 4, 134; Henry C. Dethloff, "Paddlewheels and Pioneers on Red River, 1815-1915, and the Reminiscences of Captain M. L. Scovell," *Louisiana Studies* 6 (summer 1967): 102; undated newspaper clipping in Scrapbook, vol. 11, Tappan Steamboat Collection, Special Collections, University of Arkansas Libraries, Fayetteville, Arkansas; Mary Emerson Branch, "Prime Emerson and Steamboat Building in Memphis," *West Tennessee Historical Society Papers* 38 (1984): 69-83; Lynn Willoughby, *Flowing through Time: A History of the Lower Chattahoochee River* (Tuscaloosa, 1999), 72.

34. Henry M. Shreve to Mary Shreve, August 19, 1810, Israel Shreve Revolutionary War Letters, Courtesy of Special Collections, University of Houston Libraries, Houston, Texas (first quotation); Anthony R. Gale to Nathaniel Weeks, June 16, 1817 (second quotation), and July 10, 1817, Nathaniel Weeks Papers, LSU; Hunter, *Steamboats on the Western Rivers*, 313-35.

35. "Life of Capt. C. W. Batchelor," *Waterway Journal* 8 (1896): 5; *Arkansas Gazette*, May 29, 1834; William Cage to James Winchester, April 7, 1822, James Winchester Papers, TSLA.

36. Natchez Steam Boat Company agreement, and undated steamboat agreement, both in Natchez Trace Steamboat Collection, UTX; Goodstein, *Nashville*, 35-37; Thomas H. Airey to Lambeth

and Thompson, January 28, 1836, Somdal Collection, LSUS (quotations). Even the city of Louisville owned the *Agnes* (*John Riley v. The City of Louisville*, No. 4799, 5 Rob. 184 [n.s.], New Orleans, June 1843, UNO). The occupations of the individuals in Natchez were found by comparing the names on the agreement with information in D. Clayton James, *Antebellum Natchez* (Baton Rouge, 1968).

37. Martha Jane Brazy, *An American Planter: Stephen Duncan of Antebellum Natchez and New York* (Baton Rouge, 2006), 26–27; Natchez Steam Boat Company agreement, and undated steamboat agreement (quotations), both in Natchez Trace Steamboat Collection, UTX.

38. *Sowers v. Flower et al.*, No. 1019, 2 Mart. (n.s.) 617, New Orleans, June 1824, UNO; Yater, *Two Hundred Years at the Falls of the Ohio*, 35; Paul H. Bergeron, Stephen V. Ash, and Jeanette Keith, *Tennesseans and Their History* (Knoxville, 1999), 113; Goodstein, *Nashville*, 35; Natchez Steam Boat Company agreement, UTX; Agreement of Natchitoches Steamboat Company, box 9, folder 24, Somdal Collection, LSUS; "Iron Men—Wooden Boats," vol. 1, Joseph Merrick Jones-Donald T. Wright Steamboat Collection, TU; *Williamson et al., Syndics v. Smoot*, No. 378, 7 Mart. (o.s.) 31, New Orleans, July 1819, UNO; Amite Navigation Company Document, LSU; Articles of Agreement for the Lake Steam Navigation Company, March 2, 1850, box 11, folder 422, Somdal Collection, LSUS. The percentages are from Hunter, *Steamboats on the Western Rivers*, 308–13.

39. *Arkansas Gazette*, May 29, 1834; *Shreve v. His Creditors*, No. 584, 11 Mart. (o.s.) 30, New Orleans, March 1822, UNO.

40. Undated *Cincinnati Gazette* article, as quoted in *Register of Pennsylvania* 5, no. 4 (January 30, 1830), 74–75; Taylor, *Transportation Revolution*, 69–70; Jeremy Atack, "Quantitative and Qualitative Evidence in the Weaving of Business and Economic History: Western River Steamboats and the Transportation Revolution Revisited," *Business and Economic History* 28 (fall 1999): 2–3; Hunter, *Steamboats on the Western Rivers*, 112. The dollar amount was calculated using figures from Appendix A multiplied by the average construction cost per ton, a figure that varied by decade (Haites, Mak, and Walton, *Western River Transportation*, 137).

41. Fred Bateman and Thomas Weiss, *A Deplorable Scarcity: The Failure of Southern Industrialization in a Slave Economy* (Chapel Hill, 1981), 160–61. Adding in the ancillary costs of riverboats (wood, supplies, refitting, etc.) would bring the figures more in line with expenditures on slaves, but one could also argue that the ancillary costs of slavery (food, clothing, supplies) would push that figure higher.

42. Kaye, "Second Slavery," 633–36; Robert H. Gudmestad, "Technology and the World the Slaves Made," *History Compass* 4 (January 2006): 1–11; Angela Lakwete, *Inventing the Cotton Gin: Machine and Myth in Antebellum America* (Baltimore, 2003), 47–71; Richard M. Follett, *The Sugar Masters: Planters and Slaves in Louisiana's Cane World, 1820–1860* (Baton Rouge, 2005), 22–24; Mark M. Smith, *Mastered by the Clock: Time, Slavery, and Freedom in the American South* (Chapel Hill, 1997), 112–21; and John Majewski, *Modernizing a Slave Economy: The Economic Vision of the Confederate Nation* (Chapel Hill, 2009), 4–7.

CHPATER TWO

1. *Samuel T. Williamson v. Alexander Morton, Master &c.*, No. 2427, 7 La. Ann. (n.s.) 394, New Orleans, June 1852 (quotation), UNO; Walter Johnson, "The Slave Trader, the White Slave, and the Politics of Racial Determination in the 1850s," *JAH* 87 (June 2000): 20–23; Ariela J. Gross, *What Blood Won't Tell: A History of Race on Trial in America* (Cambridge, 2008), 1–3.

2. *Samuel T. Williamson v. Alexander Morton, Master &c.*, No. 2427, 7 La. Ann. (n.s.) 394, New Orleans, June 1852 (quotations), UNO.

3. Gross, *What Blood Won't Tell*, 53–54, 71–72.

4. Louis C. Hunter, *Steamboats on the Western Rivers: An Economic and Technological History* (1949; reprint, Mineola, N.Y., 1993), 442–43; Thomas C. Buchanan, *Black Life on the Mississippi: Slaves, Free Blacks, and the Western Steamboat World* (Chapel Hill, 2004), 181; Erik F. Haites, James Mak, and Gary M. Walton, *Western River Transportation: The Era of Early Internal Development, 1810–1860* (Baltimore, 1975), 140–42. See also 1840 *Family Magazine* clipping in Iron Men—Wooden Boats scrapbook, vol. 2, Joseph Merrick Jones-Donald T. Wright Steamboat Collection, TU; Hunter, *Steamboats on the Western Rivers*, 445. By way of comparison, pilots who earned $1,350 in 1850 would make about $33,000 in modern currency. Deck and cabin crew members who earned $225 that same year would make about $5,500 in modern wages. See http://www.measuringworth.com.

5. Thomas Low Nichols, *Forty Years of American Life*, 2 vols. (London, 1864), 1:230–33; Charles Lyell, *A Second Visit to the United States of North America*, 2 vols. (New York, 1849), 2:170; A. Oakley Hall, *The Manhattaner in New Orleans; or, Phases of "Crescent City" Life* (New York, 1851), 181; Milton Rickels, *George Washington Harris* (New York, 1965), 20–21.

6. Information on Leathers is found in the finding aids from the T. P. Leathers Papers, TU, and the Thomas P. Leathers Papers, LSU. The *Natchez* was something of a franchise, as Leathers owned at least seven incarnations of the boat. The sixth one lost to the *Robert E. Lee* in the world's most famous steamboat race, but the other versions were not as noteworthy.

7. Hunter, *Steamboats on the Western Rivers*, 240–47.

8. John C. Bush Book of Travels, Bush Family Papers, WHMC; F. E. Schoolfield, "Captain Alex. F. Boss, Western Rivers Pilot," 2–4, typescript, IRL (quotation); Hunter, *Steamboats on the Western Rivers*, 243.

9. Mark Twain, *The Family Mark Twain*, vol. 1, *Life on the Mississippi* (New York, 1935), 29 (first quotation), 66 (second quotation).

10. "Smoke and Sparks," *Natchez Daily Courier*, July 6, 1855, typescript in Somdal Papers, LSUS (quotation); U.S. Congress, House, Department of the Treasury, *Report on the Internal Commerce of the United States 1887*, William F. Switzler, part 2 of *Report on the Commerce and Navigation of the United States*, 50th Cong., 1st sess., 1888, H. Exec. Doc. 6, serial 2552, 194; William James Ikerman, "The Role of the Steamboat in the Development of the Cotton Kingdom in Alabama, 1819–1860" (Master's thesis, Auburn University, 1963), 57; Ron Powers, *Mark Twain: A Life* (New York, 2005), 80–81.

11. William L. Clark to N. R. Pope, November 13, 1827, Pope-Carter Family Papers, DU (first quotation); J. W. Gosen to A. H. Hawley, October 1, 1850, J. W. Gosen Papers, TSLA (second quotation); "Memoir of Henry Dumesnil," 2, Dumesnil Family Papers, FHS; Robert T. Van Horn to parents, June 15, 1854, Van Horn Papers, WHMC; Thomas B. Eastland to James Winchester, October 8, 1823, Winchester Papers, TSLA; James Neal to Mother and Brother, April 15, 1829, Neal Family Papers, UNC.

12. Jonathan Daniel Wells, *The Origins of the Southern Middle Class, 1800–1861* (Chapel Hill, 2004), 11–12, 162–77.

13. Edmund Flagg, *Flagg's the Far West* (Cleveland, 1906), 52 (quotation); Hunter, *Steamboats on the Western Rivers*, 446; Buchanan, *Black Life on the Mississippi*, 66–67.

14. Arthur Augustus Thurlow Cunynghame, *A Glimpse at the Great Western Republic* (London, 1851), 175; Frederick Marryat, *Second Series of a Diary in America, with Remarks on its Institutions* (Philadelphia, 1840), 367 (quotation); Buchanan, *Black Life on the Mississippi*, 66–67.

15. M'Lissa Kesterman, "Steamboat Journey from Cincinnati to New Orleans in 1851," *Ohio Valley History* 7 (summer 2007): 82 (quotation); 1840 *Family Magazine* clipping in Iron Men—Wooden Boats scrapbook, vol. 2, Joseph Merrick Jones-Donald T. Wright Steamboat Collection, TU; John Habermehl, *Life on the Western Rivers* (Pittsburgh, 1901), 59–64; James T. Lloyd, *Lloyd's Steamboat Directory and Disasters on the Western Waters* (Cincinnati, 1856), 58. Jacob also became the first known black to die in a western steamboat explosion.

16. Charles Joseph Latrobe, *The Rambler in North America*, 2nd ed., 2 vols. (1836; reprint, New York, 1970), 1:296 (first quotation); Hall, *The Manhattaner in New Orleans*, 179 (remaining quotations). James Buckingham provides the exception to the rule. He met a Chinese waiter from Canton who had been in the United States for six years (James S. Buckingham, *The Slave States of America*, 2 vols. [London, 1842], 1:462).

17. Buchanan, *Black Life on the Mississippi*, 64.

18. Louisiana Swamp Doctor Manuscript (typescript), 4–6, John Q. Anderson Papers, LSU.

19. Lady Emmeline Stuart Wortley, *Travels in the United States, during 1849 and 1850* (New York, 1851), 110 (quotation); Harriet Martineau, *Retrospect of Western Travel*, 2 vols. (London, 1838), 2:10; John Francis McDermott, ed., *Before Mark Twain: A Sampler of Old, Old Times on the Mississippi* (Carbondale, 1968), 78; Buchanan, *Black Life on the Mississippi*, 65–66.

20. "Smoke and Sparks," *Natchez Daily Courier*, June 26, 1855, typescript in Somdal Papers, LSUS; Buchanan, *Black Life on the Mississippi*, 62.

21. Robert Everest, *A Journey through the United States and Part of Canada* (London, 1855), 102.

22. Habermehl, *Life on the Western Rivers*, 84–85; Buchanan, *Black Life on the Mississippi*, 55.

23. *Thomas Summers v. John Graham*, clipping in Somdal Collection, box 9, folder 346, LSUS; 1840 *Family Magazine* clipping in Iron Men—Wooden Boats scrapbook, vol. 2, Joseph Merrick Jones-Donald T. Wright Steamboat Collection, TU (quotation).

24. Ebenezer Davies, *American Scenes and Christian Slavery: A Recent Tour of Four Thousand Miles in the United States* (London, 1849), 100–101; James Thomas, *From Tennessee Slave to St. Louis Entrepreneur: The Autobiography of James Thomas*, ed. Loren Schweniger (Columbia, 1984), 85; William Ransom Hogan and Edwin Adams Davis, eds., *William Johnson's Natchez: The Ante-Bellum Diary of a Free Negro* (Baton Rouge, 1951), 508, 743; Buchanan, *Black Life on the Mississippi*, 67–68. The most recent treatment of black barbers, despite using Thomas's narrative, has no extended discussion of steamboats. See Douglas Walter Bristol Jr., *Knights of the Razor: Black Barbers in Slavery and Freedom* (Baltimore, 2009).

25. McDermott, ed., *Before Mark Twain*, 264 (quotation); Hunter, *Steamboats on the Western Rivers*, 259–63.

26. Fredrika Bremer, *America of the Fifties: Letters of Fredrika Bremer*, ed. Adolph B. Benson (New York, 1924), 261–62 (quotation); Latrobe, *Rambler in North America*, 1:281; Frederick Law Olmsted, *A Journey in the Seaboard Slave States: with remarks on their Economy* (New York, 1856), 612; Friedrich Gerstacker, *Wild Sports in the Far West: The narrative of a German wanderer beyond the Mississippi, 1837–1843*, trans. Edna L. Steeves and Harrison L. Steeves (1854; reprint, Durham, N.C., 1968), 95–97; Buchanan, *Black Life on the Mississippi*, 71.

27. T. C. Collins, *Adventures of T. C. Collins—Boatman*, comp. and ed. Herbert L. Roush Sr. (Baltimore, 1985), 56 (quotation); Hunter, *Steamboats on the Western Rivers*, 456–58.

28. George W. Featherstonhaugh, *Excursion through the Slave States* (1844; reprint, New York, 1968), 144; Habermehl, *Life on the Western Rivers*, 8; Stoughton Cooley, "The Mississippi Roustabout," *New England Magazine* 17, no. 3 (November 1894): 290; Buchanan, *Black Life on the Mississippi*, 73–75.

29. Henry Latham, *Black and White: A Journal of Three Months' Tour in the United States* (London, 1867), 150 (first and second quotations); Charles Lanman, *Adventures in the Wilds of the United States and British American Provinces*, 2 vols. (Philadelphia, 1856), 1:167 (third quotation), 177 (fourth quotation); Hiram Fuller, *Belle Brittan on a Tour at Newport, and here and there* (New York, 1858), 90 (remaining quotations); Edward King, *The Great South: A Record of Journeys in Louisiana, Texas, the Indian Territory, Missouri, Arkansas, Mississippi, Alabama, Georgia, Florida, South Carolina, North Carolina, Kentucky, Tennessee, Virginia, West Virginia, and Maryland* (Hartford, 1875), 305; Language of the River, http://riverlorian.com/languageoftheriver.htm, Jerry Hay. A cotton hook had a wooden handle that fit into the palm of the hand and a curved iron hook that protruded between the middle and ring fingers.

30. John T. Trowbridge, *The Desolate South 1865–1866: A Picture of the Battlefields and of the Devastated Confederacy*, ed. Gordon Carroll (Freeport, N.Y., 1956), 93 (first quotation); Charles Peter Grizzard, "A Glimpse of the South in the spring of 1855," 113, Beinecke Rare Book and Manuscript Library, Yale University, New Haven, Connecticut (second quotation).

31. Julian Ralph, *Dixie; or Southern Scenes and Sketches* (New York, 1896), 3–4 (quotations); Buchanan, *Black Life on the Mississippi,* 70.

32. Mrs. [Matilda Charlotte] Houstoun, *Hesperos: or, Travels in the West*, 2 vols. (London, 1850), 2:43–44 (first and second quotations); Michael Daffy as quoted in Frank Towers, *The Urban South and the Coming of the Civil War* (Charlottesville, 2004), 44 (final quotation); Hunter, *Steamboats on the Western Rivers*, 451–56; Collins, *Adventures of T. C. Collins,* 55, 66.

33. Michael Allen, ed., "Reminiscences of a Common Boatman (1849–1851)," *Gateway Heritage* 5 (fall 1984): 40 (first quotation); Samuel Wigglesworth to Thomas Wigglesworth, July 7, 1839, Wigglesworth Letters, FHS (second quotation); Buchanan, *Black Life on the Mississippi,* 72–73; Language of the River, http://riverlorian.com/languageoftheriver.htm, Jerry Hay.

34. Eric Arnesen, *Waterfront Workers of New Orleans: Race, Class, and Politics, 1863–1923* (New York, 1991), 103–4 (first quotation); undated entry after January 17, 1857, Anton Reiff Journal, LSU (second quotation); Lanman, *Adventures in the Wilds,* 167 (third quotation); Charles Peter Grizzard, "A Glimpse of the South in the spring of 1855," 36, Beinecke Rare Book and Manuscript Library, Yale University Library, New Haven, Connecticut (remaining quotations); Cooley, "Mississippi Roustabout," 294; Allen, ed., "Reminiscences of a Common Boatman," 40; Buchanan, *Black Life on the Mississippi,* 58–59.

35. *A. M. Poree, v. Cannon et al.,* typescript in Somdal Collection, LSUS; *H. M. Summers v. United States Insurance, Annuity and Trust Co.,* No. 5423, 13 La. Ann. (n.s.) 504, New Orleans, December 1858; *Robert Howes v. Steamer Red Chief, Captain and Owners,* No. 5944, 15 La. Ann. (n.s.) 321, New Orleans, May 1860, both in UNO; Hogan and Davis, eds., *William Johnson's Natchez,* 84; Judith Kelleher Schafer, *Slavery, the Civil Law, and the Supreme Court of Louisiana* (Baton Rouge, 1994), 102; Allen, ed., "Reminiscences of a Common Boatman," 43; Collins, *Adventures of T. C. Collins,* 55.

36. George Wolfe Bruce to Mother, February 5, 1854, George Wolfe Bruce Papers, UNC (first quotation); Howard Barney, "News and Views," as quoted in Ikerman, "Steamboats," 86 (second and third quotations); Thomas Bangs Thorpe, "Remembrances of the Mississippi," *Harpers's New Monthly Magazine*, 12, no. 67 (December 1855): 37 (remaining quotations).

37. King, *Great South,* 71; John A. Clark, *Gleanings by the Way* (Philadelphia, 1842), (first quotation); Report from the Secretary of the Treasury, December 12, 1838, as quoted in John H. Morrison, *History of American Steam Navigation* (New York, 1903), 225; Henry Cook Todd, *Notes upon Canada and the United States from 1832 to 1840: much in a small space, or a great deal in a little*

book (Toronto, 1840), 50; Lanman, *Adventures in the Wild*, 168; James Stuart, *Three Years in North America*, 2 vols. (Edinburgh, 1833), 2:281 (second quotation); Cooley, "Mississippi Roustabout," 300; "Memoir of Henry Dumesnil," 2, Dumesnil Family Papers, FHS.

38. Walter Havighurst, *Voices on the River: The Story of the Mississippi Waterways* (New York, 1964), 124 (first quotation); Allen, ed., "Reminiscences of a Common Boatman," 40–43; John W. Leathers to Thomas P. Leathers, December 13, 1852, Thomas P. Leathers Papers, LSU (second quotation); Paul A. Gilje, *Liberty on the Waterfront: American Maritime Culture in the Age of Revolution* (Philadelphia, 2007), 7–35.

39. January 14 and 15, 1857, entries, Anton Reiff Journal, LSU; John Geiger Diary (typescript), February 28, 1836, entry, Missouri Historical Society, St. Louis, Missouri; Dennis C. Rousey, *Policing the Southern City: New Orleans, 1805–1889* (Baton Rouge, 1996), 32.

40. *St. Louis Globe-Democrat*, January 8, 1893, as quoted in Thomas C. Buchanan, "The Slave Mississippi: African-American Steamboat Workers, Networks of Resistance, and the Commercial World of the Western Rivers, 1811–1880" (Ph.D. diss., Carnegie Mellon University, 1998), 42 (first quotation); Havighurst, *Voices on the River*, 124 (second quotation); Nichols, *Forty Years*, 1:231; Olmsted, *Seaboard Slave States*, 564 (third quotation); Habermehl, *Life on the Western Rivers*, 71–72.

41. *New Orleans Daily Delta*, May 15, 1854, typescript in Somdal Collection, Box 20, Folder 796, LSUS; F. E. Schoolfield, "Captain Alex. F. Boss, Western Rivers Pilot," 55–56, typescript, IRL (second quotation); *Chillicothe Scioto Gazette*, October 14, 1846 (third quotation); *New Orleans Picayune*, June 9, 1839, as quoted in Buchanan, *Black Life on the Mississippi*, 57; undated *Morehouse Advocate* article, as quoted in Frederick Law Olmsted, *The Cotton Kingdom: A Traveller's Observations on Cotton and Slavery in the American Slave States, 1853–1861*, ed. Arthur M. Schlesinger (New York, 1953), 299 (final quotation); undated *Pittsburgh Dispatch* article, as quoted in *National Era*, April 20, 1854. For the opposite conclusion, that the influence of the market economy "eroded class and racial barriers," see Douglas R. Egerton, "Slaves to the Marketplace: Economic Liberty and Black Rebelliousness in the Atlantic World," *JER* 26 (winter 2006): 629.

42. Petition of Helena Kimball, box 10, folder 412, Somdal Collection, LSUS; Federal Writers' Project, *Slave Narratives: A Folk History of Slavery in the United States from Interviews with Former Slaves*, vol. 11, *Arkansas Narratives*, part 5 (Washington, D.C., 1941), 69 (quotation); Jonathan D. Martin, *Divided Mastery: Slave Hiring in the American South* (Cambridge, 2004), 172–78; Sharla M. Fett, *Working Cures: Healing, Health, and Power on Southern Slave Plantations* (Chapel Hill, 2002), 159–68. For examples of enslaved Americans working in sailing vessels, see David S. Cecelski, *The Waterman's Song: Slavery and Freedom in Maritime North Carolina* (Chapel Hill, 2001), 25–56, and W. Jeffrey Bolster, *Black Jacks: African American Seaman in the Age of Sail* (Cambridge, 1997), 131–57.

43. *J. A. Lusk v. J. C. Swon—C. B. Church*, in Warranty, No. 2852, 9 La. Ann. (n.s.) 367, New Orleans, June 1854; William Wells Brown, *Narrative of William W. Brown, An American Slave* (London, 1849), 95; Buchanan, *Black Life on the Mississippi*, 23–25, 101–21; Judith Kelleher Schafer, *Becoming Free, Remaining Free: Manumission and Enslavement in New Orleans, 1846–1862* (Baton Rouge, 2003), 134–41.

44. Lewis Garrard Clarke and Milton Clarke, *Narratives of the Sufferings of Lewis and Milton Clarke* (Boston, 1846), 81; Moses Grandy, *Narrative of the Life of Moses Grandy: Late a Slave in the United States of America* (London, 1843), 47–48; Buchanan, *Black Life on the Mississippi*, 95–98.

45. Edward Russell Journal, February 2, 1835, HNOC (first and second quotations); James Hervey Otey Diary, February 4, 1860, entry, James Hervey Otey Papers, UNC; Gustavus Henry to Marion Henry, November 22, 1849, Gustavus Henry Papers, UNC (final quotation); Benjamin

Drew, *A North-Side View of Slavery: The Refugee: or the Narrative of Fugitive Slaves in Canada* (Boston, 1856), 254–55; Buchanan, *Black Life on the Mississippi,* 21–23, 90–93; Egerton, "Slaves to the Marketplace," 622.

46. Stephanie M. H. Camp, *Closer to Freedom: Enslaved Women and Everyday Resistance in the Plantation South* (Chapel Hill, 2004), 6 (first quotation), 12–34; *A. J. Morgan v. Steamer Liah Tuna,* Somdal Papers, LSUS (final quotation); Buchanan, *Black Life on the Mississippi,* 21–23, 90–93; Anthony E. Kaye, *Joining Places: Slave Neighborhoods in the Old South* (Chapel Hill, 2007), 153–76.

47. Schafer, *Slavery, the Civil Law, and the Supreme Court of Louisiana,* 96–97 (first quotation); Louis Hughes, *Thirty Years a Slave: From Bondage to Freedom* (Milwaukee, 1897), 81 (second quotation); Olmsted, *Journey in the Seaboard Slave States,* 570.

48. James Rudd Account Book, FHS; R. C. Ballard, as quoted in Buchanan, *Black Life on the Mississippi,* 82 (first quotation); Gustavus Henry to Marion Henry, November 22, 1849, Gustavus Henry Papers, UNC; *Robert G. Beverly v. Captain and Owners of steamboat Empire,* No. 6323, 15 La. Ann. (n.s.) 432, New Orleans, June 1860, UNO; Martin, *Divided Mastery,* 39, 82.

CHAPTER THREE

1. The account of the *Natchez* is in "Smoke and Sparks," *Natchez Daily Courier,* June 26, 28, July 3, 6, 10, 17, 1855, typescript in Somdal Papers, LSUS. The author identifies himself only as Tom or T.X.W. All quotations regarding the boat are drawn from this source, while the description is supplemented from other observations regarding steamboats, including Logbook of Natchez Landings, 1835–1837, UTX; Mrs. [Matilda Charlotte] Houstoun, *Hesperos: or, Travels in the West,* 2 vols. (London, 1850), 2:15; Tyrone Power, *Impressions of America during the years 1833, 1834, and 1835,* 2 vols. (London, 1836), 2:186. Boats that were less attuned to customers' desires used a gangplank (a temporary wooden plank) rather than a stage.

2. Undated *Wheeling Gazette* article, as quoted in James Hall, *The West: Its Commerce and Navigation* (1848; reprint, New York, 1970), 147 (first quotation); Amos Andrew Parker, *Trip to the West and Texas* (1835; reprint, New York, 1973), 86 (second quotation); John Francis McDermott, ed., *Before Mark Twain: A Sampler of Old, Old Times on the Mississippi* (Carbondale, 1968), 80 (third quotation); Edward King, *The Great South: A Record of Journeys in Louisiana, Texas, the Indian Territory, Missouri, Arkansas, Mississippi, Alabama, Georgia, Florida, South Carolina, North Carolina, Kentucky, Tennessee, Virginia, West Virginia, and Maryland* (Hartford, 1875), 68; James Edward Alexander, *Transatlantic Sketches, Comprising visits to the most interesting Scenes in North and South America* (Philadelphia, 1833), 243; Louis C. Hunter, *Steamboats on the Western Rivers: An Economic and Technological History* (1949; reprint, Mineola, N.Y., 1993), 264–65, 421–22; Thomas C. Buchanan, *Black Life on the Mississippi: Slaves, Free Blacks, and the Western Steamboat World* (Chapel Hill, 2004), 70–71; Erik F. Haites, James Mak, and Gary M. Walton, *Western River Transportation: The Era of Early Internal Development, 1810–1860* (Baltimore, 1975), 162; Michael Allen, ed., "Reminiscences of a Common Boatman (1849–1851)," *Gateway Heritage* 5 (fall 1984): 40; MeasuringWorth, http://www.measuringworth.com/index.html, MeasuringWorth.

3. Houstoun, *Hesperos,* 2:19; McDermott, ed., *Before Mark Twain,* 84 (quotations); Marion Bragg, *Historic Names and Places on the Lower Mississippi River* (Vicksburg, 1977), 105; William Fairfax Gray, *The Diary of William Fairfax Gray, from Virginia to Texas, 1835–1837,* ed. Paul D. Lack (Dallas, 1997), 9.

4. "Memoir of James Norman Smith," 3:30, Alexander Wallace Jones Papers, TSLA; I. A. Conn to William Conn, July 14, 1836 (first quotation), August 24, 1839 (second quotation), Gano Papers, WHMC.

5. Lady Emmeline Stuart Wortley, *Travels in the United States, during 1849 and 1850* (New York, 1851), 107 (first and second quotations); Edmund Flagg, *Flagg's the Far West* (Cleveland, 1906), 84 (third quotation); Frederick Law Olmsted, *A Journey in the Seaboard Slave States: with remarks on their Economy* (New York, 1856), 571; *Arkansas Advocate*, May 23, 1832, as quoted in Duane Huddleston, "The *Volant* and *Reindeer*: Early Arkansas Steamboats," clipping in Tappan Steamboat Collection, Special Collections, University of Arkansas Libraries, Fayetteville, Arkansas; unidentified newspaper clipping labeled April 3, 1855, and *Missouri Gazette*, April 19, 1827, clipping (final quotation), both in "Iron Men—Wooden Boats," vol. 3, Joseph Merrick Jones-Donald T. Wright Steamboat Collection, TU.

6. *Levin K. Person v. C. M. Rutherford*, No. 3585, 11 La. Ann. (n.s.) 527, New Orleans, June 1856, UNO; Frederic Bancroft, *Slave Trading in the Old South* (1931; reprint, Columbia, 1996), 280–81; Steven Deyle, *Carry Me Back: The Domestic Slave Trade in American Life* (New York, 2005), 147–48; Buchanan, *Black Life on the Mississippi*, 83–84.

7. William Wells Brown, *Narrative of William W. Brown, An American Slave* (London, 1849), 32, 38–43 (quotation); Daniel Chapman Banks Diary, April 24, 1822, entry, Daniel Chapman Banks Papers, FHS; Buchanan, *Black Life on the Mississippi*, 86.

8. Brown, *Narrative of William W. Brown*, 39 (first quotation); Thomas Hamilton, *Men and Manners in America* (Philadelphia, 1833), 304 (second and third quotations); Abraham Lincoln to Mary Speed, September 27, 1841 (typescript), Speed Family Papers, FHS (Lincoln quotations); Arthur Augustus Thurlow Cunynghame, *A Glimpse at the Great Western Republic* (London, 1851), 163.

9. John Habermehl, *Life on the Western Rivers* (Pittsburgh, 1901), 55 (quotations); McDermott, ed., *Before Mark Twain*, 84; Hunter, *Steamboats on the Western Rivers*, 419–41; Haites, Mak, and Walton, *Western River Transportation*, 163.

10. McDermott, ed., *Before Mark Twain*, 61 (first quotation), 60 (final quotation); Herbert Quick and Edward Quick, *Mississippi Steamboatin': A History of Steamboating on the Mississippi and Its Tributaries* (New York, 1926), 103 (second quotation); Robert Baird, *View of the Valley of the Mississippi: Or the Emigrant's and Traveller's Guide to the West* (Philadelphia, 1832), 323; Memoir of James Norman Smith, 3:118, in Alexander Wallace Jones Papers, TSLA.

11. Sarah Chapin, ed., "Edward Jarvis's Journal," *Filson Club Historical Quarterly* 70 (July 1996): 232–34 (first quotation); L. Jones to Nancy Smith, July 15, 1824, Margaret Yundt Kostmayer Collection, TU (second quotation); Olmsted, *Journey through the Seaboard States*, 613 (third quotation); Thomas Spence, *The Settler's Guide in the United States and British North American Provinces* (New York, 1862), 341.

12. Secretary of the Treasury to the House of Representatives, December 12, 1828, as quoted in John H. Morrison, *History of American Steam Navigation* (New York, 1903), 222 (quotation); McDermott, ed., *Before Mark Twain*, 61; Michael Allen, *Western Rivermen, 1763–1861: Ohio and Mississippi Boatmen and the Myth of the Alligator Horse* (Baton Rouge, 1990), 164–65; Michael Gillespie, *Come Hell or High Water: A Lively History of Steamboating on the Mississippi and Ohio Rivers* (Stoddard, Wisc.: 2001), 150–52; Memoir of James Norman Smith, Alexander Wallace Jones Papers, typescript, 2:148, TSLA (final quotations); Hunter, *Steamboats on the Western Rivers*, 431–35.

13. Alexander, *Transatlantic Sketches*, 252 (quotation); Chapin, ed., "Edward Jarvis's Journal," 291; Horace J. Ford Journal, March 29, 1849, entry, Historic Arkansas Museum, Little Rock, Arkansas.

14. Bragg, *Historic Names and Places*, 193; Cunynghame, *Glimpse at the Great Western Republic*, 177; Houstoun, *Hesperos*, 2:34, 38–39 (quotation).

15. Undated *St. Louis Intelligencer* article, as quoted in the *Chillicothe, Ohio, Daily Scioto Gazette*, May 26, 1852.

16. *New Orleans Daily Delta*, May 15, 1854, typescript in Somdal Collection, LSUS.

17. Samuel J. Peters Diary, December, 11, 1852, LSU (quotation); Journal, Daniel Chapman Banks Papers, April 24, 1822, FHS; Kenneth S. Greenberg, *Honor and Slavery: Lies, Duels, Noses, Masks, Dressing as a Woman, Gifts, Strangers, Humanitarianism, Death, Slave Rebellions, the Proslavery Argument, Baseball, Hunting and Gambling in the Old South* (Princeton, 1996), 87–88, 144–45; Bertram Wyatt-Brown, *Southern Honor: Ethics and Behavior in the Old South* (New York, 1982), 340–50; James Oakes, *Slavery and Freedom: An Interpretation of the Old South* (New York, 1990).

18. Hunter, *Steamboats on the Western Rivers*, 394–96.

19. Anton Reiff Journal, January 9, 20, 1857, LSU; Olmsted, *Journey in the Seaboard Slave States*, 616 (first quotation); John A. Clark, *Gleanings by the Way* (Philadelphia, 1842), 83 (second quotation); Patrick Shirreff, *A Tour through North America* (Edniburgh, 1835), 268 (third quotation); Daniel Chapman Banks Papers, April 28, 1823, entry, FHS; Horace J. Ford Journal, April 15, 1849, entry, Historic Arkansas Museum, Little Rock, Arkansas; "Western Steamboat Life," *DBR* 25 (November 1858): 601.

20. Charles Minor to Tilly Gustine, March 24, 1846, Minor Collection, UNC (first quotation); Charles Lyell, *A Second Visit to the United States of America*, 2 vols. (New York, 1849), 2:206 (second quotation); Hilliard Diary, January 25, 1850, entry, LSU (second, third, and fourth quotations); Travel Diary, February 11, 1848, entry, Eleanor Jameson Williams Baker Papers, DU (final quotation). The informal stratification of boats is not unlike that of today's cruise ships, which have an unwritten hierarchy. Travel on Carnival Cruise Lines, for instance, is very different from that on Crystal Cruises.

21. Charles Lanman, *Adventures in the Wilds of the United States and British North American Provinces*, 2 vols. (Philadelphia, 1856), 1:207; Paul Wilhelm, Duke of Wurttermberg, *Travels in North America, 1822–1824*, trans. W. Robert Nitske, ed. Savoie Lottinville (Norman, 1973), 86 (first quotation); Charles Peter Grizzard, "A Glimpse of the South in the spring of 1855," 30, Beinecke Rare Book and Manuscript Library, Yale University, New Haven, Connecticut (final quotation); George Wolfe Bruce to Mother, February 5, 1854, George Wolfe Bruce Papers, DU; February 6, 11, 1826, entries, Mississippi River Travel Diary, 1825–1826, DU; Joseph H. Ingraham, *The Sunny South: or the Southerner at Home* (1860; reprint, New York, 1968), 237–39; James S. Buckingham, *The Slaves States of America*, 2 vols. (London, 1842), 1:396–97; *McAlpin v. Lauve et al.*, No. 672, 2 La. Ann. (n.s.) 1015, New Orleans, December 1847, UNO; Anne Henry Ehrenpreis, ed., *Happy Country this America: The Travel Diary of Henry Arthur Blight* (Columbus, 1978), 253; Thomas Low Nichols, *Forty Years of American Life*, 2 vols. (London, 1864), 2:5–6; George H. Yater, *Two Hundred Years at the Falls of the Ohio: A History of Louisville and Jefferson County* (Louisville, 1979), 61; Hunter, *Steamboats on the Western Rivers*, 395–97; Frederick Way Jr., *She Takes the Horns: Steamboat Racing on the Western Waters* (Cincinnati, 1953), 43–45.

22. Nichols, *Forty Years*, 1:244 (first quotation); Edward Russell Journal, February 5, 1835, HNOC (final quotation); Bill of Fare, Steamboat *Missouri*, January 10, 1847, Missouri Historical Society, St. Louis, Missouri; Cunynghame, *Glimpse at the Great Western Republic*, 185; James Stuart, *Three Years in North America*, 2 vols. (Edinburgh, 1833), 2:277; Hamilton, *Men and Manners in America*, 295.

23. Anton Reiff Journal, February 19, 1856, entry, LSU; McDermott, ed., *Before Mark Twain,* 59; Nichols, *Forty Years,* 2:6; *Frankfort Commonwealth,* April 1, 1845, in "Advertisements—Kentucky River Steamboats," comp. J. Winston Coleman, Joseph Merrick Jones-Donald T. Wright Steamboat Collection, TU.

24. Philip Paxton [S. A. Hammett], *A Stray Yankee in Texas* (New York, 1859), 404 (first quotation); Wortley, *Travels,* 114–15 (second quotation); Ebenezer Davies, *American Scenes and Christian Slavery: A Recent Tour of Four Thousand Miles in the United States* (London, 1849), 82; John E. Crowley, *The Invention of Comfort: Sensibilities and Design in Early Modern Britain and Early America* (Baltimore, 2001), 292; Edwin Clarence Guillet, *The Great Migration: The Atlantic Crossing by Sailing Ships since 1770,* 2nd ed. (Toronto, 1963), 109–24. A few sources that use "floating palace" are Hilliard Diary, January 25, 1850, LSU; "Western Steamboat Life," *DBR* 25 (November 1858): 601; Lillian Foster, *Way-Side Glimpses, North and South* (New York, 1860), 146; Ingraham, *Sunny South,* 240; Basil Hall, *Travels in North America, in the Years 1827 and 1828,* 3 vols. (Edinburgh, 1830), 3:321; McDermott, ed., *Before Mark Twain,* xviii.

25. Miriam Badger Hill Diary, April 20, 24, 1850, entries, typescript in TU; Houstoun, *Hesperos,* 2:34 (first quotation); Ingraham, *Sunny South,* 238 (second quotation); Charles Joseph Latrobe, *The Rambler in North America,* 2nd ed., 2 vols. (1836; reprint, New York, 1970), 1:297 (final quotation); Haites, Mak, and Walton, *Western River Transportation,* 162; Hunter, *Steamboats on the Western Rivers,* 390–418.

26. McDermott, ed. *Before Mark Twain,* 103 (first quotation), xviii (third quotation); Gray, *Diary of William Fairfax Gray,* 178–79 (second quotation); Diary of Margaretta Sanders, April 14, 21, 1837, entries, Sanders Family Papers, FHS (remaining quotations); Carlos D. De Lassus Diary, July 3, 1836, entry, LSU; Maria Dyer Davies Wightman Diary, January 16, 1851, entry, DU; Cunynghame, *Glimpse at the Great Western Republic,* 139.

27. Gillespie, *Come Hell or High Water,* 70 (quotation), 71; Harriet Martineau, *Retrospect of Western Travel,* 2 vols. (London, 1838), 2:37; Charles Dickens, *American Notes for General Circulation* (London, 1850), 109; Cunynghame, *Glimpse at the Great Western Republic,* 140; Shirreff, *Tour through North America,* 269.

28. William F. Switzler, "A Trip to the South," 8, typescript in WMHC (first quotation); Cunynghame, *Glimpse at the Great Western Republic,* 207 (second quotation); Houstoun, *Hesperos,* 2:6–8 (third quotation); Fredrika Bremer, *America of the Fifties: Letters of Fredrika Bremer,* ed. Adolph B. Benson (New York, 1924), 260 (remaining quotations).

29. Olmsted, *Journey in the Seaboard Slave States,* 611 (quotation); Elizabeth Everts Bellsnyder Diary, TSLA; Charles Peter Grizzard, "A Glimpse of the South in the spring of 1855," 180, Beinecke Rare Book and Manuscript Library, Yale University, New Haven, Connecticut; Hiram Fuller, *Belle Brittan on a Tour at Newport, and here and there* (New York, 1858), 114; Martineau, *Retrospect of Western Travel,* 2:214; George W. Featherstonhaugh, *Excursion through the Slave States* (1844; reprint, New York, 1968), 133; Jack Larkin, *The Reshaping of Everyday Life, 1790–1840* (New York, 1988), 227.

30. Davies, *American Scenes,* 81 (quotation); Vesuvius and Aetna Broadside, Corliss-Respess Family Papers, FHS; Haites, Mak, and Walton, *Western River Transportation,* 31–32; Measuring-Worth, http://www.measuringworth.com/index.html, MeasuringWorth.

31. Latrobe, *Rambler in North America,* 1:296 (first quotation); Stuart, *Three Years in North America,* 2:277; Grizzard, "A Glimpse of the South in the spring of 1855," 119, Beinecke Rare Book and Manuscript Library, Yale University, New Haven, Connecticut; Featherstonhaugh, *Excursion*

through the Slave States, 134 (second quotation); Mary I. Margle to Rebecca Childress, June 7, unknown year, George Campbell Childress Papers, UTX (final second quotation); Gray, *Diary of William Fairfax Gray,* 17.

32. Vesuvius and Aetna Broadside, Corliss-Respess Family Papers, FHS (first five quotations); Olmsted, *Seaboard Slave States,* 612 (final quotation).

33. Aleksandr Borisovich Lakier, *A Russian Looks at America: The Journey of Aleksandr Borisovich Lakier in 1857,* ed. and trans. Arnold Schrier and Joyce Story (Chicago, 1979), 223.

34. "Western Steamboat Life," *DBR* 25 (November 1858): 601 (first quotation); William T. Porter, *The Big Bear of Arkansas and other sketches* (Philadelphia, 1845), 14 (second quotation); Stuart, *Three Years,* 2:323; Thomas Bangs Thorpe, "Remembrances of the Mississippi," *Harper's New Monthly Magazine* 12, no. 67 (December 1855): 34; A. Oakley Hall, *The Manhattaner in New Orleans; or, Phases of "Crescent City" Life* (New York, 1851), 185; Michel Chevalier, *Society, Manners, and Politics in the United States* (Boston, 1839), 219 (final quotation).

35. Cunynghame, *Glimpse at the Great Western Republic,* 121 (first quotation); "Smoke and Sparks," *Natchez Daily Courier,* June 26, 1855, typescript in Somdal Papers, LSUS (second quotation); Frederick Maryatt, *Second Series of a Diary in America, with Remarks on its Institutions* (Philadelphia, 1840), 227.

36. Carlos DeLassus Diary, July 5, 1836 (typescript), LSU; Anton Reiff Journal, January 9, 1856, LSU; Latrobe, *Rambler in North America,* 1:294–95 (quotation).

37. Anton Reiff Journal, January 16, 1857, LSU; Wyatt-Brown, *Southern Honor*; Greenberg, *Honor and Slavery.*

38. Edward Russell Journal, February 4, 1835, entry, HNOC (quotation); Lakier, *A Russian Looks at America,* 222; Featherstonhaugh, *Excursion through the Slave States,* 135–39; Buckingham, *Slave States of America,* 1:270; Gray, *Diary of William Fairfax Gray,* 14, 71; Martineau, *Retrospect of Western Travel,* 2:6; Latrobe, *Rambler in North America,* 1:296. There is surprisingly little scholarship regarding gambling on steamboats. John M. Findlay's *People of Chance: Gambling in American Society from Jamestown to Las Vegas* (New York, 1986) is one of the few books to address the topic, but it makes a number of dubious claims. Findlay accepts that gamblers wore flashy jewelry, argues that the river system of the interior South inhibited settlement, and believes that steamboats cut into gambling's popularity. See pages 62–76 for his discussion of gambling in the South. For a more level-headed account, see Hunter, *Steamboats on the Western Rivers,* 408–10.

39. Joshua D. Rothman, "The Hazards of Flush Times: Gambling, Mob Violence, and the Anxieties of America's Market Revolution," *JAH* 95 (December 2008): 651–77; Karen Halttunen, *Confidence Men and Painted Women: A Study in Middle-Class Culture in America, 1830–1870* (New Haven, 1982), 34 (quotation); Ann Fabian, *Card Sharps, Dream Books, and Bucket Shops: Gambling in 19th-Century America* (Ithaca, 1990), 29–38; Gerda Reith, *The Age of Chance: Gambling in Western Culture* (London, 1999), 130–38. Greenberg, *Honor and Slavery,* 135–45, connects gambling to the southern honor code, but passengers from all locales gambled on southern boats. Southerners did not seem to have an unusual affinity for, or appreciation of, gambling.

40. "Western Steamboat Life," *DBR* 25 (November 1858): 601; William Kingsford, *Impressions of the West and South during a six weeks' holiday* (Toronto, 1858), 49 (quotation); Jonathan H. Green, *Gambling Exposed* (Philadelphia, 1857), 65–68; Power, *Impressions of America,* 2:198. Thomas Ruys Smith, *River of Dreams: Imagining the Mississippi Before Mark Twain* (Baton Rouge, 2007), 145.

41. *New Orleans Picayune,* June 15, 1839; George H. Devol, *Forty Years a Gambler on the Mississippi* (1887; reprint, New York, 1968), 152; Lanman, *Adventures in the Wilds of the United States,*

172; Clark, *Gleanings by the Way,* 83; Greenberg, *Honor and Slavery,* 136–44. The gambler tied to the piston rod provided so much amusement that the crew members allowed him to keep his winnings after they let him go. Perhaps, in some sort of skewed way, he proved his masculinity by staving off death.

42. Devol, *Forty Years a Gambler on the Mississippi,* 152 (second quotation), 216–17, 295 (first quotation); Smith, *River of Dreams,* 154; Halttunen, *Confidence Men and Painted Ladies,* 24–25; Lawrence W. Levine, *Black Culture and Black Consciousness: Afro-American Folk Thought from Slavery to Freedom* (New York, 1977), 121–33; John W. Roberts, *From Trickster to Badman: The Black Folk Hero in Slavery and Freedom* (Philadelphia, 1989), 44–64.

43. Undated *Philadelphia Inquirer,* as quoted in *Niles' National Register* 25 (August 18, 1838), 388 (quotation); Cunynghame, *Glimpse at the Great Western Republic,* 205; Baird, *View of the Valley of the Mississippi,* 324–25; Power, *Impressions of America,* 2:197–98; Alexander Mackay, *The Western World; or, Travels in the United States in 1846–47,* 2 vols. (Philadelphia, 1849), 2:104; Greenberg, *Honor and Slavery,* 135–46.

44. Hunter, *Steamboats on the Western Rivers,* 393; Grizzard, "A Glimpse of the South in the spring of 1855," 30, Beinecke Rare Book and Manuscript Library, Yale University, New Haven, Connecticut; Amy G. Richter, *Home on the Rails: Women, the Railroad, and the Rise of Public Domesticity* (Chapel Hill, 2005), 37; Linda Kerber, "Separate Spheres, Female Worlds, Woman's Place: The Rhetoric of Women's History," *JAH* 75 (June 1998): 9–39; Mary P. Ryan, *Women in Public: Between Banners and Ballots, 1825–1880* (Baltimore, 1990); Judy Wajcman, *Feminism Confronts Technology* (University Park, Pa., 1991).

45. *St. Louis Missouri Republican,* March 10, 1840, as quoted in McDermott, ed., *Before Mark Twain,* xxiii (first quotation); Ingraham, *Sunny South,* 237 (second quotation); *Frankfort Commonwealth,* April 1, 1845, as transcribed in J. Winston Coleman, "Advertisements Kentucky River Steamboats," Joseph Merrick Jones-Donald T. Wright Steamboat Collection, TU.

46. Diary of Miriam Badger Hilliard, May 20, 1850, entry, TU (quotations; this diary entry is misdated April 20, 1850); Memoir of James Norman Smith, 3:26–32, Alexander Wallace Jones Papers, TSLA; Elizabeth Everts Bellsnyder Diary, undated, TSLA; Cunynghame, *Glimpse at the Great Western Republic,* 188; Latrobe, *Rambler in North America,* 1:286–88; Shirreff, *Tour,* 268.

47. Hall, *The Manhattaner in New Orleans,* 183 (first quotation); Lyell, *Second Visit,* 2:168 (second quotation).

48. *New Orleans Daily Delta,* October 6, 1859, clipping (first quotation), and "Smoke and Sparks," *Natchez Daily Courier,* July 17, 1855, typescript (remaining quotations), both in Somdal Collection, LSUS; Charles William Bradbury to Sarah Bradbury, November 7, 1835, Charles William Bradbury Papers, UNC; Marg Sanders to Uncle Joe, October 8, 1838, Sanders Family Papers, FHS.

49. *Nashville Republican Banner,* April 22, 1860, as quoted in Hunter, *Steamboats on the Western Rivers,* 414; Baird, *View of the Valley of the Mississippi,* 346 (quotations).

50. Richter, *Home on the Rails,* 60–78; Aaron W. Marrs, *Railroads in the Old South: Pursuing Progress in a Slave Society* (Baltimore, 2009), 156.

51. Grizzard, "A Glimpse of the South in the spring of 1855," 40, Beinecke Rare Book and Manuscript Library, Yale University, New Haven, Connecticut (quotations); Olmsted, *Journey in the Seaboard Slave States,* 563; Ingraham, *Sunny South,* 291; James L. Huston, "The Experiential Basis of the Northern Antislavery Impulse," *JSH* 4 (November 1990): 609–40. Antebellum southern railroads also allowed slave servants to sit with their masters, but banished all other African Americans to a separate car.

52. Frederick Piercy, *Route from Liverpool to Great Salt Lake Valley*, ed. James Linforth (Liverpool, 1855), 37–38 (first quotation); William Ransom Hogan and Edwin Adams Davis, eds., *William Johnson's Natchez: The Ante-Bellum Diary of a Free Negro* (Baton Rouge, 1951), 21, 391 (remaining quotations), 395, 513, 674; Hunter, *Steamboats on the Western Rivers*, 420–21. As the opening of the previous chapter attested, non-black minorities could enter the saloon if they were able to blend in with polite society. There are almost no references to Hispanics or Asians as cabin passengers.

53. Ehrenpreis, ed., *Happy Country this America*, 226 (first quotation); Cunynghame, *Glimpse at the Great Western Republic*, 130; Hall, *Travels in North America*, 3:309; Oliver W. Holmes and Peter T. Rohrbach, *Stagecoach East: Stagecoach Days in the East from the Colonial Period to the Civil War* (Washington, D.C., 1983), 46–55, 147–59; Larkin, *Reshaping of Everyday Life*, 229; Alice Morse Earle, *Stage-Coach and Tavern Days* (1900; reprint, New York, 1997), 363–69; Grantley F. Berkeley, *The English Sportsman in the Western Prairies* (London, 1861), 362; Eugene Alvarez, *Travel on Southern Antebellum Railroads, 1828 1860* (University, Ala., 1974), 38–39, 47–67; Marrs, *Railroads in the Old South*, 150–52.

CHAPTER FOUR

1. "Schedule of slaves, money, and other property alleged to have been lost by the Creek Indians on the 31st October 1837 by the sinking of the Steam Boat Monmouth off Prophet's Island on the Mississippi River," Letters received, 1824–1881, Special Files, M574, Roll 61, National Archives, available at Rootsweb.com; Grant Foreman, ed., *Indian Pioneer History Collection*, 37 vols. (Oklahoma City, 1937), 13:453–55; Jonathan G. Reynolds to the Mayor of New Orleans, September 14, 1837, Reel 238, Creek Agency Emigration (I consulted the microfilm version of the "Letters Received by the Office of Indian Affairs, 1824–81," which contained material on the Choctaw, Creek, Chickasaw, and Cherokee removals. The originals are housed in the National Archives in Washington. This study will refer to particular microfilm reels as, for instance, Reel 238, Creek Agency Emigration, or Reel 114, Cherokee Agency Emigration); William M. Lytle and Forrest R. Holdcamper, *Merchant Steam Vessels of the United States, 1790–1868: Documents of the United States and Other Sources,* rev. and ed. C. Bradford Mitchell, with assistance of Kenneth R. Hall (Staten Island, 1975), 20, 64, 130; Cecil Meares, "When the Steamboat *Monmouth* Sank in the Mississippi, Creek Indian Passengers Paid the Price," *Wild West* 11 (October 1998): 10. Barnett's testimony is one of the few voices from Native Americans in the South who were removed to Indian Territory on steamboats. Even though the majority of people in the "Five Civilized Tribes" were removed via steamboats, virtually all their accounts discuss land journeys rather than travel on the rivers.

2. Undated *New Orleans True American*, as reprinted in *Little Rock Arkansas Gazette*, November 28, 1837; *New Orleans Bulletin*, November 7, 1837, as reprinted in *St. Louis Daily Commercial Bulletin and Missouri Literary Register*, November 18, 1837; *New Orleans Courier*, November 2, 1837, clipping in Iron Men—Wooden Boats scrapbook, vol. 1, Joseph Merrick Jones-Donald T. Wright Steamboat Collection, TU; Marion Bragg, *Historic Names and Places on the Lower Mississippi River* (Vicksburg, 1977), 205. There is no agreement about the number of deaths on the *Monmouth*. One story fixed the casualties at 600, the boat's owner put the figure at 234, the Army claimed 296 deaths, and the usually cited number is 311. The boat, rather than being ancient as critics alleged, was one year old at the time of the accident. The *Sultana* explosion killed over 1,700 people, most

of them Union soldiers on their way home from the Civil War (Gene Eric Salecker, *Disaster on the Mississippi: The* Sultana *Explosion, April 27, 1865* (Annapolis, 1996), 53–64).

3. John Page to C. A. Harris, December 28, 1837, Reel 238, Creek Agency Emigration. Fort Gibson was about fifty miles upstream of Fort Coffee.

4. The literature on Indian Removal is immense. See, for example, Theda Perdue and Michael D. Green, *The Columbia Guide to American Indians of the Southeast* (New York, 2001), 82–90, 199–200; Ronald N. Satz, *American Indian Policy in the Jacksonian Era* (Lincoln, 1975); Stuart Banner, *How the Indians Lost Their Land: Law and Power on the Frontier* (Cambridge, 2005), 191–227; Grant Foreman, *Indian Removal: The Emigration of the Five Civilized Tribes of Indians,* 2nd ed. (Norman, 1953); John Ehle, *Trail of Tears: The Rise and Fall of the Cherokee Nation* (New York, 1988); John Missall and Mary Lou Missall, *The Seminole Wars: America's Longest Indian Conflict* (Gainesville, 2004); Arthur H. DeRosier Jr., *The Removal of the Choctaw Indians* (Knoxville, 1970), 129–47; Arrell M. Gibson, *The Chickasaws* (Norman, 1971), 168–72; Michael D. Green, *The Politics of Indian Removal: Creek Government and Society in Crisis* (Lincoln, 1982), 185–86; J. Leitch Wright Jr., *Creeks and Seminoles: The Destruction and Regeneration of the Muscogulge People* (Lincoln, 1986), 284–88; Theda Perdue and Michael D. Green, *The Cherokee Removal: A Brief History with Documents,* 2nd ed. (Boston, 2005); Muriel H. Wright, "The Removal of the Choctaws to the Indian Territory, 1830–1833," *Chronicles of Oklahoma* 6 (June 1928): 103–28. Of course, Indian Removal involved many more individuals than those living in the American South. For removal of Native Americans in the Old Northwest—where steamboats were used as well—see Stephen Warren, *The Shawnees and Their Neighbors, 1795–1870* (Urbana, 2005); Kerry A. Trask, *Black Hawk: The Battle for the Heart of America* (New York, 2006); Lucy Eldersveld Murphy, *A Gathering of Rivers: Indians, Metis, and Mining in the Western Great Lakes, 1737–1832* (Lincoln, 2000); and William J. Peterson, *Steamboating on the Upper Mississippi* (Iowa City, 1968), 134–43.

5. Perdue and Green, *American Indians of the Southeast,* 82–86; Norman K. Risjord, *Jefferson's America, 1760–1815* (Madison, 1991), 275–77; Harry L. Watson, *Liberty and Power: The Politics of Jacksonian America* (New York, 1990), 105–6; John B. Boles, *The South through Time: A History of an American Region,* 3rd ed., 2 vols. (Upper Saddle River, N.J., 2004), 1:251–53. The Seminoles might be more correctly called Florida Indians, since not all Native Americans in the present-day state of Florida were Seminoles. These people groups were closely related to the Creeks.

6. Perdue and Green, *American Indians of the Southeast,* 81–84, 88–90; Satz, *American Indian Policy in the Jacksonian Era.*

7. Lynn Willoughby, *Flowing through Time: A History of the Lower Chattahoochee River* (Tuscaloosa, 1999), 50–58; Henry deLeon Southerland Jr. and Jerry Elijah Brown, *The Federal Road through Georgia, the Creek Nation, and Alabama, 1806–1836* (Tuscaloosa, 1989), 78–81; Robbie Etheridge, *Creek Country: The Creek Indians and Their World* (Chapel Hill, 2003), 219–20; Green, *Politics of Indian Removal,* 75–76; *Little Rock Arkansas Gazette,* March 16, 1831; Harry P. Owens, *Steamboats and the Cotton Economy: River Trade in the Yazoo-Mississippi Delta* (Oxford, Miss., 1990), 4–8; John E. Rodabough, *Steamboats on the Upper Tombigbee* (Hamilton, Miss., 1985), 41–42.

8. Brad Agnew, *Fort Gibson: Terminal on the Trail of Tears* (Norman, 1980), 33–34; "Removal of the Indians," *North American Review* 31 (October 1830): 441 (quotation).

9. "Steamboat Disasters," *North American Review* 50 (January 1840): 19 (quotation); Leo Marx, *The Machine in the Garden* (New York, 1964); John F. Kasson, *Civilizing the Machine: Technology and Republican Values in America, 1776–1900* (New York, 1976); David Nye, *America as Second Cre-*

ation: Technology and Narratives of New Beginnings (Cambridge, 2003), 147–73. For contemporaries who linked steamboats and civilization or progress, see James Hall, *The West: Its Commerce and Navigation* (1848; reprint, New York, 1970), 105–10; Robert Baird, *View of the Valley of the Mississippi: Or the Emigrant's and Traveller's Guide to the West* (Philadelphia, 1832), 267; Anon., *Eighty Years' Progress of the United States,* 2 vols. (Hartford, Conn., 1867), 1:183.

10. Perdue and Green, *American Indians of the Southeast,* 91–97; DeRosier, *Removal of the Choctaw Indians,* 162; Gibson, *Chickasaws,* 163; Green, *Politics of Indian Removal,* 185; Wright, *Creeks and Seminoles,* 288; Amanda L. Paige, Fuller L. Bumpers, and Daniel F. Littlefield Jr., *The North Little Rock Site on the Trail of Tears National Historic Trail: Historical Contexts Report* (Little Rock, 2003), 19, 45; Russell Thornton, *American Indian Holocaust and Survival: A Population History since 1492* (Norman, 1987), 115–17; Satz, *American Indian Policy,* 72, 82; Michael F. Doran, "Population Statistics of Nineteenth Century Indian Territory," *Chronicles of Oklahoma* 53 (winter 1975–1976): 496. This study assumed the highest reasonable population figures for the southern Native Americans (17,000 Cherokees, 5,000 Chickasaws, 14,000 Choctaws, 19,600 Creeks, and 5,000 Seminoles). The lowest reasonable estimate would be 55,000, which would raise the percentage of Native Americans deported on riverboats to nearly two-thirds.

11. Benjamin Reynolds and George S. Gaines to John H. Eaton, February 7, 1831, in U.S. Congress, Senate, *Correspondence on the subject of emigration of Indians . . . , in five volumes,* 23rd Cong., 1st sess., 1834, S. Doc. 512, serial 244 (hereinafter cited as *Correspondence*), 1:674 (quotation); DeRosier, *Removal of the Choctaw Indians,* 116–58; Wright, "Removal of the Choctaws," 113–23; Foreman, *Indian Removal,* 19–43; F. W. Armstrong to Lewis Cass, March 30, 1833, Reel 185, Choctaw Agency Removal; *Little Rock Arkansas Gazette,* May 6, 1834; F. W. Armstrong to George Gibson, November 21, 1832, *Correspondence,* 1:400.

12. Rock Roe was also spelled Row, Rowe, and Rockroe.

13. Wright, *Creeks and Seminoles,* 284–96; Foreman, *Indian Removal,* 119–28, 152–65; Anthony F. C. Wallace, *The Long, Bitter Trail: Andrew Jackson and the Indians* (New York, 1993), 83–88 (quotation).

14. A. M. M. Upshaw to C. A. Harris, August 1, 1838, Reel 143, Chickasaw Agency Removal (first quotation); U.S. Congress, House, *Removal of Chickasaw Indians—Simeon Buckner,* 27th Cong., 2nd sess., 1842, H. Rep. 454, serial 408, 1, 8 (second and third quotations); Gibson, *Chickasaws,* 158–73; Foreman, *Indian Removal,* 206–15; Monte Ross Lewis, "Chickasaw Removal: Betrayal of the Beloved Warriors, 1794–1844" (Ph.D. diss., University of North Texas, 1981), 182–87.

15. "Financial account and explanation of John Ross for transporting a detachment of emigrant Cherokee by steamboat to Indian Territory in late 1838 and 1839," Record Group 217, Records of the Accounting Officers of the Department of the Treasury, 1775–1927, available at National Archives and Records Administration, http://arcweb.archives.gov; Winfield Scott to Nathaniel Smith, June 4, 1838, Reel 115, Cherokee Agency Emigration; Gary E. Moulton, *John Ross: Cherokee Chief* (Athens, 1978), 98–99; Foreman, *Indian Removal,* 294–312; Perdue and Green, *Cherokee Removal,* 19–24.

16. Missall and Missall, *Seminole Wars* (Gainesville, 2004), 205–7; Foreman, *Indian Removal,* 364–70; Edward A. Mueller, *Perilous Journeys: A History of Steamboating on the Chattahoochee, Apalachicola, and Flint Rivers, 1828–1928* (Eufala, Ala., 1990), 34–39.

17. Edward Deas, "Journal of Occurrences, 1837," Reel 238, Creek Agency Emigration; Louis C. Hunter, *Steamboats on the Western Rivers: An Economic and Technological History* (1949; reprint, Mineola, N.Y., 1993), 101. The average age and tonnage conclusions of steamboats used in Indian Removal are drawn from data in Lytle and Holdcamper, *Merchant Steam Vessels of the United States.*

18. Jonathan Young to C. A. Harris, June 25, 1837, Reel 114, Cherokee Agency Emigration; Gaston Litton, "The Journal of a Party of Emigrating Creek Indians, 1835–1836," *JSH* 7, no. 2 (May 1941): 233; Deas, "Journal of Occurrences," Reel 238, Creek Agency Emigration.

19. J. Brown to George Gibson, December 15, 1831, *Correspondence,* 1:427 (first quotation); Journal of J. W. Millard, Reel 143, Chickasaw Agency Emigration; J. T. Sprague to C. A. Harris, April 1, 1837, Reel 238, Creek Agency Emigration; Edward Deas, "Journal of Occurrences," Reel 238, Creek Agency Emigration; Report of Gouverneur Morris, April 9, 1838, Reel 239, Creek Agency Emigration; Phillip Mims to C. A. Harris, April 8, 1837, Reel 114, Cherokee Agency Emigration; R. E. Banta, *The Ohio* (New York, 1949), 296 (second quotation); S. T. Cross to George Gibson, November 30, 1831, in *Correspondence,* 1:812; Grant Foreman, "Journey of a Party of Cherokee Emigrants," *Mississippi Valley Historical Review* 18 (September 1931): 240; Ehle, *Trail of Tears,* 240, 322; Wright, *Creeks and Seminoles,* 286–87.

20. William Armstrong to C. A. Harris, October 4, 1837, Reel 143, Chickasaw Agency Emigration (first quotation); Deas, "Journal of Occurrences," Reel 238, Creek Agency Emigration (final quotation); and Deas to C. A. Harris, May 19, 27, 1837, Reel 238, Creek Agency Emigration.

21. F. W. Armstrong to George Gibson, October 3, 1832, in *Correspondence,* 1:671 (quotation); F. S. Bolston, "Journal of the removal of a party of hostile Creek Indians from the vicinity of Montgomery, Alabama to the new Creek Country west of Fort Gibson," Reel 237, Creek Agency Emigration; Banta, *The Ohio,* 295; Foreman, *Indian Removal,* 170; Foreman, "Journey of a Party of Cherokee Emigrants," 234–35; Milton Rickels, *George Washington Harris* (New York, 1965), 21.

22. Alexis de Tocqueville, *Democracy in America,* ed. Phillips Bradley, 2 vols. (New York, 1945), 1:353 (first quotation); *Memphis Enquirer,* October 25, 1836, November 18, 1837 (second quotation); Herbert A. Kellar, ed., "A Diary through the South in 1836: Diary of James D. Davidson," *JSH* 1 (August 1935): 355; Gerald M. Capers, *The Biography of a River Town; Memphis: Its Heroic Age,* 2nd ed. (Memphis, 2003), 48.

23. G. Reynolds to John Page, July 31, 1837, Reel 238, Creek Agency Emigration; T. T. Sloan to John Page, July 31, 1837, Reel 238, Creek Agency Emigration; A. H. Sommerville to John Page, July 31, 1837, Reel 238, Creek Agency Emigration; Jonathan B. Hagan to C. A. Harris, July 22, 1837 (first quotation), and July 27, 1837, Reel 238, Creek Agency Emigration; Jonathan B. Hagan to C. A. Harris, July 22, 1837, Reel 238, Creek Agency Emigration (remaining quotations); Jonathan Page to C. A. Harris, August 15, 1837, Reel 238, Creek Agency Emigration; Alfred Iverson to C. A. Harris, June 28, 1837, Reel 238, Creek Agency Emigration.

24. Journal of J. W. Millard, Reel 143, Chickasaw Agency Emigration (first quotation); Edward Deas, "Journal of Occurrences," Reel 238, Creek Agency Emigration (second quotation); Perdue and Green, *American Indians of the Southeast,* 47–48; DeRosier, *Removal of the Choctaw Indians,* 134.

25. William S. Colquhoun to George Gibson, November 29, 1831, in *Correspondence,* 1:592; Calvin Maynard, P. M. Fournier, W. Beckwith, and Francis Turner to J. M. Woodfin, September 21, 1837, Reel 238, Creek Agency Emigration; Lytle and Holdcamper, *Merchant Steam Vessels,* 39, 182, 208; L. Jones to Nancy Smith, July 15, 1824, Margaret Yundt Kostmayer Collection, TU (quotation); Hunter, *Steamboats on the Western Rivers,* 421–22; Erik F. Haites, James Mak, and Gary M. Walton, *Western River Transportation: The Era of Early Internal Development, 1810–1860* (Baltimore, 1975), 158. The average tonnage and passenger numbers were computed from the compilation of steamboats used in removal by water.

26. Foreman, *Indian Removal,* 171; Paige, Bumpers, and Littlefield, *North Little Rock Site,* 34;

undated *New Orleans True American* article, reprinted in *The Friend, a Religious and Literary Journal* 11 (December 2, 1837): 71–72 (first, second, and third quotations); J. M. Woodfin to George Reynolds, September 22, 1837, Reel 238, Creek Agency Emigration (remaining quotations); Lytle and Holdcamper, *Merchant Steam Vessels,* 71, 114. The notion of another middle passage echoes Ira Berlin's description of the domestic slave trade as a second middle passage (Ira Berlin, *Generations of Captivity: A History of African-American Slaves* [Cambridge, Mass., 2003], 159–244).

27. William S. Colquhoun to George Gibson, December 10, 1831, in *Correspondence,* 1:593 (first and second quotations); Litton, "The Journal of a Party of Emigrating Creek Indians," 234 (remaining quotations).

28. Memoir of James Norman Smith, Alexander Wallace Jones Papers, typescript, 2:148, TSLA; Foreman, "Journey of a Party of Cherokee Emigrants," 236–40; Edward Deas to C. A. Harris, May 29, 1838, Reel 115, Cherokee Agency Emigration; Donald Davidson, *The Tennessee,* vol. 1, *The Old River: Frontier to Secession* (New York, 1946), 270.

29. F. W. Armstrong to George Gibson, November 21, 1832, and F. W. Armstrong to Lewis Cass, March 30, 1833, both in Reel 185, Choctaw Agency Emigration; *Little Rock Arkansas Gazette,* May 6, 1834; F. W. Armstrong to George Gibson, November 21, 1832, in *Correspondence,* 1:400 (quotation); DeRosier, *Removal of the Choctaw Indians,* 152–58; Wright, "Removal of the Choctaws," 119–23.

30. *Memphis Enquirer,* October 25, 1836 (first quotation). Deas, "Journal of Occurrences," May 24, 1837, entry (second quotation); Jonathan B. Hagan to C. A. Harris, July 27, 1837 (final quotation); G. Reynolds to John Page, July 31, 1837; T. T. Sloan to John Page, July 31, 1837; A. H. Sommerville to John Page, July 31, 1837, all in Reel 238, Creek Agency Emigration; Andrew K. Frank, *Creeks and Southerners: Biculturalism on the Early American Frontier* (Lincoln, 2005), 70; Angie Debo, *The Road to Disappearance: A History of the Creek Indians* (Norman, 1979), 18; John R. Swanton, *Chickasaw Society and Religion* (1928; reprint, Lincoln, 2006), 61; Greg O'Brien, *Choctaws in a Revolutionary Age, 1750–1830* (Lincoln, 2002), 23–24.

31. George W. Carvill to Eliza Carvill, March 30, 1837, George W. Carvill Letters, WHMC (first and second quotations); *Mobile Daily Commercial Register,* July 28, 1837, as quoted in Wright, *Creeks and Seminoles,* 298; John F. Parsons, ed., "Letters on the Chickasaw Removal of 1837," *New York Historical Society Quarterly* 37 (July 1953): 280–81; T. B. Thorpe, *The Mysteries of the Backwoods; or Sketches of the Southwest* (Philadelphia, 1846), 109 (third quotation); *Little Rock Arkansas Gazette,* July 23, 1882 (fourth quotation); *Mobile Daily Commercial Register,* July 28, 1837, as quoted in Wright, *Creeks and Seminoles,* 298; A. M. M. Upshaw to C. Harris, April 10, 1838, Reel 143, Chickasaw Agency Emigration (final quotation).

32. L. G. Moses, *Wild West Shows and the Images of American Indians, 1883–1933* (Albuquerque, 1996), 15–18. This study does not lean heavily upon current historical notions of "whiteness," a primer for which may be found in David R. Roediger, "The Pursuit of Whiteness: Property, Terror, and Expansion, 1790–1860," *JER* 19 (winter 1999): 579–600.

33. *Memphis Enquirer,* December 30, 1837 (first quotation), October 25, 1836 (remaining quotations); *Little Rock Arkansas Gazette,* December 21, 1831 (second quotation); Litton, "The Journal of a Party of Emigrating Creek Indians," 233 (third quotation); J. T. Sprague to C. A. Harris, April 1, 1837, Roll 238, Creek Agency Emigration. My concept of a counter-narrative differs from the kind found in Nye, *America as Second Creation.*

34. James P. Ronda, "'We Have a Country': Race, Geography, and the Invention of Indian Territory," *JER* 19 (winter 1999): 739–55.

CHAPTER FIVE

1. James T. Lloyd, *Lloyd's Steamboat Directory and Disasters on the Western Waters* (Cincinnati, 1856), 89–93; Frederick Way Jr., *She Takes the Horns: Steamboat Racing on the Western Waters* (Cincinnati, 1953), 13–20; Louis C. Hunter, *Steamboats on the Western Rivers: An Economic and Technological History* (1949; reprint, Mineola, N.Y., 1993), 292–93; John G. Burke, "Bursting Boilers and Federal Power," *Technology and Culture* 7 (winter 1966): 4–5.

2. Frederick Marryat, *Second Series of a Diary in America, with Remarks on its Institutions* (Philadelphia, 1840), 27 (quotation); James Hall, *The West: Its Commerce and Navigation* (1848; reprint, New York, 1970), 180–82; *Report of the Commissioner of the Patents, . . . respecting applications for patents for the prevention of steam explosions,* 30th Cong., 2nd sess., 1848, S. Exec. Doc. 18, serial 529, 63–65.

3. R. John Brockmann, *Twisted Rails, Sunken Ships: The Rhetoric of Nineteenth Century Steamboat and Railroad Accident Investigation Reports, 1833–1879* (Amityville, N.Y., 2004), 93–109; Rev. H. Ruffner, "Notes of a Tour from Virginia to Tennessee, in the Months of July and August, 1838, Chapter II," *Southern Literary Messenger* 5 (February 1839): 138 (first and second quotations); George W. Carvill to Eliza Boyle, July 14, 1838, Carvill Papers, WHMC (final quotation).

4. "Smoke and Sparks," *Natchez Daily Courier,* July 6, 1855, typescript in Somdal Collection, LSUS (first quotation); "A Report on Explosions, and the Causes of Explosions, with Suggestions for their Prevention," *North American Review* 50 (January 1840): 29 (second quotation); A. Oakley Hall, *The Manhattaner in New Orleans; or, Phases of "Crescent City" Life* (New York, 1851), 173; Basil Hall, *Travels in North America, in the Years 1827 and 1828,* 3 vols. (Edinburgh, 1830), 3:311; Hunter, *Steamboats on the Western Rivers,* 332.

5. James Stuart, *Three Years in North America,* 2 vols. (Edinburgh, 1833), 2:291 (first quotation); Hall, *Manhattaner in New Orleans,* 174 (second quotation).

6. Smith Mead Nelson Diary, December 1, 1828, entry, Special Collections, Mississippi Valley Collection, McWherter Library, University of Memphis, Memphis, Tennessee (first and second quotations); Lillian Foster, *Way-Side Glimpses, North and South* (New York, 1860), 176 (final quotation).

7. Samuel Wigglesworth to Thomas Wigglesworth, July 7, 1839, Samuel Wigglesworth Letters, FHS (first quotation); Charles Casey, *Two Years on the Farm of Uncle Sam* (London, 1852), 110 (second quotation); Charles Lyell, *A Second Visit to the United States of North America,* 2 vols. (New York, 1849), 2:44; Paul Wilhelm, Duke of Wurttermberg, *Travels in North America, 1822–1824,* trans. W. Robert Nitske, ed. Savoie Lottinville (Norman, 1973), 168–69; George W. Featherstonhaugh, *Excursion through the Slave States* (1844; reprint, New York, 1968), 60–61; Hall, *The West,* 135–36; Mark M. Smith, *Mastered by the Clock: Time, Slavery, and Freedom in the American South* (Chapel Hill, 1997), 76–87.

8. *Louisville Daily Democrat,* May 24, 1853; William Ransom Hogan and Edwin Adams Davis, eds., *William Johnson's Natchez: The Ante-Bellum Diary of a Free Negro* (Baton Rouge, 1951), 258.

9. "A Report on Explosions, and the Causes of Explosions, with Suggestions for their prevention," *North American Review* 50 (January 1840): 30 (first quotation); John P. Haggott Journal, March 1845, entry, Special Collections, Mississippi Valley Collection, McWherter Library, University of Memphis, Memphis, Tennessee (remaining quotations); *Louisville Daily Democrat,* May 31, 1853.

10. Ray Samuel, Leonard V. Huber, and Warren C. Ogden, *Tales of the Mississippi* (New York,

1955), 88–94; Thomas James De la Hunt, *Perry County: A History* (Indianapolis, 1916), 173–74; K. Jack Bauer, *Zachary Taylor: Soldier, Planter, and Statesman of the Old Southwest* (Baton Rouge, 1985), 251; *New York Times,* December 18, 1901.

11. *Louisville Daily Democrat,* June 7, 1853 (quotation); Way, *She Takes the Horns,* 39, 51, 76. A map with the *Shotwell's* location is reproduced on page 76 of the Way book.

12. Undated *Peoria Register* article, as quoted in *Daily National Intelligencer,* June 2, 1837 (quotation); Aleksandr Borisovich Lakier, *A Russian Looks at America: The Journey of Aleksandr Borisovich Lakier in 1857,* ed. and trans. Arnold Schrier and Joyce Story (Chicago, 1979), 141; *Pepper v. Peytavin,* No. 751, 12 Mart. (o.s.) 671, New Orleans, February 1823, UNO; *Louisville Daily Democrat,* April 27, 1853; Hunter, *Steamboats on the Western Rivers,* 405–8.

13. Marryat, *Second Series of a Diary in America,* 20 (first quotation); Marie Fontenay de Grandfort, *The New World,* trans. E. C. Wharton (New Orleans, 1855), 81 (second quotation); undated *Peoria Register* article, as quoted in *Daily National Intelligencer,* June 2, 1837; *Harper's Weekly,* May 22, 1858; Frederick Law Olmsted, *A Journey in the Seaboard Slave States: with remarks on their Economy* (New York, 1856), 613; Edmund Flagg, *Flagg's the Far West* (Cleveland, 1906), 90–91; John Francis McDermott, ed., *Before Mark Twain: A Sampler of Old, Old Times on the Mississippi* (Carbondale, 1968), 103.

14. Way, *She Takes the Horns,* 37; Thomas C. DeLeon, *Four Years in Rebel Capitals: An Inside View of Life in the Southern Confederacy from Birth to Death* (Mobile, 1890), 45 (quotation).

15. Mark Twain, *The Family Mark Twain,* vol. 1, *Life on the Mississippi* (New York, 1935), 81 (first quotation); unidentified New Orleans papers, as quoted in an unidentified newspaper clipping in box 20, folder 790, of the Somdal Collection, LSUS (second quotation); *Louisville Daily Democrat,* May 11, 16, 17, 18, 19, 20, 21, 23, 1853; Victor M. Bogle, "The *Eclipse* vs. the *A. L. Shotwell:* Memorable Contest Almost Forgotten," *Filson Club Historical Quarterly* 35 (April 1961): 125–37.

16. *Louisville Daily Democrat,* May 26, 1853; Kenneth S. Greenberg, *Honor and Slavery: Lies, Duels, Noses, Masks, Dressing as a Woman, Gifts, Strangers, Humanitarianism, Death, Slave Rebellions, the Proslavery Argument, Baseball, Hunting and Gambling in the Old South* (Princeton, 1996), 25–32.

17. *Louisville Daily Democrat,* May 23, 1853; Greenberg, *Honor and Slavery,* 24–46; Way, *She Takes the Horns,* 43–49; Manly Wade Wellman, *Fastest on the River: The Great Race Between the* Natchez *and the* Robert E. Lee (New York, 1957). The dispute over which boat won the race was so contentious that fistfights broke out in Louisville. Most of the fracases concerned who would have to pay off their bets. The race was notable enough to merit a story in the June 2, 1853, edition of the *New York Times.*

18. *Little Rock Arkansas State Gazette,* May 23, 1837; Lloyd, *Lloyd's Steamboat Directory,* 95–101; Hogan and Davis, eds., *William Johnson's Natchez* , 176; Marryatt, *Second Series of a Diary in America,* 17–19; *Daily Cleveland Herald,* April 26, 1858; Frederick Way Jr., compiler, *Way's Packet Directory, 1848–1994: Passenger Steamboats of the Mississippi River System Since the Advent of Photography in Mid-Continent America,* rev. ed. (Athens, Ohio, 1994), 351. Steamboats periodically needed to release pressure (blow off steam) or risk an explosion, hence our current expression (Jerry Hay, "River Books and Programs," available from Language of the River, http://riverlorian.com/languageoftheriver.htm, Jerry Hay.

19. Hunter, *Steamboats on the Western Rivers,* 282–98.

20. Unidentified New Orleans newspaper article, as reprinted in the *Little Rock Arkansas State Gazette,* November 30, 1849 (first and second quotations); Simon Ashley Ferrall, *A Ramble of Six Thousand Miles through the United States of America* (London, 1832), 219 (third quotation); undated

Washington Telegraph article, reprinted in the *Little Rock Arkansas Gazette,* May 18, 1830; *Christian Journal and Literary Register,* May 1, 1830; *Mississippi Free Trader and Natchez Gazette,* February 2, 1847, January 11, 1848, September 23, 1848, and December 21, 1850; undated *New Orleans Picayune* article, reprinted in *Natchez Semi-Weekly Courier,* March 6, 1848.

21. Lloyd, *Lloyd's Steamboat Directory,* iv.

22. Unidentified New Orleans newspaper article, as reprinted in the *Little Rock Arkansas State Gazette,* November 30, 1849 (first quotation); Edwin Adams Davis, ed., *Plantation Life in the Florida Parishes of Louisiana, 1836–1854, as reflected in the Diary of Bennett H. Barrow* (New York, 1943), 303 (second quotation); unidentified New Orleans newspaper article, as reprinted in the *Little Rock Arkansas Gazette,* November 30, 1839 (final quotation); Casey, *Two Years on the Farm,* 307–8; *Memphis Enquirer,* November 30, 1838, clipping in Scrapbook, vol. 1, section 1, Tappan Steamboat Collection, Special Collections, University of Arkansas Libraries, Fayetteville, Arkansas; *Little Rock Arkansas State Democrat,* November 30, 1849.

23. Appendix D; Hunter, *Steamboats on the Western Rivers,* 271–304; Richard N. Langlois, David J. Denaulf, and Samson M. Kimenyi, "Bursting Boilers and the Federal Power Redux: The Evolution of Safety on the Western Rivers," May 1994, available at http://129.3.20.41/eps/eh/papers/9503/9503002.pdf, 6 (quotation); "Aviation Accident Statistics," National Transportation Safety Board, http://www.ntsb.gov/aviation/Table3.htm; John F. Stover, *Iron Road to the West: American Railroads in the 1850s* (New York, 1978), 208–10. Stover notes that between 1853 and 1859 there were 213 steamboat accidents that resulted in 2,304 deaths, a figure that seems out of proportion to earlier statistics. He cites various issues of the *American Railroad Journal,* which had an interest in portraying steamboat travel as especially dangerous.

24. Deposition of Samuel Clemens, taken March 9, 1858, Somdal Collection, Box 11, Folder 436, LSUS; J. L. Smith to William B. Smith, December 20, 1844, J. L. Smith Letter, LSU (quotation); Hogan and Davis, eds., *William Johnson's Natchez* , 619; Davis, ed., *Plantation Life in the Florida Parishes of Louisiana,* 318. The Smith letter incorrectly identifies the steamboat as the *Belle of Nashville* (Lloyd, *Lloyd's Steamboat Directory,* 135).

25. *Little Rock Arkansas Gazette,* October 31, 1832, May 8, 1833, and June 5, 1833 (first quotation); Rachel O'Connor to David Weeks, December 6, 1833, David Weeks and Family Papers, LSU (second quotation); Frederick to Sarah McGehee, April 5, 1833, John C. Burruss and Family Collection, LSU (final quotation); Charles E. Rosenberg, *The Cholera Years: The United States in 1832, 1849, and 1866* (Chicago, 1962), 13–98; Albert E. Cowdrey, *This Land, This South: An Environmental History* (Lexington, 1983), 86; Nancy Baird, "Asiatic Cholera's First Visit to Kentucky: A Study in Panic and Fear," *Filson Club Historical Quarterly* 48 (July 1974): 228–89. The 1848 epidemic proceeded along much the same lines as the earlier outbreak. See E. C. Prosser to Anna Butler, July 13, 1849, Anna and Sarah Butler Collection, LSU; *Natchez Semi-Weekly Courier,* December 26, 1848; *Little Rock Arkansas State Democrat,* December 29, 1848; undated *Louisville Journal* article, as quoted in the *Christian Advocate and Journal,* June 7, 1849.

26. Ari Kelman, *A River and Its City: The Nature of Landscape in New Orleans* (Berkeley, 2003), 87–95; Jo Ann Carrigan, "The Impact of Yellow Fever on Life in Louisiana," *Louisiana History* 4 (winter 1963): 5–34; Margaret Humphreys, *Yellow Fever and the South* (New Brunswick, 1992), 45–55; John Duffy, *Sword of Pestilence: The New Orleans Yellow Fever Epidemic of 1853* (Baton Rouge, 1966).

27. Dr. John W. Monette, "Observations on the epidemic Yellow Fever of the Natchez, and of the South-west," *Western Journal of Medicine and Surgery* 4 (May 1842): 335–38.

28. Drew Gilpin Faust, *This Republic of Suffering: Death and the American Civil War* (New York,

2008), 1–18; unsigned letter to "My dear mother," August 15, 1852, David Weeks and Family Papers, LSU (quotation).

29. Undated *New Orleans Picayune* article, as reprinted in the *Natchez Semi-Weekly Courier,* March 6, 1848 (first quotation); Lady Emmeline Stuart Wortley, *Travels in the United States, during 1849 and 1850* (New York, 1851), 127 (second quotation); Thomas K. Wharton, *Queen of the South: New Orleans, 1853–1862,* ed. Samuel Wilson Jr., Patricia Brady, and Lynn D. Adams (New Orleans, 1999), 169.

30. Samuel Clemens to Mary E. Clemens, June 18, 1858, and telegram to William A. Moffett, June 21, 1858, both in Mark Twain Project, http://www.marktwainproject.org, University of California, Berkeley; McDermott, ed., *Before Mark Twain,* 178–83; Ron Powers, *Mark Twain: A Life* (New York, 2005), 84–89. For one survivor's account of the *Pennsylvania* explosion, see William A. Burwell to son, June 18, 1858, Burwell Family Papers, UNC.

31. Walter Nicol Diary, UNC.

32. W. F. Weeks to John Moore, August 13, 1852, David Weeks and Family Papers, LSU (first quotation); unsigned letter to "My dear mother," August 15, 1852, and Rachel O'Connor to David Weeks, November 3, 1833, both in David Weeks Family Papers, LSU (second quotation); Andrew Macrery to Frederic Macrery, November 9, 1833, Andrew Macrery Papers, LSU.

33. St. John R. Liddell to Volney Metcalf, March 17, 1840, Moses Liddell Papers, LSU (first quotation); Lynn M. Case, ed., "The Middle West in 1837: Translations from the Notes of an Italian Count Francesco Arese," *Mississippi Valley Historical Review* 20 (December 1933): 387 (second quotation); Featherstonhaugh, *Excursion through the Slave States* 61 (final quotation); Michel Chevalier, *Society, Manners, and Politics in the United States* (Boston, 1839), 221; Marryat, *Second Series of a Diary in America,* 30; Stuart, *Three Years in North America,* 2:323.

34. Mrs. [Matilda Charlotte] Houstoun, *Hesperos: or, Travels in the West,* 2 vols. (London, 1850), 2:1 (first quotation); Samuel J. Peters Diary, December 17, 1850, entry, LSU (second quotation). See also November 18, 1848, December 14, 1850, and July 5, 1852, entries. The comments on explosions by William Johnson of Natchez are equally prosaic (Hogan and Davis, eds., *William Johnson's Natchez,* 242).

35. *Harper's Weekly,* April 10, 1858, 238

36. William Conn to John A. Gano, January 7, 1844, John Allen Gano Family Papers, WHMC (quotation); George P. Burnham, "The Steamboat Captain who was Averse to Racing," *New York Spirit of the Times,* May 14, 1846, as quoted in McDermott, ed., *Before Mark Twain,* 258–60; "Smoke and Sparks," *Natchez Daily Courier,* June 26, 28, July 3, 6, 10, 17, 1855, typescript in Somdal Papers, LSUS.

37. Thomas Hart Clay Diary, April 27, 1858, entry, Clay-Kenner Family Papers, TSLA (first and second quotations); undated newspaper clipping hand-marked 1852, Box 20, Folder 785, Somdal Collection, LSUS (third quotation); *Little Rock Arkansas Gazette,* June 6, 1838 (fourth quotation); *New Orleans Daily Delta,* March 1, 1859, typescript in Somdal Papers, LSUS (final quotation); undated *Peoria Register* article, as quoted in *Daily National Intelligencer,* June 2, 1837.

38. *Little Rock Arkansas Gazette,* May 6, 1834; Lloyd, *Lloyd's Steamboat Directory,* 83–86; Valerie Gaiennie Hyams Jr., "A History of Navigation on Red River from 1815 to 1865" (Master's thesis, Louisiana State University, 1939), 75–76; Hunter, *Steamboats on the Western Rivers,* 522–23; William E. Lass, *Navigating the Missouri: Steamboating on Nature's Highway, 1819–1935* (Norman, 2008), 112–13.

39. U.S. Congress, House, *Letter from the Secretary of the Treasury, transmitting information in relation to the surveying of the public lands north and south of Red River,* 18th Cong., 2nd sess., 1824,

H. Doc. 24, serial 114; U.S. Congress, House, *Steamboats,* 22nd Cong., 1st sess., 1832, H. Rep. 478, serial 228, 1.

40. U.S. Congress, House, *Steamboats,* 22nd Cong., 1st sess., 1832, H. Rep. 478, serial 228, 1 (quotations); Bruce Sinclair, *Philadelphia's Philosopher Mechanics: A History of the Franklin Institute, 1824–1865* (Baltimore, 1974), 171–89; R. John Brockmann, *Exploding Steamboats, Senate Debates, and Technical Reports: The Convergence of Technology, Politics, and Rhetoric in the Steamboat Bill of 1838* (Amityville, N.Y., 2002), 60–69; Burke, "Bursting Boilers and Federal Power," 8–14.

41. Hunter, *Steamboats on the Western Rivers,* 532–33; Lass, *Navigating the Missouri,* 113–41; Burke, "Bursting Boilers and Federal Power," 15–17. The same general pattern occurred on railroads in the United States, albeit at a later date. See Mark Aldrich, *Death Rode the Rails: American Railroads and Safety, 1828–1965* (Baltimore, 2006), 10–41.

42. *Mobile Examiner* article, as reprinted in the *New York Spectator,* October 29, 1838 (quotation); *Natchez Daily Courier,* July 6, 1855; Hunter, *Steamboats on the Western Rivers,* 533–41; Brockmann, *Exploding Steamboats, Senate Debates, and Technical Reports,* 123–32, Burke, "Bursting Boilers and Federal Power," 22–23.

43. *Little Rock Arkansas Gazette,* May 18, 1830 (first quotation); George W. Carvill to Eliza Boyle, July 14, 1838, George W. Carvill Letters, WHMC (second quotation); Stuart, *Three Years in North America,* 2:275 (final quotation); St. John R. Liddell to Volney Metcalfe, March 17, 1840, Moses Liddell Papers, LSU; Leonard V. Huber, comp., *Advertisements of Lower Mississippi River Steamboats, 1812–1920* (West Barrington, R.I., 1959).

44. Baron de Gerstner, as quoted in John H. Morrison, *History of American Steam Navigation* (New York, 1903), 237 (first quotation); *Louisville Daily Democrat,* June 4, 1853 (second quotation); Way, *Way's Packet Directory,* 139.

CHAPTER SIX

1. Zadok Cramer, *The Navigator: Containing Directions for Navigating the Monongahela, Allegheny, Ohio, and Mississippi Rivers,* 9th ed. (Pittsburgh, 1817), 164 (quotation); Marion Bragg, *Historic Names and Places on the Lower Mississippi River* (Vicksburg, 1977), 57; U.S. Congress, House, *Navigation on Ohio and Mississippi Rivers,* 21st Cong., 1st sess., 1830., H. Rep. 379, serial 201. Shreve originally named his boat the *Helepolis,* but the alternate spelling soon passed into standard use.

2. Henry Shreve to Charles Gratiot, July 22, 1829, Henry Miller Shreve Letters, LSUS; Little Rock *Arkansas Gazette,* February 18, 1834; Robert Baird, *View of the Valley of the Mississippi: Or the Emigrant's and Traveller's Guide to the West* (Philadelphia, 1832), 238; Tim Spell, "Uncle Sam's Toothpullers," *Nautical Research Journal* 26 (March 1980): 38–42; Robert F. Cairo, "Snag Boats on the Western Rivers, Part I," *Nautical Research Journal* 26 (June 1980): 83–93.

3. Henry Shreve to Charles Gratiot, August 23, 1829, Henry Miller Shreve Letters, LSUS (quotation); Cramer, *The Navigator,* 174; U.S. Congress, House, *Letter from the Secretary of war . . . on the Improvement of navigation of Mississippi and Ohio rivers,* 21st Cong., 2nd sess., 1830, H. Doc. 9, serial 206.

4. William Cronon, *Nature's Metropolis: Chicago and the Great West* (New York, 1991), 46–54. The literature involving the interaction between technology and the environment is immense, but may be sampled in Leo Marx, *The Machine in the Garden: Technology and the Pastoral Ideal in America* (New York, 1964); David Nye, *America as Second Creation: Technology and Narratives of*

New Beginnings (Cambridge, 2003); Carroll Pursell, *The Machine in America: A Social History of Technology* (Baltimore, 1995); Ruth Schwartz Cowan, *A Social History of American Technology* (New York, 1997); John F. Kasson, *Civilizing the Machine: Technology and Republican Values in America, 1776–1900* (New York, 1976); and Jeffrey K. Stine and Joel A. Tarr, "At the Intersection of Histories: Technology and the Environment," *Technology and Culture* 39 (October 1998): 601–40.

5. The scholarly literature on the environmental history of the South is growing. For general summaries, see Jack Temple Kirby, *Mockingbird Song: Ecological Landscapes of the South* (Chapel Hill, 2006); Mart A. Stewart, "Re-Greening the South and Southernizing the Rest," *JER* 24 (summer 2004): 242–51; Mart A. Stewart, "If John Muir Had Been an Agrarian: American Environmental History West and South," *Environment and History* 11 (2005): 139–62; Donald Davis, Craig E. Colton, Megan Kate Nelson, Barbara L. Allen, and Mikko Saikku, *Southern United States: An Environmental History* (Santa Barbara, 2006); Christopher Morris, "A More Southern Environmental History," *JSH* 75 (August 2009): 581–98; and Paul S. Sutter and Christopher J. Manganiello, eds., *Environmental History and the American South: A Reader* (Athens, 2009). Relevant specialized studies include Mart A. Stewart, *"What Nature Suffers to Groe": Life, Labor, and Landscape on the Georgia Coast, 1680–1920* (Athens, 2002); Todd Shallat, *Structures in the Stream: Water, Science, and the Rise of the U.S. Army Corps of Engineers* (Austin, Tex., 1994); Craig E. Colten, *An Unnatural Metropolis: Wresting New Orleans from Nature* (Baton Rouge, 2005); Ari Kelman, *A River and Its City: The Nature of Landscape in New Orleans* (Berkeley, 2003); and Ari Kelman, "Forests and Other River Perils," in *Transforming New Orleans and Its Environs: Centuries of Change*, ed. Craig E. Colten, 45–63 (Pittsburgh, 2000). Steamboats are typically not included in southern environmental studies, with the exceptions being Kelman and Shallat.

6. Joseph H. Ingraham, *The South-West by a Yankee*, 2 vols. (New York, 1835), 1:247 (first and second quotations); Timothy Flint, *Recollections of the Last Ten Years* (Boston, 1826), 109 (second quotation); John Banvard, *Description of Banvard's Panorama of the Mississippi River* (Boston, 1847), 21–25; John Francis McDermott, *The Lost Panoramas of the Mississippi* (Chicago, 1958); Nye, *America as Second Creation*, passim. Banvard's panorama was almost a half-mile long, still an impressive achievement. For more comments on the relation between steamboats' civilizing power on nature, see Philip Paxton [S. A. Hammett], *A Stray Yankee in Texas* (New York, 1859), 402; Edmund Flagg, *Flagg's the Far West* (Cleveland, 1906), 47; Fredrika Bremer, *America of the Fifties: Letters of Fredrika Bremer*, ed. Adolph Benson (New York, 1924), 247.

7. "Steamboat Disasters," *North American Review* 50 (January 1840): 19 (quotations); Paul F. Paskoff, *Troubled Waters: Steamboat Disasters, River Improvements, and American Public Policy, 1821–1860* (Baton Rouge, 2007), 39.

8. *Chillicothe Ohio Supporter*, September 3, 1814; Lady Emmeline Stuart Wortley, *Travels in the United States, during 1849 and 1850* (New York, 1851), 116 (first quotation); F. E. Schoolfield, "Captain Alex. F. Boss, Western Rivers Pilot," 47–52, typescript, IRL. Snag accounts are legion. See, for example, Flint, *Recollections*, 320; Michael Gillespie, *Come Hell or High Water: A Lively History of Steamboating on the Mississippi and Ohio Rivers* (Stoddard, Wisc., 2001), 71; Ebenezer Davies, *American Scenes and Christian Slavery: A Recent Tour of Four Thousand Miles in the United States* (London, 1849), 100; Lynn M. Case, ed. "The Middle West in 1837: Translations from the Notes of an Italian Count Francesco Arese," *Mississippi Valley Historical Review* 20 (December 1933): 386.

9. Arthur Augustus Thurlow Cunynghame, *A Glimpse at the Great Western Republic* (London, 1851), 173; James Edward Alexander, *Transatlantic Sketches, Comprising visits to the most interesting Scenes in North and South America* (Philadelphia, 1833), 253; J. D. B. De Bow, "Progress of the Great

West," *DBR* 4 (September 1847): 83; Emerson W. Gould, *Fifty Years on the Mississippi: or, Gould's History of River Navigation* (St. Louis, 1889), 483; Louis C. Hunter, *Steamboats on the Western Rivers: An Economic and Technological History* (1949; reprint, Mineola, N.Y., 1993), 272–77; Jerry Hay, "River Books and Programs," available from Language of the River, http://riverlorian.com/languageoftheriver.htm, Jerry Hay. As early as 1838, enterprising westerners began using diving bells to raise cargo from sunken boats. James Eads, who designed and built the first bridge across the Mississippi River, earned his fortune by designing a diving bell and salvaging items from sunken steamers.

10. Hunter, *Steamboats on the Western Rivers*, 231–33; Language of the River, http://riverlorian.com/languageoftheriver.htm, Jerry Hay.

11. Albert E. Cowdrey, *This Land, This South: An Environmental History* (Lexington, 1983), 96–97; "Reconnaissance of the Ohio River above the Falls made in 1819 by Commissioners Appointed by the States of Virginia, Kentucky, Pennsylvania, and Ohio," as quoted in Leland R. Johnson, *The Falls City Engineers: A History of the Louisville District Corps of Engineers, United States Army* (Alexandria, Va., 1974), 41 (quotations); Gould, *Fifty Years on the Mississippi*, 323–28; Nye, *America as Second Creation*, 147–204. The problems associated with states taking the lead in internal improvements is ably documented in John Lauritz Larson, *Internal Improvement: National Public Works and the Promise of Popular Government in the Early United States* (Chapel Hill, 2001), 71–108.

12. U.S. Congress, Senate, *Memorial of a number of Captains of western steamboats, praying the construction of a canal around the falls of the Ohio, on the Indiana side,* 28th Cong., 1st sess., 1843, S. Doc. 16, serial 432; Charles Joseph Latrobe, *The Rambler in North America*, 2nd ed., 2 vols. (1836; reprint, New York, 1970), 1:101–2; Martha Kreipke, "The Falls of the Ohio and the Development of the Ohio River Trade, 1810–1860," *Filson Club Historical Quarterly* 54 (April 1980): 196–217; Paul B. Trescott, "The Louisville and Portland Canal Company, 1825–1874," *Mississippi Valley Historical Review* 44 (March 1948): 686–708; Charles Bradbury to Sarah Bradbury, November 7, 1835, Charles William Bradbury Papers, UNC.

13. U.S. Congress, House, *Message from the President of the United States, transmitting a Report of the Board of Engineers on the Ohio and Mississippi Rivers,* 17th Cong., 2nd sess., 1823, H. Doc. 35, serial 65-1, 21 (quotation); D. O. Elliott, *The Improvement of the Lower Mississippi River for Flood Control and Navigation*, 3 vols. (Vicksburg, 1932), 1:279; Lawrence G. Hines, "The Early 19th Century Internal Improvements Reports and the Philosophy of Public Investment," *Journal of Economic Issues* 2 (October 1968): 387.

14. U.S. Congress, *Annals of Congress,* 18th Cong., 1st sess., 1824, 2582 (quotations); U.S. Army Corps of Engineers, *The U.S. Army Corps of Engineers: A History* (Alexandria, Va., 2007), 41; Shallat, *Structures in the Stream,* 142–43; Larson, *Internal Improvement,* 126–29; Paskoff, *Troubled Waters,* 46–48.

15. *Little Rock Arkansas Gazette,* April 3, 1833; U.S. Congress, House, *Tennessee. Petition of the citizens of Knox County, praying for an appropriation for the improvement of the navigation of the Tennessee River,* 25th Cong., 2nd sess., 1838, H. Doc. 270, serial 328 (quotation); U.S. Congress, House, *Ohio and Mississippi River. Memorial of sundry citizens of Louisville, Kentucky, praying for the improvement of the navigation of the Ohio and Mississippi Rivers,* 21st Cong., 1st sess., 1830, H. Rep. 337, serial 201; U.S. Congress, Senate, *Memorial of the Legislature of Missouri, praying that improvements may be made in the navigation of the Mississippi River,* 20th Cong., 2nd sess., 1829, S. Doc. 88, serial 182; U.S. Congress, Senate, *Resolutions of the Legislature of Tennessee, to procure an appropriation by Congress to effect the examination and removal of the Harpeth Shoals, on the*

Cumberland River, 21st Cong., 1st sess., 1830, S. Doc. 16, serial 192 (first quotation); U.S. Congress, Senate, *In the Senate of the United States . . . The Committee on Public Lands, to which was referred the memorial of the Legislature of the State of Alabama, asking a grant of land for the purpose of improving the navigation of the Coosa River,* 21st Cong., 1st sess., 1830, S. Doc. 55, serial 193 (second quotation); U.S. Congress, Senate, *Memorial of the Legislature of Missouri, praying that an appropriation be made for removing obstructions in, and repairing the harbor of, the City of St. Louis,* 23rd Cong., 1st sess., 1834, S. Doc. 21, serial 238; U.S. Congress, House, *Removal of obstructions in Red River,* 27th Cong., 3rd sess., 1843, H. Doc. 157, serial 422; *Memorial of the Citizens of St. Louis, Missouri, to the Congress of the United States* (St. Louis, 1844); *Proceedings of the St. Louis Chamber of Commerce in relation to the improvement of the navigation of the Mississippi River,* (St. Louis, 1842); Hines, "Early 19th Century Internal Improvements Reports," 384–92.

16. Paskoff, *Troubled Waters,* 73–84; Shallat, *Structures in the Stream,* 154–56.

17. Paskoff, *Troubled Waters,* 48–58; William W. Freehling, *Prelude to Civil War: The Nullification Controversy in South Carolina, 1816–1836* (New York, 1965), 301–39; Richard E. Ellis, *The Union at Risk: Jacksonian Democracy, States' Rights, and the Nullification Crisis* (New York, 1987), 158–77; Daniel Walker Howe, *What Hath God Wrought: The Transformation of America, 1815–1848* (New York, 2007), 395–410; Sean Wilentz, *The Rise of American Democracy: Jefferson to Lincoln* (New York, 2005), 379–89. That southerners of the lower Mississippi River valley looked to the federal government to promote their interests is most forcefully argued in Adam Rothman, *Slave Country: American Expansion and the Origins of the Deep South* (Cambridge, 2005).

18. U.S. Army Corps of Engineers, *The U.S. Army Corps of Engineers,* 15–40.

19. Plans for the Removal of Obstructions in the Mississippi and Ohio Rivers, 1824–1825, Record Group 77, Entry 252, NARA (quotation); Leland R. Johnson, "19th Century Engineering Part I: The Contest of 1824," *Military Engineer* 65 (May–June 1973): 66–71.

20. Plans for the Removal of Obstructions in the Mississippi and Ohio Rivers, 1824–1825, Record Group 77, Entry 252, NARA. Bruce beat out, among others, Shreve and Stephen Long. Shreve's plan does not survive, but that he submitted a bid is inferred from an outgoing letter informing him that the Corps of Engineers would "be pleased to have an opportunity of examining the modle [*sic*] of a machine for removing Sawyers, planters, &c adverted to in your letter." (J. L. Smith to H. M. Shreve, July 23, 1824, Letters Sent Relating to Internal Improvements, 1824–1830, RG 77, Entry 249, NARA).

21. U.S. Congress, Senate, *Letter from the Secretary of War, transmitting a report of the Chief Engineer, Relative to the Application of appropriation for removing obstructions to the navigation of the Ohio and Mississippi rivers,* 19th Cong., 1st sess., 1826, S. Doc. 14, serial 125; William Chase to Alexander Macomb, November 30, December 4, 7, 21, 1825 (Letters E-2656, 2660, 2664, 2671, 2681), all in Letters Received, 1819–1825, RG 77, Entry 14, NARA; Shallat, *Structures in the Stream,* 143–45; Leland R. Johnson, "19th Century Engineering Part II: The Contract of 1824," *Military Engineer* 65 (July–August 1973): 252–57.

22. U.S. Congress, Senate, *Letter from the Secretary of War, transmitting a report of the Chief Engineer, Relative to the Application of appropriation for removing obstructions to the navigation of the Ohio and Mississippi rivers,* 19th Cong., 1st sess., 1826, S. Doc. 14, serial 125, 15, 27 (quotations); Johnson, *Falls City Engineers,* 50–54. Babcock underwent another court-martial for his actions and was found guilty on four counts, but President John Quincy Adams set aside the charges.

23. U.S. Congress, House, *Letter from Henry M. Shreve,* 20th Cong., 1st sess., 1827, H. Doc. 11, serial 170, 3–4 (quotations); U.S. Congress, House, *Obstructions—the Ohio River,* 20th Cong., 2nd

sess., 1828, H. Doc. 269, serial 179; John Bruce to James Barbour, April 18, 1826, and January 1, 1827 (Letters B-85 and B-213), Letters Received, 1826–66, RG 77, Entry 18, NARA; Henry Shreve to James Barbour, February 20, 1827, and Henry Shreve to John Bruce, April 26, 1827, Henry Miller Shreve Letters, LSUS; Shallat, *Structures in the Stream,* 144–45; Johnson, "19th Century Engineering Part II," 255–56.

24. Henry M. Shreve, *Memorial of Henry M. Shreve, in relation to the Removal of Snags, Sawyers, &c., from the Great Western Rivers, by us of his Patented Steam Snag Boat* (n.p., n.d.), 4 (first quotation); "Popular Portraits with Pen and Pencil: Henry Miller Shreve," *United States Democratic Review* 22 (March 1848): 246 (second and third quotations, emphasis in original); Shreve to Charles Gratiot, November 5, 1829 (fourth quotation), and Shreve to Alexander Macomb, July 28, 1828 (final quotation), both in Henry Miller Shreve Letters, LSUS.

25. U.S. Congress, House, *Letter from the Secretary of War . . . on the Improvement of navigation of Mississippi and Ohio rivers,* 21st Cong., 2nd sess., 1830, H. Doc 9, serial 206, 8–9 (quotation); Shreve to Charles Gratiot, August 14, 1833, Henry Miller Shreve Letters, LSUS; Spell, "Uncle Sam's Toothpullers," 38–42; Cairo, "Snag Boats on the Western Waters, Part 1," 93; William E. Lass, *Navigating the Missouri: Steamboating on Nature's Highway, 1819–1935* (Norman, 2008), 78–79, 111. Based on Shreve's letters and reports, it seems the snag boats worked only in southern waters while he was superintendent.

26. U.S. Congress, House, *Ohio and Mississippi Rivers,* 22nd Cong., 2nd sess., 1833, H. Doc. 66, serial 234; Paskoff, *Troubled Waters,* 171–73; Erik F. Haites, James Mak, and Gary M. Walton, *Western River Transportation: The Era of Early Internal Development, 1810–1860* (Baltimore, 1975), 30; Johnson, *Falls City Engineers,* 78–79. The snag totals were compiled from Shreve's reports and letters in the Shreve Papers and Letters Received, 1826–66, RG 77, Entry 18, NARA.

27. "Annual Report of work done for improving the navigation of the Ohio, Mississippi, Red and Arkansas rivers, ending the 30th of September 1833," Henry Miller Shreve Letters, LSUS; Shreve to Charles Gratiot, November 1, 1833, Henry Miller Shreve Letters, LSUS; Shallat, *Structures in the Stream,* 146; U.S. Army Corps of Engineers, *U.S. Army Corps of Engineers,* 45–47; Johnson, *Falls City Engineers,* 46.

28. Shreve to James Barbour, April 26, 1827, and Annual Report, October 15, 1830, both in Henry Miller Shreve Letters, LSUS; Johnson, *Falls City Engineers,* 75–77, 88–98.

29. *Little Rock Arkansas State Gazette,* July 15, 1837 (quotation); U.S. Congress, House, *Raft of Red River,* 23rd Cong., 1st sess., 1834, H. Doc. 98, serial 256, 9–10; U.S. Congress, House, *Removal of the Raft of Red river,* 26th Cong., 1st sess., 1840, H. Rep. 426, serial 371; U.S. Congress, House, *Raft-Red River* 26th Cong., 2nd sess., 1841, H. Rep. 141, serial 388; Robert H. Gudmestad, "Steamboats and the Removal of the Red River Raft," *Louisiana History,* forthcoming; Jacques D. Bagur, *A History of Navigation on Cypress Bayou and the Lakes* (Denton, Tex., 2001), 60–90; C. Geoffrey Mangin, "Clearing the Great Raft: Impetus for Economic Growth in Louisiana's Red River Valley, 1830–1860," *North Louisiana History* 31 (fall 2000), 32–34; Norman W. Caldwell, "The Red River Raft," *Chronicles of Oklahoma* 19 (September 1941): 253–68; Grace Elizabeth Dyer, "The Removal of the Great Raft in Red River" (Master's thesis, Louisiana State University, 1948), 40–41.

30. Paskoff, *Troubled Waters,* 64–108.

31. Charles Ellet, *The Mississippi and Ohio Rivers,* 2 vols. (1853; reprint, New York, 1970), 1:58–59; Brien R. Winkley, *Man-Made Cutoffs on the Lower Mississippi River: Conception, Construction, and River Response* (Vicksburg, 1977), 3–7.

32. *Louisville Advertiser,* April 11, 1831, as quoted in *Niles' Register,* May 28, 1831 (quotations);

Martin Reuss, *Designing the Bayous: The Control of Water in the Atchafalaya Basin, 1800–1995* (College Station, 1994), 27–28.

33. *Louisville Advertiser*, April 11, 1831, as quoted in *Niles' Weekly Register*, May 28, 1831; undated *Florida Gazette* article, as quoted in *Niles' Weekly Register*, August 27, 1831 (quotation); George S. Pabis, "Delaying the Deluge: The Engineering Debate over Flood Control on the Lower Mississippi River, 1846–1861," *JSH* 64 (August 1998): 433; Ellet, *Mississippi and Ohio Rivers*, 1:58–59. Between 1884 and 1931 the Army Corps of Engineers prevented naturally occurring cutoffs, but then dug fourteen cutoffs after the disastrous 1929 flood (Winkley, *Man-Made Cutoffs*, 28–35).

34. David Blackbourn, *The Conquest of Nature: Water, Landscape, and the Making of Modern Germany* (New York, 2006), 85–99 (quotation on 85).

35. U.S. Congress, Senate, *Report of the Acting Secretary of the Interior, relative to the swamp and overflowed lands in Louisiana*, 31st Cong, 1st sess., 1850, S. Exec. Doc. 68, serial 562, 7 (first quotation); *Clarksville, Texas, Northern Standard*, November 25, 1843, typescript in Dewey A. Somdal Collection, LSUS; Pabis, "Delaying the Deluge," 135–37; undated *New Orleans Delta* article, as quoted in *Daily National Intelligencer*, March 20, 1861 (second quotation). The state of Louisiana made the Raccourci cutoff in 1848. It was four miles below Shreve's cutoff and shortened the Mississippi by nineteen miles (see Elliott, *Improvement of the Lower Mississippi River*, 1:69.

36. Reuss, *Designing the Bayous*, 29–34, 209–42; Malcolm Comeaux, "The Atchafalaya River Raft," *Louisiana Studies* 9 (winter 1970): 222–27; John McPhee, *The Control of Nature* (New York, 1989), chap. 1. Whether the most recent project is the last word on the matter is the subject of some debate. In 1950 a spokesperson for the Army Corps of Engineers confidently predicted that the Old River Control Structure would "see that Old Man River stays put." The *Washington Post* was not so sure, retorting that "if we had to bet, we would bet on the river" (Martin Reuss, "The Army Corps of Engineers and Flood-Control Politics on the Lower Mississippi," *Louisiana History* 23 (spring 1983): 138).

37. Report of work done on the Arkansas River, January 9, 1834, Henry Miller Shreve Letters, LSUS (first and second quotations); Shreve to Charles Gratiot, November 21, 1835 (Letter S-3530), Letters Received, 1826–66, RG 77, Entry 18, NARA (third quotation); John James Audubon, *John James Audubon: Writings and Drawings* (New York, 1999), 558 (final quotation); U.S. Congress, House, *Letter from Henry M. Shreve . . . upon the subject of navigation of the Mississippi River*, 20th Cong., 1st sess., 1827, H. Doc. 11, serial 170; Elliott, *Improvement of the Lower Mississippi*, 1:41–43.

38. "Annual Report of work done for improving the navigation of the Ohio, Mississippi, Red and Arkansas rivers, ending the 30th of September 1833," Henry Miller Shreve Letters, LSUS (first and second quotations); U.S. Congress, House, *Letter from Henry M. Shreve . . . upon the subject of navigation of the Mississippi River*, 20th Cong., 1st sess., 1827, H. Doc. 11, serial 170 (final quotation); Kelman, "Forests and Other River Perils," 59–61.

39. Shallat, *Structures in the Stream*, 146. Figures compiled from Shreve's letters and annual reports in Letters Received, 1826–66, RG 77, Entry 18, NARA. These numbers probably undercount the number of trees chopped down, as reports are incomplete, but they serve as a rough guide. The reasons for the cutting ban are unclear, but it is certain that the head of the Army Corps of Engineers authorized it. Shreve's men were supposed to ask for permission before cutting, but it was not always possible to find the landowner. On at least one occasion, government axmen cleared almost four acres without permission, prompting a claim for lost revenue, a complaint that probably prompted the interdiction. Shreve protested vehemently to no avail. For a discussion of translating trees felled into acreage estimates, see Appendix D.

40. Shreve to Charles Gratiot, November 18 (letter S-3524) and November 21, 1836 (letter S-3530) (quotation), both in Letters Received, 1826–66, RG 77, Entry 18, NARA; U.S. Congress, House, *Letter from Henry M. Shreve . . . upon the subject of navigation of the Mississippi River*, 20th Cong., 1st sess., 1827, H. Doc. 11, serial 170. The estimate was for December of 1836 only.

41. Kelman, "Forests and Other River Perils," 60–61; Michael Williams, *Americans and their Forests: A Historical Geography* (Cambridge, 1989), 153–55; David E. Schob, "Woodhawks and Cordwood: Steamboat Fuel on the Ohio and Mississippi Rivers, 1820–1860," *Journal of Forest History* 21 (July 1977): 124–32. See Appendix D for an explanation of these figures.

42. Cowdrey, *This Land, This South*, 90; William Fairfax Gray, *The Diary of William Fairfax Gray, from Virginia to Texas, 1835–1837*, ed. Paul D. Lack (Dallas, 1997), 16 (first quotation); William Mayo to Sidney Clay, September 11, 1830, Green Clay Papers, FHS (second quotation); Rev. H. Ruffner, "Notes of a Tour from Virginia to Tennessee, in the Months of July and August, 1838, Chapter II," *Southern Literary Messenger* 5 (February 1839): 140 (third quotation); Thomas Low Nichols, *Forty Years of American Life*, 2 vols. (London, 1864), 1:248 (final quotation). Early observations of the verdant nature of southern rivers can be found in Cunynghame, *Glimpse at the Great Western Republic*, 184, and John Francis McDermott, ed., *Before Mark Twain: A Sampler of Old, Old Times on the Mississippi* (Carbondale, 1968), 42.

43. D. J. Browne, "American Forest Trees," *North American Review* 35 (October 1832): 415 (first quotation); "Steamboats on Western Waters," *Western Monthly Magazine* 3 (June 1834): 317 (remaining quotations).

44. *Little Rock Arkansas Gazette*, January 17, 1838 (first quotation); Rev. H. Ruffner, "Notes of a Tour from Virginia to Tennessee, in the Months of July and August, 1838, Chapter II," *Southern Literary Messenger* 5 (February 1839): 140; Shreve to Charles Gratiot, January 13, 1837, Henry Miller Shreve Letters, LSUS; Kelman, "Forests and Other River Perils," 56–57. For the opinion bank caveins were "independent of the character of bank vegetation," see Elliott, *Improvements of the Lower Mississippi River*, 1:43.

45. Winkley, *Man-Made Cutoffs*, 20.

46. Edouard de Montulé, *Travels in America 1816–1817*, trans. Edward D. Seeber (1821; reprint, Bloomington, 1951); Frederick Law Olmsted, *A Journey in the Seaboard Slave States: with remarks on their Economy* (New York, 1856), 615–16; William F. Switzler, "A Trip to the South," 8, typescript in WMHC; James S. Laroe Diary, typescript, November 8, 1835, entry, LSU; Nicholas Proctor, *Bathed in Blood: Hunting and Mastery in the Old South* (Charlottesville, 2002), 61–75. It is no coincidence that Thomas Bang Thorpe's "The Big Bear of Arkansas" begins its story on a steamboat named *Invincible*. In the story, Thorpe grapples with humankind's interaction with the natural world and, since the story's hero is unable to kill the bear, seems to believe in the power of nature. See Katherine G. Simoneaux, "Symbolism in Thorpe's 'Big Bear of Arkansas,'" *Arkansas Historical Quarterly* 25 (autumn 1966): 242–44.

47. Hiram Fuller, *Belle Brittan on a Tour at Newport, and here and there* (New York, 1858, (first quotation); James Stuart, *Three Years in North America*, 2 vols. (Edinburgh, 1833), 2:299 (second quotation); Friedrich Gerstacker, *Wild Sports in the Far West: The narrative of a German wanderer beyond the Mississippi, 1837–1843*, trans. Edna L. Steeves and Harrison L. Steeves (1854; reprint, Durham, 1968), 96–97.

48. Walter Havighurst, *Voices on the River: The Story of the Mississippi Waterways* (New York, 1964), 129 (first quotation); Alexander, *Transatlantic Sketches*, 250 (second quotation); Richard White, "Trashing the Trails," in *Trails: Toward a New Western History*, ed. Patricia Nelson Limerick,

Clyde E. Milner II, and Charles E. Rankin, 26–27 (Lawrence, Kans., 1991) (final quotation).

49. *Chillicothe Scioto Gazette,* October 7, 1829 (second quotation); *Christian Advocate and Journal* (February 28, 1844): 114 (final quotation); Stewart, *"What Nature Suffers to Groe,"* 90–94; David E. Nye, *American Technological Sublime* (Cambridge, 1994); Stine and Tarr, "At the Intersection of Histories," 605.

CHAPTER SEVEN

1. Charles Lanman, *Adventures in the Wilds of the United States and British American Provinces,* 2 vols. (Philadelphia, 1856), 1:167 (first quotation); Tyrone Power, *Impressions of America during the years 1833, 1834, and 1835,* 2 vols. (London, 1836), 2:158–59 (remaining quotations); William Howard Russell, *My Diary North and South* (Boston, 1863), 185; Charles Lyell, *A Second Visit to the United States of North America,* 2 vols. (New York, 1849), 2:246–47; Thomas Spence, *The Settler's Guide in the United States and British North American Provinces* (New York, 1862), 342; Diary of Charles A. Hentz, November 11, 1845, entry, Hentz Family Papers, UNC.

2. Riverboats, of course, were not solely responsible for these dramatic changes. A steady white migration, the interstate slave trade, and Indian Removal were also important for the development of the Southwest, for instance, while the actions of English merchants and factory owners were necessary for the British addiction to cotton. Steamboats, however, are usually not recognized as being a major component in the growth of the southern political economy.

3. Dunbar Rowland, ed., *Life, Letters, and Papers of William Dunbar: of Elgin, Morayshire, Scotland, and Natchez, Mississippi* (Jackson, Miss., 1930), 381–83 (first quotation); Charles S. Davis, *The Cotton Kingdom in Alabama* (Montgomery, Ala., 1939), 117; William C. C. Claiborne to Woodson Wrenn, May 20, 1812, in *Official Letter Books of W. C. C. Claiborne, 1801–1816,* ed. Dunbar Rowland, 6 vols. (Jackson, Miss., 1917), 6:101 (second quotation); *Kimball and Lilly v. Brander et als.* No. 2625, 6 La. Ann. (o.s.) 711, New Orleans, June 1834, UNO; Walter Prichard, Fred B. Kniffen, and Clair A. Brown, eds., "Southern Louisiana and Southern Alabama in 1819: The Journal of James Leander Cathcart," *LHQ* 28 (July 1945): 824; Lewis Cecil Gray, *History of Agriculture in the Southern United States to 1860,* 2 vols. (Gloucester, Mass., 1958), 2:870.

4. William Kenner to Stephen Minor, January 10, 1812, as quoted in Leonard V. Huber, "Beginnings of Steamboat Mail on Lower Mississippi," *American Philatelist* 74 (December 1960): 189 (first quotation); Jasper Lynch to Gentlemen, July 11, 1816 (second quotation), and Jasper Lynch to Dominick Lynch, September 10, 1816, Letter Book of Jasper Lynch, Oneida County Historical Society, Utica, New York. For a contemporary of Kenner who was also dissatisfied with flatboat service, see Lewis E. Atherton, "John McDonogh and the Mississippi River Trade," *LHQ* 26 (January 1943): 37–43.

5. Logbook of Natchez Landings, 1839–1840, May 2, 1839, entry, Natchez Trace Steamboat Collection, UTX (first quotation); Frederick Law Olmsted, *A Journey in the Seaboard Slave States: with remarks on their Economy* (New York, 1856), 549; Power, *Impressions of America,* 2:195 (second quotation); James A. Watkins Manuscripts, TU; Davis, *Cotton Kingdom in Alabama,* 123 ; John Hebron Moore, *The Emergence of the Cotton Kingdom in the Old Southwest* (Baton Rouge, 1988), 159–61; Louis C. Hunter, *Steamboats on the Western Rivers: An Economic and Technological History* (1949; reprint, Mineola, N.Y., 1993), 91–92.

6. *Arkansas State Gazette,* May 30, 1838 (quotation); *Mobile Commercial Register,* June 28, 1837;

William M. Lytle and Forrest R. Holdcamper, *Merchant Steam Vessels of the United States, 1790–1868: Documents of the United States and Other Sources,* rev. and ed. C. Bradford Mitchell, with assistance of Kenneth R. Hall (Staten Island, 1975), 158; Frederick Marryat, *Second Series of a Diary in America, with Remarks on its Institutions* (Philadelphia, 1840), 15; Walter Havighurst, *Voices on the River: The Story of the Mississippi Waterways* (New York, 1964), 138; Leonard V. Huber, comp., *Advertisements of Lower Mississippi River Steamboats, 1812–1920* (West Barrington, R.I., 1959), 17.

7. Stephen F. Miller, "Plantation Labor Organization and Slave Life on the Cotton Frontier: The Alabama-Mississippi Black Belt, 1815–1840," in *Cultivation and Culture: Labor and the Shaping of Slave Life in the Americas,* ed. Ira Berlin and Philip D. Morgan, 155–69 (Charlottesville, 1993); Sam Bowers Hilliard, *Atlas of Antebellum Southern Agriculture* (Baton Rouge, 1984), 30–31; Thomas Low Nichols, *Forty Years of American Life,* 2 vols. (London, 1864), 1:234; Ira Berlin, *Generations of Captivity: A History of African-American Slaves* (Cambridge, Mass., 2003), 161–78, 274–75; Michael Tadman, *Speculators and Slaves: Masters, Traders, and Slaves in the Old South* (Madison, 1989), 64–68.

8. Horace J. Ford Journal, January 30, 1849, entry, Historic Arkansas Museum, Little Rock, Arkansas (quotation); Edwin Adams Davis, ed., *Plantation Life in the Florida Parishes of Louisiana, 1836–1854, as reflected in the Diary of Bennett H. Barrow* (New York, 1943), 80–82; "Cotton and the Cotton Planters," *DBR* 3 (January 1847): 16; Nathaniel Wiltshire to John Minor, March 24, 1816, Minor Collection, UNC; *Christian Advocate and Journal,* February 28, 1844, 114; John B. Boles, *The South through Time: A History of an American Region,* 3rd ed., 2 vols. (Upper Saddle River, N.J., 2004), 1:194–95.

9. William L. Hodge, "New Orleans: Its Present Situation and Future Prospects," *DBR* 2 (July 1846): 58 (first and second quotations); *Christian Advocate and Journal,* February 28, 1844, 114 (third quotation); Harriet E. Amos, *Cotton City: Urban Development in Antebellum Mobile* (Tuscaloosa, 1985), 21; Stuart Bruchey, ed., *Cotton and the Growth of the American Economy: 1790–1860* (New York, 1967), 80.

10. Undirected letter of Germain Musson, May 10, 1817, Germain Musson Papers, DU; *James Dalzell v. Steamboat Saxon,* No. 3269, 10 La. Ann. (n.s.) 280, New Orleans, April 1855, *Courtenay et al. vs. Mississippi Marine and Fire Ins. Co.,* No. 3152, 12 La. Ann. (o.s.) 233, New Orleans, April 1838, and *R. Y. Northern v. Williams, Phillips and Co.,* No. 1800, 6 La. Ann. (n.s.) 578, New Orleans, June 1851, all in UNO; James S. Buckingham, *The Slave States of America,* 2 vols. (London, 1842), 1:398–99; Philip Paxton [S. A. Hammett], *A Stray Yankee in Texas* (New York, 1859), 403; William Cage to James Winchester, April 7, 1822, and Samuel Seay to Winchester, Hall and Company, April 4, 1822, both in James Winchester Papers, TSLA; David O. Whitten, "Rural Life along the Mississippi: Plaquemines Parish, Louisiana, 1830–1850," *Agricultural History* 58 (July 1984): 484.

11. Byrd Douglas, *Steamboatin' on the Cumberland* (Nashville, 1961), 20–21, 88–89; R. Bruce Council, Nicholas Honerkamp, and M. Elizabeth Will, *Industry and Technology in Antebellum Tennessee: The Archaeology of Bluff Furnace* (Knoxville, 1992), 55–57; James F. Hopkins, *A History of the Hemp Industry in Kentucky,* rev. ed. (Lexington, 1998), 142–44.

12. Benjamin Drew, *A North-Side View of Slavery: The Refugee: or the Narrative of Fugitive Slaves in Canada* (Boston, 1856), 52, 185; William J. Anderson, *Life and Narrative of William J. Anderson, Twenty-Four Years a Slave* (Chicago, 1857), 32–35; Thomas C. Buchanan, *Black Life on the Mississippi: Slaves, Free Blacks, and the Western Steamboat World* (Chapel Hill, 2004), 101–10.

13. *Pearl River Navigation Company v. Stephen A. Douglas,* No. 2526, 7 La. Ann. (n.s.) 631, New Orleans, November 1852, and *Lewis Bond v. Samuel B. Frost and Owners of the Steamboat Concordia,* No. 2798, 8 La. Ann. (n.s.) 297, New Orleans, June 1853, UNO; William Kenner to John Minor,

December 25, 1819, Minor Collection, UNC; Toledano and Taylor to Peter Hickman, March 5, 1856, Hickman-Bryan Papers, WHMC (quotation).

14. Michel Chevalier, *Society, Manners, and Politics in the United States* (Boston, 1839), 221; Joseph H. Ingraham, *The South-West by a Yankee*, 2 vols. (New York, 1835), 1:137–41; Thomas K. Wharton, *Queen of the South: New Orleans, 1853–1862*, ed. Samuel Wilson Jr., Patricia Brady, and Lynn D. Adams (New Orleans, 1999), 6 (quotation); *Vicksburg Weekly Sentinel*, February 15, 1854, clipping in Somdal Collection, LSUS; William Ransom Hogan and Edwin Adams Davis, eds., *William Johnson's Natchez: The Ante-Bellum Diary of a Free Negro* (Baton Rouge, 1951), 82.

15. Alabama Cotton Sales Statements, LSU; Moses Liddell Papers, LSU; A. Ledoux to James L. Fenner, February 4, 1841, Joseph Merrick Jones-Donald T. Wright Steamboat Collection, TU; Steamboat receipts, Natchez Trace Steamboat Collection, UTX.

16. Jonathan D. Martin, *Divided Mastery: Slave Hiring in the American South* (Cambridge, Mass., 2004); Brian Schoen, *The Fragile Fabric of Union: Cotton, Federal Politics, and the Global Origins of the Civil War* (Baltimore, 2009), 122–23; *H. M. Summers v. United States Insurance, Annuity and Trust Co.*, No. 5423, 13 La. Ann. (n.s.) 504, New Orleans, December 1858, UNO.

17. U.S. Congress, House, Department of the Treasury, *Report on the Internal Commerce of the United States 1887*, William F. Switzler, part 2 of *Report on the Commerce and Navigation of the United States*, 50th Cong., 1st sess., 1888, H. Exec. Doc. 6, serial 2552, 199 (first quotation); Horace J. Ford Journal, December 13, 1848, January 11, 22, 1849, entries, Historic Arkansas Museum, Little Rock, Arkansas; *Wilcox et al. v. Halderman et al.*, No. 3533, 14 La. (o.s.) 357, New Orleans, February 1840, UNO; W. L. Bailey to J. A. Winston, January 25, 1852, and Robert Love to J. A. Winston, February 9, 1852, both in John A. Winston and Company Letters, DU; William Darby, *The Emigrant's Guide to the Western and Southwestern States and Territories* (New York, 1818), 40 (second quotation).

18. David E. Schob, "Woodhawks and Cordwood: Steamboat Fuel on the Ohio and Mississippi Rivers, 1820–1860," *Journal of Forest History* 21 (July 1977): 124–32; Charles Peter Grizzard, "A Glimpse of the South in the spring of 1855," 46, Beinecke Rare Book and Manuscript Library, Yale University, New Haven, Connecticut; Aleck Gwin to Caroline Kiger, October 23, 1852, Kiger Family Papers, UTX; James Hall, *The West: Its Commerce and Navigation* (1848; reprint, New York, 1970), 129–30; Ingraham, *Sunny South*, 298; "Steamboats on Western Waters," *Western Monthly Magazine* 3 (June 1834): 317; Wendell Holmes Stephenson, *Isaac Franklin: Slave Trader and Planter of the Old South* (Baton Rouge, 1938), 106, 114. The estimate is based on the average price of $1,400 in New Orleans in 1859 for a slave, one year before the publication of Ingraham's book, which contained the story. See Laurence J. Kotlikoff, "The Structure of Slave Prices in New Orleans, 1804 to 1862," *Economic Inquiry* 17 (October 1979): 498, for the price of slaves in New Orleans.

19. Harriet Martineau, *Retrospect of Western Travel*, 2 vols. (London, 1838), 2:8 (first quotation); Anton Reiff Journal, January 21, 1856, LSU (second quotation); *P. Pousargues v. Steamer Natchez et al.*, No. 6250, 15 La. Ann. (n.s.) 80, New Orleans, May 1860, and *Hurst v. Wallace*, No. 2402, 5 La. (o.s.) 98, New Orleans, February 1833, both in UNO.

20. Samuel Davis to Warwick Miller, June 29, 1821, Francis Hegan Miller Collection, FHS (first quotation); William F. Switzler, "A Trip to the South," 23, typescript in WHMC (second quotation); Emerson W. Gould, *Fifty Years on the Mississippi: or, Gould's History of River Navigation* (St. Louis, 1889), 125; Hogan and Davis, eds., *William Johnson's Natchez*, 36–38, 704–6. William Johnson's success in selling wood to steamboats contributed to his death. Baylor Winn, who owned riverfront property adjoining Johnson's land, shot and killed the barber on June 16, 1851, over a disputed

property line (Edwin Adams Davis and William Ransom Hogan, *The Barber of Natchez* [Baton Rouge, 1954], 262–72).

21. Mrs. [Matilda Charlotte] Houstoun, *Hesperos: or, Travels in the West*, 2 vols. (London, 1850), 2:249 (first quotation); Sarah Chapin, ed. "Edward Jarvis's Journal," *Filson Club Historical Quarterly* 70 (July 1996): 243–45 (second quotation); Edward Russell Journal, HNOC; Basil Hall, *Travels in North America, in the Years 1827 and 1828*, 3 vols. (Edinburgh, 1830), 3:356; Paul Wilhelm, Duke of Wurttemberg, *Travels in North America, 1822–1824*, trans. W. Robert Nitske, ed. Savoie Lottinville (Norman, 1973), 137; Simon Ashley Ferrall, *A Ramble of Six Thousand Miles through the United States of America* (London, 1832), 216; James Edward Alexander, *Transatlantic Sketches, Comprising visits to the most interesting Scenes in North and South America* (Philadelphia, 1833), 243.

22. Anton Reiff Journal, February 27, 1856, LSU (quotation); A. Oakley Hall, *The Manhattaner in New Orleans; or, Phases of "Crescent City" Life* (New York, 1851), 183; Michael Allen, *Western Rivermen, 1763–1861: Ohio and Mississippi Boatmen and the Myth of the Alligator Horse* (Baton Rouge, 1990), 147–48.

23. Schoen, *Fragile Fabric of Union*, 1–10, 121–26; U.S. Congress, House, Department of the Treasury, *Report on the Internal Commerce of the United States 1887*, William F. Switzler, part 2 of *Report on the Commerce and Navigation of the United States*, 50th Cong., 1st sess., 1888, H. Exec. Doc. 6, serial 2552, 216–18; Bruchey, ed., *Cotton and the Growth of the American Economy*, table 3-A.

24. Joseph H. Ingraham, *The Sunny South: or the Southerner at Home* (1860; reprint, New York, 1968), 343 (first quotation); William L. Hodge, "New Orleans: Its Present Situation and Future Prospects," *DBR* 2 (July 1846): 53–65; Hall, *Manhattaner in New Orleans*, 174–75 (remaining quotations); James A. Walker to Amanda, April 12, 1847, James A. Walker Papers, DU; Ebenezer Davies, *American Scenes and Christian Slavery: A Recent Tour of Four Thousand Miles in the United States* (London, 1849), 275; Paxton, *A Stray Yankee in Texas*, 401; Edward King, *The Great South: A Record of Journeys in Louisiana, Texas, the Indian Territory, Missouri, Arkansas, Mississippi, Alabama, Georgia, Florida, South Carolina, North Carolina, Kentucky, Tennessee, Virginia, West Virginia, and Maryland* (Hartford, 1875), 68; Alexander, *Transatlantic Sketches*, 51–55; Alexander Mackay, *The Western World: or, Travels in the United States in 1846–47*, 2 vols. (Philadelphia, 1849), 2:80; Allen, *Western Rivermen*, 143.

25. H. Didmus, *New Orleans as I found It* (New York, 1845), 14 (first quotation); *Lewis Bond v. Samuel B. Frost and Owners of the Steamboat Concordia*, No. 2798, 8 La. Ann. (n.s.) 297, New Orleans, June 1853, UNO; *Natchez Daily Courier*, July 17, 1855 (second quotation); *Kimball and James' Business Directory for the Mississippi Valley: 1844* (Cincinnati, 1844), 433.

26. Bowling Cotton Book, LSU; Lady Emmeline Stuart Wortley, *Travels in the United States, during 1849 and 1850* (New York, 1851), 123 (quotation).

27. U.S. Congress, House, Department of the Treasury, *Report on the Internal Commerce of the United States 1887*, William F. Switzler, part 2 of *Report on the Commerce and Navigation of the United States*, 50th Cong., 1st sess., 1888, H. Exec. Doc. 6, serial 2552, 191 (quotation), 199, 205.

28. *St. Louis Missouri Gazette*, May 19, 1819, as quoted in "Navigation on the Mississippi to 1819," *Waterways Journal*, November 4, 1893, 13 (first quotation); *Memorial of the Citizens of St. Louis, Missouri, to the Congress of the United States* (St. Louis, 1844), 7; *Proceedings of the St. Louis Chamber of Commerce in relation to the improvement of the navigation of the Mississippi River* (St. Louis, 1842), 30 (second quotation); George Conclin, *Conclin's New River Guide* (Cincinnati, 1855), 81; William E. Lass, *Navigating the Missouri: Steamboating on Nature's Highway, 1819–1935* (Norman, 2008), 85–116; Jeff Robert Bremer, "Frontier Capitalism: The Market Revolution in the Antebellum

Lower Missouri River Valley, 1803–1860" (Ph.D. diss., University of Kansas, 2006); Michael Allen, ed., "Reminiscences of a Common Boatman (1849–1851)," *Gateway Heritage* 5 (fall 1984): 38.

29. "Sketches of Louisville," *Western Monthly Review* 1 (March 1828): 668; "Old Days on the River," *Waterways Journal*, September 1, 1894, 3 (first and second quotations); Charles Dickens, *American Notes for General Circulation* (London, 1850), 100 (final quotation); Martha Kreipke, "The Falls of the Ohio and the Development of the Ohio River Trade, 1810–1860," *Filson Club Historical Quarterly* 54 (April 1980): 196–217; Paul B. Trescott, "The Louisville and Portland Canal Company, 1825–1874," *Mississippi Valley Historical Review* 44 (March 1948): 686–708. For accounts of people gawking at the Kentucky Giant, see Charles Casey, *Two Years on the Farm of Uncle Sam* (London, 1852), 115; Maxwell Pierson Gaddis, *Foot-prints of an Itinerant*, (Cincinnati, 1856), 326; T. C. Collins, *The Adventures of T. C. Collins—Boatman,* comp. and ed. Herbert L. Roush Sr. (Baltimore, 1985), 96; unknown to Aaron Lyle, July 12, 1846, Joseph Merrick Jones-Donald T. Wright Steamboat Collection, TU; Horace J. Ford Journal, April 18, 1849, entry, Historic Arkansas Museum, Little Rock, Arkansas.

30. Undated newspaper clipping in Scrapbook, vol. 11, Tappan Steamboat Collection, Special Collections, University of Arkansas Libraries, Fayetteville, Arkansas; U.S. Congress, House, Department of the Treasury, *Report on the Internal Commerce of the United States 1887,* William F. Switzler, part 2 of *Report on the Commerce and Navigation of the United States,* 50th Cong., 1st sess., 1888, H. Exec. Doc. 6, serial 2552, 204; Clanton W. Williams, "Early Ante-Bellum Montgomery: A Black-Belt Constituency," *JSH* 7 (November 1941): 513–15; Craig Thompson Friend, *Along the Maysville Road: The Early American Republic in the Trans-Appalachian West* (Knoxville, 2005), 251. My characterization of southern urban growth is at odds with studies that describe southern town growth as anemic. See David R. Goldfield, *Cotton Fields and Skyscrapers: Southern City and Region, 1670–1980* (Baton Rouge, 1982), 28–34.

31. For an explanation of how these figures were calculated, see Appendix E.

32. Schob, "Woodhawks and Cordwood," 124–32; Charles Peter Grizzard, "A Glimpse of the South in the spring of 1855," 46, Beinecke Rare Book and Manuscript Library, Yale University, New Haven, Connecticut; Hall, *The West,* 129–30; Ingraham, *Sunny South,* 298; "Steamboats on Western Waters," *Western Monthly Magazine* 3 (June 1834): 317; Charles Mackay, *Life and Liberty in America: or, Sketches of a Tour in the United States and Canada in 1857–8* (New York, 1859), 155. For the estimate of money paid for wood, see Appendix E.

33. *Varion v. Bell,* No. 3697, 17 La. (o.s.) 532, New Orleans, March 1841, UNO; Jefferson Foundry and Steam Engine Manufactory Ledger, 1837–1839, and Buckner and Hughs Order Book, May 1835–January 1836, both in FHS; Hogan and Davis, eds., *William Johnson's Natchez,* 594, 659. For other examples of merchants selling supplies to steamers, see *Pratt v. Flowers,* No. 967, 2 Mart. (n.s.) 333, New Orleans, April 1824, UNO; George Washington Account Book, IRL; and Clauss and Fischer Journal, 1851–1852, LSU. For the estimates of repairs and stores, see Appendix E.

34. *Black v. Savory et al.,* No. 4276, 17 La. (o.s.) 85, New Orleans, March 1841, UNO; Buchanan, *Black Life on the Mississippi,* 93–94, 138–89.

35. There are two significant, and often tedious, historical debates in play here. The first revolves around the interpretation of the South as a noncapitalist or capitalist society. For an overview of the debate, see Mark M. Smith, *Debating Slavery: Economy and Society in the Antebellum American South* (New York, 1998), and Walter Johnson, "The Pedestal and the Veil: Rethinking the Capitalism/Slavery Question," *JER* 24 (summer 2004): 299–308. The other historical controversy concerns the question of whether or not the United States experienced a "Market Revolution" between 1815

and 1860. See Charles Sellers, *The Market Revolution : Jacksonian America, 1815–1846* (New York, 1991), and Melvyn Stokes and Stephen Conway, eds., *The Market Revolution in America: Social, Political, and Religious Expressions, 1800–1880* (Charlottesville, 1996), for an explanation of the concept. Two trenchant critiques of the Market Revolution are John Majewski, "A Revolution Too Many?" *Journal of Economic History* 57 (June 1997): 476–80, and Daniel Feller, "The Market Revolution Ate My Homework," *Reviews in American History* 25 (September 1997): 408–15. A useful overview of both debates that references much more of the literature is found in Tom Downey, *Planting a Capitalist South: Masters, Merchants, and Manufacturers in the Southern Interior, 1790–1860* (Baton Rouge, 2006), 1–6.

36. Undated *Cincinnati Daily Gazette* article, as quoted in *The Ariel,* June 12, 1830 (first quotation); William Kenner to John Minor, April 15, 1814, Kenner Papers, LSU (second quotation); *Kimball and James' Business Directory,* 353–71; Chapin, ed., "Edward Jarvis Journal," 270; Ann Jennings to Rebecca Connell, April 1, 1828, George Campbell Childress Papers, UTX; "Progress of the West," *Western Monthly Review* 1 (May 1827): 26 (final quotation); Friend, *Along the Maysville Road,* 58; William J. Peterson, *Steamboating on the Upper Mississippi* (Iowa City, 1968), 388.

37. Marc Egnal, *Clash of Extremes: The Economic Origins of the Civil War* (New York, 2009), 22–25; Peterson, *Steamboating on the Upper Mississippi,* 207–9, 144–61, 381–89; Nancy Goodman and Robert Goodman, *Paddlewheels on the Upper Mississippi, 1823–1854: How Steamboats Promoted Commerce and Settlement in the West* (Stillwater, Minn., 2003), 61–70; Lass, *Navigating the Missouri,* 85–116.

38. *Arkansas Gazette,* March 16, 1831; Israel Pickens to Walter R. Lenoir, September 2, 1818, Lenoir Family Papers, UNC; *Montgomery Republican,* December 20, 1822, as quoted in William James Ikerman, "The Role of the Steamboat in the Development of the Cotton Kingdom in Alabama, 1819–1860" (Master's thesis, Auburn University, 1963), 31 (first and second quotations); John E. Rodabough, *Steamboats on the Upper Tombigbee* (Hamilton, Miss., 1985), 10 (third quotation); Helen Bartter Crocker, "Steamboats for Bowling Green: The River Politics of James Rumsey Skiles," *Filson Club Historical Quarterly* 46 (January 1972): 12; Memoir of James Norman Smith, 2:84, Alexander Wallace Jones Papers (typescript), TSLA (final quotation); Daniel Dupre, "Ambivalent Capitalists on the Cotton Frontier: Settlement and Development in the Tennessee Valley of Alabama," *JSH* 56 (May 1990): 237–40; Mell A. Frazer, *Early History of Steamboats in Alabama* (Auburn, 1907), 7. This interpretation differs from that of Sellers, who sees Americans as reluctant to embrace the Market Revolution (Sellers, *Market Revolution,* esp. 31).

39. *New Orleans Picayune,* October 17, 1858, as quoted in Judith Kelleher Schafer, *Slavery, the Civil Law, and the Supreme Court of Louisiana,* (Baton Rouge, 1994), 96–97 (first quotations); Frank Towers, *The Urban South and the Coming of the Civil War* (Charlottesville, 2004), 126, 133–34.

40. *Western Monthly Magazine and Literary Journal* 4 (December 1835), 411 (quotation). See Jonathan Daniel Wells, *The Origins of the Southern Middle Class, 1800–1861* (Chapel Hill, 2004), 60, for an illustration of the *De Bow's Review* cover.

CHAPTER EIGHT

1. Florence L. Dorsey, *Master of the Mississippi: Henry Shreve and the Conquest of the Mississippi* (New York, 1941), 209–12, 220–21, 242.

2. Eldon Hattervig, "Jefferson Landing: A Commercial Center of the Steamboat Era," *Missouri*

Historical Review 77 (April 1980): 289–91; William E. Lass, *A History of Steamboating on the Upper Missouri River* (Lincoln, 1962), 160–67.

3. Anton Reiff Journal, January 9, 1837, LSU (first and second quotations); George W. Carvill to Eliza Boyle, George W. Carvill Letters, February 29, 1852, WHMC (final quotation); Lavinia Gay to Andrew Hynes, December 1, 1844, Andrew Hynes Papers, TSLA; Mississippi River Travel Diary, 1825–1826, February 18, 21, 22, 1826, entries, DU; Louis C. Hunter, *Steamboats on the Western Rivers: An Economic and Technological History* (1949; reprint, Mineola, N.Y., 1993), 257–58.

4. John James Audubon, *John James Audubon: Writings and Drawings* (New York, 1999), 19 (quotation); T. C. Collins, *The Adventures of T. C. Collins—Boatman,* comp. and ed. Herbert L. Roush Sr. (Baltimore, 1985), 33, 57; Hunter, *Steamboats on the Western Rivers,* 250–56.

5. Samuel Wigglesworth to Thomas Wigglesworth, July 7, 1839, Samuel Wigglesworth Letters, FHS (quotation). For more adventures that stemmed from groundings, see John P. Haggott Journal, April 6, 1845, entry, Special Collections, Mississippi Valley Collection, McWherter Library, University of Memphis, Memphis, Tennessee; Arthur Augustus Thurlow Cunynghame, *A Glimpse at the Great Western Republic* (London, 1851), 171; Mrs. [Matilda Charlotte] Houstoun, *Hesperos: or, Travels in the West,* 2 vols. (London, 1850), 2:21–22; Aleksandr Borisovich Lakier, *A Russian Looks at America: The Journey of Aleksandr Borisovich Lakier in 1857,* ed. and trans. Arnold Schrier and Joyce Story (Chicago, 1979), 142; A. Oakley Hall, *The Manhattaner in New Orleans; or, Phases of "Crescent City" Life* (New York, 1851), 184.

6. John Francis McDermott, ed., *Before Mark Twain: A Sampler of Old, Old Times on the Mississippi* (Carbondale, 1968), 91 (first quotation); Charles Peter Grizzard, "A Glimpse of the South in the spring of 1855," Beinecke Rare Book and Manuscript Library, Yale University, New Haven, Connecticut (final quotation). See also Daniel Chapman Banks Diary, May 18, 1823, entry, Daniel Chapman Banks Papers, FHS; John Minor to William Minor, July 3, 1829, Minor Collection, UNC; C. C. Hardin Journal, undated, Hardin Family Papers, FHS; and Winchester and Carr to James Winchester, January 27, 1822, James Winchester Papers, TSLA; James Edward Alexander, *Transatlantic Sketches, Comprising visits to the most interesting Scenes in North and South America* (Philadelphia, 1833), 253; and Ebenezer Davies, *American Scenes and Christian Slavery: A Recent Tour of Four Thousand Miles in the United States* (London, 1849), 100.

7. *Apalachicola Commercial Advertiser,* June 13, 1846, as quoted in Edward A. Mueller, *Perilous Journeys: A History of Steamboating on the Chattahoochee, Apalachicola, and Flint Rivers, 1828–1928* (Eufala, Ala., 1990), 90 (first quotation); Coleman Rogers to Samuel Brown, January 17, 1824, Samuel Brown Papers, FHS (second quotation); Henry McDaniel to J. A. Winston, January 5, 1854, John A. Winston Papers, DU; Maria Dyer Davies Wightman Diary, March 5, 1855, entry, DU; W. N. Smith to William P. Gould, February 1855, as quoted in Charles S. Davis, *The Cotton Kingdom in Alabama* (Montgomery, 1939), 91 (final quotation), 122; McDowell, Withers, and Company to Hugh Davis, November 28, 1848, as quoted in Weymouth T. Jordan, *Hugh Davis and His Alabama Plantation* (University, Ala., 1948), 136.

8. "Steamboat Disasters," *North American Review* 50 (January 1840), 41; John F. Stover, *American Railroads,* 2nd ed. (Chicago, 1997), 10–20; Aaron W. Marrs, *Railroads in the Old South: Pursuing Progress in a Slave Society* (Baltimore, 2009), 11–18.

9. Marrs, *Railroads in the Old South,* 5. The states were Atlantic South: Delaware, Florida, Georgia, Maryland, North Carolina, South Carolina, and Virginia; Interior South: Alabama, Arkansas, Kentucky, Louisiana, Missouri, Mississippi, Tennessee, and Texas.

10. Wayne Cline, *Alabama Railroads* (Tuscaloosa, 1997), 10–16; Davis, *Cotton Kingdom in Ala-*

bama, 125; *Mississippi Free Trader and Natchez Gazette,* October 13, 1835 (quotation); John F. Stover, *The Routledge Historical Atlas of the American Railroads* (New York, 1999), 15, 17; James A. Ward, "A New Look at Antebellum Southern Railroad Development," *JSH* 39 (August 1973): 411

11. For a catalog of problems that bedeviled southern railroads, see Marrs, *Railroads in the Old South,* 18–21; R. S. Cotterill, "Southern Railroads, 1850–1860," *Mississippi Valley Historical Review* 10 (March 1924): 405; John F. Stover, *Iron Roads to the West: American Railroads in the 1850s* (New York, 1978), 90; and Ward, "A New Look at Antebellum Southern Railroad Development," 409–20.

12. J. D. B. De Bow, "Internal Improvement—Mining, Railroads, etc.," *DBR* 5 (January 1848): 87–88; Mell A. Frazer, *Early History of Steamboats in Alabama* (Auburn, 1907), 24; John Hebron Moore, *The Emergence of the Cotton Kingdom in the Old Southwest* (Baton Rouge, 1988), 164–69; John Hebron Moore, "Railroads of Antebellum Mississippi," *Journal of Mississippi History* 41 (February 1979): 53–73.

13. Cline, *Alabama Railroads,* 41. Appendix F describes the method used to calculate the figures in tables 7 and 8.

14. Marc Egnal, *Clash of Extremes: The Economic Origins of the American Civil War* New York, 2009), 102–22; Albert Fishlow, *American Railroads and the Transformation of the Ante-Bellum Economy* (Cambridge, 1965), 288–90; U.S. Congress, House, Department of the Treasury, *Report on the Internal Commerce of the United States 1887,* William F. Switzler, part 2 of *Report on the Commerce and Navigation of the United States,* 50th Cong., 1st sess., 1888, H. Exec. Doc. 6, serial 2552, 202, 215–18; Erik F. Haites, James Mak, and Gary M. Walton, *Western River Transportation: The Era of Early Internal Development, 1810–1860* (Baltimore, 1975), 9–10; Thomas D. Clark, *A Pioneer Southern Railroad from New Orleans to Cairo* (Chapel Hill, 1936), 65; Merl E. Reed, *New Orleans and the Railroads: The Struggle for Commercial Empire, 1830–1860* (Baton Rouge, 1966), 63–67.

15. J. D. B. De Bow, "Internal Improvement—Mining, Railroads, etc.," *DBR* 5 (January 1848): 87–88; "Internal Improvements," *DBR* 7 (November 1849): 459; "Southern Internal Improvements," *DBR* 10 (March 1851): 338; "Excursion to Red River," *DBR* 11 (August 1851): 223–34; "Southern and Western Rail-Road Convention," *DBR* 12 (March 1852): 319–20; "Editorial—Book Notices, etc.," *DBR* 23 (July 1857): 109–10.

16. Helen Bartter Crocker, "Steamboats for Bowling Green: The River Politics of James Rumsey Skiles," *Filson Club Historical Quarterly* 46 (January 1972): 12; Maury Klein, *History of the Louisville and Nashville Railroad* (New York, 1972), 7; Thomas D. Clark, *The Beginning of the L & N: The Development of the Louisville and Nashville Railroad from Its Memphis Branches from 1836 to 1860* (Louisville, 1933), 58–59; Marrs, *Railroads in the Old South,* 5. Much of the construction in the southern interior, moreover, was in the last five years of the decade. For instance, both the 206-mile-long railroad from New Orleans to Canton, Mississippi, and the Memphis and Ohio Railroads began construction in mid-1854, while the 483-mile-long Mobile and Ohio Railroad was less than half completed by 1856. See Stover, *Iron Road to the West,* 81, 84, 87.

17. Brian Schoen, *The Fragile Fabric of Union: Cotton, Federal Politics, and the Global Origins of the Civil War* (Baltimore, 2009), 204–8; Clark, *A Pioneer Southern Railroad,* 16, 48–50, 76, 96; John Hebron Moore, "Railroads of Antebellum Mississippi," *Journal of Mississippi History* 41 (February 1979): 78–79; Klein, *History of the Louisville and Nashville Railroad,* 5–18; Stover, *Iron Roads to the West,* 88–89.

18. See Appendix F.

19. U.S. Congress, House, Department of the Treasury, *Report on the Internal Commerce of the United States 1887,* William F. Switzler, part 2 of *Report on the Commerce and Navigation of the*

United States, 50th Cong., 1st sess., 1888, H. Exec. Doc. 6, serial 2552, 172; Stover, *Iron Road to the West*, 90–91; Stover, *American Railroads*, 2nd ed., 203.

20. U.S. Congress, House, Department of the Treasury, *Report on the Internal Commerce of the United States 1887,* William F. Switzler, part 2 of *Report on the Commerce and Navigation of the United States*, 50th Cong., 1st sess., 1888, H. Exec. Doc. 6, serial 2552, 209, 216–18.

21. Emerson W. Gould, *Fifty Years on the Mississippi: or, Gould's History of River Navigation* (St. Louis, 1889), 390; James D. Dilts, *The Great Road: The Building of the Baltimore and Ohio, the Nation's First Railroad, 1828–1853* (Stanford, 1993), 377–78; Marrs, *Railroads in the Old South*, 187–89.

22. Leonard V. Huber, comp., *Advertisements of Lower Mississippi River Steamboats, 1812–1920* (West Barrington, R.I., 1959), 48, 62 (first quotation); Memoir of James Norman Smith, 4:142, Alexander Wallace Jones Papers, TSLA, typescript (remaining quotations); James Hervey Diary, February 17, 1860, entry, James Hervey Otey Papers, UNC.

23. John Calhoun to James Calhoun, July 2, 1846, as quoted in Paul F. Paskoff, *Troubled Waters: Steamboat Disasters, River Improvements, and American Public Policy, 1821–1860* (Baton Rouge, 2007), 73 (quotation); Vicki Vaughn Johnson, *The Men and the Vision of the Southern Commercial Conventions, 1845–1871* (Columbia, Mo., 1992), 15, 101.

24. "The Late Southern Convention, Held at Vicksburg, May 9–13, 1859, Part 1," *DBR* 27 (July 1859): 101 (quotations); Johnson, *Southern Commercial Conventions*, 104–12, 124; Todd E. Shallat, *Structures in the Stream: Water, Science, and the Rise of the U. S. Army Corps of Engineers* (Austin, Tex., 1994), 154–56.

25. "The Cause of the South," *DBR* 9 (July 1850): 120–24; "The Late Southern Convention, Held at Vicksburg, May 9–13, 1859, Part 1," *DBR* 27 (July 1859): 94–103; Schoen, *Fragile Fabric of Union*, 254–59; Egnal, *Clash of Extremes*, 102–22, 268–82. That the southern trade was becoming increasingly insular contradicts James Huston's argument that mounting economic interaction between the sections helped spark the Civil War. See James L. Huston, *Calculating the Value of the Union: Slavery, Property Rights, and the Economic Origins of the Civil War* (Chapel Hill, 2003), 68–103. Egnal's *Clash of Extremes* presents perhaps the most persistent argument on the economic origins of the Civil War. The material presented in this chapter certainly reinforces his position, although I believe ideological factors cannot be completely discounted. Slavery was, after all, not just an economic system but a means of social and racial control.

26. Ward, "A New Look at Antebellum Southern Railroad Development," 416–20 (quotation on 419–20); Stover, *Iron Roads to the West*, 90–91. For a dissenting view of the supposed backwardness of southern railroads, see Marrs, *Railroads in the Old South*, 99–105. Marrs's fine book draws heavily on material from the Atlantic seaboard, where the railroads had more time to develop by 1861.

27. For discussions of how and why the Confederacy could not adequately administer its railroads, see Robert C. Black III, *The Railroads of the Confederacy* (Chapel Hill, 1952), and John E. Clark Jr., *Railroads in the Civil War: The Impact of Management on Victory and Defeat* (Baton Rouge, 2001).

EPILOGUE

1. Ron Powers, *Mark Twain: A Life* (New York, 2005), 440–48.

2. Powers, *Mark Twain,* 459 (first quotation); Mark Twain, *The Family Mark Twain*, vol. 1, *Life on the Mississippi* (New York, 1935), 106 (second quotation), 122 (third quotation), 127 (final quotation).

3. Twain, *Life on the Mississippi*, 170–74.

4. Louis C. Hunter, *Steamboats on the Western Rivers: An Economic and Technological History* (1949; reprint, Mineola, N.Y., 1993), 547–51.

5. Hunter, *Steamboats on the Western Rivers*, 561–605 (quotation on 587).

6. Thomas C. Buchanan, *Black Life on the Mississippi: Slaves, Free Blacks, and the Western Steamboat World* (Chapel Hill, 2004), 149–69.

7. Frederick Way Jr., comp., *Way's Packet Directory 1848–1994: Passenger Steamboats of the Mississippi River System Since the Advent of Photography in Mid-Continent America*, rev. ed. (Athens, Ohio, 1994), 233–35, 337–39, 395–98, 435–36; Gene Eric Salecker, *Disaster on the Mississippi: The Sultana Explosion, April 27, 1865* (Annapolis, 1996), 53–64, 177–90, 216–17.

8. John Michael Vlach, *The Planter's Prospect: Privilege and Slavery in Plantation Paintings* (Chapel Hill, 2002), 41–42, 94, 116–24, 135–38. Railroads eventually were romanticized in the same way as steamboats.

9. Jennifer L. Eichstadt and Stephen Small, *Representations of Slavery: Race and Ideology in Southern Plantation Museums* (Washington, D.C., 2002), 105–46.

APPENDIX B

1. Nathaniel Smith to Winfield Scott, August 7, 1838, in Letters Received by the Office of Indian Affairs 1824–81, Roll 115, Cherokee Agency Emigration, 1828–1854; *Little Rock Arkansas Gazette*, August 1, 1838.

APPENDIX D

1. Henry Shreve to Charles Gratiot, February 10, 1837; R. Collet to Henry Shreve, October 20, 1836; and W. Thomas to Henry Shreve, October 15, 1836, all in Letter S-3576, Letters Received, 1826–66, RG 77, Entry 18, NARA.

SELECTED BIBLIOGRAPHY

PRIMARY SOURCES

Manuscripts

Special Collections, University of Arkansas Libraries, Fayetteville, Arkansas
Steamboat *Fannie Scott* Manifest
William F. Switzler Typescripts, 1836–1837
Tappan Steamboat Collection

Historic Arkansas Museum, Little Rock, Arkansas
Horace J. Ford Journal
Duane Huddleston Collection

Beinecke Rare Book and Manuscript Library, Yale University, New Haven, Connecticut
Charles Peter Grizzard, "A Glimpse of the South in the spring of 1855"

Indiana Historical Society, Indianapolis, Indiana
Daniel French Papers

Filson Historical Society, Louisville, Kentucky
Daniel Chapman Banks Papers
Samuel Brown Papers
Buckner and Hughs Order Book, May 1835–January 1836
Green Clay Papers
Corlis-Respess Family Papers
Dumesnil Family Papers
Hardin Family Papers
Jefferson Foundry and Steam Engine Manufactory
Francis Hegan Miller Collection

James Rudd Account Book, 1830–1860
Runyon Family Papers
Sanders Family Papers
Speed Family Papers
John K. West Letter
Samuel Wigglesworth Letters

Special Collections, Howard-Tilton Memorial Library, Tulane University, New Orleans, Louisiana
Walthall Burton Papers
Benjamin Farar Papers
Miriam Badger Hilliard Diary
Joseph Merrick Jones-Donald T. Wright Steamboat Collection
Margaret Yundt Kostmayer Collection
T. P. Leathers Papers
Louisianais Records
Mississippi Navigation Company Contract, 1814
James A. Watkins Manuscripts

Historic New Orleans Collection, New Orleans, Louisiana
Morgan-Falconer Family Papers
Edward Russell Journal

Hill Memorial Library, Louisiana State University, Baton Rouge, Louisiana
Alabama Cotton Sales Statements
Amite Navigation Company Document
John Q. Anderson Papers
"Eliza Battle" Story
Hubbard S. Bosley Family Papers
John C. Burruss and Family Collection
Anna and Sarah Butler Correspondence
Clauss and Fischer Journal, 1851–1852
L. Bowling Cotton Record Book
Cotton Sales Documents
Carlos D. De Lassus Diary
A. R. Ellery Letter
Nathaniel Evans Papers
Alfred Flournoy Papers
J. Fair Hardin Collection
Mrs. Isaac H. Hilliard Diary
Orramel Hinckley and Family Papers

Charles James Johnson Papers
William Kenner Papers
James S. Laroe Diary
Thomas P. Leathers Papers
Moses Liddell Papers
Andrew Macrery Papers
E. B. Norman Collection
Sophie Cooley Pearson Collection
Samuel J. Peters, Jr. Diary
Anton Reiff Journal
J. L. Smith Letter
Succession of Isaac Franklin
Trader Register, 1841–1843
Frederick W. Treadway Journal
James Burns Wallace Diary
David Weeks and Family Papers
Nathaniel Weeks Papers

Noel Memorial Library, Louisiana State University at Shreveport, Shreveport, Louisiana
Henry Miller Shreve Letters
Dewey A. Somdal Collection
Withenbury Steamboat Reminiscences

Earl K. Long Library, University of New Orleans, New Orleans, Louisiana
Louisiana Supreme Court Archives

Maryland Historical Society, Baltimore, Maryland
Papers of Benjamin Henry Latrobe (microfiche edition)

Mississippi Department of Archives and History, Jackson, Mississippi
Jean H. Baker Collection
Natchez Steam Boat Company Stock Certificate Book
Postlethwaite Family Papers
Isaac H. Stanwood Papers
Edward A. Thorne Letters
Vesuvius Account Book, 1821–1823

Missouri Historical Society, St. Louis, Missouri
John Geiger Diary
Steamboats Collection

Western Historical Manuscript Collection, University of Missouri, Columbia, Missouri
    Bird's Landing Warehouse Ledger and Record Book
    Bush Family Papers
    George W. Carvill Letters
    John Allen Gano Family Papers
    Hickman-Bryan Papers
    John W. Honey Ship's Log, 1819
    William Franklin Switzler Papers
    Little Rock Landing Daybook, 1854–1856
    Robert Thompson Van Horn Papers
    Lewis Ziegler Account Book

New York Historical Society, New York, New York
    Belknap Family Papers
    LeBoeuf Collection
    Mississippi and Ohio Steam Boat Vesuvius Broadside

Oneida County Historical Society, Utica, New York
    Letter Book of Jasper Lynch

Rare Book, Manuscript, and Special Collections Library, Duke University, Durham, North Carolina
    John D. Dunn Papers
    Mississippi River Travel Diary, 1825–1826
    Mississippi River Travel Diary, 1838
    Mann Family Papers
    Eugene Marshall Papers
    Germain Musson Papers
    Pope-Carter Family Papers
    James A. Walker Papers
    Maria Dyer Davies Wightman Diary
    John A. Winston and Company Letters

Southern Historical Collection, University of North Carolina, Chapel Hill, North Carolina
    Rice C. Ballard Papers
    George Wolfe Bruce Papers
    Farish Carter Papers
    Charles William Bradbury Papers
    Burwell Family Papers
    Gustavus Henry Papers

Hentz Family Papers
Lenoir Family Papers
Minor Collection
Neal Family Papers
Walter Nicol Diary
James Hervey Otey Papers
Harvey Washington Walter Papers

Inland Rivers Library, Public Library of Cincinnati and Hamilton County, Cincinnati, Ohio
"Captain Alex. F. Boss, Western Rivers Pilot," by F. E. Schoolfield, typescript
Eclipse, Crew register
Empress, Crew register
General Pike, Records
George Washington, Account book
Viroqua, Crew register

Historical Society of Western Pennsylvania, Pittsburgh, Pennsylvania
New Orleans (Steamboat) Collection, 1911

Special Collections, Mississippi Valley Collection, McWherter Library, University of Memphis, Memphis, Tennessee
John P. Haggott Journal
Smith Mead Nelson Diary

Tennessee State Library and Archives, Nashville, Tennessee
Clay-Kenner Family Papers
Elizabeth Everts Bellsnyder Diary
Catherine Berry Avery Papers
J. W. Gosen Letters
Andrew Hynes Papers
John Sumner Russwurm Papers
Alexander Wallace Jones Papers
George H. Warfield Letter
James Winchester Papers

Special Collections, University Libraries, University of Houston, Houston, Texas
Israel Shreve Revolutionary War Letters

Center for American History, University of Texas at Austin, Austin, Texas
George Campbell Childress Papers

Kiger Family Papers
Natchez Trace Steamboat Collection

National Archives and Records Administration, Washington, D.C.
Record Group 75, Letters Received by the Office of Indian Affairs, 1824–81 (microfilm edition)
Record Group 77, Entry 14, Letters Received, 1819–1825
Record Group 77, Entry 18, Letters Received, 1826–66
Record Group 77, Entry 249, Letters Sent Relating to Internal Improvements, 1824–1830
Record Group 77, Entry 250, Reports on Internal Improvements
Record Group 77, Entry 252, Plans for the Removal of Obstructions in the Mississippi and Ohio Rivers, 1824–1825

Government Documents

American State Papers, Finance. *Remission of duties on goods destroyed by fire on steamboat Vesuvius at New Orleans, petition of merchants.* 17th Cong., 1st sess., 1822. App. 1, Doc. 4.
American State Papers, Post Office. *Application for carrying mail on Ohio and Mississippi Rivers in steamboats.* 22nd Cong., 2nd sess., 1833. Doc. 126.
American State Papers, Public Lands, vol. 7. *Application for donation of land for invention of steam snag boat, petition of Henry M. Shreve.* 23rd Cong., 1st sess., 1834. Doc. 1245.
American State Papers, Public Lands, vol. 7. *Operations of the General Land Office of the United States for the Year 1834.* 23rd Cong., 2nd sess., 1834. Doc. 1260.
American State Papers, Public Lands, vol. 8. *Application of Louisiana for the Establishment of a New Land Office at Natchitoches.* 24th Cong., 1st sess., 1835. Doc. 1470.
U. S. Congress. House. *Message from the President of the United States, transmitting a Report of the Board of Engineers on the Ohio and Mississippi Rivers.* 17th Cong., 2nd sess., 1823. H. Doc 35. Serial 65-1.
———. *Annals of Congress.* 18th Cong., 1st sess., 1824. Serial 2582.
———. House. *Report of the Committee of Commerce accompanied by a bill for regulating of steam boats, and for the security of passengers therein.* 18th Cong., 1st sess., 1824. H. Rept. 125. Serial 106.
———. House. *Letter from the Secretary of the Treasury, transmitting information in relation to the surveying of the public lands north and south of Red River.* 18th Cong., 2nd sess., 1824. H. Doc. 24. Serial 114.
———. House. *Letter from the Secretary of the Treasury, transmitting information collected by the Department, upon the subject of accidents on board steam boats.* 18th Cong., 2nd sess., 1825. H. Doc. 69. Serial 116.
———. House. *Pilots on the Ohio and Mississippi. Memorial of sundry owners of steam*

boats navigating Ohio and Mississippi rivers. 19th Cong., 1st sess., 1826. H. Doc. 36. Serial 133.

———. Senate. *Letter from the Secretary of War, transmitting a report of the Chief Engineer, Relative to the Application of appropriation for removing obstructions to navigation in Ohio and Mississippi rivers*. 19th Cong., 1st sess., 1826. S. Doc. 14. Serial 125.

———. Senate. *In the Senate of the United States, February 2, 1827 . . . the subject of carrying mail in steamboats from Cincinnati or Louisville to New Orleans*. 19th. Cong., 2nd sess., 1827. S. Doc. 41. Serial 145.

———. House. *Navigation of Red River*. 19th Cong., 2nd sess., 1827. H. Rpt. 96. Serial 160.

———. House. *Letter from Henry M. Shreve, to the Hon. C. A. Wickliffe, upon the subject of navigation of the Mississippi River*. 20th Cong., 1st sess., 1827. H. Doc. 11. Serial 170.

———. House. *Steamboat tonnage United States*. 20th Cong., 1st sess. 1828, H. Doc. 249. Serial 174.

———. House. *Obstructions—the Ohio River*. 20th Cong., 2nd sess., 1828. H. Rpt. 269. Serial 179.

———. Senate. *Letter from Dr. Joseph Paxton, of Hempstead County, to the Hon. A. H. Sevier, delegate to Congress from the Territory of Arkansas, in relation to the raft on Red River*. 20th Cong., 2nd sess., 1829. S. Doc 78. Serial 181.

———. Senate. *Memorial of the Legislature of Missouri, praying that improvements may be made in the navigation of the Mississippi River*. 20th Cong., 2nd sess., 1829. S. Doc. 88. Serial 182.

———. House. *Ohio and Mississippi River. Memorial of sundry citizens of Louisville, Kentucky, praying for the improvement of the navigation of the Ohio and Mississippi Rivers*. 21st Cong., 1st sess., 1830. H. Rep. 337. Serial 201.

———. House. *Navigation on Ohio and Mississippi Rivers*. 21st Cong., 1st sess., 1830. H. Rep. 379. Serial 201.

———. Senate. *In the Senate of the United States . . . Resolutions of the Legislature of Tennessee, to procure an appropriation by Congress to effect the examination and removal of the Harpeth Shoals, on the Cumberland River*. 21st Cong., 1st sess., 1830. S. Doc. 16. Serial 192.

———. Senate. *In the Senate of the United States . . . The Committee on Public Lands, to which was referred the memorial of the Legislature of the State of Alabama, asking a grant of land for the purpose of improving the navigation of the Coosa River*. 21st Cong., 1st sess., 1830. S. Doc. 55. Serial 193.

———. House. *Letter from the Secretary of War, transmitting copies of the reports of H. M. Shreve and R. Delafield on the Improvement of navigation of Mississippi and Ohio rivers*. 21st Cong., 2nd sess., 1830. H. Doc 9. Serial 206.

———. House. *Louisiana Legislature—steam explosion*. 22nd Cong., 1st sess., 1832. H. Doc. 226. Serial 220.

———. House. *Steamboats*. 22nd Cong., 1st sess., 1832. H. Rep. 478. Serial 228.

———. House. *Ohio and Mississippi Rivers.* 22nd Cong., 2nd sess., 1833. H. Doc. 66. Serial 234.

———. Senate. *Correspondence on the subject of emigration of Indians . . . in five volumes.* 23rd Cong., 1st sess., 1834. S. Doc. 512. Serial 244.

———. House. *Raft of Red River.* 23rd Cong., 1st sess., 1834. H. Doc. 98. Serial 256.

———. Senate. *Memorial of the Legislature of Missouri, praying that an appropriation be made for removing obstructions in, and repairing the harbor of, the City of St. Louis.* 23rd Cong., 1st sess., 1834. S. Doc. 21. Serial 238.

———. House. *Henry M. Shreve.* 23rd Cong., 1st sess., 1834. H. Rep. 509. Serial 263.

———. House. *Heirs of Robert Fulton.* 24th Cong., 1st sess., 1836. H. Rep. 551. Serial 295.

———. Senate. *Message from the President of the United States, with report from the Secretary of War, on the progress of the improvement on Red river.* 24th Cong., 1st sess., 1836. S. Rep. 197. Serial 281.

———. Senate. *Report from the Secretary of the Treasury.* 24th Cong., 1st sess., 1836. S. Doc. 3. Serial 279.

———. House. *Steam boilers.* 24th Cong., 1st sess., 1836. H. Doc. 162. Serial 289.

———. House. *Henry M. Shreve.* 24th Cong., 1st sess., 1836. H. Rep. 383. Serial 294.

———. Senate. *Report from the Secretary of the Treasury.* 24th Cong., 2nd sess., 1836. S. Doc. 3. Serial 279.

———. House. *Tennessee. Petition of the citizens of Knox County, praying for an appropriation for the improvement of the navigation of the Tennessee River.* 25th Cong., 2nd sess., 1838. H. Doc. 270. Serial 328.

———. Senate. *Report from the Secretary of the Treasury.* 25th Cong., 2nd sess., 1839. S. Doc. 11. Serial 314.

———. Senate. *Message from the President of the United States.* 25th Cong., 3rd sess., 1839. S. Doc. 1. Serial 311.

———. Senate. *Report from the Secretary of the Treasury.* 25th Cong., 3rd sess., 1839. S. Doc. 17. Serial 338.

———. Senate. *Resolutions of the General Assembly of Louisiana, in relation to the improvement of the Atchafalaya and Red Rivers.* 25th Cong., 3rd sess., 1839. S. Doc. 214. Serial 340.

———. Senate. *Document in relation to the prevention of explosion of steam-boilers.* 25th Cong., 3rd sess., 1839. S. Doc. 217. Serial 340.

———. House. *Steam-engines.* 25th Cong., 3rd sess., 1839. S. Doc. 21. Serial 345.

———. House. *Steam boilers.* 25th Cong., 3rd sess., 1839. H. Doc. 87. Serial 346.

———. House. *Removal of the Red River raft.* 26th Cong., 1st sess., 1840. H. Rep. 426. Serial 371.

———. Senate. *Petition of a number of citizens of Louisiana, praying for an alteration in a mail route.* 26th Cong., 1st sess., 1840. S. Doc. 274. Serial 358.

———. Senate. *Letter from the Postmaster General, in relation to the Transportation of mail in steamboats.* 26th Cong., 1st sess., 1840. S. Doc. 338. Serial 359.

———. House. *Raft—Red River.* 26th Cong., 2nd sess., 1841. H. Rep. 141. Serial 388.

———. Senate. *Report from the Secretary of the Treasury.* 26th Cong., 2nd sess., 1841. S. Doc. 61. Serial 377.

———. Senate. *Report from the Secretary of war, transmitting, in compliance with a resolution of the Senate, a report on the improvement of Red River.* 27th Cong., 1st sess., 1841. S. Doc. 64. Serial 390.

———. House. *Message from the President of the United States.* 27th Cong., 1st sess., 1841. H. Doc. 1. Serial 392.

———. Senate. *Resolutions of the General Assembly of Indiana, to procure appropriations for the improvement of the western rivers, and for purchase of the snag-boat invented by Henry M. Shreve.* 27th Cong., 2nd sess., 1842. S. Doc. 112. Serial 397.

———. House. *Caddo Indian Treaty.* 27th Cong., 2nd sess., 1842. H. Doc. 25. Serial 401.

———. House. *Removal of Chickasaw Indians—Simeon Buckner.* 27th Cong., 2nd sess., 1842. H. Rep. 454. Serial 408.

———. House. *Captain Henry M. Shreve.* 27th Cong., 2nd sess., 1842. H. Rep. 556. Serial 409.

———. House. *The Caddo Indian Treaty.* 27th Cong., 2nd sess., 1842. H. Rep. 1035. Serial 411.

———. House. *Removal of obstructions in Red River.* 27th Cong., 3rd sess., 1843. H. Doc. 157. Serial 422.

———. House. *Pilots—Ohio and Mississippi.* 27th Cong., 3rd sess., 1843. H. Rep. 178. Serial 407.

———. Senate. *Report from the Secretary of the Treasury.* 27th Cong., 3rd sess., 1843. S. Doc. 10. Serial 390.

———. Senate. *Memorial of a number of Captains of western steamboats, praying the construction of a canal around the falls of the Ohio, on the Indiana side.* 28th Cong., 1st sess., 1844. S. Doc. 16. Serial 432.

———. House. *Henry M. Shreve.* 28th Cong., 1st sess., 1844. H. Rep. 538. Serial 447.

———. Senate. *Petition of a number of Captains of steamboats and others interested in navigation of the Western waters, praying the construction of a canal around the falls of the Ohio on the Indiana side.* 28th Cong., 2nd sess., 1845. S. Doc. 25. Serial 450.

———. Senate. *Report of the Secretary of War, in answer to a resolution of the 18th December, in relation to the Removal of the raft in Red River, in Louisiana.* 29th Cong., 1st sess., 1846. S. Doc. 26. Serial 472.

———. Senate. *Memorial of the Legislature of Arkansas, asking appropriation for completing the removal of the raft in Red River.* 29th Cong., 1st sess., 1846. S. Doc. 31. Serial 472.

———. House. *Henry M. Shreve.* 29th Cong., 1st sess., 1846. H. Rpt. 369. Serial 489.

———. Senate. *Report of the Secretary of War, in answer to a resolution of the Senate, calling for a Statement of appropriations for the construction and repair of roads, fortifications, and harbors, and for the improvement of rivers, in States and Territories.* 29th Cong., 2nd sess., 1847. S. Doc. 44. Serial 494.

———. Senate. *In the Senate of the United States . . . memorial of G. R. Cox, and ninety-four others, passengers on board steamboat Yorktown, on the Mississippi River.* 30th Cong., 1st sess., 1848. S. Rep. 135. Serial 512.

———. Senate. *In the Senate of the United States . . . various Memorials and documents . . . concerning the loss of life and property in use of steamers.* 30th Cong., 1st sess., 1848. S. Rep. 241. Serial 512.

———. House. *Captain Henry M. Shreve.* 30th Cong., 1st sess., 1848. H. Rep. 30. Serial 524.

———. House. *Safety of passengers in steam vessels.* 30th Cong., 1st sess., 1848. H. Rep. 260. Serial 525.

———. Senate. *Report of the Commissioner of Patents, upon the resolution of the Senate, respecting applications for patents for the prevention of steam explosions.* 30th Cong., 2nd sess., 1848. S. Exec. Doc. 18. Serial 529.

———. Senate. *Documents related to the preservation and protection of passengers from injuries resulting from steamboat accidents.* 31st Cong., spec. sess., 1849. S. Doc. 4. Serial 547.

———. *Report of the Acting Secretary of the Interior, relative to the swamp and overflowed lands in Louisiana.* 31st Cong, 1st sess., 1850. S. Exec. Doc. 68. Serial 562.

———. Senate. *Resolution of the legislature of Louisiana, relative to the removal of Red River raft.* 31st Cong., 1st sess., 1849–1850. S. Misc. Doc. 114. Serial 563.

———. House. *Red River. Resolution of the Legislature of Louisiana, asking an appropriation for the improvement of the navigation of Red River.* 32nd Cong., 1st sess., 1852. H. Misc. Doc. 22. Serial 652.

———. Senate. *Report of the Secretary of the Treasury on the Statistics and History of the Steam Marine of the United States.* 32nd Cong., 1st sess., 1852. S. Exec. Doc. 42. Serial 619.

———. House. *Des Moines and Rock River Rapids, in the Mississippi River.* 33rd Cong., 1st sess., 1853. H. Exec. Doc. 104. Serial 725.

———. House. *Impediments in Red River.* 33rd Cong., 1st sess., 1854. H. Exec. Doc. 24. Serial 717.

———. House. *Letter from the Secretary of War, transmitting report and maps of Col. Fuller's survey of Red River.* 33rd Cong., 2nd sess., 1854–1855. H. Exec. Doc. 90. Serial 790.

———. House. *Henry M. Shreve—widow and children of.* 33rd Cong., 2nd sess., 1855. H. Rep. 88. Serial 808.

———. House. *Raft region of Red river.* 34th Cong., 1st sess., 1855–1856. H. Rep. 85. Serial 868.

———. House. *The Cholera Epidemic of 1873 in the United States.* 43rd Cong., 2nd sess., 1875. H. Exec. Doc. 95. Serial 1646.

———. House. Department of the Treasury. *Report on the Internal Commerce of the United States 1887.* William F. Switzler, part 2 of *Report on the Commerce and Navigation of the United States.* 50th Cong., 1st sess., 1888. H. Exec. Doc. 6. Serial 2552.

Kapler, Charles J., ed. *Indian Affairs: Laws and Treaties.* Washington, D.C.: Government Printing Office, 1904.

Periodicals and Newspapers

American Review (1847)
De Bow's Review (1851–1861)
The Friend, a Religious and Literary Journal (1837)
Harper's Weekly (1856–1861)
Ladies' Repository (1844)
New-England Magazine (1831)
North American Review (1827–1840)
Southern Literary Messenger (1837–1839)
Southern Quarterly Review (1846)
United States Democratic Review (1842–1848)
Waterways Journal (1888–1892)
Western Monthly Review (1827–1828)

Louisiana Supreme Court Cases

Ames et al. v. Reed, No. 948, 2 Mart. (n.s.) 236. New Orleans, March 1824.

Arthur & Co. et al. v. Dickson, No. 3265, 10 La. Ann. (n.s.) 116. New Orleans, January 1855.

Robert G. Beverly v. Captain and Owners of steamboat Empire, No. 6323, 15 La. Ann. (n.s.) 432. New Orleans, June 1860.

Black v. Savory et al., No. 4276, 17 La. (o.s.) 85. New Orleans, March 1841.

W. J. Blocker v. W. W. Whittenburg, Captain and Owner of Steamboat B. E. Clarke, No. 4167, 12 La. Ann. (n.s.) 410. New Orleans, June 1857.

Board of Selectmen v. Spalding & Rogers, No. 3048, 8 La. Ann. (n.s.) 87. New Orleans, March 1853.

Lewis Bond v. Samuel B. Frost and Owners of the Steamboat Concordia, No. 2798, 8 La. Ann. (n.s.) 297. New Orleans, June 1853.

Brannan, Patterson & Holliday v. Wm. R. Hoel, No. 6085, 15 La. Ann. (n.s.) 308. New Orleans, May 1860.

Butler v. De Hart, No. 791, 1 Mart. (n.s.) 184. New Orleans, April 1823.

Carroll v. Waters, No. 550, 9 Mart. (o.s.) 500. New Orleans, April 1821.

Jacob Clines v. Rowsell R. Frisbee, Captain and Owner of the Steamer John H. Bills, No. 4833, 5 Rob. 192. New Orleans, June 1843.

Cochran v. Smith, No. 1001, 2 Mart. (n.s.) 552. New Orleans, June 1824.

Courtnay et al. vs. Mississippi Marine and Fire Ins. Co., No. 3152, 12 La. Ann. (o.s.) 233. New Orleans, April 1838.

James Dalzell v. Steamboat Saxon, No. 3269, 10 La. Ann. (n.s.) 280. New Orleans, April 1855.

John Davis v. Nimrod Houren and another, No. 5452, 10 Rob 402. New Orleans, April 1845.

Daniel J. Dohan v. J. M. Wilson, No. 5368, 14 La. Ann. (n.s.) 353. New Orleans, May 1859.

Emmerling vs. Beebe et al., No. 3642, 15 La. (o.s.) 251. New Orleans, April 1840.

Richard England v. Theodore Gripon, owner of Steamboat Cora, No. 6316, 15 La. Ann. (n.s.) 304. New Orleans, May 1860.

Evans et al. v. Gray et al., No. 730, 12 Mart. (o.s.) 507. New Orleans, January 1823.

Fearn Putnam & Co. v. W. A Richardson, No. 4756, 12 La. Ann. (n.s.) 752. New Orleans, November 1857.

Frisby v. Sheridan, No. 1060, 3 Mart. (n.s.) 242. New Orleans, January 1825.

Gilly et al v. Logan et al., No. 942, 2 Mart. (n.s.) 196. New Orleans, February 1824.

Honore v. White et al., No. 809, 1 Mart (n.s.) 219. New Orleans, May 1823.

Robert Howes v. Steamer Red Chief, Captain and Owners, No. 5944, 15 La. Ann. (n.s.) 321. New Orleans, May 1860.

Hunt v. Morris et al., No. 331, 6 Mart. (o.s.) 676. New Orleans, June 1819.

Hunt v. Norris et al., No. 179, 4 Mart. (o.s.) 517. New Orleans, December 1816.

Hurst v. Wallace, No. 2402, 5 La. (o.s.) 98. New Orleans, February 1833.

Kimball and Lilly vs. Brander et als., No. 2625, 6 La. Ann. (o.s.) 711. New Orleans, June 1834.

M. C. Lisk v. M. A. Mathis, No. 4000, 11 La. Ann. (n.s.) 418. New Orleans, May 1856.

J. A. Lusk v. J. C. Swon—C. B. Church, in Warranty, No. 2852, 9 La. Ann. (n.s.) 367. New Orleans, June 1854.

Lynch v. Postlethwaite, No. 369, 7 Mart. (o.s.) 69. New Orleans, July 1819.

McAlpin v. Lauve et al., No. 672, 2 La. Ann. (n.s.) 1015. New Orleans, December 1847.

McIntosh v. Forstall et al., No. 1162, 3 Mart. (n.s.) 571. New Orleans, May 1825.

McNeill et al v. A. Glass and Company, No. 739, 1 Mart. (n.s.) 261. New Orleans, May 1823.

Nancarrow v. Young et al., No. 345, 6 Mart. (o.s.) 662. New Orleans, June 1819.

R. Y. Northern v. Williams, Phillips and Co., No. 1800, 6 La. Ann. (n.s.) 578. New Orleans, June 1851.

Peabody et al. v. Carrol, No. 511, 9 Mart. (o.s.) 295. New Orleans, February 1821.

Pearl River Navigation Company v. Stephen A. Douglas, No. 2526, 7 La. Ann. (n.s.) 631. New Orleans, November 1852.

Pepper v. Peytavin, No. 751, 12 Mart. (o.s.) 671. New Orleans, February 1823.

Levin K. Person v. C. M. Rutherford, No. 3585, 11 La. Ann. (n.s.) 527. New Orleans, June 1856.

P. Pousargues v. Steamer Natchez et al., No. 6250, 15 La. Ann. (n.s.) 80. New Orleans, May 1860.

Pratt v. Flowers, No. 967, 2 Mart. (n.s.) 333. New Orleans, April 1824.

Reese and Seger v. Steamer Mary Foley et al., No. 1892, 6 La. Ann. (n.s.) 71. New Orleans, February 1851.

Riley et al. v. Hart et al., No. 661, 3 La. Ann. (n.s.) 184. New Orleans, February 1848.

John Riley v. The City of Louisville, No. 4799, 5 Rob. 184. New Orleans, June 1843.

Shreve v. His Creditors, No. 584, 11 Mart. (o.s.) 30. New Orleans, March 1822.

Sowers v. Flower et al., No. 1019, 2 Mart. (n.s.) 617. New Orleans, June 1824.

State v. The New Orleans Navigation Company, No. 642, 11 Mart. (o.s.) 38. New Orleans, March 1822.

The State of Louisiana, for the use of the Charity Hospital of New Orleans v. Samuel W. Fullerton, No. 5280, 7 Rob. 210. New Orleans, April 1844.

H. M. Summers v. United States Insurance, Annuity and Trust Co., No. 5423, 13 La. Ann. (n.s.) 504. New Orleans, December 1858.

Varion v. Bell, No. 3697, 17 La. (o.s.) 532. New Orleans, March 1841.

Walton et al. v. Grant et al., No. 975, 2 Mart. (n.s.) 494. New Orleans, May 1824.

Wilcox et al. v. Halderman et al., No. 3533, 14 La. (o.s.) 357. New Orleans, February 1840.

Williamson et al., Syndics v. Smoot, No. 378, 7 Mart. (o.s.) 31. New Orleans, July 1819.

Samuel T. Williamson v. Alexander Morton, Master &c., No. 2427, 7 La. Ann. (n.s.) 394. New Orleans, June 1852.

Books and Printed Sources

Aggregate Amount of each description of Persons within the United States of America, and the Territories thereof, agreeably to actual enumeration made according to law, in the year 1810. New York: L. M. Cornwall, n.d.

Alexander, James Edward. *Transatlantic Sketches, Comprising visits to the most interesting Scenes in North and South America.* Philadelphia: Key and Biddle, 1833.

Allen, Michael, ed. "Reminiscences of a Common Boatman (1849–1851)." *Gateway Heritage* 5 (fall 1984): 36–49.

Anderson, William J. *Life and Narrative of William J. Anderson, Twenty-Four Years a Slave.* Chicago: Daily Tribune, 1857.

Audubon, John James. *John James Audubon: Writings and Drawings.* New York: Library of America, 1999.

Baird, Robert. *View of the Valley of the Mississippi: Or the Emigrant's and Traveller's Guide to the West.* Philadelphia: H. S. Tanner, 1832.

Banvard, John. *Description of Banvard's Panorama of the Mississippi River.* Boston: John Putnam, 1847.

Berkeley, Grantley F. *The English Sportsman in the Western Prairies.* London: Hurst and Blackett, 1861.

Bremer, Fredrika. *America of the Fifties: Letters of Fredrika Bremer.* Edited by Adolph B. Benson. New York: American-Scandinavian Foundation, 1924.

Brown, William Wells. *Narrative of William W. Brown, An American Slave.* London: Charles Gilpin, 1849.

Buckingham, James S. *The Slave States of America.* 2 vols. London: Fisher, 1842.

Case, Lynn M., ed. "The Middle West in 1837: Translations from the Notes of an Italian Count Francesco Arese." *Mississippi Valley Historical Review* 20 (December 1933): 381–99.

Casey, Charles. *Two Years on the Farm of Uncle Sam.* London: R. Bentley, 1852.

Chapin, Sarah, ed. "Edward Jarvis's Journal." *Filson Club Historical Quarterly* 70 (July 1996): 227–303.

Chevalier, Michel. *Society, Manners, and Politics in the United States.* Boston: Weeks, Jordan, and Company, 1839.

Clark, John A. *Gleanings by the Way.* Philadelphia: W. J. and J. K. Simon, 1842.

Clarke, Lewis Garrard, and Milton Clarke. *Narratives of the Sufferings of Lewis and Milton Clarke.* Boston: Bela Marsh, 1846.

Collins, T. C. *The Adventures of T. C. Collins—Boatman,* compiled and edited by Herbert L. Roush Sr. Baltimore: Gateway Press, 1985.

Compendium of the Enumeration of the Inhabitants and Statistics of the United States as obtained at the Department of State, from the Returns of the Sixth Census. Washington, D.C.: Thomas Allen, 1841.

Conclin, George. *Conclin's New River Guide.* Cincinnati: U. P. James, 1855.

Cooley, Stoughton. "The Mississippi Roustabout." *New England Magazine* 17, no. 3 (November 1894): 290–301.

Cramer, Zadok. *The Navigator: Containing Directions for Navigating the Monongahela, Allegheny, Ohio, and Mississippi Rivers,* 7th ed. Pittsburgh: Cramer, Spear and Eichbaum, 1811.

Crockett, David. *The Autobiography of David Crockett.* New York: C. Scribner's Sons, 1923.

Cumings, Samuel. *The Western Pilot: Containing charts of the Ohio River, and the Mississippi, from the Mouth of the Missouri to the Gulf of Mexico.* Cincinnati: N. and G. Guilford, 1834.

Cunynghame, Arthur Augustus Thurlow. *A Glimpse at the Great Western Republic.* London: R. Bentley, 1851.

Darby, William. *The Emigrant's Guide to the Western and Southwestern States and Territories.* New York: Kirk and Mercer, 1818.

Davies, Ebenezer. *American Scenes and Christian Slavery: A Recent Tour of Four Thousand Miles in the United States.* London: J. Snow, 1849.

Davis, Edwin Adams, ed. *Plantation Life in the Florida Parishes of Louisiana, 1836–1854, as reflected in the Diary of Bennett H. Barrow.* New York: Columbia Univ. Press, 1943.

Davis, Edwin Adams, and John C. L. Andreassen, eds. "From Louisville to New Orleans in 1816: Diary of William Newton Mercer." *Journal of Southern History* 11 (August 1945): 390–402.

De Bow, J. D. *The Seventh Census of the United States: 1850.* Washington, D.C.: Robert Armstrong, 1853.

DeLeon, Thomas C. *Four Years in Rebel Capitals: An Inside View of Life in the Southern Confederacy from Birth to Death.* Mobile: Gossip Printing, 1890.

Devol, George H. *Forty Years a Gambler on the Mississippi.* 1887. Reprint, New York: Johnson Reprint Corporation, 1968.

Dewees, William B. *Letters from an Early Settler of Texas,* compiled by Cara Cardelle. Louisville: Morton and Griswold, 1852.

Dickens, Charles. *American Notes for General Circulation.* London: Chapman and Hall, 1850.

Didmus, H. *New Orleans as I found It.* New York: Harper and Brothers, 1845.

Drew, Benjamin. *A North-Side View of Slavery. The Refugee: or the Narrative of Fugitive Slaves in Canada.* Boston: J. P. Jewett, 1856.

Ehrenpreis, Anne Henry, ed. *Happy Country this America: The Travel Diary of Henry Arthur Blight.* Columbus: Ohio State Univ. Press, 1978.

Ellet, Charles. *The Mississippi and Ohio Rivers.* 2 vols. 1853. Reprint, New York: Arno, 1970.

Everest, Robert. *A Journey through the United States and part of Canada.* London: J. Chapman, 1855.

Featherstonhaugh, George W. *Excursion through the Slave States.* 1844. Reprint, New York: Negro Universities Press, 1968.

Federal Writers' Project. *Slave Narratives: A Folk History of Slavery in the United States from Interviews with Former Slaves,* vol. 11, *Arkansas Narratives,* part 5. Washington, D.C.: Federal Writers' Project, 1941.

Ferrall, Simon Ashley. *A Ramble of Six Thousand Miles through the United States of America.* London: Effingham and Wilson, 1832.

Flagg, Edmund. *Flagg's the Far West.* Cleveland: A. H. Clark, 1906.

Flint, Charles Louis. *Eighty Years' Progress of the United States,* vol. 1. Hartford, Conn.: L. Stebbins, 1867.

Flint, Timothy. *Recollections of the Last Ten Years.* Boston: Cumings and Hilliard, 1826.

Foreman, Grant, ed. *Indian Pioneer History Collection,* 37 vols. Oklahoma City: Oklahoma Historical Society, 1937.

———, ed. "Journey of a Party of Cherokee Emigrants." *Mississippi Valley Historical Review* 18 (September 1931): 232–45.

Foster, Lillian. *Way-Side Glimpses, North and South.* New York: Rudd and Carleton, 1860.

Fuller, Hiram. *Belle Brittan on a Tour at Newport, and here and there.* New York: Derby and Jackson, 1858.

Gaddis, Maxwell Pierson. *Foot-prints of an Itinerant.* Cincinnati: Methodist Book Concern, 1856.

Gerstacker, Friedrich. *Wild Sports in the Far West: The narrative of a German wanderer beyond the Mississippi, 1837–1843,* translated by Edna L. Steeves and Harrison L. Steeves. 1854. Reprint, Durham: Duke Univ. Press, 1968.

Gould, Emerson W. *Fifty Years on the Mississippi: or, Gould's History of River Navigation.* St. Louis, Mo.: Nixon-Jones, 1889.

de Grandfort, Marie Fontenay. *The New World.* Translated by E. C. Wharton. New Orleans: Sherman, Wharton, and Co., 1855.

Grandy, Moses. *Narrative of the Life of Moses Grandy: Late a Slave in the United States of America.* London: Gilpin, 1843.

Gray, William Fairfax. *The Diary of William Fairfax Gray, from Virginia to Texas, 1835–1837.* Edited by Paul D. Lack. Dallas: DeGolyer Library and William P. Clements Center for Southwest Studies, Southern Methodist University, 1997.

Green, Jonathan H. *Gambling Exposed.* Philadelphia: T. B. Peterson and Brothers, 1857.

Habermehl, John. *Life on the Western Rivers.* Pittsburgh: McNary and Simpson, 1901.

Hall, A. Oakley. *The Manhattaner in New Orleans; or, Phases of "Crescent City" Life.* New York: J. S. Redfield, 1851.

Hall, Basil. *Travels in North America, in the Years 1827 and 1828.* 3 vols. Edinburgh: Cadell, 1830.

Hall, James. *The West: Its Commerce and Navigation.* 1848. Reprint, New York: Burt Franklin, 1970.

Hamilton, Thomas. *Men and Manners in America.* Philadelphia: Carey, Lea and Blanchard, 1833.

Hogan, William Ransom, and Edwin Adams Davis, eds. *William Johnson's Natchez: The Ante-Bellum Diary of a Free Negro.* Baton Rouge: Louisiana State Univ. Press, 1951.

Houstoun, Mrs. [Matilda Charlotte]. *Hesperos: or, Travels in the West.* 2 vols. London: J. W. Parker, 1850.

Hughes, Louis. *Thirty Years a Slave: From Bondage to Freedom.* Milwaukee: South Side Printing, 1897.

Ingraham, Joseph H. *The South-West by a Yankee.* 2 vols. New York: Harper and Brothers, 1835.

———. *The Sunny South: or the Southerner at Home.* 1860. Reprint, New York: Negro Universities Press, 1968.

Jeffrey, Thomas E., ed. *Papers of Benjamin Henry Latrobe,* microfiche ed. Clifton, N.J.: Published for the Maryland Historical Society by James T. White and Company, 1976.

Journal of the Proceedings of the South-Western Convention. Memphis: n.p., 1845.

Kellar, Herbert A., ed. "A Diary through the South in 1836: Diary of James D. Davidson." *Journal of Southern History* 1 (August 1935): 345–77.

Kimball and James' Business Directory for the Mississippi Valley: 1844. Cincinnati: Kendall and Barnard, 1844.

King, Edward. *The Great South: A Record of Journeys in Louisiana, Texas, the Indian Territory, Missouri, Arkansas, Mississippi, Alabama, Georgia, Florida, South Carolina, North Carolina, Kentucky, Tennessee, Virginia, West Virginia, and Maryland.* Hartford, Conn.: American Publishing Company, 1875.

Kingsford, William. *Impressions of the West and South during a six weeks' holiday.* Toronto: A. H. Armour, 1858.

Lakier, Aleksandr Borisovich. *A Russian Looks at America: The Journey of Aleksandr Borisovich Lakier in 1857.* Edited and translated by Arnold Schrier and Joyce Story. Chicago: Univ. of Chicago Press, 1979.

Lanman, Charles. *Adventures in the Wilds of the United States and British American Provinces.* 2 vols. Philadelphia: John W. Moore, 1856.

Latham, Henry. *Black and White: A Journal of Three Months' Tour in the United States.* London: Macmillan, 1867.

Latrobe, Charles Joseph. *The Rambler in North America,* 2nd ed. 2 vols. 1836. Reprint, New York: Johnson Reprint Corporation, 1970.

Latrobe, J. H. B. *The First Steamboat Voyage on the Western Waters.* Baltimore: J. Murphy, 1871.

———. *A Lost Chapter in the History of the Steamboat.* Baltimore: J. Murphy, 1871.

Litton, Gaston, ed. "The Journal of a Party of Emigrating Creek Indians, 1835–1836." *Journal of Southern History* 7, no. 2 (May 1941): 224–42.

Lloyd, James T. *Lloyd's Steamboat Directory and Disasters on the Western Waters.* Cincinnati: James T. Lloyd, 1856.

Lyell, Charles. *A Second Visit to the United States of North America.* 2 vols. New York: Harper and Brothers, 1849.

Mackay, Alexander. *The Western World: or, Travels in the United States in 1846–47.* 2 vols. Philadelphia: Lea and Blanchard, 1849.

Mackay, Charles. *Life and Liberty in America: or, Sketches of a Tour in the United States and Canada in 1857–8.* New York: Harper and Brothers, 1859.

Marestier, Jean Baptiste. *Memoir on Steamboats of the United States of America,* translated by Sidney Withington. 1824. Reprint, Mystic, Conn.: Marine Historical Association, 1957.

Marryat, Frederick. *A Diary in America, with Remarks on its Institutions.* Edited by Sydney Jackman. New York: Knopf, 1962.

———. *Second Series of a Diary in America, with Remarks on its Institutions.* Philadelphia: T. K. and P. G. Collins, 1840.

Martineau, Harriet. *Retrospect of Western Travel.* 2 vols. London: Saunders and Otley, 1838.

McDermott, John Francis, ed. *Before Mark Twain: A Sampler of Old, Old Times on the Mississippi.* Carbondale: Southern Illinois Univ. Press, 1968.

Memorial of the Citizens of St. Louis, Missouri, to the Congress of the United States. St. Louis: Chambers and Knapp, 1844.

Merrick, George Byron. *Old Times on the Upper Mississippi: The Recollections of a Steamboat Pilot from 1854 to 1863.* Cleveland: Arthur H. Clark, 1909.

Montulé, Edouard de. *Travels in America 1816–1817,* translated by Edward D. Seeber. 1821. Reprint, Bloomington: Indiana Univ. Press, 1951.

Nichols, Thomas Low. *Forty Years of American Life.* 2 vols. London: J. Maxwell and Company, 1864.

Olmsted, Frederick Law. *The Cotton Kingdom: A Traveller's Observations on Cotton and Slavery in the American Slave States, 1853–1861.* Edited by Arthur M. Schlesinger. New York: Alfred A. Knopf, 1953.

———. *A Journey in the Seaboard Slave States: with remarks on their Economy.* New York: Dix and Edwards, 1856.

Parker, Amos Andrew, *Trip to the West and Texas.* 1835. Reprint, New York: Arno Press, 1973.

Parsons, John F., ed. "Letters on the Chickasaw Removal of 1837." *New York Historical Society Quarterly* 37 (July 1953): 273–83.

Paxton, Philip [S. A. Hammett]. *A Stray Yankee in Texas.* New York: Redfield, 1859.

Piercy, Frederick. *Route from Liverpool to Great Salt Lake Valley.* Edited by James Linforth. Liverpool: Franklin D. Richards, 1855.

Porter, William T. *The Big Bear of Arkansas and other sketches.* Philadelphia: Carey and Hart, 1845.

Power, Tyrone. *Impressions of America during the years 1833, 1834, and 1835.* 2 vols. London: Richard Bentley, 1836.

Prichard, Walter, Fred B. Kniffen, and Clair A. Brown, eds. "Southern Louisiana and Southern Alabama in 1819: The Journal of James Leander Cathcart." *Louisiana Historical Quarterly* 28 (July 1945): 733–921.

Proceedings of the St. Louis Chamber of Commerce in relation to the improvement of the navigation of the Mississippi River. St. Louis: Chambers and Knapp, 1842.

Ralph, Julian. *Dixie; or Southern Scenes and Sketches.* New York: Harper and Brothers, 1896.

Read, Frederick Brent, ed. *Up the Heights of Fame and Fortune, and The Routes taken by the Climbers to become Men of Mark.* Cincinnati: William H. Moore, 1873.

Rowland, Dunbar, ed. *Life, Letters, and Papers of William Dunbar: of Elgin, Morayshire, Scotland, and Natchez, Mississippi.* Jackson: Press of the Mississippi Historical Society, 1930.

———, ed. *Official Letter Books of W. C. C. Claiborne, 1801–1816.* 6 vols. Jackson, Miss.: State Department of Archives and History, 1917.

Russell, William Howard. *My Diary North and South.* Boston: T.O.H.P. Burnham, 1863.

Shirreff, Patrick. *A Tour through North America.* Edinburgh: Oliver and Boyd, 1835.

Shreve, Henry M. *Memorial of Henry M. Shreve, in relation to the Removal of Snags, Sawyers, &c., from the Great Western Rivers, by the use of his Patented Steam Snag Boat.* N.p., n.d.

Spence, Thomas. *The Settler's Guide in the United States and British North American Provinces.* New York: Davis and Kent, 1862.

Stuart, James. *Three Years in North America.* 2 vols. Edinburgh: R. Cadell, 1833.

Suppiger, Joseph, Salomon Koepfli, and Kaspar Koepfli. *Journey to New Switzerland: Travel Account of the Koepfli and Suppiger Family to St. Louis on the Mississippi and the Founding of New Switzerland in the State of Illinois,* translated by Raymond J. Spahn and edited by John C. Abbott. Carbondale: Southern Illinois Univ. Press, 1987.

Thomas, James. *From Tennessee Slave to St. Louis Entrepreneur: The Autobiography of James Thomas.* Edited by Loren Schweniger. Columbia: Univ. of Missouri Press, 1984.

Thorpe, Thomas Bangs. *The Mysteries of the Backwoods; or Sketches of the Southwest.* Philadelphia: Carey and Hart, 1846.

———. "Remembrances of the Mississippi." *Harper's New Monthly Magazine* 12, no. 67 (December 1855): 25–41.

Todd, Henry Cook. *Notes upon Canada and the United States from 1832 to 1840: much in a small space, or a great deal in a little book.* Toronto: Rogers and Thompson, 1840.

de Toqueville, Alexis. *Democracy in America.* Edited by Phillips Bradley. 2 vols. New York: Vintage Books, 1945.

Trowbridge, John T. *The Desolate South 1865–1866: A Picture of the Battlefields and of the Devastated Confederacy.* Edited by Gordon Carroll. Freeport, N.Y.: Duell, Sloan, and Pearce, 1956.

Twain, Mark. *The Family Mark Twain,* vol. 1, *Life on the Mississippi.* New York: Harper and Brothers, 1935.

Wharton, Thomas K. *Queen of the South: New Orleans, 1853–1862.* Edited by Samuel Wilson Jr., Patricia Brady, and Lynn D. Adams. New Orleans: Historic New Orleans Collection, 1999.

Wortley, Lady Emmeline Stuart. *Travels in the United States, during 1849 and 1850.* New York: Harper and Brothers, 1851.

Wurttemberg, Duke of [Paul Wilhelm]. *Travels in North America, 1822–1824.* Translated by W. Robert Nitske. Edited by Savoie Lottinville. Norman: Univ. of Oklahoma Press, 1973.

SECONDARY SOURCES

Agnew, Brad. *Fort Gibson: Terminal on the Trail of Tears.* Norman: Univ. of Oklahoma Press, 1980.

Aldrich, Mark. *Death Rode the Rails: American Railroads and Safety, 1828–1965.* Baltimore: Johns Hopkins Univ. Press, 2006.

Allen, Michael. "The Riverman as Jacksonian Man," *Western Historical Quarterly* 21 (August 1990): 305–20.

———. *Western Rivermen, 1763–1861: Ohio and Mississippi Boatmen and the Myth of the Alligator Horse.* Baton Rouge: Louisiana State Univ. Press, 1990.

Alvarez, Eugene. *Travel on Southern Antebellum Railroads, 1828–1860.* University, Ala: Univ. of Alabama Press, 1974.

Amos, Harriet E. *Cotton City: Urban Development in Antebellum Mobile.* Tuscaloosa: Univ. of Alabama Press, 1985.

Andrews, Thomas G. *Killing for Coal: America's Deadliest Labor War.* Cambridge: Harvard Univ. Press, 2008.

Anfinson, John O. *The River We Have Wrought: A History of the Upper Mississippi.* Minneapolis: Univ. of Minnesota Press, 2003.

Arnesen, Eric. *Waterfront Workers of New Orleans: Race, Class, and Politics, 1863–1923.* New York: Oxford Univ. Press, 1991.

Atack, Jeremy. "Economies of Scale in Western River Steamboating: A Comment." *Journal of Economic History* 38 (June 1978): 457–66.

————. "Quantitative and Qualitative Evidence in the Weaving of Business and Economic History: Western River Steamboats and the Transportation Revolution Revisited." *Business and Economic History* 28 (fall 1999): 1–11.

Atack, Jeremy, Erik F. Haites, James Mak, and Gary M. Walton. "The Profitability of Steamboating on the Western Rivers: 1850." *Business History Review* 49 (fall 1975): 346–54.

Atherton, Lewis E. "John McDonogh and the Mississippi River Trade." *Louisiana Historical Quarterly* 26 (January 1943): 37–43.

Bagur, Jacques D. *A History of Navigation on Cypress Bayou and the Lakes.* Denton: Univ. of North Texas Press, 2001.

Baird, Nancy. "Asiatic Cholera's First Visit to Kentucky: A Study in Panic and Fear." *Filson Club Historical Quarterly* 48 (July 1974): 228–40.

Baldwin, Leland D. *The Keelboat Age on Western Waters.* Pittsburgh: Univ. of Pittsburgh Press, 1941.

————. "Shipbuilding on the Western Waters, 1793–1817." *Mississippi Valley Historical Review* 20 (June 1933): 29–44.

Bancroft, Frederic. *Slave Trading in the Old South.* 1931. Reprint, Columbia: Univ. of South Carolina Press, 1996.

Banner, Stuart. *How the Indians Lost Their Land: Law and Power on the Frontier.* Cambridge: Harvard Univ. Press, 2005.

Banta, R. E. *The Ohio.* New York: Rinehart, 1949.

Bateman, Fred, and Thomas Weiss. *A Deplorable Scarcity: The Failure of Southern Industrialization in a Slave Economy.* Chapel Hill: Univ. of North Carolina Press, 1981.

Bates, Alan L. *The Western Rivers Engineroom Cyclopoedium.* Louisville: Cyclopoedium Press, 1996.

————. *The Western Rivers Steamboat Cyclopoedium.* Leonia, N.J.: Hustle Press, 1968.

Bauer, K. Jack. *Zachary Taylor: Soldier, Planter, and Statesman of the Old Southwest.* Baton Rouge: Louisiana State Univ. Press, 1985.

Baxter, Maurice G. *The Steamboat Monopoly: Gibbons v. Ogden, 1824.* New York: Knopf, 1972.

Bergeron, Paul H., Stephen V. Ash, and Jeanette Keith. *Tennesseans and Their History.* Knoxville: Univ. of Tennessee Press, 1999.

Berlin, Ira. *Generations of Captivity: A History of African-American Slaves.* Cambridge, Mass.: Harvard Univ. Press, 2003.

Berlin, Ira, and Philip D. Morgan, eds. *Cultivation and Culture: Labor and the Shaping of Slave Life in the Americas.* Charlottesville: Univ. Press of Virginia, 1993.

Black, Robert C., III. *The Railroads of the Confederacy.* Chapel Hill: Univ. of North Carolina Press, 1952.

Blackbourn, David. *The Conquest of Nature: Water, Landscape, and the Making of Modern Germany.* New York: W. W. Norton, 2006.

Bogle, Victor M. "The *Eclipse* vs. the *A. L. Shotwell*: Memorable Contest Almost Forgotten." *Filson Club Historical Quarterly* 35 (April 1961): 125–37.

Boles, John B. *The South through Time: A History of an American Region,* 3rd ed. 2 vols. Upper Saddle River, N.J.: Pearson, 2004.

Bolster, W. Jeffrey. *Black Jacks: African American Seaman in the Age of Sail.* Cambridge: Harvard Univ. Press, 1997.

Bond, Bradley G. *Political Culture in the Nineteenth-Century South: Mississippi, 1830–1900.* Baton Rouge: Louisiana State Univ. Press, 1995.

Bragg, Marion. *Historic Names and Places on the Lower Mississippi River.* Vicksburg: Mississippi River Commission, 1977.

Branch, Mary Emerson. "Prime Emerson and Steamboat Building in Memphis." *West Tennessee Historical Society Papers* 38 (1984): 69–83.

Brasseaux, Carl A., and Keith P. Fontenot. *Steamboats on Louisiana's Bayous: A History and Directory.* Baton Rouge: Louisiana State Univ. Press, 2004.

Brazy, Martha Jane. *An American Planter: Stephen Duncan of Antebellum Natchez and New York.* Baton Rouge: Louisiana State Univ. Press, 2006.

Bremer, Jeff Robert. "Frontier Capitalism: The Market Revolution in the Antebellum Lower Missouri River Valley, 1803–1860." Ph.D. diss., University of Kansas, 2006.

Bristol, Douglas Walter, Jr. *Knights of the Razor: Black Barbers in Slavery and Freedom.* Baltimore: Johns Hopkins Univ. Press, 2009.

Brock, Eric, and Gary Joiner. *Red River Steamboats.* Charleston, S.C.: Arcadia Publishing, 1999.

Brockmann, R. John. *Exploding Steamboats, Senate Debates, and Technical Reports: The Convergence of Technology, Politics, and Rhetoric in the Steamboat Bill of 1838.* Amityville, N.Y.: Baywood Publishing, 2002.

———. *Twisted Rails, Sunken Ships: The Rhetoric of Nineteenth Century Steamboat and Railroad Accident Investigation Reports, 1833–1879.* Amityville, N.Y.: Baywood Publishing, 2004.

Bruchey, Stuart, ed. *Cotton and the Growth of the American Economy: 1790–1860.* New York: Harcourt, Brace and World, 1967.

Buchanan, Thomas C. *Black Life on the Mississippi: Slaves, Free Blacks, and the Western Steamboat World.* Chapel Hill: Univ. of North Carolina Press, 2004.

———. "The Slave Mississippi: African-American Steamboat Workers, Networks of Resistance, and the Commercial World of the Western Rivers, 1811–1880." Ph.D. diss., Carnegie Mellon University, 1998.

Burke, John G. "Bursting Boilers and Federal Power." *Technology and Culture* 7 (winter 1966): 1–23.

Cairo, Robert F. "Snag Boats on the Western Rivers, Part I." *Nautical Research Journal* 26 (June 1980): 83–93.

———. "Snag Boats on the Western Rivers, Part II." *Nautical Research Journal* 26 (December 1980): 167–76.

Caldwell, Norman W. "The Red River Raft." *Chronicles of Oklahoma* 19 (September 1941): 253–68.

Camp, Stephanie M. H. *Closer to Freedom: Enslaved Women and Everyday Resistance in the Plantation South.* Chapel Hill: Univ. of North Carolina Press, 2004.

Capers, Gerald M. *The Biography of a River Town; Memphis: Its Heroic Age,* 2nd ed. Memphis: Lightning Press, 2003.

Carrigan, Jo Ann. "The Impact of Yellow Fever on Life in Louisiana." *Louisiana History* 4 (winter 1963): 5–34.

Carson, W. Wallace. "Transportation and Traffic on the Ohio and the Mississippi before the Steamboat." *Mississippi Valley Historical Review* 7 (June 1920): 26–38.

Cecelski, David S. *The Waterman's Song: Slavery and Freedom in Maritime North Carolina.* Chapel Hill: Univ. of North Carolina Press, 2001.

Clark, John E., Jr. *Railroads in the Civil War: The Impact of Management on Victory and Defeat.* Baton Rouge: Louisiana State Univ. Press, 2001.

Clark, Thomas D. *The Beginning of the L & N: The Development of the Louisville and Nashville Railroad from Its Memphis Branches from 1836 to 1860.* Louisville: Standard Printing, 1933.

———. *A Pioneer Southern Railroad from New Orleans to Cairo.* Chapel Hill: Univ. of North Carolina Press, 1936.

Cline, Wayne. *Alabama Railroads.* Tuscaloosa: Univ. of Alabama Press, 1997.

Coleman, J. Winston, Jr. "Kentucky River Steamboats." *Register of the Kentucky Historical Society* 63 (October 1965): 299–322.

Colten, Craig E. *An Unnatural Metropolis: Wresting New Orleans from Nature.* Baton Rouge: Louisiana State Univ. Press, 2005.

Comeaux, Malcolm. "The Atchafalaya River Raft." *Louisiana Studies* 9 (winter 1970): 217–27.

Cotterill, R. S. "Southern Railroads, 1850–1860." *Mississippi Valley Historical Review* 10 (March 1924): 396–405.

———. "Southern Railroads and Western Trade, 1840–1850." *Mississippi Valley Historical Review* 3 (March 1917): 427–41.

Council, R. Bruce, Nicholas Honerkamp, and M. Elizabeth Will. *Industry and Technology in Antebellum Tennessee: The Archaeology of Bluff Furnace.* Knoxville: Univ. of Tennessee Press, 1992.

Cowan, Ruth Schwartz. *A Social History of American Technology.* New York: Oxford Univ. Press, 1997.

Cowdrey, Albert E. *This Land, This South: An Environmental History.* Lexington: Univ. Press of Kentucky, 1983.

Cox, Thomas H. *Gibbons v. Ogden, Law, and Society in the Early Republic.* Athens: Ohio Univ. Press, 2009.

Crocker, Helen Bartter. "Steamboats for Bowling Green: The River Politics of James Rumsey Skiles." *Filson Club Historical Quarterly* 46 (January 1972): 9–23.

Cronon, William. *Nature's Metropolis: Chicago and the Great West.* New York: W. W. Norton, 1991.

Crowley, John E. *The Invention of Comfort: Sensibilities and Design in Early Modern Britain and Early America*. Baltimore: Johns Hopkins Univ. Press, 2001.

Davidson, Donald. *The Tennessee*, vol. 1, *The Old River: Frontier to Secession*. New York: Rinehart, 1946.

Dahlinger, Charles W. "The *New Orleans*." *Pittsburg Legal Journal* 59 (October 1911): 579–91.

Daniels, Wilson. "Steam-boating on the Ohio and Mississippi Before the Civil War." *Indiana Magazine of History* 11 (June 1915): 99–127.

Davis, Charles S. *The Cotton Kingdom in Alabama*. Montgomery: Alabama State Department of Archives and History, 1939.

Davis, Donald, Craig E. Colton, Megan Kate Nelson, Barbara L. Allen, and Mikko Saikku. *Southern United States: An Environmental History*. Santa Barbara, Calif.: ABC-CLIO, 2006.

Davis, Edwin Adams, and William Ransom Hogan. *The Barber of Natchez*. Baton Rouge: Louisiana State Univ. Press, 1954.

Dayton, Fred Erving. *Steamboat Days*. New York: Tudor Publishing, 1925.

Debo, Angie. *The Road to Disappearance: A History of the Creek Indians*. Norman: Univ. of Oklahoma Press, 1979.

De la Hunt, Thomas James. *Perry County: A History*. Indianapolis: W. K. Stewart, 1916.

DeRosier, Arthur H., Jr. *The Removal of the Choctaw Indians*. Knoxville: Univ. of Tennessee Press, 1970.

Dethloff, Henry C. "Paddlewheels and Pioneers on Red River, 1815–1915, and the Reminiscences of Captain M. L. Scovell." *Louisiana Studies* 6 (summer 1967): 91–134.

Deyle, Stephen. *Carry Me Back: The Domestic Slave Trade in American Life*. New York: Oxford Univ. Press, 2005.

Dilts, James D. *The Great Road: The Building of the Baltimore and Ohio, the Nation's First Railroad, 1828–1853*. Stanford: Stanford Univ. Press, 1993.

Dohan, Mary Helen. *Mr. Roosevelt's Steamboat: The First Steamboat to Travel the Mississippi*. New York: Dodd, Mead, and Company, 1981.

Doran, Michael F. "Population Statistics of Nineteenth Century Indian Territory." *Chronicles of Oklahoma* 53 (winter 1975–1976): 492–515.

Dorsey, Florence L. *Master of the Mississippi: Henry Shreve and the Conquest of the Mississippi*. New York: Houghton Mifflin, 1941.

Douglas, Byrd. *Steamboatin' on the Cumberland*. Nashville: Tennessee Book Company, 1961.

Downey, Tom. *Planting a Capitalist South: Masters, Merchants, and Manufacturers in the Southern Interior, 1790–1860*. Baton Rouge: Louisiana State Univ. Press, 2006.

Duffy, John. *Sword of Pestilence: The New Orleans Yellow Fever Epidemic of 1853*. Baton Rouge: Louisiana State Univ. Press, 1966.

Dupre, Daniel. "Ambivalent Capitalists on the Cotton Frontier: Settlement and Development in the Tennessee Valley of Alabama." *Journal of Southern History* 56 (May 1990): 215–40.

Durham, Walter T. *James Winchester: Tennessee Pioneer.* Gallatin, Tenn.: Sumner County Library Board, 1979.

Dyer, Grace Elizabeth. "The Removal of the Great Raft in Red River." Master's thesis, Louisiana State University, 1948.

Earle, Alice Morse. *Stage-Coach and Tavern Days.* 1900. Reprint, New York: Macmillan, 1997.

Egerton, Douglas R. "Markets without a Market Revolution: Southern Planters and Capitalism." *Journal of the Early Republic* 24 (summer 2004): 207–21.

———. "Slaves to the Marketplace: Economic Liberty and Black Rebelliousness in the Atlantic World." *Journal of the Early Republic* 26 (winter 2006): 617–39.

Egnal, Marc. *Clash of Extremes: The Economic Origins of the American Civil War.* New York: Hill and Wang, 2009.

Ehle, John. *Trail of Tears: The Rise and Fall of the Cherokee Nation.* New York: Random House, 1988.

Eichstadt, Jennifer L., and Stephen Small. *Representations of Slavery: Race and Ideology in Southern Plantation Museums.* Washington, D.C.: Smithsonian Institution Press, 2002.

Elliott, D. O. *The Improvement of the Lower Mississippi River for Flood Control and Navigation.* 3 vols. Vicksburg, Miss.: U.S. Waterways Experiment Station, 1932.

Ellis, Richard E. *The Union at Risk: Jacksonian Democracy, States' Rights, and the Nullification Crisis.* New York: Oxford Univ. Press, 1987.

Etheridge, Robbie. *Creek Country: The Creek Indians and Their World.* Chapel Hill: Univ. of North Carolina Press, 2003.

Evans, W. A. "Steamboats on the Upper Tombigbee in the Early Days." *Journal of Mississippi History* 4 (October 1942): 216–24.

Fabian, Ann. *Card Sharps, Dream Books, and Bucket Shops: Gambling in 19th-Century America.* Ithaca: Cornell Univ. Press, 1990.

Faust, Drew Gilpin. *This Republic of Suffering: Death and the American Civil War.* New York: Alfred A. Knopf, 2008.

Feldman, Jay. *When the Mississippi Ran Backwards: Empire, Intrigue, Murder, and the New Madrid Earthquakes.* New York: Free Press, 2005.

Feller, Daniel. *The Jacksonian Promise: America, 1815–1860.* Baltimore: Johns Hopkins Univ. Press, 1995.

———. "The Market Revolution Ate My Homework." *Reviews in American History* 25 (September 1997): 408–15.

Fett, Sharla M. *Working Cures: Healing, Health, and Power on Southern Slave Plantations.* Chapel Hill: Univ. of North Carolina Press, 2002.

Findlay, John M. *People of Chance: Gambling in American Society from Jamestown to Las Vegas.* New York: Oxford Univ. Press, 1986.

Fishbaugh, Charles Preston. *From Paddle Wheels to Propellers.* Indianapolis: Indiana Historical Society, 1970.

Fishlow, Albert. *American Railroads and the Transformation of the Ante-Bellum Economy*. Cambridge: Harvard Univ. Press, 1965.

Follett, Richard. *The Sugar Masters: Planters and Slaves in Louisiana's Cane World, 1820–1860*. Baton Rouge: Louisiana State Univ. Press, 2005.

Foreman, Grant. *Indian Removal: The Emigration of the Five Civilized Tribes of Indians*, 2nd ed. Norman: Univ. of Oklahoma Press, 1953.

———. "River Navigation in the Early Southwest." *Mississippi Valley Historical Review* 15 (June 1928): 34–55.

Fossier, Albert A. *New Orleans: The Glamour Period, 1800–1840*. New Orleans: Pelican Publishing Company, 1957.

Foster, James Fleetwood. *Ante-Bellum Floating Palaces of the Alabama River and the "Good Old Times in Dixie."* Selma, Ala.: Coffee Printing Company, 1960.

Frank, Andrew K. *Creeks and Southerners: Biculturalism on the Early American Frontier*. Lincoln: Univ. of Nebraska Press, 2005.

Frazer, Mell A. *Early History of Steamboats in Alabama*. Auburn: n.p., 1907.

Freehling, William W. *Prelude to Civil War: The Nullification Controversy in South Carolina, 1816–1836*. New York: Harper and Row, 1965.

Friend, Craig Thompson. *Along the Maysville Road: The Early American Republic in the Trans-Appalachian West*. Knoxville: Univ. of Tennessee Press, 2005.

Gandy, Joan W., and Thomas H. *The Mississippi Steamboat Era in Historic Photographs: Natchez to New Orleans, 1870–1920*. New York: Dover Publications, 1987.

Gibson, Arrell M. *The Chickasaws*. Norman: Univ. of Oklahoma Press, 1971.

Gilje, Paul A. *Liberty on the Waterfront: American Maritime Culture in the Age of Revolution*. Philadelphia: Univ. of Pennsylvania Press, 2007.

Gillespie, Michael. *Come Hell or High Water: A Lively History of Steamboating on the Mississippi and Ohio Rivers*. Stoddard, Wisc.: Heritage Press, 2001.

———. *Wild River, Wooden Boats: True Stories of Steamboating and the Missouri River*. Stoddard, Wisc.: Heritage Press, 2000.

Goldfield, David R. *Cotton Fields and Skyscrapers: Southern City and Region, 1607–1980*. Baton Rouge: Louisiana State Univ. Press, 1982.

Goodman, Nancy, and Robert Goodman. *Paddlewheels on the Upper Mississippi, 1823–1854: How Steamboats Promoted Commerce and Settlement in the West*. Stillwater, Minn.: Washington County Historical Society, 2003.

Goodstein, Anita Shafer. *Nashville, 1780–1860: From Frontier to City*. Gainesville: Univ. of Florida Press, 1989.

Graham, Philip. *Showboats: The History of an American Institution*. Austin: Univ. of Texas Press, 1951.

Gray, Lewis Cecil. *History of Agriculture in the Southern United States to 1860*. 2 vols. Gloucester, Mass.: Peter Smith, 1958.

Grayson, Frank Y. *Thrills of the Historic Ohio River*. Cincinnati: N.p., n.d.

Green, Jerry E. "Steubenville, Ohio, and the Nineteenth-Century Steamboat Trade." *Ohio History* 113 (winter/spring 2004): 18–30.

Green, Michael D. *The Politics of Indian Removal: Creek Government and Society in Crisis.* Lincoln: Univ. of Nebraska Press, 1982.

Greenberg, Kenneth S. *Honor and Slavery: Lies, Duels, Noses, Masks, Dressing as a Woman, Gifts, Strangers, Humanitarianism, Death, Slave Rebellions, the Proslavery Argument, Baseball, Hunting and Gambling in the Old South.* Princeton: Princeton Univ. Press, 1996.

Gross, Ariela J. *What Blood Won't Tell: A History of Race on Trial in America.* Cambridge: Harvard Univ. Press, 2008.

Gruenwald, Kim M. *River of Enterprise: The Commercial Origins of Regional Identity in the Ohio Valley, 1790–1850.* Bloomington: Indiana Univ. Press, 2002.

Gudmestad, Robert H. "Steamboats and the Removal of the Red River Raft." *Louisiana History,* forthcoming.

———. "Technology and the World the Slaves Made." *History Compass* 4 (January 2006): 1–11.

Guillet, Edwin Clarence. *The Great Migration: The Atlantic Crossing by Sailing Ships since 1770,* 2nd ed. Toronto: Univ. of Toronto Press, 1963.

Haites, Erik F., and James Mak. "Economies of Scale in Western River Steamboating." *Journal of Economic History* 36 (September 1976): 689–703.

———. "Economies of Scale in Western River Steamboating: A Reply." *Journal of Economic History* 38 (June 1978): 467–70.

———. "Ohio and Mississippi River Transportation, 1810–1860." *Explorations in Economic History* 8 (winter 1970): 153–80.

———. "Steamboating on the Mississippi: A Purely Competitive Industry." *Business History Review* 45 (spring 1971): 52–78.

Haites, Erik F., James Mak, and Gary M. Walton. *Western River Transportation: The Era of Early Internal Development, 1810–1860.* Baltimore: Johns Hopkins Univ. Press, 1975.

Halttunen, Karen. *Confidence Men and Painted Women: A Study in Middle-Class Culture in America, 1830–1870.* New Haven: Yale Univ. Press, 1982.

Hammack, James Wallace, Jr. *Kentucky and the Second American Revolution: The War of 1812.* Lexington: Univ. Press of Kentucky, 1976.

Hattervig, Eldon. "Jefferson Landing: A Commercial Center of the Steamboat Era." *Missouri Historical Review* 77 (April 1980): 277–99.

Havighurst, Walter. "Travelers' Tales by Steamboat in the 1840s." *Queen City Heritage* 57 (summer/fall 1999): 27–36.

———. *Voices on the River: The Story of the Mississippi Waterways.* New York: Macmillan, 1964.

Hawthorne, Lloyd. "Captain Henry M. Shreve: Master of the Red." *North Louisiana Historical Association Journal* 2 (spring 1971): 1–6.

Henkin, David. *The Postal Age: The Emergence of Modern Communications in Nineteenth-Century America*. Chicago: Univ. of Chicago Press, 2006.

Hilliard, Sam Bowers. *Atlas of Antebellum Southern Agriculture*. Baton Rouge: Louisiana State Univ. Press, 1984.

Hines, Lawrence G. "The Early 19th Century Internal Improvements Reports and the Philosophy of Public Investment." *Journal of Economic Issues* 2 (October 1968): 384–92.

Holly, David C. *Tidewater by Steamboat: A Saga of the Chesapeake*. Baltimore: Johns Hopkins Univ. Press, 1991.

Holmes, Oliver W., and Peter T. Rohrbach. *Stagecoach East: Stagecoach Days in the East from the Colonial Period to the Civil War*. Washington, D.C.: Smithsonian Institution Press, 1983.

Hopkins, Arthur E. "Steamboats at Louisville and on the Ohio and Mississippi Rivers." *Filson Club Historical Quarterly* 17 (July 1943): 143–62.

Hopkins, James F. *A History of the Hemp Industry in Kentucky*, rev. ed. Lexington: Univ. of Kentucky Press, 1998.

Horsman, Reginald. *Race and Manifest Destiny: The Origins of American Racial Anglo-Saxonism*. Cambridge: Harvard Univ. Press, 1981.

Howe, Daniel Walker. *What Hath God Wrought: The Transformation of America, 1815–1848*. New York: Oxford Univ. Press, 2007.

Humphreys, Margaret. *Yellow Fever and the South*. New Brunswick: Rutgers Univ. Press, 1992.

Huber, Leonard V., comp. *Advertisements of Lower Mississippi River Steamboats, 1812–1920*. West Barrington, R.I.: Steamship Historical Society of America, 1959.

———. "Beginnings of Steamboat Mail on Lower Mississippi." *American Philatelist* 74 (December 1960): 187–200.

Hulbert, Archer B. "Western Ship-Building." *American Historical Review* 21 (July 1916): 720–33.

Hunter, Louis C. "The Invention of the Western Steamboat." *Journal of Economic History* 3 (November 1943): 201–20.

———. *Steamboats on the Western Rivers: An Economic and Technological History*. 1949. Reprint, Mineola, N.Y.: Dover Publications, 1993.

Huston, James L. *Calculating the Value of the Union: Slavery, Property Rights, and the Economic Origins of the Civil War*. Chapel Hill: Univ. of North Carolina Press, 2003.

———. "The Experiential Basis of the Northern Antislavery Impulse." *Journal of Southern History* 4 (November 1990): 609–40.

Hyams, Valerie Gaiennie, Jr. "A History of Navigation on Red River from 1815 to 1865." Master's thesis, Louisiana State University, 1939.

Ikerman, William James. "The Role of the Steamboat in the Development of the Cotton Kingdom in Alabama, 1819–1860." Master's thesis, Auburn University, 1963.

James, D. Clayton. *Antebellum Natchez*. Baton Rouge: Louisiana State Univ. Press, 1968.

John, Richard R. *Spreading the News: The American Postal System from Franklin to Morse.* Cambridge: Harvard Univ. Press, 1995.

Johnson, Leland R. *The Falls City Engineers: A History of the Louisville District Corps of Engineers, United States Army.* Alexandria, Va.: Office of History Headquarters, 1974.

———. "19th Century Engineering Part I: The Contest of 1824." *Military Engineer* 65 (May–June 1973): 66–71.

———. "19th Century Engineering Part II: The Contract of 1824." *Military Engineer* 65 (July–August 1973): 252–57.

Johnson, Vicki Vaughan. *The Men and the Vision of the Southern Commercial Conventions, 1845–1871.* Columbia: Univ. of Missouri Press, 1992.

Johnson, Walter. "Clerks All! Or, Slaves with Cash." *Journal of the Early Republic* 26 (winter 2006): 641–51.

———. "The Pedestal and the Veil: Rethinking the Capitalism/Slavery Question." *Journal of the Early Republic* 24 (summer 2004): 299–308.

———. "The Slave Trader, the White Slave, and the Politics of Racial Determination in the 1850s." *Journal of American History* 87 (June 2000): 13–38.

Jordan, Weymouth T. *Hugh Davis and His Alabama Plantation.* University, Ala.: Univ. of Alabama Press, 1948.

Kane, Adam I. *The Western River Steamboat.* College Station: Texas A & M Univ. Press, 2004.

Kasson, John F. *Civilizing the Machine: Technology and Republican Values in America, 1776–1900.* New York: Hill and Wang, 1976.

Kaye, Anthony E. *Joining Places: Slave Neighborhoods in the Old South.* Chapel Hill: Univ. of North Carolina Press, 2007.

———. "The Second Slavery: Modernity in the Nineteenth-Century South and the Atlantic World." *Journal of Southern History* 75 (August 2009): 627–50.

Kelman, Ari. "Forests and Other River Perils." In *Transforming New Orleans and Its Environs: Centuries of Change,* edited by Craig E. Colten, 45–63. Pittsburgh: Univ. of Pittsburgh Press, 2000.

———. *A River and Its City: The Nature of Landscape in New Orleans.* Berkeley: Univ. of California Press, 2003.

Kerber, Linda. "Separate Spheres, Female Worlds, Woman's Place: The Rhetoric of Women's History." *Journal of American History* 75 (June 1998): 9–39.

Kesterman, M'Lissa. "Steamboat Journey from Cincinnati to New Orleans in 1851." *Ohio Valley History* 7 (summer 2007): 78–84.

Kirby, Jack Temple. *Mockingbird Song: Ecological Landscapes of the South.* Chapel Hill: Univ. of North Carolina Press, 2006.

Klein, Maury. *History of the Louisville and Nashville Railroad.* New York: MacMillan, 1972.

Kolchin, Peter. "The South and the World." *Journal of Southern History* 75 (August 2009): 565–80.

Kotlikoff, Laurence J. "The Structure of Slave Prices in New Orleans, 1804 to 1862." *Economic Inquiry* 17 (October 1979): 496–518.

Kreipke, Martha. "The Falls of the Ohio and the Development of the Ohio River Trade, 1810–1860." *Filson Club Historical Quarterly* 54 (April 1980): 196–217.

Kussart, Mrs. S. *Navigation on the Monongahela River,* compiled and indexed by Richard T. Wiley. N.p., 1971.

Lakwete, Angela, *Inventing the Cotton Gin: Machine and Myth in Antebellum America.* Baltimore: Johns Hopkins Univ. Press, 2003.

Larkin, Jack. *The Reshaping of Everyday Life, 1790–1840.* New York: HarperCollins, 1988.

Larson, John Lauritz. *Internal Improvement: National Public Works and the Promise of Popular Government in the Early United States.* Chapel Hill: Univ. of North Carolina Press, 2001.

———. *The Market Revolution in America: Liberty, Ambition, and the Eclipse of the Common Good.* New York: Cambridge Univ. Press, 2010.

Lass, William E. *A History of Steamboating on the Upper Missouri River.* Lincoln: Univ. of Nebraska Press, 1962.

———. *Navigating the Missouri: Steamboating on Nature's Highway, 1819–1935.* Norman: Arthur H. Clarke, 2008.

Leahy, Ethel C. *Who's Who on the Ohio River and Its Tributaries.* Cincinnati: E. C. Leahy Publishing, 1931.

Leavitt, Penelope M., and James S. Moy. "Spalding and Rogers' Floating Palace, 1852–1859." *Theatre Survey* 25 (May 1984): 15–28.

Levine, Lawrence W. *Black Culture and Black Consciousness: Afro-American Folk Thought from Slavery to Freedom.* New York: Oxford Univ. Press, 1977.

Lewis, Monte Ross. "Chickasaw Removal: Betrayal of the Beloved Warriors, 1794–1844." Ph.D. diss., University of North Texas, 1981.

Lytle, William M., and Forrest R. Holdcamper. *Merchant Steam Vessels of the United States, 1790–1868: Documents of the United States and Other Sources.* Revised and edited by C. Bradford Mitchell, with assistance of Kenneth R. Hall. Staten Island, N.Y.: Steamship Historical Society of America; distributed by Univ. of Baltimore Press, 1975.

Maass, Alfred A. "Brownsville's Steamboat *Enterprize* and Pittsburgh's Supply of General Jackson's Army." *Pittsburgh History* 77 (spring 1994): 22–29.

———. "Daniel French and the Western Steamboat Engine." *American Neptune* 56 (winter 1996): 29–44.

Majewski, John. *Modernizing a Slave Economy: The Economic Vision of the Confederate Nation.* Chapel Hill: Univ. of North Carolina Press, 2009.

———. "A Revolution Too Many?" *Journal of Economic History* 57 (June 1997): 476–80.

Mak, James, and Gary M. Walton. "The Persistence of Old Technologies: The Case of Flatboats." *Journal of Economic History* 33 (June 1973): 444–51.

———. "Steamboats and the Great Productivity Surge in River Transportation." *Journal of Economic History* 32 (September 1972): 616–40.

Mangin, C. Geoffrey. "Clearing the Great Raft: Impetus for Economic Growth in Louisiana's Red River Valley, 1830–1860." *North Louisiana History* 31 (fall 2000): 32–42.

Marrs, Aaron W. *Railroads in the Old South: Pursuing Progress in a Slave Society.* Baltimore: Johns Hopkins Univ. Press, 2009.

Martin, Jonathan D. *Divided Mastery: Slave Hiring in the American South.* Cambridge: Harvard Univ. Press, 2004.

Marx, Leo. *The Machine in the Garden: Technology and the Pastoral Ideal in America.* New York: Oxford Univ. Press, 1964.

McCall, Edith. *Conquering the Rivers: Henry Miller Shreve and the Navigation of America's Inland Waterways.* Baton Rouge: Louisiana State Univ. Press, 1984.

McDermott, John Francis. *The Lost Panoramas of the Mississippi.* Chicago: Univ. of Chicago Press, 1958.

McPhee, John. *The Control of Nature.* New York: Farrar, Straus, and Giroux, 1989.

Meares, Cecil. "When the Steamboat *Monmouth* Sank in the Mississippi, Creek Indian Passengers Paid the Price." *Wild West* 11 (October 1998): 10–12.

Meier, Kathryn M. "The Removal of the Great Raft from the Red River." *North Louisiana History* 31 (summer 2000): 24–34.

Miller, Stephen F. "Plantation Labor Organization and Slave Life on the Cotton Frontier: The Alabama-Mississippi Black Belt, 1815–1840." In *Cultivation and Culture: Labor and the Shaping of Slave Life in the Americas,* edited by Ira Berlin and Philip D. Morgan, 155–69. Charlottesville: Univ. Press of Virginia, 1993.

Missall, John, and Mary Lou Missall. *The Seminole Wars: America's Longest Indian Conflict.* Gainesville: Univ. Press of Florida, 2004.

Moore, John Hebron. *The Emergence of the Cotton Kingdom in the Old Southwest.* Baton Rouge: Louisiana State Univ. Press, 1988.

———. "Railroads of Antebellum Mississippi." *Journal of Mississippi History* 41 (February 1979): 53–81.

———. "Simon Gray, Riverman: A Slave Who Was Almost Free." *Mississippi Valley Historical Review* 49 (December 1962): 472–84.

Morris, Christopher. "A More Southern Environmental History." *Journal of Southern History* 75 (August 2009): 581–98.

Morrison, John H. *History of American Steam Navigation.* New York: Agrosy-Antiquarian, 1903.

Moses, L. G. *Wild West Shows and the Images of American Indians, 1883–1933.* Albuquerque: Univ. of New Mexico Press, 1996.

Moulton, Gary E. *John Ross: Cherokee Chief.* Athens: Univ. of Georgia Press, 1978.

Mueller, Edward A. *Perilous Journeys: A History of Steamboating on the Chattahoochee, Apalachicola, and Flint Rivers, 1828–1928.* Eufala, Ala.: Historic Chattahoochee Commission, 1990.

Murphy, Lucy Eldersveld. *A Gathering of Rivers: Indians, Metis, and Mining in the Western Great Lakes, 1737–1832*. Lincoln: Univ. of Nebraska Press, 2000.

Nelson, Scott Reynolds. *Steel Drivin' Man: John Henry, the Untold Story of an American Legend*. New York: Oxford Univ. Press, 2006.

Neville, Bert. *Directory of River Packets in the Mobile-Alabama-Warrior-Tombigbee Trades (1818–1932), with Illustrations, Charts and Tables of Landings*. Selma, Ala.: Coffee Printing Company, 1962.

———. *Directory of Tennessee River Steamboats (1821–1928), with Illustrations*. Selma, Ala.: Coffee Printing Company, 1963.

Nye, David. *America as Second Creation: Technology and Narratives of New Beginnings*. Cambridge: MIT Press, 2003.

———. *American Technological Sublime*. Cambridge: MIT Press, 1994.

Oakes, James. *Slavery and Freedom: An Interpretation of the Old South*. New York: W. W. Norton, 1990.

O'Brien, Greg. *Choctaws in a Revolutionary Age, 1750–1830*. Lincoln: Univ. of Nebraska Press, 2002.

O'Brien, Michael. *Conjectures of Order: Intellectual Life and the American South, 1810–1860*. 2 vols. Chapel Hill: Univ. of North Carolina Press, 2004.

Owens, Harry P. *Steamboats and the Cotton Economy: River Trade in the Yazoo-Mississippi Delta*. Oxford: Univ. of Mississippi Press, 1990.

Pabis, George S. "Delaying the Deluge: The Engineering Debate over Flood Control on the Lower Mississippi River, 1846–1861." *Journal of Southern History* 64 (August 1998): 421–54.

Paige, Amanda L., Fuller L. Bumpers, and Daniel F. Littlefield Jr. *The North Little Rock Site on the Trail of Tears National Historic Trail: Historical Contexts Report*. Little Rock: American Native Press Archives, 2003.

Paskoff, Paul F. *Troubled Waters: Steamboat Disasters, River Improvements, and American Public Policy, 1821–1860*. Baton Rouge: Louisiana State Univ. Press, 2007.

Penick, James Lal, Jr. *The New Madrid Earthquakes*, rev ed. Columbia, Mo.: Univ. of Missouri Press, 1981.

Penningroth, Dylan C. *The Claims of Kinfolk: African American Property and Community in the Nineteenth-Century South*. Chapel Hill: Univ. of North Carolina Press, 2003.

Perdue, Theda, and Michael D. Green. *The Cherokee Removal: A Brief History with Documents*, 2nd ed. Boston: Bedford/St. Martin's, 2005.

———. *The Columbia Guide to American Indians of the Southeast*. New York: Columbia Univ. Press, 2001.

Peterson, William J. *Steamboating on the Upper Mississippi*. Iowa City: State Historical Society of Iowa, 1968.

Pfaff, Caroline S. "Henry Miller Shreve: A Biography." *Louisiana Historical Quarterly* 10 (April 1927): 192–240.

Powers, Ron. *Mark Twain: A Life.* New York: Free Press, 2005.

Powles, James M. "*New Orleans*: First Steamboat Down the Mississippi." *American History* 40 (June 2005): 48–55.

Proctor, Nicholas. *Bathed in Blood: Hunting and Mastery in the Old South.* Charlottesville: Univ. of Virginia Press, 2002.

Pursell, Carroll. *The Machine in America: A Social History of Technology.* Baltimore: Johns Hopkins Univ. Press, 1995.

Quick, Herbert, and Edward Quick. *Mississippi Steamboatin': A History of Steamboating on the Mississippi and Its Tributaries.* New York: Henry Holt, 1926.

Ray, Kristofer. *Middle Tennessee, 1775–1825: Progress and Popular Democracy on the Southwestern Frontier.* Knoxville: Univ. of Tennessee Press, 2007.

Reed, Merl E. *New Orleans and the Railroads: The Struggle for Commercial Empire, 1830–1860.* Baton Rouge: Louisiana State Univ. Press, 1966.

Reith, Gerda. *The Age of Chance: Gambling in Western Culture.* London: Routledge, 1999.

Renoff, Gregory J. *The Big Tent: The Traveling Circus in Georgia, 1820–1930.* Athens: Univ. of Georgia Press, 2008.

Reps, John W. *Cities of the Mississippi: Nineteenth-Century Images of Urban Development.* Columbia: Univ. of Missouri Press, 1994.

Reuss, Martin. "The Army Corps of Engineers and Flood-Control Politics on the Lower Mississippi." *Louisiana History* 23 (spring 1983): 131–48.

———. *Designing the Bayous: The Control of Water in the Atchafalaya Basin, 1800–1995.* College Station: Texas A & M Press, 1994.

Richter, Amy G. *Home on the Rails: Women, the Railroad, and the Rise of Public Domesticity.* Chapel Hill: Univ. of North Carolina Press, 2005.

Rickels, Milton. *George Washington Harris.* New York: Twayne Publishers, 1965.

Risjord, Norman K. *Jefferson's America, 1760–1815.* Madison: Univ. of Wisconsin Press, 1991.

Roberts, John W. *From Trickster to Badman: The Black Folk Hero in Slavery and Freedom.* Philadelphia: Univ. of Pennsylvania Press, 1989.

Rodabough, John E. *Steamboats on the Upper Tombigbee.* Hamilton, Miss.: Tombigbee Press, 1985.

Roediger, David R. "The Pursuit of Whiteness: Property, Terror, and Expansion, 1790–1860." *Journal of the Early Republic* 19 (winter 1999): 579–600.

Ronda, James P. "'We Have a Country': Race, Geography, and the Invention of Indian Territory." *Journal of the Early Republic* 19 (winter 1999): 739–55.

Rosenberg, Charles E. *The Cholera Years: The United States in 1832, 1849, and 1866.* Chicago: Univ. of Chicago Press, 1962

Ross, Margaret. "The New Madrid Earthquake." *Arkansas Historical Quarterly* 27 (summer 1968): 83–104.

Rothman, Adam. *Slave Country: American Expansion and the Origins of the Deep South.* Cambridge: Harvard Univ. Press, 2005.

Rothman, Joshua D. "The Hazards of Flush Times: Gambling, Mob Violence, and the Anxieties of America's Market Revolution." *Journal of American History* 95 (December 2008): 651–77.

Rousey, Dennis C. *Policing the Southern City: New Orleans, 1805–1889.* Baton Rouge: Louisiana State Univ. Press, 1996.

Ryan, Mary P. *Women in Public: Between Banners and Ballots, 1825–1880.* Baltimore: Johns Hopkins Univ. Press, 1990.

Ryder, F. Van Loon. "The 'New Orleans': The First Steamboat on Our Western Waters." *Filson Club Historical Quarterly* 37 (January 1963): 29–37.

Salecker, Gene Eric. *Disaster on the Mississippi: The* Sultana *Explosion, April 27, 1865.* Annapolis: Naval Institute Press, 1996.

Samuel, Ray, Leonard V. Huber, and Warren C. Ogden. *Tales of the Mississippi.* New York: Hastings House, 1955.

Satz, Ronald N. *American Indian Policy in the Jacksonian Era.* Lincoln: Univ. of Nebraska Press, 1975.

Schafer, Judith Kelleher. *Becoming Free, Remaining Free: Manumission and Enslavement in New Orleans, 1846–1862.* Baton Rouge: Louisiana State Univ. Press, 2003.

———. *Slavery, the Civil Law, and the Supreme Court of Louisiana.* Baton Rouge: Louisiana State Univ. Press, 1994.

Schob, David E. "Woodhawks and Cordwood: Steamboat Fuel on the Ohio and Mississippi Rivers, 1820–1860." *Journal of Forest History* 21 (July 1977): 124–32.

Schoen, Brian. *The Fragile Fabric of Union: Cotton, Federal Politics, and the Global Origins of the Civil War.* Baltimore: Johns Hopkins Univ. Press, 2009.

Schwartz, Ruth Cowan. *A Social History of American Technology.* New York: Oxford Univ. Press, 1997.

Sellers, Charles. *The Market Revolution: Jacksonian America, 1815–1846.* New York: Oxford Univ. Press, 1991.

Shallat, Todd. *Structures in the Stream: Water, Science, and the Rise of the U.S. Army Corps of Engineers.* Austin: Univ. of Texas Press, 1994.

Simoneaux, Katherine G. "Symbolism in Thorpe's 'Big Bear of Arkansas.'" *Arkansas Historical Quarterly* 25 (autumn 1966): 240–47.

Sinclair, Bruce. *Philadelphia's Philosopher Mechanics: A History of the Franklin Institute, 1824–1865.* Baltimore: Johns Hopkins Univ. Press, 1974.

Smith, Jonathan Kennon. *Genealogical Abstracts from Reported Deaths, the Nashville Christian Advocate, 1897–1899.* Jackson, Tenn.: Smith, 2002.

Smith, Mark M. *Debating Slavery: Economy and Society in the Antebellum American South.* New York: Cambridge Univ. Press, 1998.

———. *Mastered by the Clock: Time, Slavery, and Freedom in the American South.* Chapel Hill: Univ. of North Carolina Press, 1997.

Smith, Thomas Ruys. *River of Dreams: Imagining the Mississippi Before Mark Twain.* Baton Rouge: Louisiana State Univ. Press, 2007.

Southerland, Henry deLeon, Jr., and Jerry Elijah Brown. *The Federal Road through Georgia, the Creek Nation, and Alabama, 1806–1836.* Tuscaloosa: Univ. of Alabama Press, 1989.

Spell, Tim. "Uncle Sam's Toothpullers." *Nautical Research Journal* 26 (March 1980): 38–42.

Stephenson, Wendell Holmes. *Isaac Franklin: Slave Trader and Planter of the Old South.* Baton Rouge: Louisiana State Univ. Press, 1938.

Stewart, Mart A. "If John Muir Had Been an Agrarian: American Environmental History West and South." *Environment and History* 11 (2005): 139–62.

—— "Re-Greening the South and Southernizing the Rest." *Journal of the Early Republic* 24 (summer 2004): 242–51.

——. *"What Nature Suffers to Groe": Life, Labor, and Landscape on the Georgia Coast, 1680–1920.* Athens: Univ. of Georgia Press, 2002.

Stine, Jeffrey K., and Joel A. Tarr. "At the Intersection of Histories: Technology and the Environment." *Technology and Culture* 39 (October 1998): 601–40.

Stokes, Melvyn, and Stephen Conway, eds. *The Market Revolution in America: Social, Political, and Religious Expressions, 1800–1880.* Charlottesville: Univ. of Virginia Press, 1996.

Stover, John F. *American Railroads,* 2nd ed. Chicago: Univ. of Chicago Press, 1997.

——. *Iron Roads to the West: American Railroads in the 1850s.* New York: Columbia Univ. Press, 1978.

——. *The Railroads of the South, 1865–1900: A Study in Finance and Control.* Chapel Hill: Univ. of North Carolina Press, 1955.

——. *The Routledge Historical Atlas of the American Railroads.* New York: Routledge, 1999.

Sutter, Paul S., and Christopher J. Manganiello, eds. *Environmental History and the American South: A Reader.* Athens: Univ. of Georgia Press, 2009.

Swanton, John R. *Chickasaw Society and Religion.* 1928. Reprint, Lincoln: Univ. of Nebraska Press, 2006.

Tadman, Michael. *Speculators and Slaves: Masters, Traders, and Slaves in the Old South.* Madison: Univ. of Wisconsin Press, 1989.

Taylor, George Rogers. *The Transportation Revolution, 1815–1860.* New York: Rinehart, 1951.

Thornton, Russell. *American Indian Holocaust and Survival: A Population History since 1492.* Norman: Univ. of Oklahoma Press, 1987.

Towers, Frank. *The Urban South and the Coming of the Civil War.* Charlottesville: Univ. of Virginia Press, 2004.

Trask, Kerry A. *Black Hawk: The Battle for the Heart of America.* Macmillan: New York, 2006.

Trescott, Paul B. "The Louisville and Portland Canal Company, 1825–1874." *Mississippi Valley Historical Review* 44 (March 1948): 686–708.

Tyson, Carl Newton. *The Red River in Southwestern History.* Norman: Univ. of Oklahoma Press, 1981.

U.S. Army Corps of Engineers. *The U.S. Army Corps of Engineers: A History.* Alexandria, Va.: Office of History Headquarters, 2007.

Vlach, John Michael. *The Planter's Prospect: Privilege and Slavery in Plantation Paintings.* Chapel Hill: Univ. of North Carolina Press, 2002.

Wade, Richard C. *The Urban Frontier: Pioneer Life in Early Pittsburgh, Cincinnati, Lexington, Louisville, and St. Louis.* Chicago: Univ. of Chicago Press, 1964.

Wajcman, Judy. *Feminism Confronts Technology.* University Park: Penn State Univ. Press, 1991.

Wallace, Anthony F. C. *The Long, Bitter Trail: Andrew Jackson and the Indians.* New York: Hill and Wang, 1993.

Ward, James A. "A New Look at Antebellum Southern Railroad Development." *Journal of Southern History* 39 (August 1973): 409–20.

Warren, Stephen. *The Shawnees and Their Neighbors, 1795–1870.* Urbana: Univ. of Illinois Press, 2005.

Waschka, Ronald W. "River Transportation at Memphis before the Civil War." *West Tennessee Historical Society Papers* 45 (1991): 1–18.

Watson, Alan D. "Sailing under Steam: The Advent of Steam Navigation in North Carolina to the Civil War." *North Carolina Historical Review* 75 (January 1998): 29–68.

Watson, Harry L. *Liberty and Power: The Politics of Jacksonian America.* New York: Hill and Wang, 1990.

Way, Frederick, Jr. *She Takes the Horns: Steamboat Racing on the Western Waters.* Cincinnati: Young and Klein, 1953.

———, comp. *Way's Packet Directory 1848–1994: Passenger Steamboats of the Mississippi River System Since the Advent of Photography in Mid-Continent America,* rev. ed. Athens: Ohio Univ. Press, 1994.

Wellman, Manly Wade. *Fastest on the River: The Great Race Between the Natchez and the Robert E. Lee.* New York: Henry Holt, 1957.

Wells, Jonathan Daniel. *The Origins of the Southern Middle Class, 1800–1861.* Chapel Hill: Univ. of North Carolina Press, 2004.

White, John H. "A Portrait of the 1826 Steamboat *Tecumseh.*" *Ohio Valley History* 9 (fall 2009): 59–66.

White, Richard. "Trashing the Trails." In *Trails: Toward a New Western History,* edited by Patricia Nelson Limerick, Clyde E. Milner II, and Charles E. Rankin, 26–39. Lawrence, Kans.: Univ. of Kansas Press, 1991.

Whitham, William B. "Steamboats on Western Rivers." *Gateway Heritage* 5 (spring 1985): 2–11.

Whitten, David O. "Rural Life along the Mississippi: Plaquemines Parish, Louisiana, 1830–1850." *Agricultural History* 58 (July 1984): 477–87.

Wilentz, Sean. *The Rise of American Democracy: Jefferson to Lincoln.* New York: W. W. Norton, 2005.

Williams, Clanton W. "Early Ante-Bellum Montgomery: A Black-Belt Constituency." *Journal of Southern History* 7 (November 1941): 495–525.

Williams, David. *Americans and Their Forests: A Historical Geography.* New York: Cambridge Univ. Press, 1989.

Willoughby, Lynn. *Flowing through Time: A History of the Lower Chattahoochee River.* Tuscaloosa: Univ. of Alabama Press, 1999.

Winkley, Brien R. *Man-Made Cutoffs on the Lower Mississippi River: Conception, Construction, and River Response.* Vicksburg: U.S. Army Corps of Engineers, 1977.

Wright, J. Leitch, Jr. *Creeks and Seminoles: The Destruction and Regeneration of the Muscogulge People.* Lincoln: Univ. of Nebraska Press, 1986.

Wright, Muriel H. "The Removal of the Choctaws to the Indian Territory, 1830–1833." *Chronicles of Oklahoma* 6 (June 1928): 103–28.

Wyatt-Brown, Bertram. *Southern Honor: Ethics and Behavior in the Old South.* New York: Oxford Univ. Press, 1982.

Yater, George H. *Two Hundred Years at the Falls of the Ohio: A History of Louisville and Jefferson County.* Louisville: Heritage Corporation, 1979.

WEBSITES

Fast Facts. www.census.gov/history. U. S. Census Bureau. Accessed March 20, 2007.

"Financial account and explanation of John Ross for transporting a detachment of emigrant Cherokee by steamboat to Indian Territory in late 1838 and 1839." Record Group 217. Records of the Accounting Officers of the Department of the Treasury, 1775–1927. National Archives and Records Administration. Available at http://arc web.archives.gov. Accessed April 2005.

Historical Census Browser. http://fisher.lib.virginia.edu/collections/stats/histcensus/index.html. University of Virginia, Geospatial and Statistical Data Center. Accessed March 20, 2007.

Langlois, Richard N., David J. Denaulf, and Samson M. Kimenyi. "Bursting Boilers and the Federal Power Redux: The Evolution of Safety on the Western Rivers." May 1994. Available at http://129.3.20.41/eps/eh/papers/9503/9503002.pdf. Accessed October 7, 2010.

Language of the River. http://riverlorian.com/languageoftheriver.htm. Jerry Hay. Accessed December 2, 2009.

Mark Twain Project. http://www.marktwainproject.org. University of California, Berkeley. Accessed June 1, 2009.

MeasuringWorth. http://www.measuringworth.com/index.html. MeasuringWorth. Accessed March 20, 2007.

National Transportation Safety Board. "Aviation Accident Statistics." Available at http://www.ntsb.gov/aviation/Table3.htm. Accessed October 7, 2010.

INDEX